TEACHING JEWISH HOLIDAYS

HISTORY, VALUES, AND ACTIVITIES

ROBERT GOODMAN

A.R.E. Publishing, Inc.
Denver, Colorado

Published by:
A.R.E. Publishing, Inc.
Denver, Colorado

Library of Congress Catalog Number 97-71133
ISBN 0-86705-042-X

Printed in the United States of America
10   9   8   7   6   5   4   3   2   1

DEDICATION

To Mary Rubin Goodman, the light of my life. Her support and
insights have been an ongoing source of strength and inspiration to me.

ACKNOWLEDGEMENTS

My thanks to Mordecai Levow, who encouraged me to write the original version of this work. His assistance made it possible for me to be awarded the Emanuel Gamoran N.A.T.E. Curriculum Award in 1976 for the original work, *A Guide To the Teaching of the Holidays and Festivals*, which was published by the Milwaukee Bureau of Jewish Education.

My deepest appreciation to Nachama Skolnik Moskowitz (NSM), Director of Curriculum, Jewish Education Center of Cleveland, who deserves special appreciation for the more than 300 creative activities she added, and to Julius Becker (JB), former Director of Art Education for the Board of Jewish Education of Metropolitan Chicago, for permission to use many of his innovative art projects.

Grateful thanks to Carolyn Starman Hessel, Executive Director of the Jewish Book Council and Resource Editor CAJE *Jewish Education News*, for what is surely the most comprehensive bibliography on the Jewish holidays ever to be published.

A special thank-you also to all who field tested some of the activities, and who shared their ideas and feedback with me. These include the creative teachers, administrators, and staff at Temple Sinai of Denver, Colorado and Temple Emanuel of San Jose, California, as well as the following individuals whose activities are included herein and whose contributions are noted by their initials: Judie Moses (JM); Sy Hefter (SH); Eleanor Byers (EB); Pauline Tannenbaum (PT); Emily Gannes (EG), Phyllis Mintzer (PM); Margaret Lasakow (ML); Betty Rinsler (BR); Ord Matek (OM); Fred W. Marcus (FWM): Audrey Friedman Marcus (AFM); Rabbi Raymond A. Zwerin (RAZ).

To Audrey Friedman Marcus and Rabbi Raymond Zwerin of A.R.E. Publishing, my gratitude for their support, confidence, and encouragement, and for their superb editing.

CONTENTS

INTRODUCTION

ABOUT THIS BOOK

The holidays and festivals of the Jewish calendar are taught every year at every grade level in every Jewish Religious School. This reality is both positive and negative. On the positive side, children become connected to Jewish continuity and to an ongoing, developing Jewish tradition; on the negative side, they become bored with the annual repetition of the same activities and observances. The publication of the second edition of this book obviates this negative side.

While many books on Jewish holidays and festivals contain a bit of background and a few activities, there has never been a book on the subject as encyclopedic as this one. *Teaching Jewish Holidays* (formerly *A Teachers Guide to Jewish Holidays*) brings together in one concise, easy to access volume an astounding array of over 1,000 activities for every age group, as well as complete background material on every holiday in the Jewish cycle.

No longer will teachers have to devote many hours gathering from many sources sufficient material and ideas to prepare their lessons. Here you will find a resource book and teachers guide all in one volume. Its comprehensive content makes it an invaluable compendium for teachers of children and adults, youth leaders, camp counselors, Rabbis, Havurah facilitators, indeed, anyone who works in Jewish education.

THE CONTENTS

Each chapter herein deals with one holiday/festival, or in those instances where it is reasonable to do so (e.g., Sukkot and Hoshana Rabbah), two are combined. Chapters contains the following sections which are described below: Vocabulary, Background, Central Themes, Scope and Sequence, and Activities. In the final section of the book is an Appendix and a comprehensive Bibliography (see below for descriptions).

Vocabulary

In this section can be found a extensive listing of the vocabulary related to the holiday. While the definitions and explanations are concise, pertinent material from traditional sources is included as appropriate.

Background

This section contains background information about the holiday, including its origins, biblical and Rabbinic references, central themes, home observances, highlights from the liturgy, and special aspects of the holiday, such as specific observances, customs, and the like. Information about the Jewish calendar can be found in the chapter on Rosh Chodesh.

Scope and Sequence

This section includes suggestions for specific emphases for each grade level. Varying the point of view every year and creating a spiral curriculum will help to avoid repetition in the classroom. It can also spark a deeper understanding of our heritage with each passing year.

You need not feel bound to follow the Scope and Sequence as it is presented in each chapter. The various topics will give you some ideas about what you might wish to stress at each grade level. You will, of course, need to take into consideration the abilities of your students and the time available to teach any given holiday.

Activities

For most holidays, there is a detailed and lengthy listing of activities, arranged by age group in the following categories: Preschool/Kindergarten, Primary, Intermediate, Seconday, All-school, and Family. In each of these sections, you will find suggestions of other materials pertinent to the holiday that are published by A.R.E. and by other publishers. Among the hundreds of activities presented here are: affective exercises, role play, drama, discussion, research, debate, brainstorming, worship services, creative writing, puzzles of various sorts, games, crafts, singing, cooking, reading books, guest speakers, surveys, *tzedakah* projects, and other imaginative strategies. Many of the activities integrate science and social studies. In this edition, there are many more activities that engage higher level thinking skills.

Some of the holiday chapters also contain skits and readings. These can be modified to fit the needs of your educational program. Some of these utilize humor, while others are serious. Most of these can be used as is, without memorization, lengthy preparation, or elaborate props.

Appendix

The Appendix contains the blessings associated with Shabbat and the other holidays. Each is listed in Hebrew, English, and transliteration. If desired, this section can be copied and sent home for family use.

Bibliography

A General Bibliography on Jewish holidays is followed by a separate listing of resources for each of the holidays covered in the book. (Some, like Rosh HaShanah and Yom Kippur, are combined into one list.) In both the General Bibliography and those for the various holidays, there is a section of books and materials called For Students and one entitled For Teachers and Parents. When they are available on the subject, audiocassettes, videos, and CD-ROMs are also listed.

USING THE BOOK

You will find this book very easy to use. As you plan to teach a specific holiday, review for yourself the vocabulary and background in the chapter on that holiday. Make a note of the specific facts you feel are important and that you want to convey to students. Then look over the various activities for students in the age category of your class (don't forget to check the activities in other age groups for those that you can modify and adapt), and decide on those which are appropriate and most

comfortable for you. Check the Bibliography for useful resources for you and for students. (Hopefully, your school has a teacher resource center or even a shelf where a variety of these resources are available for research and use.) You are now ready to write your lesson plans. You will find an infinite number of choices to help you in this task.

CONCLUSION

It is sad but true that many of the children in our schools do not experience the Jewish holidays at home. Further, we serve an increasing number of children of intermarried parents who may not have the knowledge and skills to transmit our Jewish traditions and heritage. The sole contact for these children with the celebration and observance of the holidays may be at Religious School. Therefore, it is incumbent on us as Jewish educators to provide them with knowledge of each of the holidays; with ongoing review of what has been learned; and with joyous celebrations, the memory of which will stay with them and inform their Jewish practice throughout their lives. We can involve families in meaningful holiday observance and provide them with a vocabulary of Jewish life through: carefully planned and engaging family education programs, interesting and informative take-home materials, and frequent suggestions for home observance.

The quest for "spirituality" has become an overriding concern in the post-modern era. Yet, what is Jewish spirituality? Is it a feeling of closeness to God? Is it a feeling of being immersed in a 4000-year-old tradition? Is it a feeling of working in partnership with God to promote *Tikkun Olam* (repairing the world)? However we chose to define Jewish spirituality, it does imply a deepening identity with one's heritage. That deepening should certainly be one of our primary educational goals.

In the process of teaching the Jewish holidays and festivals, it is important to emphasize the values central to each holiday. Finding ways to relate those values to the lives of our students is an effective way of making the holidays and festivals meaningful. The book *Teaching Mitzvot: Concepts,*

Values, and Activities by Barbara Binder Kadden and Bruce Kadden can be particularly helpful. Six of its 36 units deal specifically with holidays and provide a wealth of interesting ideas. In addition, a number of profoundly insightful books about Jewish beliefs and values have been written in recent years. *To Life* by Harold Kushner and *For Those Who Cannot Believe* by Harold M. Schulweis, to name just two of these, help to give thinking Jews marvelous insights into the profound Jewish values that are reflected in the Jewish holidays and festivals.

May your teaching be a celebration!

CHAPTER ONE

SHABBAT

VOCABULARY

Ayshet Chayil: "A Woman of Valor" is devoted to her husband and family, cares for the poor, and practices acts of loving-kindness . . . she is worth far more than precious jewels. As part of the Friday evening home ritual prior to dinner, the husband and children recite Proverbs 31:10-31 to their wife and mother. It is a sign of great honor and prestige to be called an *Ayshet Chayil*.

Besamim: Spices, in particular those used as a part of the Havdalah service. Often put in a beautiful spice box, these cloves and other fragrant spices serve as a last, poignant reminder of the sweetness of the Shabbat now coming to an end. (For blessing, see Appendix, page 251.)

Birkat HaMazon: The Grace After Meals. In Yiddish it is called *Benschen*. It is recited only when bread has been eaten. Thanking God for our food is based on the command in Deuteronomy 8:10: "When you eat and are satisfied, you shall bless the Lord your God for the land God has given to you." The Shabbat Grace after Meals begins with Psalm 126, *"Shir HaMa'alot."*

Birkat Horim: "Blessing of Parents." Parent places hands on the head of each child, saying for each boy: "May God make you as Ephraim and Manasseh" (Genesis 48:20), and for each girl: "May God make you as Sarah, Rebekah, Rachel, and Leah" (after Ruth 4:12). For both boys and

girls, the Priestly Blessing (Numbers 6:24-26) is also recited. (For blessings, see Appendix, page 251.)

Candles: At least two candles (*Nayrot*) are lit approximately 20 minutes before sundown prior to Shabbat or a festival. For Shabbat the two candles refer to the two versions of the fourth commandment (Exodus 20:8 and Deuteronomy 5:12).

Candle Lighting: In Hebrew *Hadlakat Nayrot*, in Yiddish *Benschen Licht*. The candles are usually lit and blessed by the woman of the house, but other members of the family are permitted to light and bless the candles (*Mishnah Shabbat* 2:61). (For blessings, see Appendix, page 251.)

Challah/Challot: Originally, this referred to the portion of each batch of dough that was twisted off and set aside as an offering to the Tabernacle (Numbers 15:18-21) and then to the Temple in Jerusalem. Today, *challah* refers to the special Shabbat loaf which is braided to remind us of the portion twisted off as an offering. Two *challot* are used at each Shabbat meal to remind us of the double portion of manna available to the Israelites in the Wilderness each Friday, enough to last through Shabbat (Exodus 16:13-26).

Cholent: "Warm things" in Yiddish. It is a Shabbat dish consisting of meat, potatoes, and beans in a stew prepared on Friday and kept in the oven until Saturday lunch. The term *cholent* is used among Ashkenazim; the Hebrew word *chamim* is used among Sephardim.

Eliyahu HaNavi: "Elijah the Prophet." Seen as the forerunner of the Messiah, Elijah plays an important role in Jewish messianic hopes. The song *"Eliyahu HaNavi"* is sung as part of the Havdalah service in the hope that the Messiah will speedily arrive. (Since Shabbat is deemed to be a foretaste of the messianic era, Messiah need not and would not arrive on that day. Once Shabbat is over, however, Messiah is beckoned.)

Erev Shabbat: "Shabbat Eve." *Erev* Shabbat refers to all day Friday and the time preceding the beginning of Shabbat, as well as the Friday evening portion of Shabbat itself.

Haftarah: This is the portion from the Prophets (*Nevi'im*) or Writings (*Ketuvim*) which is read in the synagogue after reading from the Torah. A *Haftarah* portion is read on Shabbat, holidays, and on fast days. There is usually a noticeable link between the Torah portion and the *Haftarah* portion in the form of a common theme, word, name, or event.

HaMotzi: The blessing over bread. The wording, ". . . Who brings forth bread from the earth," is taken from Psalm 104:14. (For blessing, see Appendix, page 251.)

Havdalah: "Separation." The Havdalah ceremony consists of a series of blessings recited at the termination of Shabbat to emphasize the difference between Shabbat and the ordinary weekdays. A special braided candle, spices, and wine are used as part of the ceremony. (For blessings, see Appendix, page 251.)

Kabbalat Shabbat: "Welcoming the Shabbat." Before the Ma'ariv service on Friday evening comes the Kabbalat Shabbat service, consisting of Psalms 95-99 and Psalm 29, *"Lecha Dodi"* (the famous poem made into a hymn), and Psalms 92-93.

Kiddush: "Sanctification." The term refers to the blessing over the wine for any holiday or life cycle occasion, but especially when Shabbat (or the Festivals) are consecrated. This blessing can be said over two loaves of bread if wine is not available. On Friday evening, the first paragraph consists of Genesis 2:1-3, followed by ". . . *Boray Pri HaGafen.*" This in turn is followed by the body of the *Kiddush*, which reminds us of the Exodus from Egypt. The festival *Kiddush* differs from the Shabbat *Kiddush*.

L'cha Dodi: "Come, my friend." Written by Rabbi Solomon Alkabetz (1505-1584), a Kabbalist of Safed, this poem set to music likens the Shabbat to a bride in the refrain, "Come, my friend, to meet the bride; let us welcome the Shabbat." It has been described as one of the finest pieces of religious poetry ever written.

Maftir: "One who concludes." It is the term given to the three or more concluding verses of the weekly Torah portion. It also refers to the person who reads these verses and then blesses (and reads) the *Haftarah*. A child celebrating a Bar/Bat Mitzvah usually reads the *Maftir* and then the *Haftarah*.

Melaveh Malkah: "Accompanying the Queen." Shabbat is said to begin/enter like a bride, but conclude/go out like a queen. At the conclusion of the Shabbat, known as *Motza'ay Shabbat*, a festive meal and celebration take place as if in honor of the "queen." The meal is accompanied by songs and hymns.

Mezuzah: "Doorpost." *Mezuzah* refers to the parchment scrolls on which are written Deuteronomy 6:4-9 and 11:13-21. These scrolls are placed inside a container and affixed to the doorposts of a home occupied by Jews. The *mezuzah* is fastened in a slanting position to the upper part of the doorpost on the right side as one enters the room, home, school, or synagogue.

Motza'ay Shabbat: Means "Conclusion of the Shabbat," at which time the Havdalah service takes place.

Muktzeh: "Set aside" or "Stored away." The term refers to objects related to work which may not be handled on the Shabbat so that Jews will not forget the holiness of the day. Money, work objects, and other items designated for non-Shabbat use are set apart from those objects which are for Shabbat use. *Muktzeh* also refers to the 39 acts of work prohibited on Shabbat.

Neshamah Yetayrah: "Additional soul." Tradition teaches that a Jew possesses an additional soul or oversoul on Shabbat. This enables one to derive an extra measure of satisfaction from the day. Smelling the sweet spices of Havdalah serves to compensate for the departure of the additional soul as Shabbat comes to an end.

Oneg Shabbat: "Shabbat delight." The term refers to gatherings held either Friday evening or Shabbat afternoon devoted to community singing, study, cultural discussions, or socializing. In the 1920s, the poet H. N. Bialik introduced the custom of *Oneg* Shabbat through Torah study and the singing of *zemirot*. More commonly, the term refers to the reception held in the synagogue after Shabbat services.

Pikuach Nefesh Docheh et HaShabbat: "Saving a life postpones the Shabbat." While many laws have been established to preserve the holiness of the day, Shabbat laws may be suspended if health is endangered or in order to save a life. For example, if a woman goes into labor on Shabbat, her husband is permitted to drive her to the hospital. The basic principle underlying this dictum is that the *mitzvot* are to live by and not to die from. Similarily, Shabbat was made for humankind and not humankind for Shabbat.

Sedra/Sidrot: "Order." The term refers to the order of the weekly Torah portions. Torah is divided into 54 *sidrot*. On some weeks, especially in a non-leap year, two *sidrot* are combined several times so that the Torah will be completed in one year. The term *parashah* is used interchangeably with *sedra*;

however, the term *parashah* also refers to the divisions of each weekly *sedra*. There are seven *parashiyot* in each *sedra*, plus *Maftir*.

Seudah Shelisheet: "Third Meal" in Hebrew; in Yiddish, *Shallish S(h)eudos*. In years past, two meals a day was the norm especially among the poor. The Hasidim, especially, insisted that a third meal be added to Shabbat so as to further emphasize the joy of the day. Eaten on Saturday at sunset, it developed into a festive communal gathering accompanied by *zemirot* and lasting long into the evening. The term is sometimes used interchangeably with *Melavah Malkah*.

Shabbat Beresheet: The first Shabbat after Simchat Torah on which the first *sedra* of the year (Genesis 1:1-6:8) is read.

Shabbat Chazon: "Shabbat of the Vision," the Shabbat preceding Tishah B'Av. Its name derives from the *Haftarah* (Isaiah 1:1-27) which begins with the word *Chazon*, vision.

Shabbat Chol HaMo'ed: The Shabbat occurring in the middle of Sukkot or Passover is marked by special Torah readings and festival poems. In addition, Song of Songs is read on Passover and Ecclesiastes is read on Sukkot.

Shabbat HaChodesh: "Shabbat of the Month." This is the Shabbat that coincides with the first of Nisan, the month of Passover, and the celebration of Jewish freedom. Exodus 12:1-20 is read in addition to the regular weekly *sedra*.

Shabbat HaGadol: "The Great Shabbat," the Shabbat preceding Passover, at which time it is customary for the Rabbi to deliver a sermon dealing with the rites and dietary laws pertaining to Passover. Its name derives either from a corruption of "Shabbat *Haggadah*" or from its *Haftarah* portion (Malachi 4:5-6) which ends with the words: "Behold, I will send you Elijah . . . before that great and awesome day of God."

Shabbat Mevarchin: "The Shabbat of Blessing" is a Shabbat that precedes a new month. A special blessing is recited for the new moon and the name of the month and the date of Rosh Chodesh are announced.

Shabbat Nachamu: "Shabbat of Comfort," the Shabbat that follows Tishah B'Av. Its name is derived from the *Haftarah* of the day (Isaiah 40: 1-26) which begins with the words "*Nachamu, Nachamu, Ami* — Be comforted, be comforted, My people . . . " This is the first of seven consecutive weeks in which the *Haftarah* portions read are prophecies of comfort. The *sedra* read is the Ten Commandments.

Shabbat Parah: "Shabbat of the Red Heifer" — the Shabbat that occurs one week before Shabbat HaChodesh. Numbers 19:1-22 is read in addition to the regular *sedra*.

Shabbat Queen (Shabbat HaMalkah): Shabbat has been described in folk literature and in poetry as the crowning glory of the week — as royalty. It is said that Shabbat enters as a bride and departs as a queen.

Shabbat Rosh Chodesh: "Shabbat of the New Month" — when a new month coincides with the Shabbat. Isaiah 66:1-24 is read as a special *Haftarah* in place of the regular *Haftarah*.

Shabbat Shekalim: "Shabbat of the Shekel," the Shabbat immediately preceding the month of Adar (Adar II in a leap year). Exodus 30:11-16 is read in addition to the regular *sedra*. This reading makes mention of the ancient coin (*shekel*) which was collected as an offering of the people for the Tabernacle.

Shabbat Shirah: "Shabbat of the Song," the Shabbat on which "*Shirat HaYam*" (The Song of the Sea) is read. This song of victory marked the redemption of the Hebrew slaves from Egyptian slavery. The song is part of the *sedra Beshalach* (Exodus 13:17-17:16).

Shabbat Shuvah: "Shabbat of Repentance," the Shabbat between Rosh HaShanah and Yom Kippur. Its name derives from the *Haftarah* for that day (Hosea 14:2-10) which begins with the word *Shuvah*, return or repent.

Shalom Aleichem: "Peace be unto you." This is the traditional Jewish greeting. The usual response is "*Aleichem HaShalom,*" meaning "Unto you be peace."

Shomer Shabbat: "Keeper of Shabbat." A *Shomer Shabbat* is a Shabbat observer, while a *M'chalayl Shabbat* is one who desecrates the Shabbat. The term *Shomer Shabbat* usually refers to a person who observes Shabbat according to *halachah* — Jewish law. There are, however, according to some Jews, gradations of Shabbat observance, as modern life often raises the issue of religious compromise.

Shemoneh Esray: "Eighteen." The core of the worship service, this group of prayers in the weekday liturgy consists of three introductory blessings of praise to God, 13 intermediary petitions or requests of God, and three final blessings of praise. For Shabbat, the 13 intermediary petitions are replaced by one blessing which hallows the sanctity of Shabbat. The other six blessings remain the same. Also known as the *Amidah* (Standing) or *HaTefilah* (The Prayer).

Siddur: The Shabbat and Festival Prayer Book, as differentiated from *Machzor*, the High Holy Day Prayer Book. The *Siddur* contains selections from the Bible and post-biblical literature. It can also be seen as an open-ended anthology of Jewish literature and values.

T'chum Shabbat: The "Shabbat limit" beyond which travel on the Shabbat is prohibited. The traditional distance is 2000 cubits in any one direction, but various considerations (*ayruv*) make possible extensions of the distance that one may walk on the Shabbat.

Zemirot: "Songs" sung during Shabbat meals and/or melodies sung during Shabbat worship services. The words to some *zemirot* are in the *Siddur*. Others are simply a part of the Jewish folk repertoire developed over time.

BACKGROUND

Shabbat represents one of the most unique and significant contributions of the Jewish people to world civilization. In looking for antecedents to Shabbat, it can be noted that prior to the Israelite development of Shabbat, there was no fixed rest day in the ancient world. In Mesopotamia where the lunar calendar was used, the 7th, 14th, 21st, and 28th day of each month were considered to be unlucky. Therefore, certain activities were not scheduled on these days out of fear that they would fail.

Among the Babylonians, the *Sapattu* occurred on the 15th day of the month, the day of the full moon. It was called the "day of the quieting of the gods." It may have been a day when certain special ceremonies were performed. While there appears to be a linguistic connection between the Babylonian *Sapattu* and the Hebrew Shabbat, the two have little else in common.

From the idea of a weekly day of rest, came the idea of a Sabbatical year (*sh'mitah*) during which the soil was allowed to lie fallow in order to replenish itself. After seven times seven years, there is a jubilee year (*yovel*) — a time of returning property to its original tribal ownership and of releasing slaves from their period of indenture.

Whatever its antecedents, the biblical Shabbat (Saturday) represents a radical departure from anything that preceded it. Though a Jewish creation, the idea of the Sabbath has been adopted by both Christian and Moslem traditions. Christianity chose Sunday as its Sabbath and Islam, the youngest of these religions, chose Friday as its Sabbath.

Shabbat in the Bible

Genesis 2:1-3: "The heaven and the earth were finished, and all their array. And on the seventh day God finished the work which God had been doing, and God ceased on the seventh day from all the work which God had done. And God blessed the seventh day and declared it holy, because on it God ceased from all the work of creation which God had done."

Exodus 16:4-5, 29: "And God said to Moses, "I will rain down bread (i.e., manna) for you from the sky. and the people shall go out and gather each day that day's portion . . . . But on the sixth day, when they apportion what they have brought in, it shall prove to be double the amount they gather each day . . . . Mark that God has given you the Sabbath; therefore God gives you food for two days on the sixth day."

Exodus 20:8-11: "Remember the Sabbath day and keep it holy. Six days you shall labor and do all your work, but the seventh day is a Sabbath of the Eternal your God: you shall not do any work — you, your son or daughter, your male or female slave, or your cattle, or the stranger who is within your settlements. For in six days, God made heaven and earth, the sea and all that is in them, and rested on the seventh day; therefore God blessed the Sabbath day and hallowed it."

Exodus 31:13-18: "And God spoke to Moses saying: Speak to the Israelite people and say: 'Nevertheless, you must keep My Sabbaths, for this is a sign between Me and you throughout the generations, that you may know that I the Eternal have consecrated you. You shall keep the Sabbath, for it is holy for you. One who profanes it shall be put to death: whoever does work on it, that person shall be cut off from his kin. Six days may work be done, but on the seventh day there shall be a Sabbath of complete rest, holy to the Eternal; whoever does work on the Sabbath day shall be put to death. The Israelite people shall keep the Sabbath, observing the Sabbath throughout the generations as a covenant for all time: it shall be a sign for all time between Me and the people of Israel. For in six days, God made heaven and earth, and on the seventh day, God ceased from work and was refreshed."

Deuteronomy 5:12-15: "Observe the Sabbath day and keep it holy, as the Lord your God has commanded you. Six days you shall labor and do all your work, but the seventh day is a Sabbath of the Lord your God: you shall not do any work, you, your son or your daughter, your male or female slave, your ox or your ass, or any of your cattle or the stranger in your settlements, so that your male and female slave may rest as you do. Remember that you were slaves in the land of Egypt and the Eternal your God freed you from there with a mighty hand and an outstretched arm; therefore, the Eternal your God has commanded you to observe the Sabbath day."

Isaiah 58:13-14: "If you refrain from trampling the Sabbath, from pursuing your affairs on My holy day; if you call the Sabbath 'delight,' God's holy day honored; and if you honor it and go not your ways nor look to your affairs nor strike bargains — then you can seek the favor of the Eternal. I will set you astride the heights of the earth, and let you enjoy the heritage of your father Jacob, for the mouth of the Eternal has spoken."

Doing Shabbat
For the observant Jew, there is a carefully orchestrated choreography for the Shabbat. What follows is a brief schematic of a typical traditional Shabbat. A more detailed account can be found in *The First Jewish Catalog*, edited by Siegel, Strassfeld, and Strassfeld, pp. 105-114.

Friday Preparations
Cleaning the home for Shabbat.
Preparation of food and baking of *challah*.
Bathing and visit to the *mikvah*.
Dressing for Shabbat.
Putting money in the *tzedakah* box.

Friday Night
Lighting the Shabbat candles to mark the formal

beginning of the Shabbat.
Kabbalat Shabbat: Beginning of the Shabbat eve worship service in the synagogue.
Ma'ariv Service: The evening service after which one returns home for dinner.
Blessing of the children by parents.
Sing *"Shalom Aleichem"* at the table.
A Woman of Valor: Husband (and children) read(s) selections from Proverbs 31 to the woman of the home.
Singing of *Kiddush*.
Washing of the hands with appropriate blessing.
HaMotzi.
The first meal of the Shabbat.
Singing of *zemirot* during and after the meal.
Birkat HaMazon (Grace after Meals) is sung.
Family Time and/or study of Torah before going to sleep.

Shabbat Morning
Shacharit – Morning Worship Service, includes reading of Torah.
Musaf Service – after the Shacharit Service, this additional service is recited.
Return home for the second Shabbat meal.
A short version of the *Kiddush* is sung.
HaMotzi.
The second meal is usually a meat meal and it consists of food kept warm from the previous day (*cholent/chamim*).
Mealtime may also include singing or discussion of a selection from the Torah.
Birkat HaMazon is sung.
Afternoon – time for a walk, a nap, reading, fellowship.
Study of *Pirke Avot* (Ethics of the Fathers) or a passage from the Bible.

Concluding the Sabbath
At the Minchah Service (afternoon), the beginning of the following week's Torah portion is read.
Seudah Shlisheet, the third meal, takes place.
Ma'ariv Service (evening) takes place approximately 43 minutes after sunset.

Havdalah marks the conclusion of the Shabbat and the beginning of the week.
Melaveh Malkah (Escorting the Queen) celebration.

Central Themes

- Shabbat is considered the symbol of the perfect life. It is the one day when Jews can forget their troubles and have a foretaste of the world to come. Exodus 20:8-11 and Deuteronomy 5:12-15 point out that Shabbat is the common possession, the entitlement of all, rich and poor, human and beast. Therefore, the very idea of Shabbat bespeaks the equality of all people, and the necessity for human rights and individual freedom. Shabbat is not the possession of one segment of society, but is the common possession of everyone. Shabbat is a universal, democratic concept. Shabbat is unlike the *Shappatu* in ancient Babylonia, which limited the day of rest to the wealthy and the powerful. Judaism mandated that Shabbat should be for all of God's creatures. The animals were also to rest on Shabbat. Just as God rested on the seventh day, so, too, should all of God's creatures have a chance to do the same.

- Shabbat serves as a sign and as a tangible symbol of the covenant between God and Israel (Exodus 31:13-18). In the words of Ahad Ha'am: More than Jews have kept the Sabbath, the observance of the Sabbath has kept the Jews alive.

- Shabbat emphasizes differences: Shabbat vs. the other six days, special vs. mundane, faithfulness vs. faithlessness, etc. It teaches that it is important not to take for granted that which is special and different. The brief but beautiful ceremony of Havdalah marks the conclusion of the Shabbat and the beginning of the work week. It sets the other six days apart from Shabbat.

- Shabbat teaches hope. Just as Jews could always look forward to the joy of Shabbat no matter how difficult life might be, so, too, has the Jew always looked forward to a better world. Shabbat and Shabbat joy teach optimism and

hope for a better world for all of God's creatures. Part of that hope stems from the idea that we are partners with God in the work of creation. Our task is to fix that which is broken so as to improve the world (*Tikkun Olam*).

- Shabbat teaches the *mitzvah* of *Talmud Torah* (study). Judaism considers prayer and study of equal importance. A large portion of the Shabbat morning worship service is devoted to the reading or chanting of Torah and *Haftarah*. Many synagogues have Hebrew and English texts with accompanying commentaries so that the worshiper can both follow the portions and reflect upon their meaning. At home, at mealtime and during the Sabbath day, it is appropriate to read and then discuss passages of Torah.

- Shabbat teaches the *mitzvah* of *Hachnasat Orchim* (welcoming guests/hospitality). It is a *mitzvah* to welcome the stranger and those who are without family to share a Shabbat meal. This reinforces a sense of community and the belief that every Jew cares about every other Jew.

- While most of the Jewish holidays and festivals have historical roots, Shabbat goes back to the very act of creation itself. Just as God rested on the "day" after creation, we, too, are commanded to make Shabbat a day of rest for ourselves and for all of God's creatures.

- Shabbat is the fourth commandment in both versions of the Ten Commandments — Exodus 20:8-11 and Deuteronomy 5:12-15. In Exodus we are commanded to "remember" the Shabbat because God created the world in six days and then rested. In Deuteronomy we are reminded to "observe" the Shabbat because we did not have that luxury when we were slaves in Egypt.

- One of the central activities of Shabbat in addition to prayer and study is eating. Ideally, it is one day of the week when everyone shares leisurely meals accompanied by discussion and singing. Usually the foods eaten have become family traditions over the years, passed on to each succeeding generation. Eating well and enjoying family sharing time go hand-in-hand with the observance of Shabbat.

- *Tzedakah* is an important Jewish value word. It means "righteousness" or "doing righteous acts," which would include acts of charity. It is a long-standing custom for Jews to have a *pushke* or charity box in the home, and to put money in it before the lighting of the Shabbat or Festival candles. This is to remind us that, even as we prepare to enjoy the beauty of the day ahead, we must also consider the needs and well-being of others.

- Harold M. Schulweis (*For Those Who Can't Believe: Overcoming the Obstacles to Faith*, p. 207) cites an "imaginative Rabbinic legend" which notes that each day of the week was paired with a partner: Sunday with Monday, Tuesday with Wednesday, Thursday with Friday. But that left Shabbat without a partner. So it asked God to be its partner. Schulweis puts it this way: "The Sabbath is the thanksgiving prayer affirming the life of the universe."

- Harold Kushner (*To Life! A Celebration of Jewish Being & Thinking*, pp. 105-106) notes that there is nothing inherently holy in the day itself. Only if we take the time to sanctify it does it become holy. Only when we choose to observe Shabbat does it take on meaning. We can become observant one step at a time, gradually adding to our repertoire of Jewish observance. This process has a connection to the idea that humankind is a partner with God in the ongoing act of creation.

Shabbat and the Contemporary Jew
In a previous section, the choreography of Shabbat observance was outlined . . . from the time of preparation before the Shabbat actually begins until Havdalah, which marks its termination. The observant Jew knows what to do because it is a natural part of his or her life. The non-observant Jew, on the other hand, may not know where to

begin. He or she may be overwhelmed by the fullness of activities and expectations, by the details of ritual, and by the prayers associated with Shabbat observance.

In this contemporary world with its many demands and challenges, Shabbat observance has many permutations. In some homes, while the husband goes to synagogue, the wife stays home to prepare the Friday Shabbat meal. *Erev* Shabbat is celebrated at home around the dinner table. The family will worship in synagogue with the rest of the community on Saturday morning. In other homes, the family ushers in the Shabbat with dinner and then, as a family, goes to synagogue. Saturday morning may or may not see them attending services again in the synagogue. Late Friday evening services for some Jewish families and for single people have been a spiritual blessing.

One of the key elements of Shabbat for the modern Jew is that it offers a change of pace, a respite from the work week — the opportunity to set aside cares and anxieties and to do something different from the every day. This may involve reading a good book, going on a picnic, going to synagogue, studying *Pirke Avot* or the week's Torah portion. It may be the only time of the week that families can spend significant time together. Just as the soil needs time to replenish itself, so, too, do Jews need an opportunity to dedicate one day a week to personal and family "re-jew-venation."

SCOPE AND SEQUENCE

Grade	Themes/Ideas
Kindergarten	What is Shabbat — the kinds of things we do at home to celebrate Shabbat.
Grade One	Basic Shabbat blessings — candles, *motzi*, wine, Shabbat stories.
Grade Two	Shabbat in the synagogue — what makes Shabbat different from the rest of the week?

Grade Three   *Oneg* Shabbat and Havdalah — planning a *Seudah Shlisheet* and Havdalah service for children and families.

Grade Four   Shabbat vocabulary: Part One.

Grade Five   Shabbat vocabulary: Part Two (more difficult terms).

Grade Six   Shabbat worship — planning a creative Shabbat worship service; analyze Shabbat prayers.

Grade Seven   Shabbat in the Bible.

Grade Eight   Origin of the Shabbat; post-biblical sources.

Grade Nine   The meaning of the Shabbat in light of Jewish tradition; review of Shabbat terminology.

Grade Ten   The meaning of Shabbat for the contemporary Jew.

Grade Eleven   Shabbat in the eyes of Jewish thinkers.

Grade Twelve   Summary and recapitulation — the role Shabbat plays in students' lives and the role it could play.

ACTIVITIES

Preschool/Kindergarten

1. Add to the housekeeping corner items for Shabbat: white playdough (make-believe *challah*), actual *challah* (it can be baked and then covered with shellac), candlesticks, *challah* cover, special wine cups, prayer book, *kipot*, dress-up clothes (for the students and the dolls), a plastic juice bottle with purple colored water (glue the cap on so students can't open it), etc. (NSM)

2. Place the following on a table and have students figure out what goes together (you might use the words "in pairs" where appropriate): 2 *challot*, 2 candlesticks, 2 candles, a *challah* cover/a *challah*, *Kiddush* cup/grape juice bottle, Havdalah candle/candle holder, spice box/spices (shown separately), etc. (NSM)

3. Place a variety of Shabbat ritual objects on a table. Review the names of the items and then ask children to close their eyes. Remove something and have students open their eyes and see if they can identify what's missing. (NSM)

4. Ask parents to send in pairs of candlesticks which would be okay for students to touch. Leave them randomly on a table for students to explore. They might make pairs, sort according to characteristics, put candles in the holes, etc. (NSM)

5. Have a variety of breads available for students to smell and taste, including *challah*. How are these the same? Different? You might develop a simple graphic check list for students to use in their comparisons. Or, allow students to sort the breads according to characteristics they consider important. Can students pick out the *challah* based only on taste, smell, or touch? (NSM)

6. Blindfold two children, turn them around, and set them off in the general direction of each other. The pair attempts to shake hands and greet each other with *"Shabbat Shalom,"* *"Good Shabbos,"* or *"Shalom Aleichem."*

7. Have the class make *challah*. Take photos of the process, especially of the transformation from raw ingredients to the final product. Later, students can put these pictures in the order of the baking process. Another option: Take pictures of the class baking other bread and have students do a comparison of the process and product. Place the pictures in a

center for students working alone or in pairs to put in order, compare, and/or discuss. (NSM)

8. Pin a picture of a Shabbat symbol on each child's back. Each child walks around asking the other children questions about the picture on his/her back in order to guess what it is. Or, children may stand in front of the class and ask questions of the entire class in order to figure it out.

9. If possible, obtain different kinds of *challah* from a bakery (in a long braid, in a round shape, egg, no egg, with raisins, sweet, etc). Have students observe, smell, and taste them. What is the same? What is different? Why are all of these considered *challah*? (NSM)

10. Place Shabbat ritual objects in a "feelie bag." Have students reach in and identify the objects by touch. (NSM)

11. Demonstrate the things our bodies do on Shabbat: hands light the candles, tongues taste the grape juice or wine, noses smell the *challah* or spice box, etc. (NSM)

12. Using your class calendar, count the days until the next Shabbat. (NSM)

13. Play Duck, Duck, Goose, but use the words, "Shabbat, Shabbat, *Shalom!*" (NSM)

14. If you have a class which meets on Friday, establish a special routine to welcome Shabbat. Include special cleanup and a Kabbalat Shabbat. If you have a snack or eat lunch together, place special centerpieces on the table(s). Discuss or study the weekly Torah portion. It is nice, also, to invite special (pre)Shabbat guests. (NSM)

15. Have a hunt for Shabbat symbols. Cut out five cardboard *challot*, five *Kiddush* cups, and five

candles. Before the children arrive, hide these in the classroom. Divide the class into teams. Have teams search for the symbols. A *challah* is worth 5 points, a *Kiddush* cup is 3 points, and a candle is 2 points. Give the team with the most points special duties during the Shabbat celebration.

16. Have youngsters pretend to call the Sabbath Queen on the telephone. What would she say to them? What would they say to her?

17. Make rhythm instruments out of orange juice cans filled with beans, aluminum pie plates strapped together with marbles inside, round oatmeal boxes for drums. Use the instruments to accompany *zemirot*.

18. Ask one child to leave the room. Then hide a Shabbat object. When the child returns, he/she looks for the missing object. The other students assist in the search by saying *Kar* (cold), *Cham* (warm), *Kar Me'od* (very cold) and *Cham Me'od* (very warm).

19. Ask around and see which adults in your congregation have fine artwork depicting Shabbat. Divide students into small groups to study the pictures up close. Ask: What is the artist trying to convey about Shabbat? Have each group make a list of their thoughts on large chart paper. Post the papers around the room and compare the concepts the artists work with. (NSM)

20. Read to the children *Bim and Bom: A Shabbat Tale* by Daniel Swartz. Have them sing the song and make illustrations for the book. (For additional stories about Shabbat, see the Bibliography, pages 263-265.)

21. Have older students complete The Instant Lesson *Symbols of Shabbat* by Debra Marcovic and Lisa Ranchwerger.

22. Help children complete pages 1-5 in *Jewish Preschool/Kindergarten Copy Pak*™ by Nancy Cohen Nowak.

23. Do one of the movement activities related to *Shabbat in Creative Movement for a Song* by JoAnne Tucker (pages 11, 22, 26, 30, 42).

24. Do one or more of the Shabbat art projects in *100+ Jewish Art Projects for Children* by Nina Streisand Sher and Margaret A. Feldman (pages 60, 61, 62).

25. Complete some of the activities in *The Jewish Preschool Teachers Handbook* by Sandy Furfine Wolf and Nancy Cohen Nowak (pages 47-53).

Primary

1. Bring in pictures related to Shabbat (photographs, pictures from magazines, drawings, etc.). Mount them on pieces of cardboard. Laminate the pictures. Then, using a jigsaw, cut each picture into puzzle pieces. Divide the class into groups of 3 to 5 students. Each group receives the same or a different picture. The group to put its picture together first wins. If there are four groups and four different pictures, then the game can be repeated four times.

2. Choose different children to be "Shabbat Queen for a Day." Discuss why each wants to be the Queen.

3. To contrast the loudness of every day and the quiet and restfulness of Shabbat, play a loud song and then a quiet, soothing song. Have students discuss with their parents what their family can do to make Shabbat special (e.g., have a lovely dinner, light candles, go to synagogue, take a Shabbat walk together, etc.).

4. Make a *challah* cover out of men's handkerchiefs, burlap, or fabric scraps. Decorate with sequins, rick-rack, etc.

5. Make a Havdalah candle. Moisten some blue and white paper straws, insert string through each straw, and roll one straw around the other.

6. Have a non-Jewish friend take pictures of a family preparing for Shabbat, the table blessings, dinner, worship services, etc., all the way through Havdalah. Either make photo duplicates, or copy the pictures with a color copier so that there are enough sets for small groups of students to work with them. Have students put them in order of the progression of Shabbat. Students can also write captions for the pictures or create a story to share with the class. (NSM)

7. Use clay or wood, turnips, wooden spools, or even soap to make Shabbat candlesticks.

8. Make beautiful Shabbat candles out of sheets of beeswax (available at hobby art supply stores). Cut the 7½" x 16" sheets in halves or thirds on the bias. Place a wick on the long straight edge and secure it in place. Roll wax snugly over wick and continue to roll evenly. (JB)

9. Play a modified game of *Charades*. Have a student act out one of the blessings for Shabbat dinner or Havdalah. The others have to guess which blessing the child is representing. You might have students close their eyes and listen for the sounds related to the blessings. For the candle blessings they might listen for the matches and/or the sound of fabric swishing as arms are circled before the blessing. For the *Kiddush* they might listen for the sound of swallowing, etc. (NSM)

10. In anticipation of Shabbat, have children help polish the silver *Kiddush* cup or the silver ornaments which adorn the Torah. (This activity requires good supervision.) (NSM)

11. Bake a round *challah*. With younger children, use a ready-to-bake biscuit mix. Say the

blessing and eat the *challah* in class and/or send one home with each child to be used on Shabbat.

12. Prepare foods for a traditional Shabbat dinner. Invite parents to help with this project.

13. Seat children in a circle. Have class members take turns telling why a particular Shabbat symbol is their favorite.

14. Ask students to close their eyes. Pass around a fresh *challah*, but don't tell them what it is. Have the children describe its feel and smell, taste it with eyes still closed, and describe its taste. If desired, have them write or dictate poems or essays about the experience.

15. Have students imagine themselves to be a specific Shabbat ritual or a Shabbat object and then pantomime it. Other students guess what it is.

16. Teach the children the basic Shabbat blessings in Hebrew (candles, short *Kiddush, HaMotzi*). Explain the meaning of each. (For blessings, see Appendix, page 251.)

17. Have students interview the synagogue Administrator. Find out what special preparations the synagogue has to make in order to celebrate Shabbat. In all likelihood, the students will have many questions to ask about these logistical preparations.

18. Have students complete the Instant Lessons *Mastering the Shabbat Table Service, Erev Shabbat, Yom Shabbat,* and *Motzei Shabbat.*

19. Perform the play "Shabbat Shalom" from *Class Acts: Plays & Skits for Jewish Settings* by Stan J. Beiner (page 21). Invite parents and/or other classes to the performance.

20. Complete the activity pages in *Shabbat Shalom Copy Pak 1-4*™ by Marji Gold-Vukson.

21. Do one of the movement activities related to Shabbat in *Creative Movement for a Song* by JoAnne Tucker (pages 11, 22, 26, 30, 42).

22. Do one or more of the Shabbat art projects in *100+ Jewish Art Projects for Children* by Nina Streisand Sher and Margaret A. Feldman (pages 58, 59, 64, 66).

Intermediate

1. Ask students to keep a diary for ten weeks, summarizing at the conclusion of each Shabbat what they did and how they felt during the Shabbat just ended. See if their feelings and attitudes change during the ten-week period. Ask them to try to have different kinds of Shabbat experiences during the ten weeks. Collect the diaries, read them, and make private comments to each student. Ask for volunteers to share with the class some of what they have written. (These diaries also provide an informal survey of Shabbat observance.)

2. The following paragraph about Shabbat contains five errors. Ask students are to locate the mistakes, cross them out, and write in the correct information above each error.

From the beginning of Shabbat, which is welcomed by the beautiful *Oneg* Shabbat service, until the conclusion of Shabbat with its lovely *Haftarah* ceremony, Jews find special peace and beauty in Shabbat. On Friday evenings, after the candles are lit and the *Kiddush* is sung, we say *HaMotzi* over the three loaves of *challah* to remind us of the triple portion of food given to our ancestors in the Wilderness of Sinai. The *zemirot* are the special foods which are a part of Shabbat meals.

(Corrections: *Kabbalat* for *Oneg*; Havdalah for *Haftarah*; two for three; double for triple; songs for foods.)

3. Have each student create a book of original holiday poems which they can take home with them at the end of the year. Call it *My Book of Holiday Poems*, and have each child design a cover for his/her book. Suggest a different form for each holiday poem (e.g., haiku, diamante, limerick, etc.). For the Shabbat poem, put key Shabbat words on the blackboard. Have the students write at least one four-line poem using a minimum of two Shabbat terms. The poem may be serious, silly, or somewhere in between.

4. Have each student make a cassette tape of the blessings over candles, wine, and bread to take home and use as a teaching device for the rest of the family.

5. Give each student three pieces of paper. On each piece, the student writes one question about Shabbat to ask the class. Collect the questions and use them for a Shabbat Quiz.

6. In each group of words or phrases, have students find and underline the one that does not belong:
    a. *Kiddush, HaMotzi, Hallel, Hadlakat Nayrot*
    b. Shacharit, Havdalah, Kri'at HaTorah, Musaf
    c. Spice Box, Candle, Wine, *Challah*
    d. Kabbalat Shabbat, *Melaveh Malkah, Oneg Shabbat, Ma Nishtanah*

    Answers: a. = *Hallel*; b. = *Havdalah*; c. = *Challah*; d. = *Ma Nishtanah*

7. Brainstorm the key themes of Shabbat. Write the list on the blackboard. Then give each student 10 to 15 minutes to write a prayer which reflects one of the themes. Use some or all of the prayers for a Religious School worship service. Or, the Rabbi may wish to invite some of the students to read their prayers as part of the congregational Shabbat worship service.

8. Seat students in a circle on chairs or on the floor. Each child makes a sentence beginning with "Shabbat is" and completed by a feeling, mood, or characteristic of Shabbat. Variation: This can also be done as a game. The first student makes up a sentence with "Shabbat is ___ " and a word beginning with "A" that relates in some way to Shabbat. The second student makes a sentence with "Shabbat is ___ " and a word beginning with "B," and so on. (Skip the letters Q and X.)

9. Find pictures, newspaper and magazine articles, articles from the synagogue bulletin, photocopies of relevant materials from texts, original essays, and art work which deal with Shabbat. If the class is particularly successful in gathering materials, the display can be placed at the entrance to the school or in the hall.

10. Search through daily or weekly cartoons in the newspaper and collect cartoons. White out the dialogue to make them open-ended. Divide the class into groups of 3 to 5 students. Each group is given the same cartoon and asked to write a dialogue for the cartoon related to Shabbat. After 10 to 15 minutes, the small groups share their results with the remainder of the class.

11. Have the class make up their own words to traditional Shabbat melodies.

12. Have students create a paper bag representation of one of the members of Tevye's family in *Fiddler On The Roof*. Give each student a paper bag, crayons, a scissors, colored paper, and glue. After they have made their puppets, have them use their puppets to act out the Shabbat scene from the musical. Find other applications for Shabbat paper bag puppets.

13. Make a spice box out of a match box or other small box. Decorate with foil, sequins, etc. Or, use a Leggs panty hose "egg." Cover with

tissue paper in different colors. Poke holes in the shell and put in various spices. Have a Havdalah service using these boxes.

14. On an 8½" x 11" sheet of paper, have students make up a Shabbat "Coat of Arms." This can include such things as pictures of ritual objects, slogans, general Jewish symbols, and whatever else students think will meaningfully depict Shabbat.

15. Divide students into pairs. Give each pair a printed Torah and a Jewish calendar which has the Shabbat Torah portion listed (these are often available from a local Jewish funeral home). Have students work their way through the year by looking up the various Torah portions read during the course of the year, including the ones for special Shabbatot. (NSM)

16. Make Shabbat decals, T-shirts, and/or banners (JB). Use the following techniques:
    a. Apply textile paints (which are wash fast and sun fast) in one of two ways: (1) Paint directly onto the cloth or place a blotter under cloth; (2) Cut a stencil and paint with a stencil brush (dauber).
    b. Use fabric crayons for rapid results. In addition to the fabric crayons, you will need tracing paper, polyester fabric, and a heating iron. Follow these steps: (1) Make the drawing on tracing paper in pencil; if the picture has any lettering, do it back-wards; (2) Color the design solidly with crayons; (3) Tack or tape cloth to a board; (4) Turn design over, colors touching the cloth — hold design firmly; (5) Iron entire tracing, then lift off. Design in color is embedded in cloth; (7) Print several more if desired.
    c. Use Magic Markers. Tack or tape cloth to a board. Draw a heavy black line over pencil sketch. Color all areas between black lines.

17. After studying the 39 types of work prohibited on Shabbat (*Muktzeh*), divide students into groups of 3 to 4. Give each group a magazine to cut up, looking for pictures of things which are in keeping with Shabbat and which things are not. Paste the pictures into a mural or collage. (NSM)

18. Divide students into groups. Give each group one of the passages from the Torah about Shabbat (see above, pages 5 and 6). Have each create a mural depicting their passage. (NSM)

19. Have a sing-down. Only songs which have the word "Shabbat" or are traditionally sung on Shabbat may be used. (NSM)

20. Have students research the categories of work that, according to tradition, are not permitted on Shabbat. Discuss the following questions: Is full observance of Shabbat a "practical" aim? What happens when business obligations force a person to work on Shabbat? What constitutes a reasonable, attainable form of Shabbat observance for the non-Orthodox Jew today?

    Have students think about what they do on Shabbat, or what they would like to do. Either as a large group or in small groups, examine the following list of activities to see which they feel are appropriate for Shabbat. (Each group may add other items to the list if desired.)
    a. Read a good book
    b. Rest
    c. Pray in synagogue
    d. Go to the movies
    e. Read a comic book
    f. Play with the dog
    g. Play football
    h. Attend an *Oneg* Shabbat
    i. Visit friends
    j. Take a walk in the park
    k. Build a model airplane
    l. Play chess
    m. Study Torah
    n. Wash the family car(s)

o. Watch a ball game
p. Play ping pong
Follow up by having each student make a personal contract regarding Shabbat observance for the next month.

21. Have students research how Shabbat was celebrated in the shtetls of Eastern Europe. Invite a guest speaker who knows about the shtetl experience to describe it to the class. Or, if this is not possible, view a video on the subject. Resource: *The Shtetl* (Behrman House)

22. Ask students to pretend that they are speaking with someone who knows nothing about Judaism. Take turns having students come to the front of the class and explain Shabbat and the feelings that it evokes so that the listener will better understand why Shabbat is special.

23. Ask each student to bring in a Jewish object or artifact which is special to him or her and which pertains to Shabbat (e.g., a *Kiddush* cup which has been a family possession for a long time, a special *kipah*, a book, photograph, cassette tape). Students tell each other why the object is special to them.

24. Create a museum using the ritual items students have brought from home (Activity #23 immediately above). Have each student write a one paragraph description of the item. The class can take the museum from room to room or other classes can come in to view the display. In either case, the students who bring the objects from home serve as museum guides.

25. Choose a poem or story about Shabbat (for suggestions, see Bibliography, pages 263-265). Ask students to close their eyes and block out all extraneous thoughts, concentrating on what is being read. Then have them open their eyes and react to the reading.

26. Darken a room and light one candle. Students sit in a circle around the candle. Each person looks at the candle and thinks about what it would be like to be a candle looking out at a Jewish home on Shabbat. Divide the group into pairs. Each partner becomes one of the candles, and each relates to the other what he/she saw and felt. After a few minutes, reassemble the group and elicit responses from them.

27. Give each student a sheet of paper and pencil to write down what he/she considers to be the ten most essential Shabbat words. In pairs, students have five minutes to talk using only their combined lists of 20 words (minus duplications). First, each partner speaks for two minutes using only the ten words on the list; then they may converse using both lists of words.

28. Invite an elderly person to describe Shabbat in the country of their birth or when they first came to this country.

29. Shabbat is welcomed as a bride and leaves as a queen. Have students role play a meeting between *Shabbat Kallah* and *Shabbat Malkah*. Two volunteers interact, discussing their common love, namely Shabbat.

30. Ask for two volunteers to portray two symbols or objects related to Shabbat. (These two are the only ones to know what the symbols or objects are.) The pair interacts in pantomime. The class must figure out what the symbol or object is.

31. Perform or do a readers theater version of the play "A Love for Learning" from *Kings and Things: 20 Jewish Plays for Kids 8 to 18* by Meridith Shaw Patera (page 136). Relate the love of learning to study on Shabbat.

32. Do one or more of the Shabbat art projects in *100+ Jewish Art Projects for Children* by Nina

Streisand Sher and Margaret A. Feldman (pages 63, 65, 67).

Secondary

1. Ahad Ha'am said: "More than the Jews have kept the Sabbath, the Sabbath has kept the Jews." Have each student write a paragraph or two describing in his/her own words what this quotation means. Follow up with a class discussion.

2. Give each student a story geared to a younger age group. Each student writes a review of the story for the synagogue bulletin or library.

3. Provide each student with one age appropriate story to read. Give the same story to each of several students. Students who have read the same story are then grouped together. Each group works out a consensus statement that summarizes the story and its key ideas. Each group summarizes and/or acts out its story for the other students.

4. Read the two versions of the fourth commandment (Exodus 20:8-11 and Deuteronomy 5:12-15). Compare and contrast them. Ask: Why should we remember Shabbat each week? What connection does Shabbat have to the creation of the heaven and the earth? Who is commanded to keep the Shabbat? Who is left out? What is the connection between Shabbat and the Exodus?

5. Divide the class into groups of 3 to 5 students each. Give the groups 10 to 15 minutes to make up questions about Shabbat to ask the other groups. Reassemble the whole group for a Shabbat Quiz. The teacher administers the questions, giving teams 1 point for correct answers to easy questions and 2 points for correct answers to difficult questions. The team with the most points wins.

6. As a class, devise a "Shabbat Attitude Survey." Each student then surveys five to ten people.

Have the class tabulate the results the following week. Some possible questions: The thing I like best about Shabbat is _____. For me the most meaningful aspect of Shabbat is _____. The hardest part of Shabbat is _____. Celebrating Shabbat teaches me _____.

7. Divide the class into six groups. Ask each group to examine and summarize for the class one of the following passages related to Shabbat:
    a. Genesis 2:1-2
    b. Exodus 31:12-17
    c. Isaiah 56:1-7
    d. Exodus 20:8-11
    e. Deuteronomy 5:12-15
    f. Isaiah 58:13-14

8. Read the following statement to the class. Ask students to agree or disagree with it and explain their response. "Judaism was founded long before Christianity or Islam came into being. Shabbat was a part of Judaism from its earliest days. When Christianity was established, adherents wanted to have a Sabbath, but to make it distinctively Christian, they celebrated it on Sundays. About 600 years later, Islam also wanted a Sabbath, but since Saturday and Sunday were taken, Islam chose Friday as its Sabbath."

9. As a class, have students write a Shabbat Manual of observance. Use existing manuals as resources.
    Resources: *The Art of Jewish Living: Shabbat Seder* by Ron Wolfson; *Gates of Shabbat: Shaarei Shabbat* by Mark Dov Shapiro.

10. Most communities, no matter how affluent they may seem to be, have invisible minorities as well as people living below the poverty line. These people should receive our help throughout the year, and not just during the Thanksgiving season. To reinforce the idea that we

shouldn't take God's gifts for granted (especially the good food we enjoy on Shabbat), organize an in-school food drive. Ask students to bring one item of non-perishable food or one paper product to Religious School each week. Students go along when the items are donated to a local food pantry. Discuss how a food or clothing drive is truly an act of *tzedakah*.

11. Invite a local church group to visit the synagogue. Kabbalat Shabbat is a good service for them to observe. After the service, the Rabbi, minister, and/or students studying comparative religion can explain some of the main tenets of Judaism and Christianity and some of the differences between the two religions. Be sure students extend a warm welcome to the guests.

12. Rabbi Harold Kushner speaks about remembering that we were once slaves in Egypt as a reason for observing the Shabbat (*To Life! A Celebration of Jewish Being & Thinking*, p. 95). He notes that slavery in the past was a matter of who owned a person's body. In the modern world, however, slavery is more a matter of who owns a person's soul and who owns a person's time. Ask students if they agree or disagree with Kushner. In what ways can people be slaves in the modern world without living in a politically repressive climate? Are there ways that we enslave ourselves?

13. We read in *parasha Mishpatim* (Exodus 21:2), which comes immediately after the Ten Commandments: "When you acquire a Hebrew slave, he shall serve six years; in the seventh year, he shall be freed, without payment." Discuss the connection between this important statement and the observance of the Shabbat. How do slaves and former slaves fit into the Shabbat picture?

14. Discuss the importance of lighting candles at the beginning of Shabbat. Examine the flame as a symbol of light and hope, as opposed to the darkness that is outside the home. How

does this represent our hope for a better world? Are there other benefits from lighting Shabbat candles?

15. Compare and contrast the lighting of the Shabbat candles and the Havdalah candle. Discuss: What is the significance of the braided candle that is used for Havdalah? How does the candle symbolize Judaism's concept of relationships and interdependence?

16. Using a Hebrew and/or English text, examine the *Kiddush* carefully. Find the passages which reflect the following ideas:

    a. God completed the act of creation and ceased from acts of creation on the seventh day.

    b. God rested from all manner of work on the seventh day.

    c. God blessed and sanctified the seventh day.

    d. God has made the Shabbat as a reminder of the work of creation.

    e. God made the Shabbat as a remembrance of the Exodus from Egypt and freedom from slavery.

    f. God set Israel apart from all other peoples. Israel has a special relationship with God.

    g. The Shabbat is a sacred inheritance of the Jewish people.

17. Play Shabbat music or music from *Fiddler on the Roof*. Ask students to close their eyes and think about Shabbat memories, particularly about what they did on Shabbat when they were younger. Thoughts may be shared with the total group, or you may may divide the class into small groups for sharing.

18. Have students imagine they are living in a ghetto in Europe in the Middle Ages or in a *shtetl* in the nineteenth century. Together, they discuss what preparations need to be made for the forthcoming celebration of Shabbat.

Discuss how Shabbat in that time differs from Shabbat in this place today.

19. Present a situation involving the observance of Shabbat which is not clear-cut in terms of how one is to act. In pairs or small groups, students act out the situation. Each group then discusses the situation and their reaction to the way they role played it. Reassemble the class and elicit feedback.

All-School

1. Assign students to cross-graded groups via name tags cut out in the shapes of symbols of various Jewish holidays. Everyone goes to a big room where large sheets of butcher paper are marked with name tag symbols. Each group has candles, wine, and *challah*. A Confirmation student assigned to each group leads the Shabbat table service and tells a short story. Everyone enjoys lunch and sings *zemirot*. Then all participate in various art projects:
   a. Make candlesticks out of tuna cans.
   b. Make a spice box by sticking cloves into an orange.
   c. Make a *challah* board. Sand a piece of scrap wood from a lumber yard. Put the family name on it and varnish it.
   d. Make *challah* covers by crayoning on flour sacks cut into long strips.
   e. Using a shoe box, make a Shabbat box. Fill it with Shabbat items.
   f. Make a Havdalah candle. Soften three Chanukah candles by dipping them in boiling water. Then weave them together.

2. Plan a school-wide program or family education program with Shabbat activity stations. Stations can include:
   a. Make Shabbat ritual objects: candlesticks, *Kiddush* cup, *challah* cover, Havdalah set.
   b. Learn Shabbat Blessings: candles, *Kiddush*, Havdalah.
   c. Shabbat Foods/*Cholent*: Explanation and/or demonstration.

d. The Weekly Torah Portion: Display a *Sefer Torah*, a Torah Commentary, and a *Tikkun*. Explain how the weekly *parashah* is selected and read.
   e. Quiz: Participants take an age-appropriate short quiz to reinforce what was learned in each of the other stations.

3. Plan a "lock-in" sleepover for one grade or for the youth group, beginning with a Friday evening Kabbalat Shabbat service and dinner and concluding with Havdalah. Go through a full day of Shabbat observance, celebration, and singing.

Family

1. Obtain a nice stuffed animal and a notebook. Develop a rotating schedule in which students take home both the animal and notebook for a weekend. Send along a note asking the families to write their "guest's" weekend adventures in the notebook. When the animal and journal are returned, you will be able to read to the class all kinds of family customs, including Shabbat observance. (NSM)

2. Organize a family education program for two to four-year-olds (there are three already designed Shabbat programs in *Head Start on Holidays: Jewish Programs for Preschoolers and Their Parents* by Roberta Louis Goodman and Andye Honigman Zell).

3. Use Shabbat as a time to send home Jewish books, tapes, videos, games, or CD-ROMs on a rotating basis. Enclose the item going home in a plastic resealable bag with a special Shabbat "logo." Include a sheet that families can fill in with their reactions. (NSM)

4. Work with students to create a Shabbat Kit to send home to their families. Students may make a *challah* cover, small *challah*, *Kiddush* cup, matchbox cover, candlesticks, and two candles. Also include information on how to use the items, along with some background on

Shabbat. Include a response sheet, asking families to share with you their experience with the kit. You might wish to send home two more candles the next week. (NSM)

5. Help match families so that they can enjoy Shabbat dinner together. (NSM)

6. Invite families for a "make it and take it" Havdalah workshop. Have stations for making dipped and braided candles, spice boxes, and decorated *Kiddush* cups. Also include a station for learning the blessings (see Appendix, page 251), with time for families to write something on the theme of Shabbat, separation, or other similar theme. If the workshop is timed right, families could spread out (either in the building, or outside if possible) and do their own Havdalah; it's a beautiful sight to see many Havdalah candles flickering in the dark. Have a songleader sit in a central area quietly playing his/her guitar. As families finish, they go and sit with the song leader. When all families have joined together, sing some appropriate, quiet songs as a group. (NSM)

7. Send home information describing the traditional blessing parents give their children on Shabbat. Also send home short biographies (or a list of names parents will recognize) of famous Jews. Be sure to include males and females. Suggest that parents consider blessing their children in the name of any of these people, describing a value or virtue which that person embodies. For example: "May you be like Emma Lazarus who used poetry to express her deepest thoughts." (NSM)

8. Organize a class Shabbat dinner. Such occasions enable children to put into practice what they have learned in Religious School while at the same time teaching parents the how-to of Shabbat without the risk of embarrassment. Following dinner, the families participate in worship services.

9. Invite families to class or do the following exercise at a Shabbaton. Seat everyone on the floor in two rows facing each other with knees touching. Unroll a Torah Scroll across their knees so that participants can see and touch the Torah (make sure the Torah doesn't touch the floor). Describe the Torah and encourage participants to ask questions about how the Torah is made, what materials are used, how a scribe works, etc. Show the group the *sedra* for that week. With the Torah open, discuss the meaning and relevance of the *sedra* with the students. Or, do this exercise using many long tables placed end to end. Have the participants look at the unrolled Torah from either side of the tables.

10. Send home materials to help families study a selected part of the weekly Torah portion. Each family member is given a few verses to study and summarize for the rest of the family. (Younger children will need some help with this.) Each family member reads their selection from the Torah and then restates it in his/her own words. To conclude, the family discusses the meaning of the passage from the Torah.

11. Suggest that families do something special to celebrate Shabbat. They might go to a different synagogue or take part in a special event, one in which they would not normally participate. Upon returning home, all share feelings and reactions.

12. Encourage families to plan a festive meal for the celebration of Shabbat. Include at least one traditional dish.

13. Suggest that families listen to Jewish music together or read selections from a Jewish humor book.

BIBLIOGRAPHY
See pages 263-265.

CHAPTER TWO

ROSH HASHANAH

VOCABULARY

Apples and Honey: On the eve of Rosh HaShanah, prior to the kindling of the festival lights and the recitation of *Kiddush*, a piece of apple is dipped in honey. *Shehecheyanu* is pronounced and the words "May it be God's will to grant us a good and a sweet year," are said. On the second night of Rosh HaShanah, it is customary to taste a fruit which has not been eaten during the past season so that the *Shehecheyanu* can again be recited. (See Appendix, pages 252 and 253, for these blessings in Hebrew and English.)

Aseret Y'may Teshuvah: "Ten Days of Repentance" — the period between Rosh HaShanah and Yom Kippur. According to the Talmud *(Rosh HaShanah* 16b), on Rosh HaShanah the wholly righteous are inscribed in the Book of Life. For others, judgment is suspended until Yom Kippur, when their good works and acts of repentance can still tilt the balance in their favor . . . so that they may live. During this period, emphasis is placed on the sincerity of one's repentance. Perfunctory acts of repentance carry no weight.

Avinu Malkaynu: "Our Father, Our King" — this prayer, one of the best known in the High Holy Day liturgy, dates from the period of the Talmud. The complete prayer consists of 44 requests for God's blessings and requests for forgiveness of sins, as well as for protection from misfortune. Each supplication begins with the refrain, *"Avinu Malkaynu."* The prayer reflects two aspects of God:

the loving parent Who accepts us with compassion and the stern ruler who establishes and enforces rules.

Ba'al Tokayah: "Master of the *Tekiah*" — the person who sounds the *shofar* during the High Holy Day period.

Elul: The sixth month of the Jewish year (August/September). As the month immediately before Rosh HaShanah, it is a time of preparation. The *shofar* is sounded each day. Elul is 29 days long and its zodiac sign is Virgo.

Hineni: "Behold me." In this dramatic prayer which occurs early in the *erev* Rosh HaShanah worship service, the Rabbi stands before the open Ark and speaks to God on behalf of the congregation. The prayer begins: "Behold me, of little merit, trembling and afraid as I stand before You to plead for Your people. Let them not be put to shame because of me, nor I because of them . . . ."

Kittel: A white garment worn on the Holy Days. It represents the ideal of purity and symbolizes the confidence on the part of the Jew that God's forgiveness will come when the Jew resolves to sin no more.

L'Shanah Tovah Tikatayvu (V'tichataymu): "May you be inscribed (and sealed) for a good year." This is the Rosh HaShanah greeting which expresses the hope that all friends and loved ones will be written and sealed in the Book of Life, and granted happiness and fulfillment in the year ahead.

Machzor: "Cycle." The High Holy Day prayer book.

Makri: "Calling out." The *Makri* is the person who calls out the names of the various sounds to be blown on the *shofar.*

Malchuyot: "Kingship." *Malchuyot* is the first section of the middle part of the Shofar Service that comprises the intermediate blessings of the *Amidah* of the Musaf Service. It stresses God's sovereignty over all the creatures of the universe.

Musaf Amidah: The Musaf service follows Shacharit on Shabbat and Festivals. During the weekdays, the intermediate blessings take the form of petitions, but on Shabbat and the festivals, these blessings are replaced by a single intermediate prayer in praise of God. The *Amidah* for the High Holy Days, however, is by far the longest *Amidah* of any Jewish worship service. Between the three introductory blessings and the three final blessings comes a special series of prayers known as the Shofar Service which consists of three parts: *Malchuyot, Zichronot,* and *Shofarot.*

Rosh HaShanah: "Head of the Year." The term does not occur in the Bible. Ezra 3:6 and Nehemiah 8:1-11 refer to the first day of the seventh month as a festival; however, Ezra states: "From the first day of the seventh month, they began to offer burnt offerings to the Lord . . . " The passage in Nehemiah states: "And Ezra the Priest brought the Law before the congregation, both men and women, and all that could hear with understanding. Upon the first day of the seventh month . . . And Nehemiah . . . said unto all the people: 'This day is holy unto the Lord your God . . . .'" By the time the Mishnah was completed (ca. 217 C.E.), the term Rosh HaShanah was in common usage. Furthermore, one tractate of the Mishnah is entitled *Rosh HaShanah.*

Selichot: "Forgiveness." At midnight on the Saturday evening before Rosh HaShanah (or a week earlier if Rosh HaShanah begins on a Monday or Tuesday), a special synagogue service is held during which sins of the past year are confessed. The service consists of supplications, penitential prayers, and religious poetry (*piyyutim*) reflecting the theme of forgiveness from sin. The Selichot liturgy is based largely on the Psalms, supplemented by a considerable amount of recent additional readings.

Shabbat Shuvah: "Shabbat of Repentance" — the Shabbat between Rosh HaShanah and Yom Kippur. A special *Haftarah* is read which consists of Hosea 14:2-10, Micah 7:18-20, and Joel 2:15-27. The name for this Shabbat is taken from Hosea 14:2 which begins with the words: "Return, 0 Israel . . . (*Shuvah Yisrael*)." On this Shabbat, it is customary for Rabbis to deliver sermons on the theme of repentance.

Shehecheyanu: "The One who has kept us alive." This prayer is recited at the beginning of Rosh HaShanah and the festivals, at joyous life cycle events, for new ventures, on the eating of new foods, on the donning of a new garment, and the like.

Shevarim: One of the sounds of the *shofar.* It consists of three short broken notes.

Shofar: The *shofar* is made from the horn of a ram or other clean animal, but not from the horn of a cow or an ox. It is sounded every morning during Elul, on Rosh HaShanah morning during the Musaf service before the Torah is returned to the Ark, and again at the conclusion of Yom Kippur.

Shofarot: Plural of *Shofar. Shofarot* is the third section of the middle part of the Shofar Service that comprises the intermediate blessings of the *Amidah* of the Musaf service. It contains verses from the Bible which recall God's revelation at Sinai to the accompaniment of the blowing of the *shofar* (Exodus 19:19), and shows the connection between the blowing of the *shofar* and acts of faith.

Tashlich: "Cast/Throw." On the first day of Rosh HaShanah, or on the second day if the first day of Rosh HaShanah occurs on Shabbat, after the Minchah service, it is a tradition to go to a river or a stream to cast sins symbolically into the water. The key passage in this ceremony, which sometimes involves throwing pocket lint or bread crumbs into the water, is Micah 7:19: "The Eternal will have compassion upon us; the Eternal will subdue our iniquities. And You will cast (*tashlich*) all their sins into the depths of the sea." Metaphorically, as the eyes of fish never close, so God always watches for our sins to be cast away.

Tekiah: One of the sounds of the *shofar*. It consists of one deep note which ends abruptly.

Tekiah Gedolah: "Great *Tekiah*." This final sound in the sequence of *shofar* sounds is a greatly prolonged *tekiah*.

Teruah: One of the sounds of the *shofar*, it consists of nine short broken notes making a wavering sound.

Tishre: The seventh month of the Jewish year (September/October). It is 30 days long, and its zodiac sign is Libra. The first of Tishre is Rosh HaShanah, the tenth is Yom Kippur, the fifteenth is Sukkot, the twenty-second and twenty-third are Shemini Atzeret and Simchat Torah. While the month of Nisan has been the first month in the Jewish calendar since biblical times, the first of Tishre marks the anniversary of the creation of the world which, according to tradition, took place over 5700 years ago. In the course of time, the first of Tishre came to be considered the religious new year, the first of Nisan became the beginning of the year for matters of state, the fifteenth of Elul became the new year for purposes of establishing

the tithe for livestock and agricultural products, and the 15th of Shevat (Tu B'Shevat) became the new year of the trees.

Un'taneh Tokef: "Let us recount the power" and holiness of this day. This prayer was originally uttered, according to legend, by the martyred Rabbi Amnon of Mayence as he was about to die. It may have been written, however, by Rabbi Kalonymus ben Meshulam in the eleventh century. The prayer describes, in poignant terms, the heavenly day of judgment. It states that only God knows who will live and who will die during the coming year. It states that God, like a shepherd counting sheep, each year counts us and decides what will become of each of us.

Yamim Nora'im: "Days of Awe" — the ten days beginning with Rosh HaShanah and concluding with Yom Kippur. The expression was coined in the late Middle Ages. It reflected the terror felt by Jews as a result of horrible persecutions that were then occurring, and also of the awe of God who stands in judgment during the *Yamim Nora'im*. This term is contrasted with *Yamim Tovim*, "festive days," which reflect the joyful side of the Jewish festivals.

Yom HaDin: "Day of Judgment" — one of the names for Rosh HaShanah, since on this day God judges the actions of Jews. It is also a time for self-examination, self-assessment, and self-judgment.

Yom HaZikron: "Day of Remembrance" — one of the names for Rosh HaShanah, it reflects the idea that God remembers each individual and passes judgment at this season. The second part of the intermediate blessings of the *Amidah* of the Musaf service is called *Zichronot*.

Yom Teruah: "Day of the Sounding of the *Shofar*" — one of the names for Rosh HaShanah. It comes from Numbers 29:1: "In the seventh month, on the first day of the month, you shall observe a sacred occasion: you shall not work at your occupations. You shall observe it as a day when the horn is sounded."

Zichronot: "*Remembrances.*" *Zichronot* is the second section of the Shofar Service that comprises the intermediate blessings of the *Amidah* of the Musaf service on Rosh HaShanah. It stresses God's remembrance of acts of faith performed by Jews throughout the ages.

BACKGROUND

Rosh Hashanah is the first day of Tishre, the seventh month of the Jewish calendar year (corresponding to September/October). The moon, though waxing, is but a thin sliver in the shape of the Hebrew letter *resh*. This is the beginning of the Ten Days of Repentance, the *Yamim Nora'im* — the awesome days — when, according to tradition, all of humankind awaits the divine decree.

Rosh HaShanah is considered to be the birthday of the world, the day on which Sarah first learned that she would have a child, the day on which Isaac was born, and the day on which Hannah learned that she would have a son.

The holiday is referred to by several names in the Tanach: *Yom Teru'ah* (Numbers 29:1) – day of the sounding of the *shofar*; *Shabaton* and/or *Zicharon Teru'ah* (Leviticus 23:24) – a holy convocation; *Mikrah Kodesh* – a holy assembly (Leviticus 23:23/ Numbers 29:1 — although this may be more a description of the day than a name for it). The words "*rosh hashanah*" occur only in Ezekiel 40:1 where they seem to refer to the beginning of the year and not to a specific celebration. The first of Tishre, however, is cited several times: Leviticus 23:23 and Nehemiah 8:2. Clearly, Rosh HaShanah existed in some form during biblical times, but the observance took on major importance much later in Jewish history.

In Rabbinic literature, the holiday is referred to by four names: *Yom Teru'ah* – day of sounding the horn; *Yom HaDin* – day of judgment; *Yom*

HaZikaron – day of remembrance; and, Rosh HaShanah.

There are four new years in the Jewish calendar: Nisan 1 – the reign of kings; Elul 15 – for assessing tithes; Tishre 1 – for judgment and for spiritual growth; and, Shevat 15 – for the trees.

Four New Years

The Mishnah makes reference to four different New Years. *Rosh HaShanah* 1:1 states: ". . . the first of Nisan (March/April) is the New Year for kings and festivals; the first of Elul (August/September) is the New Year for the tithing of cattle. Rabbis Elazer and Shimon say that it falls on the first of Tishre. The first of Tishre (September/October) is the New Year for the reckoning of years (of foreign kings), of the Sabbatical years (every seven years), and of Jubilee years (every 50 years), as well as the New Year for the planting of trees and vegetables. The first of Shevat (January/February) is the New Year for the (fruit) trees according to the House of Shammai, while the House of Hillel says that it falls on the 15th of Shevat."

The first of Nisan can be considered to be the legal New Year. This was the date around which the reign of Israelite kings was calculated. The dates of each of the festivals of the Jewish year are calculated from the first day of Nisan. Accordingly, Pesach, which begins on the fifteenth of Nisan, is the first festival of the year, while Rosh HaShanah takes place on the first day of the seventh month of Tishre — in the exact middle of the year.

The first of Elul is the New Year for tithing. When the Mishnah speaks of cattle, it actually refers to all animals that are counted as part of the tithe. Any animal born before Elul 1st was counted as part of the tithe for the year ending with that date.

The first of Tishre, the biblical Day of Memorial, became Rosh HaShanah — the beginning of the religious year.

The 15th of Shevat marks the beginning of the fruit crop in Israel. It is the New Year for the fruit trees. This same Mishnah cites two conflicting dates for the New Year of the Trees. The House of Shammai favored the 1st of Shevat, because Shammai was the spokesperson for the conservative, upper-class Jews who, being able to afford to take good care of their land and their trees, could probably have trees ready to welcome spring early. The House of Hillel, on the other hand, favored the 15th of Shevat. More liberal and clearly more attuned to the needs of the struggling masses, Hillel believed that the trees belonging to the working class needed those extra 15 days in order to recuperate from the previous year's winter. *Halachah is* according to Hillel.

Central Themes

- The mood of this holiday is serious and solemn, but not morbid.

- White is worn to reflect an optimism that God will accept our prayers.

- It is a time for genuine soul-searching and moral self-examination.

- It is a time to appreciate the blessings of the past year.

- It is a time to pray for life and peace, not only for loved ones, but for all people everywhere.

- It is a time to reflect upon our own actions during the past year and to make amends (*teshuvah*) for our failures.

- For sins against God, prayer, generousity, and repentance bring forgiveness; for sins against others, we must obtain forgiveness from them.

- Some holidays and festivals link us to historical events (i.e., Passover/the Exodus, Shavuot/Torah on Mount Sinai, Chanukah/victory of the Maccabees etc.). Rosh HaShanah, on the other hand, celebrates the birth of the world, embodying the unique idea that we are partners with God in an ongoing creation process and are committed to the task of *Tikkun Olam* (repairing the world).

- The idea of a birthday of the world begs the issue of universalism and particularism. A people with a covenantal relationship with God must also recognize that the world belongs to all of God's creatures.

Highlights of the Liturgy

Selichot takes place at midnight on the Saturday evening prior to Rosh HaShanah. If Rosh HaShanah falls on a Monday or Tuesday, Selichot is observed on Saturday evening of the previous week. Selichot serves to usher in the High Holy Days.

The blessing over Rosh HaShanah candles is the same as that blessing for other festivals. (See Appendix, page 251, for blessing.)

Key prayers of the holiday include:

Hineni: A dramatic prayer, in which the Rabbi asks for the strength to be a good leader and prays for the welfare of the congregation.

Avinu Malkaynu: An acknowledgement that God as a loving parent and Sovereign has dominion over our lives.

Un'taneh Tokef: A powerful, poem describing the forthcoming day of judgment (see page 23 for a description).

Amidah of the Musaf service: This section containing the blowing of the *shofar* is divided into three parts, each of which has a separate theme:

Malchuyot - stresses God's dominion over all the creatures of the universe.

Zichronot - deals with the historical experiences of the Jewish people and the role that God has played in those events.

Shofarot - describes the revelation at Sinai to the accompaniment of the *shofar*.

Torah and Haftarah Readings

The traditional Torah portion for the first day of Rosh HaShanah is Genesis 21 about the birth of Isaac and his growth to manhood. In Reform congregations, Genesis 22, the account of the binding of Isaac *(Akaydat Yitzchak)* is read.

The traditional Torah portion for the second day is Genesis 22. In Reform congregations Genesis 1, the account of Creation, is read.

The *Maftir* for the first and second days is Numbers 29:1-6 which describes the special offerings for the day including a burnt offering, a meal offering, and a sin offering.

The traditional *Haftarah* for the first day is I Samuel 1:1-2:10, describing the birth of Samuel. This story parallels the story of the birth of Isaac. In Reform congregations either this Samuel passage is read or Nehemiah 8, which describes Ezra assembling the people to read Torah to them on the first day of the seventh month.

The traditional *Haftarah* for the second day is Jeremiah 31:2-20, which contains words of consolation to the people. In Reform congregations either the Jeremiah passage above or Isaiah 58:6-13 is read. In the latter, Isaiah reminds the people that to improve the welfare of all is the best kind of fast.

The Shofar
The sounds of the *shofar* help to intensify the spirit of reverence and solemnity which characterizes the Rosh HaShanah worship service. The soundings of the *shofar* are:

Tekiah: A deep note which ends abruptly.

Shevarim: Three brief notes.

Teruah: A wavering or weeping sound consisting of nine short broken notes.

Tekiah Gedolah: A prolonged *Tekiah*.

The person who blows the *shofar* is known as the *Ba'al Tokayah*.

The great sage and scholar, Saadia Gaon (882-952), presents ten reasons for sounding the *shofar* during the Days of Awe. Each is a reminder of an important event or idea.

1. Rosh HaShanah marks the beginning of creation. Just as the trumpets are sounded at a coronation, so, too, God is hailed as Sovereign of the world on this day (Psalm 88:6).

2. The *shofar* serves as a reminder of the Jew's duty to return to God by calling the sinner to repentance. It serves to herald the beginning of the High Holy Days.

3. When the Torah was given to Israel at Mount Sinai, the event was accompanied by loud blasts of the *shofar* (Exodus 19:16).

4. The sound of the *shofar* serves as a reminder of the words of the prophets which are likened to the call of a trumpet (Ezekiel 33:4-5).

5. The *shofar* serves as a reminder of the destruction of the Temple, since the armies which conquered the Temple in Jerusalem sounded trumpet blasts as a battle cry.

6. In the *Akedah* account read on this holiday (Genesis 22:1-19), a ram is substituted for Isaac as an offering to God. Hence, the sounding of the ram's horn.

7. The sound of the trumpet fills the listener with fear and trepidation as he or she stands before God in prayer. Amos 3:6 states: "Shall the horn be blown in a city and the people not tremble?"

8. The prophet Zephaniah (1:14-16) speaks of the day of judgment — the "Day of God" when trumpets will be sounded.

9. Isaiah (27:13) declares that the great *shofar* will herald the coming of the messianic age and the redemption of Israel.

10. The *shofar* serves as a reminder of the future resurrection of the dead and the eternal life that awaits the righteous.

Customs

- We greet one another with the words *"Shanah Tovah Tikatayvu"* — May you be inscribed for a good year" (see "The Three Books," page 44).

- The white *kittel* worn on Rosh HaShanah represents the idea of purity and symbolizes confidence that God will forgive sins as long as we resolve to sin no more.

- A piece of apple is dipped in honey on the eve of Rosh HaShanah, reflective of the hope for a sweet New Year. The person performing this act says: "May it be God's will to grant us a good and a sweet year." (See Appendix, page 252, for the blessing in Hebrew.)

- On the afternoon of Rosh HaShanah, it is a custom to walk to a place of flowing water, a river, lake, ocean, even a well, to perform the ceremony of Tashlich (see Vocabulary for this chapter). Pocket lint or bread crumbs are cast into the water as words of *teshuvah* and hymns are recited.

- Greeting cards for the New Year are often sent to one another, althought this is a very recent custom.

- In some communities, families "go walking" about the neighborhood and drop in on each other to offer greetings. Sweets and cold drinks are shared.

SCOPE AND SEQUENCE

A suggested grade-by-grade curriculum for Rosh HaShanah follows. It should be viewed as a starting point in developing a Rosh HaShanah curriculum for your school.

Grade	Themes/Ideas
Kindergarten	Head of the Year – a new start at the beginning of the year. Apples and Honey – starting the New Year on a sweet, hope-filled note.
Grade One	Home preparations for Rosh HaShanah, including cleaning the home, the festive meal, and learning the *Shehecheyanu.*
Grade Two	New Year's resolutions – how to be a better person in the coming year. A brief look at *Avinu Malkaynu* — God as a parent and a ruler.
Grade Three	The concept of the Book of Life — no one is perfect, but people should strive toward perfection and, hopefully, come a little closer to it each year.
Grade Four	The *shofar* and its many uses. The meaning of the *shofar.* Introduction to Rosh HaShanah vocabulary.
Grade Five	Comparison of the Jewish New Year with the secular New Year. Key Rosh HaShanah terms.
Grade Six	*Yom HaDin* — how God judges us and how we judge ourselves. Confession to God. Resolutions to ourselves and apologies to the people we may have wronged during the past year.
Grade Seven	Biblical selections read on Rosh HaShanah with emphasis upon the *Akedah* (Genesis 22).
Grade Eight	An examination of the content and meaning of key prayers such as *Al Chayt, Avinu Malkaynu, Zochraynu, Hineni,* and the Shofar Service.
Grade Nine	*Yom HaZikaron* — remembering our actions in order not to repeat our mistakes in the coming year.

The past year as a link in the chain of Jewish tradition.

Grade Ten   Summary and review: The meaning of Rosh HaShanah to students as they confirm their faith and commitment.

Grade Eleven   Writing creative prayers for a youth service to be led by high school students.

Grade Twelve   The essence of Rosh HaShanah.

ACTIVITIES

Preschool/Kindergarten

1. Put apple, honey jar, *shofar*, toy Torah (in white), New Year's card, wine cup, candles, *Machzor* in a "feelie box." Have students identify the items by touch. (NSM)

2. Play *Pass the Shofar*. This variation of *Hot Potato* resembles musical chairs, except that all of the students are seated. Music is played and the *shofar* is passed from student to student. When the music stops, the person with the *shofar* is out and one chair is removed. The last person left wins. Variations: The person left with the *shofar* sings a song, recites a prayer, or tells a story.

3. Create a discovery center with sandwich bread, pita, dinner rolls, Shabbat *challah*, and High Holy Day (sweet, round) *challah*. Let students discover the differences through sight, smell, touch, and taste. (NSM)

4. Have a birthday party for the world. (NSM)

5. Make prints using apples. Mount as a display or make greeting cards out of the prints.

6. Have someone blow the *shofar*. Ask: Which notes are faster? Which are slower? What does

the sound of the *shofar* remind us to do? (NSM)

7. Cut painting paper in the shape of a *shofar*. Have students paint the shape. (NSM)

8. Make applesauce, strudel, or another apple recipe. (NSM)

9. Create a sequencing game out of *shofrot* drawn in different sizes. Students sequence the *shofrot* from small to large. Or, make a matching game by drawing *shofrot* of slightly different shapes and randomly tracing each one on a piece of posterboard. Students have to place each *shofar* into the correct space. (NSM)

10. Read to the class *Sammy Spider's First Rosh Hashanah* by Sylvia Rouss. Let the children make original illustratrations for the book, then sequence their illustrations in the correct order of the story.

11. In a science center, place different types of honey. Have students observe/explore their color, smell, taste, and viscosity (their drip speed). Perhaps provide a chart for students to record their observations. (NSM)

12. In an art center, provide paper plates, yarn, buttons, markers, glue, and other art supplies. Have students create happy and sad (or angry faces). Use these when you talk about behaviors; students can identify good and bad behavior using the correct face. (NSM)

13. Help children complete pages 6, 7, and 8 in *Jewish Preschool/Kindergarten Copy Pak*™ by Nancy Cohen Nowak.

14. Organize a family education program for two to four-year-olds. (There are two already designed programs in *Head Start on Holidays: Jewish Programs for Preschoolers and Their Parents* by Roberta Louis Goodman and

Andye Honigman Zell. One is about the High Holy Days in general and one is specifically about Rosh HaShanah.)

15. Do one or more of the Rosh HaShanah art projects in *100+ Jewish Art Projects for Children* by Nina Streisand Sher and Margaret A. Feldman (pages 1 and 4).

Primary

1. Teach the concepts that (a) we are partners in God's creation of the world, and (b) creation is not finished — we are helping God continue the process. Tell children that God created corn. We can create popcorn. Then make popcorn. Eat it after first saying a blessing. Then tell the children that God created lemons, water, and sugar cane. We can create lemonade. Make lemonade and share it. Talk about this experience of partnership with God in the continuation of creation. (EG)

2. Take turns making Rosh HaShanah resolutions. Check up on each other throughout the year to see if the resolutions are being taken seriously.

3. Everyone forms a circle. One student becomes the world and steps into the center of the circle. Each person then approaches the world and offers it a gift, telling the world what the pretend gift is. Remaining in a circle, each person in turn becomes a *shofar* and makes a *shofar* sound announcing the birthday of the world. Everyone joins together in making one loud *shofar* sound. Then students sit down and discuss how they felt during this experiential activity.

4. Read to the children *The World's Birthday: A Rosh Hashanah Story* by Barbara Diamond Goldin. Discuss other ways candles can go out — we can blow them out, they can get wet, they can be deprived of oxygen, etc. Then decorate a cake for the birthday of the world.

5. Sitting in a circle, discuss students' Tishre symbols (e.g., *shofar*, apples and honey, *sukkah*, *lulav*, *etrog*, Torah). Each child takes a turn and tells which is his/her favorite and why.

6. Whip around the room and have each student complete this sentence: I can become a better person by _____. Discuss the responses and the concept of working to improve our behavior during the coming year.

7. Become a *shofar*: Students stand up, close their eyes tightly, and imagine that each is a huge *shofar*. Then remain standing with eyes closed, make *shofar* sounds, open eyes, and sit down. Discuss what they thought about and how they felt during this activity.

8. Bring apples and honey to class. Before eating, recite as a class, in Hebrew and English, "May it be Your will, O Eternal Our God, to grant us a sweet and a good year." (See Appendix, page 252, for blessing in Hebrew.)

9. During a class session, bake a round *challah* with raisins.

10. Give each student water color markers and paper. Ask students to draw a picture of something they did that wasn't nice. Throw the papers into the water table, face down. Watch the bad behavior disappear. You might follow this up with a discussion of Tashlich. Read *A Rosh Hashanah Walk* by Carol Levin (Kar-Ben Copies, Inc.), a book which explains the custom of Tashlich in simple rhyme. (NSM)

11. Have each student write down something that he/she did that wasn't nice; keep all ideas private. (Younger students could dictate their thoughts to the teacher, or draw a picture.) When all are done, have students tear up their sheets and throw them in the trash can. Ceremoniously, take the trash can outside to the dumpster and get rid of their not-nice behavior. (NSM)

12. Have a Rosh HaShanah coin toss. Prepare five cardboard squares, each at least one foot square. On each place a picture of an important symbol related to Rosh HaShanah. From 5' or 6' away, students try to throw the coins on the five squares. When a coin lands on one of the five squares, the student must say something about the symbol depicted on that square. Give healthy food treats as prizes for correct responses and accurate coin tossing. Variations: Toss small bean bags; don't give out prizes until everyone has had a turn.

13. Create a calendar which shows the entire period of the *Yamim Nora'im/Aseret Y'may Teshuvah*. Ask students to write in each space one thing which they would do to repent for something they did during the year (e.g., asking forgiveness of the person they hurt, righting a wrong, etc.). (NSM)

14. Many children have never had an opportunity to sound a *shofar*. Bring a *shofar to* class and give each child an opportunity to try to make it sound. (Wipe the mouthpiece with rubbing alcohol between students.) Then see if anyone is able to make the correct sounds for *Tekiah*, *Shevarim*, and *Teruah*. If possible, provide some other wind instruments for shape and sound comparison. If they close their eyes, can students recognize the sound of the *shofar*?

15. Ask: If Rosh HaShanah is considered the birthday of the world, what "present" could we give the world? (Example: Clean up the grounds around your school.) (NSM)

16. Tell or read stories about children not behaving nicely. Temporarily omit the ending. Discuss with students what the child in the story might have done differently. (NSM)

17. Take a "field trip" to the sanctuary before Rosh HaShanah and during the *Yamim Nora'im*. What changes to students notice? (Look for

the Torahs dressed in white, special flowers, different prayer books, etc.). (NSM)

18. Make a sorting game out of pictures of people doing the right and wrong things (watch out for pictures that might frighten the children). Find pictures in magazines, newspapers, stories, and clip art. Have students sort the pictures. (Place a self-check device on the back, perhaps smiley faces and faces with a frown). (NSM)

19. Ask a Rabbi or Cantor to come to the class dressed in what he/she wears for Rosh HaShanah/Yom Kippur services. Ask students why the Rabbi dresses differently for the High Holy Days. Ask them how they will dress at services. (NSM)

21. Blindfold two children. Turn them around and set them off in the general direction of each other. They attempt to shake hands and say "*L'Shanah Tovah Tikatayvu*," "*Gut Yontif*," or "Rosh HaShanah Greetings" to each other.

22. Point out to the class that some actions evoke pride and good feelings, while others evoke sadness and even shame. Divide the class into groups of 4 or 5 students. Have the groups sit in small circles. Hold up a picture of a happy face. Each person in the group responds to this picture by telling the other members of that group about one positive, happy memory from the past year. Now hold up a sad face. Each person in turn shares one experience which was not happy and which did not evoke happy memories. Then each person in the group reacts to the responses of the other members of their group with suggestions and comments. The class reassembles and briefly discusses the activity.

23. Create a maze. Students take a trip through "holidayland," visiting each of the High Holy Days along the way. Begin with Selichot and

end with Yom Kippur or Simchat Torah. Number the items. Students must trace their way through the maze to get from one place to the next.

24. Complete the Instant Lessons *Rosh ha Shanah* and *A Long, Penitent Season* by Ira J. Wise.

25. Bake a birthday cake for the world, then have a party to celebrate.

26. Do one or more of the Rosh HaShanah art projects in *100+ Jewish Art Projects for Children* by Nina Streisand Sher and Margaret A. Feldman (pages 3 and 5).

27. Complete pages 1, 2, and 3 in *Jewish Holiday Copy Pak™ K-3* by Marji Gold-Vukson.

Intermediate

1. Ask students to share with each other their memories of special High Holy Day experiences. Did they spend time with grandparents? Did they eat special foods? What made the experiences so memorable?

2. Seat students in chairs or on the floor in a circle. Each child makes a sentence beginning with "Rosh HaShanah is _____ " and completes it with a feeling, mood, or characteristic of Rosh HaShanah. Variation: Make this into a game. The first student makes a sentence with "Rosh HaShanah is _____ " and an "A" word, the second student uses a "B" word, and so on (skip Q, X, and Z). The adjective or noun used must, in some way, relate to the holiday.

3. Discuss: How would you compare and contrast Rosh HaShanah and January first? What might the connection be between noise making on New Year's Eve (December 31st) and blowing the *shofar* on Rosh HaShanah? How has Judaism infused this custom of "making a sound" with spirituality?

4. Divide the class into small groups to write High Holy Day slogans or mottos that reflect the values and themes of Rosh HaShanah. The slogans can deal with the themes of repentance, introspection, self-evaluation, etc.

5. Give each student a blank sheet of paper and a pencil. Read a list of Rosh HaShanah related words to the class and ask the students to write down the first word or phrase that comes to mind after hearing each word. In small groups or as a class, compare responses and share feedback.

6. Have students make a display of pictures, newspaper and magazine articles, articles from synagogue bulletins, photocopies of pertinent materials, original essays and art work which deal with Rosh HaShanah and the High Holy Days in general. Local Jewish and secular newspapers often have short articles about the Jewish New Year. Be sure they check the food section, too. Place the display at the entrance to the school or in the hall.

7. Have each child make a dictionary of Rosh HaShanah terms and then illustrate it.

8. Make Rosh HaShanah Cards. Use appropriate symbols and Hebrew expressions. Here are several different and creative ways to make Rosh HaShanah cards. (JB)
   a. Make cards from plastic throwaways. First plan the design. Then, after trimming the edges, use a nail or a stylus to press the design into the plastic. (Be sure to make all letters backwards.) Print as many cards as desired in the same way as you would print a linoleum block.
   b. Make cards using the student's name as the design. Have students draw a symbol first (e.g., an open Torah, tablets, a *shofar*, a whale, a *shin*, etc.). Then have them write their name in stylized Hebrew to fill the symbol drawing. The name thus

becomes part of the symbol and can be used for the design of the cover of the card or the inside.

c. Make cards from water mono-prints. The results are rapid, surprising, and unpredictable. You will need spray paints (one can will last for 60 pupils), a shallow tray or a pail, paper, and water. Follow these steps: (1) Place tray on a table covered with newspaper. (2) Have students stand around table and pinch their noses while the teacher sprays. (3) The teacher sprays paint into the tray for a few seconds with two cans, one in each hand. Student drops his/her paper on top and removes it quickly to pick up the moving colors. (4) Wipe the nozzle hole immediately after spraying to prevent sealing of hole. (5) Use the painted side for the front of the card and write the message inside.

d. Make cards from rubbings. When thin paper is placed over a texturized or raised surface and rubbed hard with a black crayon. A textural effect is produced. Try it first with a coin or a notebook cover. A search around the synagogue and also at home will reveal many forms suitable for texture rubbings. Have children do several rubbings and mount them on cards.

e. Rubbing and printing with cardboard provides two results from one design. You will need cardboard, scissors, paste, water-based ink, a brayer and black crayolas. Follow this procedure: (1) Have students cut their design out of cardboard. (2) Glue each piece to a second cardboard. (3) Cover entirely with a coat of shellac. (4) Run a color-filled brayer over the design. (5) Place the card over the wet ink. (6) Rub hard with the palm of the hand. (7) Lift card off and the print is complete. (8) When the design is dry, make a rubbing as described in the previous paragraph.

9. As a class, devise a survey of attitudes and feelings regarding the High Holy Days. After the class decides upon 4 or 5 questions to use as the basis for the survey, each student surveys 5 to 10 people. The results are then tabulated question-by-question the following week. Possible questions can include:

The thing I like best about the High Holy Days is ____.
For me the most meaningful aspect of the High Holy Days is ____.
The hardest part of the High Holy Days is ____.

High Holy Days observance teaches me ____.

10. Explain the Talmudic legend of the three books found in *Rosh HaShanah* 16b (see page 44). Hand each student a piece of paper with "My Personal Balance Sheet" written at the top of the page. The two columns below are headed "Deeds I Am Proud Of" and "Deeds I Am Not Happy About." About one-third of the way from the bottom of the sheet, write across the page: "Suggestions for Improvement." Ask students to fill in some items in each column. Then collect the sheets and give them out to other students, making sure that no student receives his/her own sheet. Ask the students to read over the sheet they have received, and write in a few suggestions for improvement at the bottom of the page. This exercise provides students with an opportunity for "safe" feedback without violating their sense of privacy.

11. Write a sentence or statement with all of the letters run together and with extra letters added. Students must remove the superfluous letters and write in correct message in the space provided. For example:

EMADONAIQABWILLIXABLESSZ
NOKYOUVWITHONAPEACEND =
ADONAI WILL BLESS YOU WITH
PEACE

Here is the Rosh HaShanah message:

AZMAYROYOUYEBERIINSCRONOIABE
DHANDITSEAOULEDIFORUAGOODMI
YEARIS
MAY YOU BE INSCRIBED
AND SEALED FOR A GOOD YEAR

12. Read and discuss one or more of the stories in *Days of Awe: Stories for Rosh Hashanah and Yom Kippur* by Eric Kimmel.

13. Students become detectives. Pass out a paragraph which contains five errors. The student's task is to locate the mistakes, cross them out, and write in the correct information above each error. If done orally as a team competition, the first team to spot a mistake gets a point, and then gets two points for supplying the correct information. If the first team does not have the correct information, the second team is given an opportunity to supply it and score two points. A sample paragraph reads:

During Tishre, which is the month before Rosh HaShanah and Yom Kippur, the Selichot service takes place. This service is usually held at midnight on the Sunday evening before Rosh HaShanah. During the High Holy Days, Jews use a special prayer book called a Tashlich. The Shabbat after Rosh HaShanah is called Shabbat HaGadol. There are several names for Rosh HaShanah: *Yom Teruah* means "The Day of the Blowing of the *Shofar*, "*Yom HaDin* means "Day of Judgment," and *Yom HaZikaron* means "Day of Repentence."

(Corrections: Elul for Tishre; Saturday evening for Sunday evening; *Machzor* for Tashlich, Shabbat Shuvah for Shabbat HaGadol, and Day of Remembrance for Day of Repentance.)

14. Brainstorm the key themes of Rosh HaShanah. List of themes on the blackboard. Then give each student 15-20 minutes to write

a prayer related to the holiday of Rosh HaShanah and the High Holy Days which reflects one or more of the themes of the holiday. Use the prayers as a start on a class prayer book.

15. Obtain a classroom set of Jewish calendars (Jewish funeral homes or bagel stores often distribute these). Ask groups of students to study August, September, and October, looking for the beginnings of Elul and Tishre and days on which the High Holy Days occur. Have them color these according to a code you provide and note the Hebrew months and days. Students could also do observations of the moon, drawing their sightings onto the calendar. Pull this into a discussion of the Hebrew calendar and the importance of this time of year.

16. Give students a sheet of paper and ask them to write at least one Rosh HaShanah resolution. Discuss in pairs. Each partner reacts to the other's resolutions with comments and suggestions, if any. Collect the resolutions and, later in the year, return them to students. Have students work with the same partners, reporting successes and/or failures in following the resolutions. As a class, discuss the activity and the feelings it evoked. Ask: Why do you think we need a day to make New Year's resolutions?

17. Have each student bring a cassette tape to class and record a special Rosh HaShanah greeting. This can include appropriate Hebrew phrases, Rosh HaShanah resolutions, and more. The students take the tapes home and listen to them with their families.

18. Ask each student to keep a diary for the month of Tishre. Each day, in addition to any general comments or observations, the student writes down three types of things:
    a. Good things I have done today.
    b. Things I should not have done today.

c. I would like to change what happened today. At the conclusion of Yom Kippur, each student writes an essay which involves that long hard look at self and how he/she can be a better person in the forthcoming year.

19. Read/study *"Avinu Malkaynu"* with students. Have students write their own *"Avinu Malkaynu"* prayer. Encourage them to take their prayer to synagogue on Rosh HaShanah and read it during the congregational reading of *"Avinu Malkaynu."*

20. Role play a meeting between Ms. Rosh HaShanah and Mr. Everyday. Divide the class into pairs. Each partner is first one person and then the other. They speak to each other, share their feelings and thoughts. Reverse roles and then repeat the process.

21. Divide students into groups of two or three. Give each group a *Siddur* and a *Machzor.* Ask them to go through the two books and develop a list of comparisons. Have them record their findings on a sheet with two columns: Things Which Are the Same, and Things Which are Different. (NSM)

22. Two particularly good stories dealing with Rosh HaShanah are "If Not Higher," by I.L. Peretz and "Three Who Ate" by David Frishman. (See page 58 for a dramatization of the latter.) For additional story sources, see the General Bibliography and the Rosh HaShanah Bibliography at the conclusion of the book. As a follow-up activity, have students rate each story from 1 to 10. Give each child an opportunity to draw a book jacket with the title, author, and rating sometime during the year. Display the jackets on the bulletin board.

23. Do the Rosh HaShanah art projects in *100+ Jewish Art Projects for Children* by Nina

Streisand Sher and Margaret A. Feldman (pages 2 and 6).

24. Complete pages 1, 2, and 3 in *Jewish Holiday Copy Pak™ 4-6* by Marji Gold-Vukson.

Secondary

1. Ask: Why do you think the *Akedah* account (Genesis 22: 1-19) might be read on Rosh HaShanah? Do the dramatic reading of Genesis 22.1-19 and then discuss its implications. Traditionally, Abraham is pictured as the hero because his trust in God was so great that he was willing to sacrifice Isaac. What was heroic about Abraham's act? Who was the more heroic, Abraham or Isaac?

2. Besides the *Akedah*, in what other ways did God test Abraham? (e.g., the three strangers, Sodom and Gomorrah). Look at the *Akedah* from the viewpoint of Isaac. He trusted his father just as his father trusted God. If you were Isaac, would you expect your father to intercede with God on your behalf? Why or why not? What could Abraham have said to God to save Isaac?

3. Working in pairs, one student is Abraham and the other Isaac. Either orally or silently, read Genesis 22:1-19. Point out that this story can be seen as a sermon against child sacrifice, and that God intended to test Abraham's faith, not to kill Isaac. In each pair, Abraham tells Isaac how he feels about what God commanded him to do. Isaac listens. Isaac then tells Abraham about how he feels about being led to Mount Moriah to die. Reverse roles and repeat the interaction. The pairs then discuss how they felt in each role. Which role did each person prefer? Why? As a class, discuss the feelings evoked by this exercise. What insights were gleaned from it?

4. *"Avinu Malkaynu"* means "Our Father, Our King." In gender-sensitive liturgy, it might

become "Our Parent, Our Sovereign." It suggests that God is both loving parent and Source of order in the world. Ask: What image of God do you have when you recite/chant this prayer? To which aspect of God do we direct our prayers?

5. Divide the class into six groups. Ask each group to examine and summarize for the class one of the passages related to the *shofar*. They are: Exodus 19:16-19, Exodus 20:15-18, Psalm 81:4-5, Psalm 150, Isaiah 27:13, and Zechariah 9:14-16. After the groups have had ten minutes to examine their passage, one representative from each group summarizes the passage and explains its significance to the rest of the class.

6. Discuss the feelings the *shofar* evokes. Research the different situations in ancient times that the Israelites blew the *shofar* (e.g., to assemble the people, to muster troops, to break down walls). When, in addition to Rosh HaShanah morning, is the *shofar* blown in modern times?

7. Discuss the *midrash* about the three books which God is said to open on Rosh HaShanah (see page 44). Ask students if they believe that this literally happens or if is meant to be symbolic. Have them explain their answers. Discuss: How is it possible for God to judge us and for us to judge ourselves both at the same time? What could you do to make self-evaluation a part of your life at other times besides at Rosh HaShanah? What can you do to assure that you are honest with yourself? What steps can you take to improve?

8. Encourage students to go on the Internet and to bring back to class information on alternative Rosh HaShanah observance ideas culled from such Jewish sites as: Jewish Family – http://www.Jewishfamily.com/; Virtual Jerusalem – http://virtual.co.il/; America Online – use Key Word Jewish Community,

then once in that section, locate the youth section and check out Sparks e-zine and the boards. (NSM)

9. Have students participate in the dramatic reading of Genesis 22:1-19 (see page 35). Select students to play the parts of narrator, Abraham, Isaac, and Angel/God. Afterward, discuss the Points to Ponder.

All-School

1. Have the older students do the dramatic reading of Genesis 22:1-19 (see page 35) for students in Grades 1 to 6.

2. Using 9" x 12" sheets of construction paper, make a graffiti board for the school on which students can write their hopes for the year to come.

3. In three hours, either as a Shabbaton or as a special learning activity during the regular Religious School session, organize a compressed celebration of Rosh HaShanah. Or, do this as a Shabbaton for families as a preparation for the observance of Rosh HaShanah. (This is also an excellent project for a *Havurah*.)

Family

1. Suggest that families work together to prepare the Rosh HaShanah evening meal. They might bake a special rounded *challah*, prepare apples and honey, and look through Jewish cookbooks to find special foods that are appropriate for Rosh HaShanah.

2. Send home sentences for families to complete and discuss around the dinner table. Because there is no right answer, these sentence completions are a great equalizer between parents and children. Some suggested sentences:

I like Rosh HaShanah because _____
Rosh HaShanah is special to me because _____

On Rosh HaShanah I feel _____
On Rosh HaShanah I plan to _____

3. Send home a copy of the Torah portion read on Rosh HaShanah for home study. If the *Akedah* story is selected, suggest they discuss how family members might react if they were in the position of Abraham and Isaac. Each member of the family is given a few verses to study and summarize for the rest of the family. When all are ready, the family members read the selection from the Torah and then restate it in their own words. To conclude, the family discusses the meaning of the passage from the Torah.

4. Suggest that families share happy and sad memories from the past year at the dinner table. Each family member discusses what they hope to accomplish during the coming year.

5. Send home instructions for making High Holy Day designs using strip letters. (Students who know how to do Hebrew lettering can do this.) Here is a method that will make instant calligraphers out of student artists. You will need construction paper, a paper cutter, paste, a ruler, and an idea for copy. Follow these steps: (1) Out of 9" x 12" pieces of paper, cut a supply of uniform strips of paper 1/4" wide (or narrower). One or two 9" x 1 2" sheets will provide enough strips for a class. Hand out the strips to the students. (2) Make guide lines to establish letter heights. (3) Pencil in the letters to make the desired message (*L'Shanah Tovah,* Rosh HaShanah, etc.). (4) Cover each sketched letter stroke with a strip, centering the strip and pasting it down. Several strips or parts of strips will be necessary to complete a letter. You might want to make a chart for the class of a simplified block Hebrew alphabet, or provide each person with a photocopy of such an alphabet. (JB)

GENESIS 22:1-19

A Dramatic Reading

Cast of Characters
Narrator
God
Abraham
Isaac
Angel

Narrator: There came a time when God put Abraham to the test. And God said to him:

God: Abraham.

Narrator: And Abraham answered.

Abraham: Here I am.

Narrator: Then God said:

God: Take your son, your precious one, Isaac, whom you love, and go to the land of Moriah; there you shall offer him as a burnt offering on one of the hills that I will point out to you.

Narrator: Early the next morning, Abraham split wood for the burnt offering, saddled his donkey, took with him two of his young men and his son Isaac, and set out for the place that God had told him about. On the third day, as he looked up, Abraham saw the place from afar. He said to his young men:

Abraham: Stay here with the donkey while I and the boy go up to worship; then we will return to you.

Narrator: Abraham took the wood for the sacrifice and gave it to Isaac, his son, to carry. He himself carried the firestone and the knife; and the two walked on together. Then Isaac broke the silence and said to his father:

Isaac: Father!

Narrator: And Abraham said:

Abraham: Here I am, my son!

Narrator: And Isaac said:

Isaac: I see the firestone and the wood, but where is the lamb for the burnt offering?

Narrator: Abraham replied:

Abraham: God will provide for the burnt offering, my son.

Narrator: And the two walked on together. They came to the place of which God had told to Abraham. Abraham built an altar there. He laid on the wood. He tied up his son Isaac. He laid him on the altar on top of the wood. An angel appeared and said:

Angel: Do not raise your hand against the boy, nor do the least thing to him; for now I know you stand in awe of God, since you did not withhold from Me your own son, your precious one.

Narrator: As Abraham looked up, his eyes fell upon a ram caught in the thicket by its horns. So he took the ram and offered it as a burnt offering in place of his son. And Abraham named that place "*Adonai* Sees," as it is said to this day: 'On the mountain of *Adonai* [all] is seen.' The Angel of God called to Abraham out of heaven a second time and said:

Angel: By Myself do I swear, says God, that because you have done this, and did not withhold your son, your precious one, from Me, I will bless you greatly, and make your descendants as numerous as the stars of the heaven and the sands of the seashore; and your descendants shall come to possess the gates of your enemies. All the nations of the earth shall be blessed through your descendants, because you obeyed My command.

Narrator: Abraham then returned to his servants and they left together for Beersheva. And Abraham stayed in Beersheva.

Points to Ponder:

Why do you think this selection from the Torah is read in Reform synagogues on Rosh HaShanah?

Do you think that Genesis 22:1-19 is an actual event or do you think that it was written to present a certain message?

Some people feel that Genesis 22:1-19 is a "mini-sermon." If this were indeed the case, what would be the topic of the sermon?

What does Genesis 22:1-19 tell us about Abraham's faith in God?

What is the significance of the first line which states: "And God put Abraham to the "test"?

Do you think that God intended for Isaac to die after Abraham waited almost 100 years to have a son who could be his heir?

If you were in Abraham's position, what would you have done?

BIBLIOGRAPHY

See pages 266-268.

CHAPTER THREE
YOM KIPPUR

VOCABULARY

Al Chayt: "For the Sin." *Al Chayt* is one of the prayers in the *Vidui* (Confession). This prayer and the *Ashamnu* are recited by the entire congregation collectively, even by those who have not been guilty of any of the sins mentioned in these prayers. Their participation symbolizes their regret that they were unable to prevent others from committing such sins. There are various versions of the *Al Chayt* prayer, some with as many as 44 verses.

Ashamnu: "We Have Sinned." Shorter than the *Al Chayt* prayer, it serves as the other part of the service of public confession.

G'mar Chatimah Tovah: This expression, "be sealed (in the Book of Life) for good," is the traditional greeting used between Rosh HaShanah and Yom Kippur.

Kaparot: "Sacrificial Rites." On the morning preceding Yom Kippur, it is customary to recite certain prayers and give offerings of charity to the poor. These prayers ask God for a year of life, and health, not only for the person offering the prayers, but also for all people everywhere.

Ki Anu Amecha: "For we are Your people." Repeated in each of the Yom Kippur worship services, this prayer asks God to forgive our failings because we are God's people and children, and God is our protector.

Kittel: A white robe worn traditionally during the High Holy Days as a symbol of purity. It is reflective of Isaiah 1:18: "Though your sins be as scarlet, they shall be white as snow."

Kol Nidre: "All vows." The name of this best known of all the Yom Kippur petitions is chanted at the beginning of the Ma'ariv service on Yom Kippur eve. It has a haunting melody. A free translation reads: "Let all vows, oaths, and promises that we make . . . to You, O God, between this Yom Kippur and the next, be excused should we, after honest effort, find ourselves unable to fulfill them . . . ."

While the origins of the prayer are uncertain, during the Middle Ages and subsequently thereafter, Jews were often forced to vow allegiance to Christianity, while continuing to practice Judaism in secret. Through this prayer they begged God to forgive them and release them from such vows made under duress. Today, *Kol Nidre* remains a part of the liturgy because of its historical associations, its inspirational melody, and its great beauty.

Mechilah: "Forgiveness" — which is one of the basic motifs of the Yom Kippur liturgy. The Talmud (*Yoma* 85b) records the words of Rabbi Eleazur ben Azariyah: "For transgressions against God, the Day of Atonement atones; but for transgressions against another person, the Day of Atonement does not atone, unless and until one has made peace with that person, and redressed the wrongs that were done." It is customary, therefore, for Jews to ask each other for forgiveness on the day preceding Yom Kippur.

Ne'ilah: "Closing" — this is the concluding service for Yom Kippur. As the last rays of the sun fade, the gates of prayer to God begin to close. As Ne'ilah draws to a close, one long, loud blast of the *shofar* is sounded. At this service, the Jew expresses confidence in God's willingness to forgive, and asks to be "sealed" in the Book of Life. The Talmud (*Megillah* 31a) questions whether the word *Ne'ilah* refers to the closing of the gates of heaven or the gates of the ancient Temple, or whether it refers to the closing service itself.

Scapegoat (Seir L'Azazel): For more than 2000 years, the Jew has served as scapegoat, being falsely blamed for all sorts of woes and calamities. Leviticus 16 tells how, on the Day of Atonement, the High Priest would take two goats, one designated "for *Adonai*" as a Temple offering, and one for Azazel. All of the sins of the people were symbolically placed upon the goat for Azazel which was then allowed to escape into the wilderness, bearing those sins away. Hence the term escape goat — scapegoat.

Schlag Kapores: A Yiddish expression meaning "Swinging Atonement." This custom takes place on the afternoon before Yom Kippur. A person takes a live chicken and swings it around and around, making a circle above the head. A formula is recited, asking that the life of the chicken be taken in place of the person who is swinging the chicken. The animal is then killed and either eaten for the Yom Kippur eve meal or is given to charity. Some people believe that the circle was meant to keep away the evil spirits. Even though this custom is considered by many to be a superstition, it still persists among some Jews.

Seir L'Azazel: See Scapegoat, above.

Sh'ma Kolaynu: "Hear Our Voice." This prayer is recited near the end of services on Yom Kippur. It asks God to have mercy upon the worshipers and to accept their prayers.

Tallit: A prayer shawl. Even though used for morning worship only, the *tallit* is worn for the *Kol Nidre* worship service. The reason for this exception is that the *tallit* helps to create a special atmosphere for worship and accentuates the idea of purity.

Teshuvah: "Repentance" or "Returning." One who sins — i.e., strays from the accepted norms of behavior — must make *teshuvah* — "return" to the right path. A perfunctory observance of Yom Kippur without a conscious effort to confess one's shortcomings to God, to divest oneself of one's mistakes, renders Yom Kippur meaningless.

Tzedakah: "Righteousness," but used in the sense of "charity." The giving of *tzedakah* is customary at this time of year. In some congregations, people pay their synagogue dues before Yom Kippur so that they may begin their prayers without a feeling of owing human beings or God. Many congregations make appeals for funds for the synagogue or for State of Israel Bonds on Yom Kippur.

Vidui: "Confession." Jews direct their confessions to God without the assistance of any intermediary. Confession is effective only when it goes hand-in-hand with sincere repentance. In the Yom Kippur liturgy, the two key prayers in the public confession are *Ashamnu* and *Al Chayt*.

Yizkor: "God will remember" or "May God Remember." Yizkor refers to the Memorial Service which is held on Yom Kippur (and the last day of the three Festivals). The service involves both a commemoration of death and a quest for a higher level of spirituality. In Conservative and Orthodox synagogues, Yizkor is held after the morning service on Yom Kippur while, in Reform synagogues, it usually takes place after the afternoon service and prior to Ne'ilah.

Yom Kippur: "Day of Atonement." The tenth day of the month of Tishre is a day for fasting and introspection.

Yom Tzom: "Fast Day." Yom Kippur and Tishah B'Av are two of the most important fast days in the Jewish calendar. The fast is for 25 hours from just prior to the beginning of Yom Kippur until after the conclusion of Ne'ilah.

Yonah: The biblical Book of Jonah. This short but significant work, one of the minor prophets in the second portion of the Bible (*Nevi'im*), comprises almost the entire afternoon *Haftarah* reading for Yom Kippur. Micah 7:18-20 is also read. The Book of Jonah contains a message of religious universalism. All people, be they Jew or non-Jew, are entitled to God's blessings and to God's forgiveness for their sins and wrongdoings. The story is an eloquent statement against religious parochialism and may be viewed as one of history's first sermons. Jonah, like most prophets, was accustomed to not being heard by his people, for prophetic messages more often than not fell on deaf ears. When the people of Ninevah, Israel's arch enemy, repent of their sins, Jonah experiences a terrible dilemma: how can he return home having enabled this nation to repent? The enemy accepts his message while his own people ignore him. Indeed, Jonah can be read on many levels. It is a whale of a story!

BACKGROUND

Yom Kippur is the tenth day of Tishre, the seventh month of the Jewish calendar year. The moon is waxing and is between half crescent and full. This is the most solemn day of the year. It is said that those not inscribed in the Book of Life on Rosh HaShanah are given the Ten Days of Repentance in which to pray for forgiveness and to perform good deeds so as to be "sealed" in the Book of Life on Yom Kippur.

Yom Kippur is considered to be the Sabbath of Sabbaths. It is the one day in the Jewish year which is equal in importance to the Sabbath.

Because fasting for two days would be a severe hardship, this is the only major holiday which in the Diaspora has no second day observance.

There are several references to this day in the Torah — all of Leviticus 16, and especially 16:29-31; Numbers 29:7-11; Leviticus 25:9-10; and Leviticus 23:27-32. The latter is the longest and the most detailed of the citations: " . . . the tenth day of this seventh month is a day of atonement . . . a sacred occasion for you. You shall practice self-denial, and you shall bring an offering by fire to the Lord; you shall do no work throughout the day . . . . For this is a day of atonement, to cleanse you from all your sins, so that you shall be clean before God . . . . Do no work whatsoever; it is . . . a Sabbath of complete rest for you . . . on the ninth day of the month at evening, from evening to evening, you shall observe your Sabbath."

In the Jubilee (50th year), the *shofar* is to be sounded on the Day of Atonement proclaiming liberty throughout the land for all slaves and the return of land to its original tribal owners (Leviticus 25:9-10).

From the Talmud we learn that on this day Moses descended (for the second time) with the Ten Commandments along with God's pardon for the sin of the golden calf (*Baba Batra* 121a). On this the holiest day of the year (Yom Kippur), the holiest person in Israel (the High Priest), entered the holiest place in the world (the Holy of Holies in the Temple), to recite the holiest word (the tetragrammaton — the four letter Name of God). There he made atonement for himself, for his family, and then for all of his people Israel. It is reported that as he said the holy Name, the people outside the Temple would respond with the words, "Blessed be the honored Name and majesty forever and ever" (Mishnah, *Yoma* 6:2).

Since this was such an intense occasion, there was always the possibility that the *Kohen Gadol* could succumb to some physical or emotional infirmity while in the inner sanctum. Because no one would be able to go in after him, a rope was affixed around his ankle so that he might be drawn out. Indeed, the experience was so filled with awe that friends of the High Priest feared for his life and would welcome him after he emerged from the Temple, escort him home, and spend the evening in company together with him (*Yoma* 5:1, 7:4).

By the end of the biblical period, it was already evident that Yom Kippur was the most significant of holy days — not only for its religious importance, but for its social component as well. For on that day (and on the 15th of Av), young maidens of Jerusalem would go out to dance in the vineyards dressed in fine white attire, while the eligible men looked on. And what did the maidens say? "Young man, raise your eyes and see your chosen one" (*Ta'anit* 4:8).

Central Themes
- "Great is repentance, for on account of an individual who repents, the sins of all the world are forgiven" (*Yoma* 86b)

- "Repent one day before your death." But how does one know the day of death? Therefore, let one repent every day" (*Pirke Avot* 2:15).

- No person is so wicked and so depraved as to be incapable of repenting and becoming a decent human being. There is always a possibility of changing one's ways. As we are taught, the gates of repentance are always open.

- Maimonides taught that even the worst person who repents — even in old age — will be forgiven (*Yad, Teshuvah* 2:1).

- No matter how good and pious a person may be, there is still need for improving one's character. Every person must strive continually for self-improvement. Yet, the affirmation that we can improve is the ultimate expression of optimism.

- For sins against God, the day atones; for sins against others, one must seek them out and ask their forgiveness. Such forgiveness should not be withheld if it is tendered sincerely.

- How can one know if repentance is sincere and forgiveness granted? If one does not again commit the same sin under similar circumstances.

- On this day, we are invited to see ourselves as we really are; serious self-examination is required. We are also reminded of our responsibility to and for the Jewish community as a whole. Thus, the confessions of each person take place in the context of group worship.

- Leviticus 16 introduces the concept of the scapegoat. It is one of the great ironies of history that the people that introduced the concept to the world became history's most frequent victim of scapegoating.

Why Fast
- Fasting is seen as a means for setting aside one's physical desires and stressing one's spiritual needs in their place. The day is devoted to prayer, repentance, and self-examination.

- Fasting and abstaining from all bodily nourishment for about 25 hours can serve as an expression of submission to God.

- Fasting promotes the realization of human weakness and of dependence upon God.

- When people fast, they are all equal and all have the same basic needs. One person does not go hungry while another eats lavishly.

- Fasting helps direct thoughts toward the spiritual — the needs of the psyche and the soul.

- Fasting is a form of self-discipline.

- Fasting shows repentance for the wrongs people have committed and for the good they have failed to do. In biblical times, sacrifices to God were offered to expiate sins. Today, we offer a sacrifice of the heart. By fasting, we demonstrate that repentance consists of more than uttering right sounding words.

- Fasting serves to awaken feelings of compassion in people. When people feel hunger, they tend to become more sensitive to the needs of others and to feel motivated to try to help them.

Customs and Home Observances

The meal prior to the onset of Yom Kippur is a festive one. As on Rosh HaShanah, a round *challah* is served. Pieces are dipped in honey and the following is said: "May God give you a good and sweet year." There is no *Kiddush* said on Yom Kippur. Just prior to lighting the holiday candles before the onset of the Yom Kippur, Yizkor (Memorial) candles are lit in memory of the deceased. Usually one 24-hour candle is lit for each close relative remembered. The following words may be recited: *"Nishmat Adam Nayr Adonai"* (The human spirit is the light of the Eternal One.)

Prior to leaving for the synagogue, sons are blessed with the words: "May God inspire you to live in the tradition of Ephraim and Manasseh, who carried forward the life of our people." Daughters are blessed with the words: "May God inspire you to live in the tradition of Sarah and Rebekah, Rachel and Leah, who carried forward the life of our people." The *Shehecheyanu* prayer is said. (For blessings in Hebrew and English, see Appendix, pages 251 and 253.)

Some follow the custom of not wearing leather shoes on Yom Kippur because: (1) since a worshiper prays for forgiveness from sin, he/she should not be wearing anything from a slain animal, or (2) because Moses was commanded to remove his shoes at the Burning Bush, so, too, should we remove shoes (or wear canvas shoes) while praying on Yom Kippur.

The last service on Yom Kippur (Ne'ilah), ends with one long blast of the *shofar*. This may symbolize a triumph for another year over sin and sinfulness.

A break-the-fast ensues — usually a light meal of dairy products. Sephardim often start that meal with several bites of bread dipped in olive oil.

According to tradition, construction of the *sukkah* should begin just as soon as Yom Kippur has ended. This is often expressed symbolically by putting just a few boards together and saving further construction for the following days.

Highlights of the Liturgy

It is customary for worshipers to remain in the synagogue all day and to devote themselves to prayer and meditation throughout Yom Kippur. In earlier times, worshipers actually remained overnight, sleeping on the *shul* benches. To facilitate ongoing thought and meditation, the *Machzor* contains devotional prayers and readings that can be perused or studied in between the various services of the day.

There are five services on Yom Kippur, more than on any other day in the year — Shacharit, Musaf, Yizkor, an Afternoon Service, and the concluding Ne'ilah service. Many congregations have in addition separate services for teens and for children and for families. Some synagogues offer a "Tot Yontif" experience for very young children who attend with their parents.

Yizkor is an additional service held in Conservative and Orthodox synagogues at the conclusion of the morning service. Reform congregations usually observe Yizkor between the Afternoon Service and Ne'ilah.

Kol Nidre is at once the single most famous hymn of the day, it is also the name by which the *erev* Yom Kippur Service is known. Chanted three times at the very beginning of the evening service to a haunting melody, this is a request for the annulment of all vows in the coming year that might be made under duress, threat, or coercion.

Inserted into the *Avot* section of the *Amidah* is the *Zochraynu* prayer — "Remember us unto life, O Sovereign who delights in life, and inscribe/seal us in the Book of Life for Your sake, O God of life."

On Yom Kippur, the entire congregation recites the *Vidui* (Confession) consisting of: *Ashamnu* — a listing of sins in alphabetical order followed by a plea for forgiveness; *Tavo* — " . . . let our prayers come before You (*tavo*) . . . for we are not so arrogant and stiff-necked as to say we have not sinned . . . we have sinned, we have transgressed, we have done perversely"; and *Al Chayt,* which details our every sin, introducing each with the phrase *"Al Chayt Shechatanu Lefanecha* — For the sin that we have commited . . ."

Most moving is the *Un'taneh Tokef* which declares that life and death are in God's power. "On Rosh HaShanah it is written and on Yom Kippur it is sealed . . . Who shall live and who shall die . . . But *teshuvah, tefilah,* and *tzedakah* temper the decree."

Torah and Haftarah Readings
For the morning of Yom Kippur, the traditional Torah Reading is Leviticus 16:1-34, the ancient scapegoat ritual. *Maftir* is Numbers 29:7-11, the additional sacrifices that were offered on Yom Kippur. Six people are called to the Torah to read the Torah blessings. Reform synagogues read Deuteronomy 29:9-14 and 30:11-20, which asks that we choose to follow God's way and live.

The morning *Haftarah* reading is Isaiah 57:14-58:14, wherein the Prophet describes the ideal fast — acts of *tzedakah* and *gemilut chesed.*

The traditional reading for the Afternoon Service is Leviticus 18:1-30, which details forbidden relationships. The beginning of the chapter warns: "You shall not copy the practices of the land of Egypt where you dwelt, or the land of Canaan to which I am taking you; nor shall you follow their customs. My norms alone shall you observe, and faithfully follow My laws: I *Adonai* am your God" (3-4). Reform congregations read Leviticus 19:1-37, which details moral imperatives — acts that make one holy.

The afternoon *Haftarah* reading is the book of Jonah, a reluctant prophet who flees from God's command to go to Ninevah and tell the people there to repent. The story serves as a reminder that, in addition to having a special relationship with Israel, God cares for all peoples. This message of religious universalism is unique.

The Three Books
A legend: On Rosh HaShanah, God opens three books — the Book of Life for those who lived a

blameless life during the past year, the Book of Death for those who performed no good deeds during the past year, and a huge book for those whose lives were a mixture of the good and the bad. Since just about everyone falls into this latter category, it is taught that God spends the period from Rosh HaShanah through Yom Kippur weighing the good and bad deeds of each person. On Yom Kippur, a decision on each individual is reached for entry into either the Book of Life or the Book of Death. It was believed that the power of life and death was in God's hands (*Rosh HaShanah* 16b). While some hold to the literal interpretation of this legend, others understand the High Holy Days as a time of self-judgment, and a time for taking a serious look at one's actions and priorities.

SCOPE AND SEQUENCE

Grade	Themes/Ideas
Kindergarten	Saying "I'm sorry" to friends and family members you have hurt during the past year, and asking: "How can I make things up to you for what I did?"
Grade One	Home observance, including preparations for Yom Kippur, the festive meal, behavior during the Day of Atonement, and breaking the fast. What can students do to observe this day and what might their parents do?
Grade Two	What is Yom Kippur like in the synagogue? Students can examine in brief the various worship services. Learn that parents might spend the entire day at the synagogue. What might the students do while the parents are engaged in prayer?
Grade Three	Why do we fast? How do we feel physically and emotionally when we fast?

Grade Four	The concept of confession, as well as making amends. Examine the terms Yom Kippur, *Mechilah*, *Teshuvah*, and *Vidui*.
Grade Five	Examine the concept of repentance as "returning to the right path" after "missing the mark." Investigate interesting customs related to Yom Kippur.
Grade Six	Jonah and the concept of religious universalism. Why is Jonah read on Yom Kippur? What message does Jonah bring to the modern Jew?
Grade Seven	Discuss Torah and *Haftarah* readings other than Jonah. Include Leviticus 16, Deuteronomy 29:9-14 and 30:11-20. Why do different congregations read different Torah sections?
Grade Eight	A brief look at key prayers and a careful examination of *Kol Nidre*. Why is it included in the liturgy? What meaning does *Kol Nidre* have for the contemporary Jew?
Grade Nine	A close look at the concept of the scapegoat. Read Leviticus 16 carefully. Examine the impact of the scapegoat idea upon Jewish history. How does scapegoating play a role in your life and in the lives of others you know?
Grade Ten	What are the key concepts of Yom Kippur? If a non-Jewish neighbor asked you about Yom Kippur, what would you say? What special meaning does it hold for you?
Grade Eleven	Examine the difference between sins against God and sins against

humanity. How do Jews deal with each on Yom Kippur? What can I do to better myself?

Grade Twelve	Write creative Yom Kippur prayers for inclusion in the youth service. Study the overall format of the Yom Kippur liturgy.

ACTIVITIES

Note: For additional activities, consult the previous chapter, on Rosh HaShanah. Many of those activities are applicable for Yom Kippur as well.

Preschool/Kindergarten

1. Use tin foil to create art on the subject of "Look and see a nicer me."

2. Students sit in a circle and take turns completing the sentence, "I'm sorry that, during the past year I did not _____." After everyone has had a turn, each student completes a second sentence: "During the coming year I hope to _____." Students may react to the statements of others either after each sentence has been completed, or at the conclusion of the activity.

3. Read with students prayers special to Yom Kippur (e.g., *Al Chayt* or *Ashamnu*). Have them create their own prayers using the pattern of the originals (i.e., beginning each line, "*Al Chayt Shechatanu* — I have done wrong by . . ." or, a poem that lists alphabetically things that people do wrong). (NSM)

4. Provide each student with a lunch-size bag. Ask each to decorate the bag with something they want to do better in the coming year. (You may wish to write the child's dictation about their picture as well.) Send the bag home, along with a note suggesting that the bag be used to pack the child's lunch after Yom Kippur. (NSM)

5. It is customary to give *tzedakah* on Yom Kippur. Have each student create a *tzedakah* box which they can use for Yom Kippur and for the other holidays during the coming year. (NSM)
Resource: *100+ Jewish Art Projects for Children* by Nina Streisand Sher and Margaret A. Feldman (pp. 78 and 79).

6. Before asking God for forgiveness on Yom Kippur, we ask for forgiveness from others we have hurt or wronged. Have students make "I'm Sorry" cards to give to their parents before dinner on *erev* Yom Kippur. (NSM)

7. Arrange for your class to bake something to contribute to the congregation's break-the-fast. Perhaps they can also make some centerpieces for the tables. (NSM)

8. Help children complete pages 9 and 10 in *Jewish Preschool/Kindergarten Copy Pak*™ by Nancy Cohen Nowak.

9. Complete some of the activities in *The Jewish Preschool Teachers Handbook* by Sandy Furfine Wolf and Nancy Cohen Nowak, pages 58-62.

Primary
1. Have each student write something from the past year which he/she would do away with. Then burn the papers in the flame of a candle as a symbol of making a new start. Or have students write out on paper the times they missed the mark and throw the paper into a garbage can.

2. Using fabric paints, have each student make a personalized T-shirt to reflect both the themes of Yom Kippur and his/her personal feelings at this time of year. After the shirts have been completed, the students take turns explaining them to the rest of the class.

3. Together with the class, count the number of days between Rosh HaShanah and Yom Kippur. Label these as *Aseret Y'may Teshuvah*. (NSM)

4. On Yom Kippur, the Rabbi and Cantor wear white robes instead of the black robes that are worn at other times. Ask: Why do you think white robes are worn on Yom Kippur? What do black and white garments suggest to you?

5. If you took students into the sanctuary to explore changes immediately before Rosh HaShanah, take them back again after Yom Kippur. Have them note any changes they see. (If the class meets shortly after Yom Kippur, see if students can help change the Torah covers from white back to their normal color.) (NSM)

6. Use large sheets of brown wrapping paper and make a simulated *Kotel* (Western Wall). Make slits or holes in the wall. Children think about something that happened during the past year that they feel sorry about, or a wrong that was done to them that they are now willing to forgive. Each student writes this on a piece of paper (or dictates it), puts his/her name on it, and folds it up. They tuck the notes into a crevice on the wall, just as people place notes to God in crevices of the *Kotel*. Leave the notes there for a week or two and then throw them away, or keep them there for several months and then return them to the students. Discuss the act of writing down one's very personal thoughts.

7. As a class, make a large whale out of poster board. Each child pretends to be in the whale and must compose a prayer to get out.

8. Have students practice *Kapparot*, substituting their *tzedakah* money for a chicken. (Most who do this use money in multiples of 18.) Then have the class decide where the money should be donated. (NSM)

9. The Jonah story lends itself to illustration. You will need cardboard for covers (front and back), drawing paper, coloring materials, knowledge of the story. Have students follow this procedure:

   a. Design a cover to fit a 9" x 12" page in the shape of the whale. Include title and author.

   b. Use the cover as a pattern and cut the pages in the same shape.

   c. Write the story of Jonah as it is recounted in the Bible. Then add new and original legends to the book.

   d. Bind the book. Place it in the class library for all to read. Take it home to share with family members.

10. Have students write their good and bad deeds on rocks and then weigh each pile.

11. Give each student a plastic bandage. Ask them to write on it the name of a person with whom they had a broken relationship. Have them think of ways to repair the break. Share with the group if desired.

12. Teach students the traditional greeting one says between Rosh HaShanah and Yom Kippur — *G'mar Chatimah Tovah*. Encourage them to say it to Jewish people they know. Perhaps have them record — on a Jewish calendar with the *Yamim Nora'im* marked — the number of times they say it daily. (NSM)

13. Brainstorm what students could do when Yom Kippur services seem too long. (Make sure you know what options are okay with the Rabbi.) (NSM)

14. Have students create a sign which they can hang on their door knob to remind them of the good behaviors they want to do. (NSM)

15. Listen to *Kol Nidre*. Ask students to pay special attention to the music. Is the music happy? sad? some other emotion? How does listening to this music help us get ready for the full day of prayer on Yom Kippur? (For very young children, ask: How does listening to this music help adults get into the mood for Yom Kippur?) (NSM)

16. The word *"Chayt"* means "missing the mark." An archer who misses the bulls-eye says, *"Chatati,"* I missed. Create a large bulls-eye for your class. Have students write down one thing which they did during the past year in which they missed the mark. When done, students tape their papers to the target, off center. Take the target and fold or tear it up, physically representing the sins they are getting rid of. (NSM)

17. Many congregations hold a food drive during the High Holy Days. They pass out grocery bags on Rosh HaShanah and encourage congregants to return them full of non-perishable food and paper items when they come for *Kol Nidre*. If your congregation is planning such a drive, speak to the coordinator to find out what your students can do to assist (e.g., staple instructions to the bags, sort the food after it arrives, accompany the food to the place receiving it, etc.).

18. Complete The Instant Lessons *Yom Kippur* and *The Feather Story*.

19. Perform or do a readers theater performance of "The Magic Seed" in *Kings and Things: 20 Jewish Plays for Kids 8 to 18* by Meridith Shaw Patera (page 37). Discuss how the themes of justice and mercy relate to the High Holy Days.

20. Do one or more of the Yom Kippur art projects in *100+ Jewish Art Projects for Children* by Nina Streisand Sher and Margaret A. Feldman (pages 11, 12, and 13).

21. Complete pages 4 and 5 in *Jewish Holiday Copy Pak™ K-3* by Marji Gold-Vukson.

Intermediate

1. Take themes such as "I'm sorry," disappointment over uncompleted goals, sadness, soul searching, meditation, and act them out using pantomime. Ask for volunteers, giving each volunteer a different feeling to portray. The class attempts to guess what is being portrayed.

2. Have each student write a paragraph about Yom Kippur. Then have them write five factual questions about their paragraph. Duplicate a set of all the paragraphs followed by the student questions. Use for individual assignments, learning centers, enrichment.

3. Have students write short essays in response to the following:
    a. What things have I done during the past year which are good and of which I am proud?
    b. What have I done during the past year that I would like to improve upon?
    c. What have I neglected to do that I could have and should have done during the past year?
    d. What do I hope to do in the coming year that I was unable to do in the year now ending?

4. Find the five mistakes in the following paragraph about Yom Kippur. Put a line through the mistakes and write in the corrections above the errors:

    Yom Kippur, meaning Day of Repentance, is the holiest day in the Jewish year, the Sabbath of Sabbaths. Yom Kippur begins with the beautiful prayer *Al Chayt,* which means "all vows." During this day of fasting, Jews remain in the synagogue for the entire day. During the Yizkor service, Jews remember their friends and relatives who are no longer living. Throughout the day, Jews offer special *Vidui* prayers of praise to God. During the afternoon service, the book of Micah is read. It is about a prophet who tries to run away from God. The closing service is called Musaf and ends with a long blast of the *shofar.*

    (Corrections: Atonement for Repentance, *Kol Nidre* for *Al Chayt,* prayers of confession for prayers of praise, Jonah for Micah, and Ne'ilah for Musaf.)

5. Unscramble the Words: This review activity helps the students to become reacquainted with key Yom Kippur terms. It is suggested that, during a review lesson, a list of Yom Kippur terms be put on the blackboard or given to the students in the form of a handout. The following scrambled words may be used:

    EAPRNTEENC (REPENTANCE)

    VATHEUSH (TESHUVAH)

    TOPACSAGE (SCAPEGOAT)

    RIN KOLED (KOL NIDRE)

    HEANIL (NEILAH)

    OKZIRY (YIZKOR)

    DIUIV (VIDUI)

    NGAITSF (FASTING)

6. Have each student write a note to someone present who was not adequately thanked for something special they did for him or her. Give out the notes during the class. Share them if students are willing. Allow time to write similar notes to family and friends outside of the class.

7. Have each child write a poem for inclusion in his/her poetry book. This time write an acrostic. Write the letters of Yom Kippur down the left-hand side of a piece of paper. Each student writes a line beginning with each letter. Share the poems.

8. Have students read Leviticus 16, which describes the ceremony of sending the scape-

goat into the desert (a Yom Kippur Torah reading). Working in pairs, have students make a list of ways that people miss the mark today (i.e., sin), things which could metaphorically be sent into the desert. Post these on a "goat" in the center of a bulletin board. (NSM)

9. Present the following groups of three statements to students, one of which is incorrect. Students decide which is incorrect and explain why in the space that follows the questions. Here are a few sample statements. (The false statements are noted with an F.)

Rosh HaShanah is observed on the first two days of Tishre.
Tashlich is a ceremony of symbolically throwing away one's sins.
Selichot are *shofar* sounds. (F)

The High Holy Day prayer book is called a *Piyyut*. (F)
Yom Kippur is the tenth day of the Ten Days of Repentance.
Many Jews pray for an entire day on Yom Kippur.

Avinu Malkaynu means "Our Father, Our King."
Kol Nidre means "All vows."
Al Chayt means "For the sacrifices." (F)

10. Each student writes a letter to himself/herself describing shortcomings and accomplishments during the past year. Have students outline what they hope to accomplish in the forthcoming year, with particular emphasis on areas where they hope for improvement. Collect the sealed letters and put them away until the spring. At that time, return them to the students to give them a chance to see how they have measured up to their own hopes for themselves since Yom Kippur.

11. Divide the class into groups of 3 to 5 students. Give groups 10 or 15 minutes to make up questions about Yom Kippur and the High

Holy Days which will be given to the other groups. All the groups then assemble for the Yom Kippur Quiz. Administer the questions, giving 1 point for correct answers to easy questions and 2 points for correct answers to difficult questions. The team with the most points wins. This is an effective review activity.

12. Send home information to parents about ways of helping students younger than 13 make appropriate fasting decisions. Almost all students could be encouraged to give up a dessert or a pre-bedtime snack on *erev* Yom Kippur. (NSM)

13. Divide the class into teams of 3-5 students. The task of each group is to write one or more headlines to describe or reflect the mood and/or themes of Yom Kippur. Teams can prepare one main headline and several sub-headlines or several main headlines. Decide which team has the best headlines. This can also be handled as a brainstorming activity for the whole class. In this case, write the suggested headlines on the blackboard and have the class decide which they like best.

14. Prepare a special edition of a class newspaper devoted to Yom Kippur and the High Holy Days. Students can write about how Yom Kippur is observed and its underlying themes. Include interviews with the Rabbi, principal, Cantor, and other synagogue staff, descriptions of home celebrations, etc.

15. "You've committed a sin," shouted a little boy as his big brother ate something on Yom Kippur. Ask students: In your view, is this act a sin? If so, how serious is it? is it as serious, for instance, as stealing?

16. Read and discuss one or more of the stories in *Days of Awe: Stories for Rosh Hashanah and Yom Kippur* by Eric Kimmel.

17. Ask: Why do you think that Yom Kippur is called the Sabbath of Sabbaths?

18. Ask: Do you know anyone who actually attempts to make amends with people they have hurt during the past year? Do you? Brainstorm some ways to make amends with family and friends for the pain we inadvertently or intentionally caused them.

19. Write a Yom Kippur prayer. Ask students to think for a few minutes about what Yom Kippur means to them. Have them write down their thoughts in the form of a prayer or meditation. When these are completed, collect them and put them together in a High Holy Day Book of Prayers and Meditations. Duplicate the booklet and give to each student to take home to share with his/her family. Or, if the students are already making individual prayer books, add these prayers to those books.

20. Compile a class *Al Chayt*. Each student lists several personal shortcomings or failings during the past year, but does not write down his/her name on the paper. Collect the papers and put together a personalized version of the *Al Chayt*. Each line can begin with "For the wrongdoing we have committed by _____, we are sorry." Insert items from students' papers.

21. Complete one or more of the Instant Lessons *T'shuvah, She Wrote* and *Missing the Mark*, both by Ira J. Wise.

22. Do one or more of the Yom Kippur art projects in *100+ Jewish Art Projects for Children* by Nina Streisand Sher and Margaret A. Feldman (pages 8 and 9).

23. Perform or do a readers theater performance of "The Teardrop" (page 146) or "Justice and Mercy" (page 34) in *Kings and Things: 20 Jewish Plays for Kids 8 to 18* by Meridith Shaw Patera. Discuss how the themes of justice and mercy relate to the High Holy Days.

24. Complete pages 4 and 5 of *Jewish Holiday Copy Pak™ 4-6* by Marji Gold-Vukson.

Secondary

1. Provide a Catholic Bible (one with the Apocrypha; you can find one in a library). Have students search through to find the Books of Maccabees. Then ask them to find Maccabees in a Tanach. When they can't, explain that the Rabbis who were putting together the Hebrew Bible felt at that time that Chanukah was too recent in history. They also felt that these books were not holy enough to be put into our Bible. But the Catholics saved the books in a collection of additional writings called the Apocrypha. (The Book of Judith is also in the Apocrypha; it was probably written during the time of the Hasmoneans.) (NSM)

2. There are some people who, on Yom Kippur, go home from the synagogue in the middle of the day and take a nap. They say that doing this helps them forget how hungry they are. Discuss with students whether or not they accept this reasoning and why? Ask: Would you do it? Do you think that doing this is in the spirit of the day, or is it contrary to the purpose of fasting?

3. Discuss: Why fast on Yom Kippur? Why do you fast (if you do)? Is it because everyone expects you to fast on Yom Kippur? Explain your reasoning for fasting or not fasting.

4. Have students analyze what, in their opinion, is the key message of Yom Kippur. What is its meaning and importance for each of them?

5. Honor 13-year-olds (and those older) who fast for the first time all the way through the day. Some suggestions: Say *Shehecheyanu,* make an award certificate, have a special class snack, or other observance of your choosing. (NSM)

6. Yizkor occurs four times a year (Yom Kippur, end of Sukkot, end of Pesach, Shavuot). Examine the meaning of the Hebrew word *"Yizkor"* (God will remember). Why do we have a memorial service on special holidays? How does the Yizkor service enhance our feeling of closeness with loved ones who have died? How do these memories enhance the meaning of this holy day for us?

7. Discuss how Jews are expected to maintain a balance between self and the rest of the world by examining Hillel's statement: "If I am not for myself, who will be for me? If I am for myself alone, what am I? If not now, when?" (*Pirke Avot* 1:14) This quotation raises a number of questions: What is the relationship between love of self and caring about others? How does performing righteous acts keep a person's ego in check? What would the world be like without *tzedakah*? What would it be like If everyone thought only about themselves? What does "If not now, when?" mean? When must acts of *tzedakah* begin, and why? How do the High Holy Days, and especially Yom Kippur, remind us of this double responsibility of taking care of ourselves and taking care of others as well?

8. Encourage students to go out on the Internet and to bring back to class information on alternative Yom Kippur observance ideas culled from such Jewish sites as: "Jewish Family" (http://www.jewishfamily.com/); "Virtual Jerusalem" (http://virtual.co.il/); America Online – use Key Word "Jewish Community," then once in that section, locate the youth section and check out Sparks e-zine and the boards. (NSM)

9. Discuss why the Book of Jonah is read on Yom Kippur. What is its central message? Is it an effective way to get that message across? What does the story of Jonah teach us about

ourselves? about human beings in general? about God's relationship to the entire world?

10. As a class, read Leviticus 16 to see how the scapegoat symbolically carried the sins of the people as it went into the wilderness. Discuss how the concept of using someone as a scapegoat developed from this ancient ritual. Explore various situations in which Jews and others were blamed for things that they did not cause. Discuss the irony that the people who "invented" the scapegoat should end up being history's scapegoat.

11. In pairs, follow this procedure:
    a. Each student finds a partner who is not a friend outside of school, someone whom that student does not know well. One student becomes A and the other B. Each pair finds a comfortable place to sit.
    b. A boasts about things that he/she did during the past year while B listens without talking.
    c. B boasts about his/her accomplishments during the past year while A listens without talking.
    d. A confesses one or more failings during the past year, while B listens without speaking.
    e. B confesses while A listens.
    f. A and B feedback to each other. They consider such questions as: How did you feel when you boasted? How did you feel when you confessed failings? How did your feelings differ? What did you learn from this experience?
        Afterward, sit in a circle to process the activity. Discuss feelings, learning, aspirations for the future.

12. Divide the class into groups of 3-5 students each. Write three sentences on the blackboard and have students address the following three statements in the manner described below:

I am concerned about doing _____ during the coming year.

The group can help me with my concern by _____.

I can help to resolve/deal with my concern by _____.

Step 1: With each group working at the same time, students take turns completing the first statement.

Step 2: Students may react to the statements made by other students in the group.

Step 3: Repeat steps 1 and 2 for the second statement.

Step 4: Repeat steps 1 and 2 for the third statement.

Step 5: React to, comment upon, and discuss the other students' concerns and how sharing their concerns can be helpful to each other.

13. The *Kol Nidre* begins the Yom Kippur eve worship service. It petitions God to cancel out vows made in haste, in anger, or under duress. For a personal experience related to the prayer, follow this procedure:

Step 1: Give out a sheet of paper to each student with two headings on it: Promises I Have Made and Can Fulfill, and Promises I Have Made but Cannot Fulfill. Each student has ten minutes to write down as many things as he/she can think of in both categories.

Step 2: Explain that sometimes people make false promises or promises that cannot be kept for various reasons. Sometimes promises are made because people talk too much or speak without thinking first. One way to get out of the habit of idle talk and into more considered communicating is to treasure moments of silence. Ask the students to find a partner at this time. Once the partners are situated, ask

the students to imagine that each one is about to make a false promise. With their partners, each student sits in silence for the next five minutes, and may only communicate with the other student using gestures, facial expressions, and mirror images — but no words!

Step 3: Share in words what was communicated in silence during the previous five minutes.

Step 4: Lists of fulfilled and unfulfilled promises are shared with partners. They can make suggestions to each other about how to shorten the list of unfulfilled promises. Discuss the problem of idle talk and how it can cause trouble.

Step 5: Hand out a copy of the *Kol Nidre* prayer (in English) to each student. Read it to the class once, asking students to follow the text as you read. Then ask the students to reread the prayer and discuss it with their partners.

Step 6: Reassemble the class and discuss the connection between the *Kol Nidre* and this learning activity. What feelings were evoked during this exercise?

14. Have students read and analyze Leviticus 16 as to what it means to them. First, as a class, read the chapter, which describes the ancient scapegoat ritual. Examine together the psychological function of the ritual. Briefly explain how this concept has come to haunt the Jewish people for the past 2000 years. Next, describe the *Tashlich* ceremony. Discuss how it relates to the scapegoat ritual and how it may, in effect, be a more up-to-date version of that ritual. Then, in small groups, discuss how people use scapegoats in their daily lives and how they "pass the buck" in their dealings with others. Ask students to give examples of times they themselves have done this. Discuss:

Why do people need scapegoats? Who are our modern-day scapegoats? What can we do about this?

15. Assign parts for a reading of "The Book of Jonah: A Dramatization" (see page 55). If the Narrator parts are divided among 8-10 students, there can be enough parts for about 20 students. After completing this contemporary dramatic rendering, do one or more of the following activities related to the Book of Jonah: (1) Consider the Points to Ponder found at the conclusion of the dramatic reading; (2) Discuss the content and meaning of the story to help students to understand its complex, multi-faceted meaning; (3) Present the dramatization to the other classes or as part of the Yom Kippur Youth Worship Service.

16. Put Jonah on trial. Divide the class into two groups. Group A is the pro-Jonah group, while group B is the anti-Jonah group. A prepares arguments to demonstrate Jonah's innocence, while B prepares arguments to show Jonah's guilt. Each group selects a lawyer to present its case. The Rabbi, Director of Education, and the teacher serve as the judges. The judges evaluate the arguments for the defense and the prosecution. After rendering a verdict, discuss the question: What would you have done if you had been in Jonah's place?

17. Divide the class into groups, assigning to each one of the worship services for Yom Kippur from your congregation's *Machzor*. Give each group an opportunity to investigate their assigned service. Have them consider such questions as: Are there aspects of the service that look familiar from Shabbat or weekday services? Which prayers ask God's forgiveness? To what readings do students especially relate? When the original investigations are completed, create new groups, being sure that one person from each of the first groups is in each newly constituted group. Ask students to teach each other about what they learned in their original groups, moving in order from the *erev* Yom Kippur service through Ne'ilah. (NSM)

18. Read "Three Who Ate," by David Frishman (see page 55 below), or present it in the form of a dramatization. This story, which takes place in the late nineteenth century in Eastern Europe, vividly portrays the power and the mood of Yom Kippur. After the story has been read by the class or presented to the class, discuss its significance, considering the following in particular:

    a. How does this story reflect the belief that the account of "The Three Books" (see page 44) is more than just a *midrash*?

    b. How does this story reflect the important teaching that "The saving of a life postpones the Shabbat" (*Pikuach Nefesh Docheh et HaShabbat*)? Think of examples from contemporary life (e.g., a woman who goes into labor on the Shabbat may use the phone and ride to the hospital so as not to endanger her life or the unborn).

19. Prior to giving a short lecture on the origins of Yom Kippur, customs and observances, and highlights of the liturgy (see Overview, page 43), assign students to one of four listening teams: Team 1 is to ask at least two questions. Team 2 is to tell which points they agreed with and why. Team 3 is to tell which points they disagreed with and why. Team 4 is to give specific examples or applications of the material. Present the lecture. Afterward, give teams a few minutes to complete their assignments. Then call on each team to question, agree, and so forth. (Adapted from *Active Learning: 101 Strategies to Teach Any Subject* by Mel Silberman.)

20. Complete one or both of the Instant Lessons *The Yom Kippur Crisis* by Peter A. Oppenheim

and Diane E. Berg and *Did Darth Vader Repent?* by Steven Bayar.

21. Perform the play "Forgiveness" in *Class Acts: Plays & Skits for Jewish Settings* by Stan J. Beiner (page 25).

All-School

1. Have a school-wide essay contest: "Why Jews Need Yom Kippur." Divide the entries into K-3, 4-6, 7-9 and 10-12. Pick the best entry or entries from each grade grouping.

2. Students in Grades 4 and up can present "Three Who Ate" (see page 58) as a dramatic reading. Then each class can discuss the pros and cons of what the Rabbi in the story and his assistants did. Take a vote in each class to see how many students agree and disagree with the Rabbi's decision, then make a tally for the whole school.

3. Yom Kippur is an ideal time to organize an ongoing food drive through the Religious School. Link up with a local food pantry. Place inexpensive plastic trash bins or grocery carts at conspicuous points throughout the building, and label them with signs that say "Food Donations for the Needy." Students can bring non-perishable food items and paper products in addition to their regular *tzedakah* contributions. When the bins are filled, deliver them to the food pantry.

4. Have a "Jonah Day." Build a very large fish that younger children can crawl into. Older students can present "The Book of Jonah: A Dramatization" (see page 55). This can be followed by a school-wide debate about the fate of Jonah. Argue the pros and cons of punishing Jonah for running away from God vs. the pros and cons of forgiving him for his actions. At the conclusion of the brief debate, take a vote. For other ideas, consult the activities above.

Family

1. Send home a coded message for families to figure out. If desired, they can then design their own code for sending holiday messages to each other. An example of a simple code follows. To decode, move each letter back one letter in order.

   Z P N L J Q Q V S J T
   YOM KIPPUR IS

   D P O T J E F S F E U P C F U I F
   CONSIDERED TO BE THE

   T B C C B U I P G T B C C B U I T
   SABBATH OF SABBATHS

2. Organize a family education program for two to four-year-olds (there is an already designed High Holy Day program in *Head Start on Holidays: Jewish Programs for Preschoolers and Their Parents* by Roberta Louis Goodman and Andye Honigman Zell).

3. Prepare a handout to send home with the students that will include the following:
   a. The Festival candle lighting prayer (For blessings in Hebrew and English, see Appendix, page 253.)
   b. The blessing for the children to be said by father or mother (For blessings, see Appendix, page 251.)
   c. Instructions for dipping the *challah* in honey with the words: "May God give you a good and a sweet year."
   d. A reminder that a memorial candle should be lit for members of the family who have died.

4. Encourage families to talk about the highlights and sad times of the past year. Suggest that they discuss what each person can do to bring happiness to the entire family.

5. Send home some sentences for families to complete that express their thoughts and

feelings about fasting on Yom Kippur. Some suggestions:

I fast because _____.
Fasting enables me to _____.
After fasting I feel _____.
The best way to get through a day of fasting is by _____.
Fasting makes me think about _____.
The reason we fast on Yom Kippur is _____.
Fasting is important to me because _____.

6. Ask families to talk about ways that each family member can help the other members reach their own personal goals. Think of ways to share both feelings and tasks.

THE BOOK OF JONAH: A DRAMATIZATION

Robert Goodman

Cast of Characters
Narrator
God
Jonah
Sailor 1
Sailor 2
Captain
Servant
King

Narrator: In the book of Second Kings, chapter 14, verse 25 we are told that Jonah, the son of Amittai, served as a prophet in Israel during the reign of King Jeroboam II, who ruled from 785-745 B.C.E. One day, God spoke to the prophet Jonah:

God: Listen, Jonah. Arise and go to Nineveh, the capital of Assyria. Tell the people that they have done wicked things and that they will be destroyed if they do not sincerely repent of their sins.

Narrator: Jonah listened carefully to the words and was very upset. He thought to himself:

Jonah: God wants me to go to Nineveh even though Assyria is the great enemy of my people. That in itself seems like a crazy idea, but there is something else that bothers me even more. Here I am a prophet of Israel, yet my own people do not listen to my words. I tell them to repent of their sins, and they do not pay attention to me. If I go to Ninevah and tell the people to repent, and they listen to me, then it will be very embarrassing to me and to the people of Israel. What can I do? Ah yes, I know. I will simply run away!

Narrator: So Jonah went to the port of Yafo and bought a ticket on a ship that was sailing to Tarshish far away. Soon the ship set sail. At first, all went well, but then a great storm began to toss the ship to and fro. The waves were so high and the storm so fierce, that all the sailors were afraid that they would drown.

Narrator: But something else was very strange: while they were in a terrible storm, nearby ships sailed by in calm waters. The sailors spoke:

Sailor 1: This is very strange. Perhaps one of the gods that we pray to is angry with us. Let each of us pray to our gods to save us.

Sailor 2: That might work, but let's also throw some of our cargo into the sea in order to make the ship lighter.

Captain: Wait a minute! We have a passenger who is sleeping in the hold of the ship. Let us wake this man whose name is Jonah and ask him to pray to his God. I will speak to this stranger. (Captain wakes up Jonah.)

Jonah: Oh, hello Captain! My, the sea is rough; there must be quite a storm out there! I must have slept through everything.

Captain: Why do you sleep? Get up and pray to your gods to call off this storm just as we have all done! Perhaps your prayers can save us!

Narrator: But neither the prayers nor throwing of cargo overboard seemed to help. Finally the sailors decided to cast lots to see who was at fault. They believed that whoever picked up the paper with the "X" marked on it was the person responsible for the storm. So they cast lots, and the lot fell upon Jonah. Then the sailors and Jonah spoke to each other.

Sailor 1: Tell us, who are you? What is your country and why does this evil fall upon us?

Jonah: My name is Jonah and I am a Hebrew. I fear *Adonai*, the God of heaven, who made the sea and the dry land.

Sailor 2: What have you done wrong to bring us this harm? Please tell us!

Jonah: God commanded me to go to Ninevah, but I didn't want to go. I bought passage on this ship and planned to travel in the opposite direction. Now I see that I cannot

run from God because God is everywhere. It's my fault that you are suffering.

Sailor 1: What shall we do so that the sea will once again be calm? We must do something because the storm is getting worse every minute.

Jonah: Pick me up and throw me into the sea, and then the storm will cease.

Sailor 2: We cannot do that; we would be sending you to your death. Let us try to row harder in order to return to Yafo.

Narrator: The harder the sailors rowed, the less it seemed to help. Finally, having no choice, they picked up Jonah and threw him into the sea. But they were very afraid and offered a sacrifice to the God of Israel, Jonah's God.

Sailor 1: We beg You, O God, do not make us die for the sake of this man. We do not want to be guilty of causing an innocent man to die. But look, now that we have thrown Jonah into the sea, the storm has stopped. You must be very great indeed, O God of the people Israel.

Narrator: After the sailors had cast Jonah into the stormy sea, a great fish came along and swallowed him up. For three days and three nights, Jonah remained inside the belly of the giant fish. Somehow Jonah remained alive and well during those three days. On the third day, he offered a prayer to God:

Jonah: O God, I realize that I have done evil. I did not obey your command

and I tried to escape from You. But now I know that a person cannot run away from You because You, O God, are everywhere. I now understand that what You commanded me to do was right, and I am ready to obey Your command. I pray that you will forgive me!

Narrator: For three days and three nights, the giant fish swam toward the north in the very direction that Jonah was supposed to have gone in the first place. When God heard Jonah's sincere prayer, God knew that now Jonah was ready to do what he had been commanded to do. So God spoke to the fish:

God: O great fish, you have done your job well. Now spit forth your passenger Jonah on dry land close to the city of Nineveh. Jonah will go and speak to the king and to all the people of Assyria.

Narrator: So the fish spit Jonah onto the dry land. And God spoke to Jonah, commanding him for the second time to go to Ninevah to tell the people of their sinfulness. Jonah listened to God's command, entered the city, and began to proclaim the word of God.

Jonah: O people of Ninevah, listen to me — you have sinned so greatly that in 40 days your city will be destroyed, unless you truly repent of your evil deeds.

Narrator: The people of Ninevah listened to Jonah because they believed that he was a true prophet of God. They proclaimed a fast and put on sackcloth. Even the king heeded the words of Jonah.

Servant: King, have you heard the proclamation of the prophet of Israel called Jonah? He has declared that unless we give up our evil doing and repent fully, our great city will be destroyed in 40 days.

King: This is horrible! I, too, will cover myself with ashes and sackcloth. I shall declare a time of public fasting for the entire land. Perhaps if we all turn away from his evil, God will spare us, and allow us to live.

Narrator: And God saw that the people of Ninevah were truly repenting of their evil ways. So God decided not to destroy them. But this kind and just action of God's greatly upset Jonah. It disturbed him because he had been successful with the non-Jews, but a failure with his own people, who should have listened to him but didn't. Jonah then turned to God with a bitter prayer.

Jonah: O God, because I know that You are a gracious, compassionate, and merciful God, I knew that You would spare the people of Nineveh. Because I knew this would happen, I did not want to come to proclaim Your word. I beg You, O Lord, take my life from me because I cannot bear the shame of returning to my people.

Narrator: Late in the day, Jonah left the city and built himself a booth so as to escape the hot afternoon sun. He sat in the lengthening shadows to see what would happen to the city. Although he begged God to take his life, he really did not want to die. During the night, God caused a gourd to grow so that Jonah had shade over his head which protected him from the sun. For a short while, the plant gave Jonah relief from the sun and heat, but then God caused a worm to eat the roots of the plant which caused it to die. Then God made a strong east wind blow and caused the sun to beat down on Jonah's head. Nearly fainting, Jonah called out to God.

Jonah: O God, it is better for me to die than to live. How could You be so cruel as to cause this plant to die, leaving me exposed to the brutal sun? Indeed, I am very angry for what you have done, O God.

God: Listen to me well, Jonah! You are upset over the death of something that you did not create, did not help to grow, and did not tend to. Yet you are bitter that it has died. If you can care about something you had no part in fashioning, then shouldn't I, the Creator of all, be concerned with the well-being of all my creatures? The people of Nineveh need My help as much as your people, and are you to tell Me that I should ignore them?

Narrator: And so ends the story of Jonah. There are those who believe that the book is a true story written by Jonah himself. There are others who believe that it was written centuries after Jonah lived. What do you think? What is really important: the events of the story, or the ideas it tries to get across?

Points to Ponder:

Discuss the questions raised by the Narrator at the end of the reading.

There are people who see the story of Jonah in very symbolic terms — Jonah means "dove" in Hebrew, which is the symbol of innocence and purity. Amittai, his father's name, means "truth," which reflects Israel's way of life. Nineveh was chosen as representative of the nations because Jonah lived when Nineveh was the capital of the greatest nation in the world; accordingly, it was probably the most evil in the eyes of Israel. How do you explain these symbols if Jonah was not innocent and did not want to save the Ninevites?

Perhaps the key message of the story is the universality of God. To the author of Jonah, God is concerned with all people, Jews and non-Jews alike. Could this book have been meant to counteract this notion?

Ezra made major reforms in Jewish life around 450 B.C.E. He was far too strict in the eyes of many, bringing hardship to some Jews. Could this book have been written as a reaction to Ezra?

Based on the Book of Jonah, do you think God prefers sin or goodness from the nations of the world?

What does the story say about the ability of a person to flee from his conscience? Can we replace "God" with "conscience" and see experiences in our own lives that are similar to those of Jonah? What part does our conscience play in our lives?

THREE WHO ATE

David Frishman
(Adapted by Robert Goodman)

Cast of Characters
Narrator A
Narrator B
Rabbi
Congregant

Narrator A: Even if I live many years and grow to be very old, I shall never forget the day and what was done on it; nor shall I ever forget the men, for they were no ordinary people, but great heroes.

Narrator B: I, too, remember those days. The year was 1870, and the place was Eastern Europe, the area around Poland. Those were bitter times. We Jews were treated badly. Yes, very badly.

Narrator A: Then a great calamity fell upon us. Cholera, the dreaded disease, had broken out and spread throughout the land. By day and by night, men, women, and children, young and old, died like flies. And those who were left, hung between life and death, not sure when their turn would come.

Narrator B: The summer came to an end and then came the Ten Days of Repentance. And finally the most solemn day of all, Yom Kippur arrived. Yes, I shall remember that day as long as I live.

Narrator A: It was the evening of Yom Kippur, the time for the chanting of that haunting melody, *Kol Nidre*. Usually, for *Kol Nidre*, the Cantor and two members of the congregation stand before the Ark. But not this year. This year it was the Rabbi and his two assistants.

Narrator B: Hush! Quiet! What is happening? The Rabbi slowly rises to his feet and begins to speak. It is so quiet in the synagogue that we could hear a pin drop. The Rabbi speaks:

Rabbi: With the consent of the All Present and with the permission of this congregation, we begin our prayers to God, and begin to look inside ourselves in the hope that we will be better people in the year ahead. (He remains standing at the *bimah*.)

Narrator A: And a great fear fell upon me and upon all the people young and old.

In that moment, when the Rabbi mounted the platform, I began to wonder: Is he going to give a sermon — is he going to lecture the people when they are falling dead like flies? But the Rabbi neither preached nor lectured. He only called to remembrance the souls of those who had died during the last few days.

Narrator B: But how long it lasted! How many names he mentioned! The list was so long! And it seemed to me that the Rabbi would have been better off calling out the names of those who remained alive, because they were so few.

Narrator A: I shall never forget that night and the praying, because it was not really praying, but one long, loud groan rising from the depth of the human heart. It was a collective cry of pain and hurt from all of us.

Narrator B: That night no one left the synagogue. On and on we prayed, hoping against hope that our prayers would help bring the plague to an end.

Narrator A: By early in the morning, there were some people missing. Two of the congregation had fallen during the night and died before our eyes. They lay wrapped in their prayer shawls and white robes.

Narrator B: They kept on bringing messages to the synagogue, but nobody wanted to know or to ask questions for fear it might be about a member of his or her family. It was horrible! But the Day of Atonement that followed was more awful still!

Narrator A: The Rabbi is old, perhaps even 80 years old, but he is tall and straight as a fir tree. His long beard is white like silver, but the thick, long hair of his head is whiter still, and his face pale.

Narrator B: I stood in awe of him. I knew he was a man of God, a great scholar, a man whose advice was sought by people throughout the world.

Narrator A: I knew also that he was inclined to be lenient in his decisions, and that no one dared to oppose him. What I saw that day is carved, even burned in my memory.

Narrator B: The Musaf service is over, and the people are waiting to hear what the Rabbi will say. And the Rabbi began to speak:

Rabbi: On this, the holiest of the days of the year, on this day of repentance and prayer, on the day when we choose between life and death, we see death making the choice for us. (Speaking with great pain in his voice.) And when trouble comes to a person, that person must look to his or her deeds. We need to consider our concerns and God's. We also need to be concerned about our body, our health, or well-being. Indeed, how we take care of ourselves is important to God, because by looking after ourselves, we are able to serve God.

Narrator A: I was a child then, but I remember how I began to tremble when I heard those words, because I was beginning to understand what was about to happen.

Rabbi: And people shall live by my commandments and not die by them.

There are times when one must turn aside from the Law, if by so doing a whole community may be saved.

Narrator B: I was shaking with fear. What does the Rabbi want? What does he mean by these words? What does he wish to accomplish? And suddenly I see that he is overcome with grief and weeping. What has happened? Why does he weep? And there I stand in the corner, in silence, and I too, begin to cry. And then I again hear him speak.

Rabbi: With the consent of the all-knowing God and with the consent of this congregation, we give you permission to eat and drink on this Day of Atonement. Yes, you may eat!

Narrator A: Silence! Not a sound is heard in the synagogue, not a breath is drawn. And then a voice is heard from the congregation.

Congregant: Rabbi, are you asking us to eat on Yom Kippur, on this day of fasting? But that is a sin! We have never in our adult lives eaten on this, the holiest day of the year. Now you ask us to eat?

Rabbi: Yes, I call upon you to eat on this Day of Atonement because of the cholera. (*In a begging tone.*) Please, eat; today we must eat. This is a time to turn aside from the Law. We are to live by the commandments, and not die because of them!

Narrator B: But no one in the synagogue moved. The Rabbi stood and begged them to eat.

Rabbi: Please, I beg you to eat so that you may live! Listen, I take responsibility for our eating on this day. You are innocent of any wrongdoing.

Narrator A: No one stirs. And presently he begins in a changed voice. Now he does not beg, he commands.

Rabbi: I give you leave to eat. I — I — I! What would you have of me? Why will you torment me till my strength fails? Think well! Do you not think that I have not struggled with myself from early this morning until now?

Narrator B: Then the Rabbi grows white as chalk and lets his head droop with sadness. The *Shamash* of the synagogue comes over to him and the Rabbi whispers a few words. He speaks with his assistants and they, too, agree with whatever he said to them. And then he spoke one more time:

Rabbi: It is God's will. I am an old man, and I have never in all my years knowingly broken a religious commandment, but this is a divine commandment and I know that it is the will of God.

And so let it be! So that you, my dear friends, will live, I shall eat because then you, too, will eat!

Narrator A: I shall never in all my life forget that moment. The *Shamash* brought out of the Rabbi's study a cup of wine and little rolls of bread. And there, on that tragic Yom Kippur Day, the Rabbi, our great Rabbi, stood on the pulpit and ate. And we, too, ate — and we lived!

Points to Ponder

Why was it necessary for the Rabbi to eat first in order for the congregation to eat?

How was it in keeping with Jewish values for the Rabbi to command the people to eat? You may wish to look at the *parashah Nitzavim* (Deuteronomy 29-30).

How does this story illustrate that the synagogue is the focus of Jewish life, is the place where Jews gathered and shared special experiences?

Do you agree or disagree with the decision the Rabbi made. Why or why not?

What do you think might have happened in your own synagogue under similar circumstances?

BIBLIOGRAPHY

See pages 266-268.

CHAPTER FOUR

SUKKOT AND HOSHANA RABBAH

VOCABULARY

Aravah: Willow — one of the *Arba'ah Minim.* According to a *midrash*, it is shaped like, and symbolic of, the mouth. Since the willow has neither taste nor aroma, it represents homiletically those Jews who perform no good deeds and who are ignorant of Torah.

Arba'ah Minim: The "Four Species" mentioned in the Torah, which grow in *Eretz Yisrael* and are used in the celebration of Sukkot. They are the *etrog* (also called fruit of the *hadar* tree; a citron), *lulav* (palm), *hadas* (myrtle), and *aravah* (willow).

Chag Adonai: "Festival of *Adonai*." This name for Sukkot suggests that, in ancient times, Sukkot was one of the most important festivals in the Jewish calendar. The term is found in Leviticus 23:39: "Mark, on the fifteenth day of the seventh month, when you have gathered in the yield of your land, you shall observe a Festival of *Adonai* seven days . . . ."

Chag HaAsif: "Festival of the Harvest" or "Festival of the Ingathering." In Israel, Sukkot marks the end of the agricultural year, when the last crops of the season are harvested. It is a time when people would express their joy and gratitude to God for the blessings of a good crop and for health and life. Deuteronomy 16:15 states: "You shall hold a festival for *Adonai* your God seven days, in the place that *Adonai* will choose; for *Adonai* your God will bless all your crops and all

your undertakings, and you shall have nothing but joy" (see also Exodus 23:16).

Chag HaSukkot: "Festival of the Booths." One of the four names for Sukkot, the term is used in Leviticus 23:34: "On the fifteenth day of this seventh month there shall be a Festival of the Booths to God for seven days."

Chol HaMo'ed: "Intermediate Days of the Festival" — these are the third through the sixth days of Sukkot.

Etrog: A citron fruit of the *hadar* tree, this is one of the *Arba'ah Minim.* According to a *midrash*, it is shaped like and is symbolic of the heart. Since the *etrog* has both taste and aroma, it represents homiletically those Jews who have a knowledge of Torah and perform good deeds.

Hadas: Myrtle — one of the *Arba'ah Minim.* According to a *midrash*, its leaves are shaped like and are symbolic of the eye. Since the myrtle has aroma but no taste, it represents homiletically those Jews who perform good deeds, but who do not know Torah.

Hakafah/Hakafot: "Circle(s)" or "Circling." It is a relatively modern custom to march around (*hakafah*) the sanctuary with the Torah during holidays so that congregants can kiss it and show it honor. *Hakafot* are especially associated with Sukkot,

Hoshana Rabbah, and Simchat Torah (see Hoshana Rabbah below).

Hakhayl: "Assemble." Once every seven years, according to Deuteronomy 31:10-13, the Israelites were commanded to assemble on Sukkot (on the steps of the Temple in Jerusalem), to bring their offerings, to listen to the reading of the Torah, and to become acquainted with its laws. In recent years, an effort was made to reinstate this practice in symbolic fashion in Israel.

Hallel: Psalms 113-118. During the morning worship services on Sukkot, the *Hallel* Psalms are chanted while the four species are waved as a reminder of God's dominion over all of nature. The *Hallel* is recited only on joyous occasions. Some scholars believe that these Psalms were assembled for use at the rededication of the Temple after the Maccabean victory over Antiochus in 165 B.C.E.

HeChag: "The Festival." One of the four names for the festival, it underscores the idea that Sukkot was the most significant of the ancient festivals, surpassing both Pesach and Shavuot in importance. Serving as the culmination of the harvest season, Sukkot occupied a key place in the life of the ancient Israelites.

Hoshana: "Save us, please." Hoshana prayers are recited while making *hakafot* around the synagogue during Sukkot. The word comes from Psalm 118:25: "We beseech You, *Adonai*, save now! We beseech You, *Adonai*, make us now to prosper." The word is also associated with a willow branch. Both meanings apply to Hoshana Rabbah. To accommodate the second meaning of the term, some hold willow twigs as they chant Psalm 118.

Hoshana Rabbah: "The Great Hoshana." Hoshana Rabbah occurs on the seventh day of Sukkot. On this day, seven *hakafot* are made around the synagogue with the *lulav* and *etrog* in hand while reciting the Hoshana prayer: "Save now, we

beseech you, *Adonai*" (Psalm 118:25). On each of the previous days of Sukkot, there is only one *hakafah* with *lulav* and *etrog*. After the *hakafot* on Hoshana Rabbah, it is a custom to beat willow branches until all of the leaves fall off. This symbolizes the casting off of sins.

Kohelet: The Book of Ecclesiastes, which is read on the eighth day of Sukkot. It begins with the somber words, "Vanity of vanities, all is vanity . . ." Authorship is ascribed to King Solomon in his later years, reflecting of the passage of time and the changes that age brings, and yet . . . life is always the same — "There is nothing new under the sun." Possessions and pleasures are of no lasting consequence — merely a striving after wind. Sukkot, though a joyous festival, occurs in the autumn when summer's light begins to lessen and intimations of the winter of life are in the air.

Layl HaChotam: "The Night of Sealing." While one tradition has it that the fate of human beings is decided by God on Yom Kippur, there is also a tradition that the divine decision is not finalized until Hoshana Rabbah, the last night of Sukkot. Accordingly, this name is given to *erev* Hoshana Rabbah. The customary greeting on this evening and the days leading up to it is: "*G'mar Chatimah Tovah*" (May the final sealing decree be good).

Lulav: Palm — one of the *Arba'ah Minim.* The *lulav,* according to a *midrash,* is shaped like, and is symbolic of, the spine. Since the date palm has taste but no aroma, it represents homiletically those Jews who know Torah, but do not practice good deeds.

Masechet Sukkah: A tractate of the Mishnah which contains a detailed description of the rules and regulations pertaining to Sukkot, with particular emphasis upon the construction and use of a *sukkah.* The tractate begins: "If a *sukkah* is more than 20 cubits high (30'), it is not valid (Rabbi Judah declares it valid), and if it is not ten handbreadths high or has not three sides or if what is unshaded is more than what is shaded, it is not valid . . . " (*Sukkah* 1:1).

S'chach: Evergreen twigs and leaves that are used to cover the roof of the *sukkah*. The shade created by the roof covering must exceed the areas exposed to sunlight, but one must be able to see stars through the *s'chach*.

Shalosh Regalim: Three Pilgrimage Festivals. On Pesach, Shavuot, and Sukkot, Israelites journeyed on foot (to Jerusalem) to offer sacrifices (at the Temple) in accordance with the injunction in Deuteronomy 16:16-17.

Simchat Bayt HaSho'ayvah: "The Joy of the Place of the Water Drawing." In the days of the Temple in Jerusalem, on each of the six intermediate days of Sukkot, priests filled containers with water drawn from the Pool of Siloam in the valley to the south of the Temple Mount. The water was then brought to the Temple in a joyous ceremony that included singing and dancing (*Sukkot* 5:1-5). The origin of the water drawing celebration is not known, but the festival was believed to have been linked to the people's prayers for rain. In recent years, some *yeshivot* in Jerusalem have instituted a *Simchat Bayt HaSho'ayvah* ceremony.

Sukkah: Booth. The term refers to the special, temporary structure erected for use during the festival of Sukkot. Tradition holds that the Israelites lived in *sukkot* during their 40 years of wandering through the wilderness of Sinai. Such booths were also used as temporary shelters by farmers during the fall harvest period in ancient Israel.

Sukkot: This term is the plural of *sukkah*, the name of the festival, and the name of a tractate in the Talmud.

Tikkun Layl Hoshana Rabbah: On the eve of Hoshana Rabbah, people gather to study the collection of readings by this name, which includes all of Deuteronomy, the 150 Psalms, and selections

from mystical writings. Deuteronomy is read because on Simchat Torah the annual cycle of reading the Torah is completed. Psalms are read because they like the Torah are divided into five books, and their author, King David (according to tradition), spent his nights in study and prayer.

Ushpizin: Each day during Sukkot, a short prayer may be recited whereby one of the seven *Ushpizin* (guests) — Abraham, Isaac, Jacob, Joseph, Moses, Aaron, and David — is welcomed to join with the family in their *sukkah*. This custom derives from a mystical understanding of the phrase: *"U'Fros Alaynu Sukkat Sh'lomecha"* — as these leaders saved our people in their times, so may the *Shechinah* (Divine Presence) shelter us today beneath wings of peace. As they are welcomed to join us, so, too, is God's presence invited.

Z'man Simchataynu: "The Season of Our Rejoicing." Sukkot is a time to rejoice in gratitude for what we might at other times of the year take for granted — for the fall harvest and for all the harvests of one's life. *Midrash Tehillim* 80:56 states: "In the world to come, all prayers will be eliminated except for prayers of thanksgiving, which will never be abolished."

BACKGROUND

Sukkot

Sukkot begins at the full moon, on the eve of the 15th of Tishre, four days after Yom Kippur. While it occurs so close to the Day of Atonement, it is remarkably different from it both in mood and in content.

As the third of the *Shalosh Regalim*, Sukkot marks the end of summer, ushers in the fall harvest, and anticipates the beginning of the rainy season in Israel. Between Pesach and Sukkot, little if any rain falls, therefore, between Sukkot and the following Pesach, farmers depend on the rains to get them through the following dry season.

The three Pilgrimage Festivals were originally agricultural celebrations. At one time the festival of

Sukkot, which marked the fall harvest, may not have been linked to a particular day, but rather to the day on which the harvest was completed. Only later (see also Leviticus 23:24), was the period of Sukkot fixed to Tishre 15-22.

Exodus 23:14-16 refers to the three Pilgrimage Festivals in essentially agricultural terms: "Three times a year you shall hold a festival for Me: You shall observe the Feast of Unleavened Bread, eating unleavened bread for seven days as I have commanded you, at the set time in the month of Aviv, for in it you went forth from Egypt; and none shall appear before Me empty-handed; and the Feast of the Harvest, of the first fruits of your work, of what you sow in the field; and the Feast of Ingathering at the end of the year, when you gather in the results of your work from the field." Note that only in the case of Pesach is there even a suggestion of more than an agricultural interpretation for one of the Pilgrimage Festivals. In post-biblical literature, more universal interpretations were given to each of these festivals.

Reflecting a later time frame than Exodus 23:14-16 is Leviticus 23:39-43, which clearly links the agricultural and historical aspects of Sukkot: "Mark, on the 15th day of the seventh month, when you have gathered in the yield of your land, you shall observe the festival of *Adonai* to last seven days: a complete rest on the first day, and a complete rest on the eighth day. On the first day you shall take the product of the *hadar* tree, branches of palm trees, boughs of leafy trees, and willows of the brook, and you shall rejoice before *Adonai* your God seven days. You shall observe it as a festival of the Lord for seven days in the year; you shall observe it in the seventh month as a law for all time, throughout the generations. You shall live in booths seven days; all citizens in Israel shall live in booths, in order that future generations may know that I made the Israelite people live in booths when I brought them out of the land of Egypt. I am *Adonai* Your God."

In the course of time, Sukkot took on additional significance. Just as Pesach was linked to the Exodus and Shavuot to the giving of the Torah at Mount Sinai, Sukkot was seen as a tangible reminder of the wilderness experience. According to later thinking, the Israelites used *sukkah*-like structures during their 40 years of wandering in the Sinai. Therefore, the *sukkah* came to be seen as more than a shelter used by farmers during the harvest season. Sukkot, by taking on this historical significance, became relevant to Jews living outside of Israel in non-agricultural settings.

There are a dozen or so references to this festival in the Tanach. Some are quite interesting and raise more questions than they answer. Exodus 23:16 states that the Festival of the Ingathering was celebrated at the end of the year (*b'tzayt hashanah*), not at the beginning. Deuteronomy 31:10-12 states that the Torah was read every seventh year to the assembled people on Sukkot. Nehemiah 8:14-18 implies that that Torah was read before the people (on the first of the seventh month) and studied on Sukkot for seven days. These verses also include olive branches as one of the four species and omit willow. And, there is a reference here that the festival was not celebrated from the days of Joshua until the return from Babylonian exile. The so-called Psalms of enthronement (47, 93, 96-99) have led some to think that Sukkot at first was a time for reaffirming the covenant between God and the people. As if to reaffirm that idea, I Kings 8:2 states: "All the men of Israel gathered before King Solomon at the festival in the month of Etanim — that is, the seventh month . . . to bring up the Ark (of the Covenant) and place it in the Temple."

The Rabbis in the Talmud emphasize Leviticus 23:39-43, which reminds us that we dwelled in booths during the desert experience after the Exodus. Every celebrant is to rejoice with the *Arba'ah Minim* for all seven days of the festival. Reference is also made to the *Simchat Bayt HaSho'ayvah* — when on *Chol HaMo'ed* the people would sing and dance with torches as they carried up water from springs into Jerusalem.

Over the centuries, Sukkot has evolved. Today, the first two days of the holiday are considered Sukkot, the third through the sixth are *Chol*

HaMo'ed Sukkot, the seventh day is called Hoshana Rabbah, the eighth day is Shemini Atzeret, and the ninth day, which is a separate festival, is Simchat Torah.

On the eve of Simchat Torah, all of the Torah scrolls are taken out of the Ark and carried as part of the seven *hakafot* around the synagogue. At the end of each *hakafah,* there is singing and dancing. The *hakafot* are repeated for the morning service on Simchat Torah. The custom of *hakafot* on Simchat Torah originated in the sixteenth century in order to endear the Torah to the children of Israel.

Central Themes

- Sukkot is a Festival of Thanksgiving for the abundance of the harvest and for the mercies shown to the Israelites as they wandered through the desert after leaving Egypt.

- To today's urban dweller, Sukkot and the building of a *sukkah* are reminders that we were once farmers, and that only now after nearly 2000 years of being kept away from our land do we had the opportunity to work the soil once again.

- Sukkot is the link between the modern Jew and nature. It is also known by the following names: Chag HaAsif ("Feast of the Harvest/Ingathering"), Chag Adonai ("Feast of *Adonai*" – which reflects the connection between God and the People during Sukkot in ancient Israel), HeChag ("The Festival" – which may indicate that Sukkot was the most important of the ancient Pilgrimage Festivals), and Z'man Simchataynu ("The Season of Our Rejoicing" – which reflects the joyous nature of the Festival). The latter name also refers to Simchat Torah.

- The development of the three Pilgrimage Festivals is reflective of the creative genius of the Jewish people. The broader, more universal interpretations given to each festival make it possible for Jews of every age and in every location to celebrate each of these festivals joyfully and meaningfully.

- The *sukkah* unites the past, present, and future. It is the functional booth of wilderness dwellers and of yesterday's farmers, it is the symbolic reminder today of our connectedness to the land and to all of nature, and it points to the continuity of the Jewish people. Despite obstacles and persecutions, still Jews build and harvest, create and survive. Therefore, even when the present is fraught with difficulty the *sukkah* reminds us that one need only look upward to find the source of inspiration and encouragement.

- The *sukkah* lends a sense of needed perspective. We have surrounded ourselves with machines and devices by which and with which we live our lives. The genie of technology is most seductive. It is important therefore to get in touch periodically with nature so as to remind ourselves that "The earth is the Lord's and the fullness thereof" (Psalm 24:1).

- The *sukkah*, according to Maimonides, helps remind Jews to live modestly even in days of prosperity, so as to keep one's values in perspective.

- The Kabbalistic practice of *Ushpizin* reflects the importance of *Hachnasat Orchim*, hospitality, in Jewish life. It is customary for families to invite people to eat with them at any time of year, but especially on Shabbat, at the *Seder*, and in the *sukkah*.

- The Festival of Sukkot reinforces the Jew's sense of community. *Kol Yisrael Arayvin Zeh BaZeh.* That Jews are responsible for one another is the key teaching of Judaism. Eating together on Sukkot reinforces this sense of community.

- Without a doubt, the Pilgrims modeled their Thanksgiving celebration on the biblical Sukkot. One of the lesser known names for Sukkot is *Chag HaHoda'ah* (Festival of Thanksgiving).

- It is also likely that the first celebration of Chanukah was a delayed celebration of Sukkot.

The Maccabees and their followers were so busy fighting the Syrian-Greeks that they were unable to celebrate Sukkot. This may explain why they celebrated the rededication of the Temple for eight days.

• Sukkot is closely connected to nature. In showing gratitude to God for many blessings, one also feels a sense of responsibility to guard and protect God's world. The principle of *Bal Tashchit* (do not destroy) originally referred to trees in a battle zone (Deuteronomy 20:19), but it has come to be Judaism's ecology phrase. Humanity was not given the world to misuse and destroy; rather, the world is to enjoy and to preserve for future generations.

The Sukkah
The sixth tractate of the second division of the Mishnah is called *Sukkah*. It's very first verses contain a detailed description of the rules and regulations pertaining to the construction and use of a proper *sukkah*:

1. It must be less than 30' high.
2. The walls must be strong enough to withstand ordinary gusts of wind.
3. The shade offered by the roof covering of the *sukkah* must be sufficient to block out most of the sun's rays, while airy enough so that the stars are visible through the roof at night.
4. There must be at least three walls, made of any material.
5. The *sukkah* must be a temporary structure, so a screened in porch or a screened house cannot serve as a *sukkah*.
6. It is considered a *mitzvah* to eat one's meals in the *sukkah*.
7. One is not obliged to sleep in the *sukkah*, particularly in colder climates. One is not required to eat in the *sukkah* when it is raining.
8. The *sukkah* can be adorned or decorated with pictures, hanging gourds, fruit, tapestries, etc.
9. There is no prescribed minimum size; however, the *sukkah* must be large enough to accommodate at least one person.

Upon entering a *sukkah*, one pronounces the blessing over dwelling in a booth. Additionally, *Shehecheyanu* is said upon entering the *sukkah* for the first time. (For blessing in Hebrew and English, see Appendix, page 250.)

Midrash of the Four Species
The four agricultural species used on Sukkot are mentioned in Leviticus 23:40: "On the first day you shall take the product of the *hadar* tree (*etrog*), branches of palm trees (*lulav*), boughs of leafy trees (*hadas* – myrtle), and willows (*aravah*) of the brook, and you shall rejoice before *Adonai* your God seven days."

A *midrash* equates taste with knowledge of Torah and aroma with being righteous. Using taste and aroma it describes four types of Jews (*Leviticus Rabbah* 30):

The *etrog* is shaped like the human heart; it has both taste and aroma and accordingly represents those Jews who have a knowledge of Torah and do good deeds.

The *lulav* is long and narrow like the human spine. Since the fruit of the palm tree, the date, has taste but no aroma, it represents Jews who know Torah, but do not practice good deeds.

The *hadas* leaf is shaped like the human eye. Since it has aroma but no taste, it symbolizes those who perform good deeds, but who do not know Torah.

The *aravah* leaf has the shape of a mouth. Since it has neither taste nor aroma, it represents those Jews who perform no good deeds and are ignorant of Torah as well.

Before a worship service on Sukkot or immediately before reciting the *Hallel*, a blessing is said over the four species by each worshiper as he/she takes them in hand. They are waved in six directions: East, West, North, South, up and down, to indicate that God is everywhere. (For blessing, see Appendix, page 250.)

The *lulav* is not used on Shabbat, because it was feared that people would carry it through the streets to the synagogue, thereby violating the prohibition against carrying on the Sabbath.

Hoshana Rabbah

Hoshana Rabbah is the seventh day of Sukkot. On the first six days, only one *hakafah* is made around the sanctuary with the *lulav* and *etrog*. On Hoshana Rabbah seven circuits are made.

Mishnah *Sukkah* 4:5 describes the special ceremony in the Temple that took place on Hoshana Rabbah: "How was the rite of the willow branch fulfilled? There was a place below Jerusalem called Motza. There they went and cut themselves young willow branches. They came and set these up at the sides of the Altar so that their tops were bent over the Altar. They then blow on the *shofar* a sustained, a quavering, and another sustained blast. Each day they went in a procession a single time around the Altar saying, 'Save now, we beseech You, *Adonai*, send now prosperity' (Psalm 118:25). But on the seventh day, they went in procession seven times around the Altar . . . ."

The ceremony of beating the ground with the willow branches can be explained thusly: just as the tree, after losing its leaves, gets renewed life when God sends rain and warmth, so too, can humankind gain fresh strength to deal with life's challenges by renewed faith in God and trust in the guidance of God's unseen hand.

Hoshana Rabbah also has a solemn character. It has been suggested in various sources, among them the *Zohar* and Rashi on Talmud *Yoma* 21b, that while God's judgments are sealed on Yom Kippur, the final verdict can be delivered on Hoshana Rabbah. In a sense, the prayers of this day represent one last chance to make impassioned pleas for forgiveness for one's sins.

Linked to this belief is the practice of holding an all night prayer and study session on Hoshana Rabbah during which selections from the anthology *Tikkun Layl Hoshana Rabbah* are read. The book lends its name to the evening. It contains the entire books of Deuteronomy and Psalms, as well as selections from Bible, Mishnah, and other devotional works.

Torah and Haftarah

The traditional Torah Portion for the first and second day of Sukkot is Leviticus 22:26-23:44. It begins with the rules for the use of sacrificial animals, and then proceeds to a comprehensive description of the festivals of the Jewish year, concluding with a discussion of Sukkot. *Maftir* for the first two days is Numbers 28:12-16 describing the sacrificial offerings for Sukkot; then, Numbers 29, verses 12-16, 20-28, 23-31, and 26-34, are read on each succeeding day of the festival. Exodus 33:12-34:26 is read on Shabbat of *Chol HaMo'ed*. Numbers 29:26-34 is read on Hoshana Rabbah. Deuteronomy 14:22-16:17 is read on Shemini Atzeret with Numbers 29:35-30:1 as the *Maftir*.

In Reform congregations, Leviticus 23:33-44 and 39-44 are read the first two days; Exodus 23:14-17 on the third; Exodus 34:12-24, Deuteronomy 16:13-17 and 9-13 on the fourth, fifth, and sixth days; and Deuteronomy 11:10-15 on the seventh day. Exodus 33:12-34:26 is read on the Shabbat of Sukkot.

In all synagogues, the *Haftarah* for the first day of Sukkot is Zechariah 14:1-21, a description of life in Israel at the end of days. I Kings 8:2-21 is read on the second day. In it King Solomon speaks to the people, probably on Sukkot, about the Holy Temple in Jerusalem. Ezekiel 38:18-39:16 is read on Shabbat *Chol HaMo'ed*, I Kings 8:54-9:1 is read on Shemini Atzeret, and Joshua 1:1-18 is the *Haftarah* for Simchat Torah.

SCOPE AND SEQUENCE

Grade	Themes/Ideas
Kindergarten	The *sukkah* as a home, a roof over our heads; why the *sukkah* should be beautiful.
Grade One	The harvest and food: why we should count our blessings and thank God for those blessings; the importance of giving food to the poor.
Grade Two	A look at how we observe Sukkot in the synagogue, including how to build a *sukkah*.

Grade Three	An examination of Sukkot and nature, including the concept of closeness to the land, what grows on the land, and how nature plays a role in our lives.	

Grade Three An examination of Sukkot and nature, including the concept of closeness to the land, what grows on the land, and how nature plays a role in our lives.

Grade Four A close look at the four species and how they are variously interpreted.

Grade Five A comparison of the similarities and differences between Sukkot and the American festival of Thanksgiving; Sukkot vocabulary.

Grade Six Special Sukkot customs and practices; Sukkot vocabulary continued.

Grade Seven Biblical selections related to and read on Sukkot.

Grade Eight The origin and development of Sukkot.

Grade Nine An overview of Hoshana Rabbah.

Grade Ten The meaning and significance of Sukkot for Jews today.

Grade Eleven A close look at how to build a *sukkah*; *Mitzvot* related to Sukkot and *Ushpizin*.

Grade Twelve If you had five minutes to explain Sukkot to a non-Jew, what would you say?

ACTIVITIES

Note: Many of the strategies included in this section may also be utilized for Shemini Atzeret and Simchat Torah. Accordingly, this listing of strategies will be more comprehensive than the Simchat Torah listing, which may be considered a supplement to the activities below.

Preschool/Kindergarten

1. Take a class trip to a farm or farmer's market to purchase fruits and vegetables. Use this as a way to open up a discussion on harvest. Relate the discussion back to biblical times. (NSM)

2. Cut open fruits and vegetables. Which have seeds? skin? Match the color/taste of the juice with fresh fruit or vegetable. (NSM)

3. Place seeds from fruits and vegetables in a resealable plastic bag with a wet paper towel. Keep the bag near a window. Watch what happens. Plant the sprouts and continue to watch the growth. (NSM)

4. Make bingo/lotto games with fruits and vegetables (teacher stores have stickers that can be used for this). Label the top of the game "S-U-K-O-T." (Use this acceptable spelling of the holiday, as it is not possible to play bingo with six letters or two the same.) (NSM)

5. Draw a picture in which one or more objects related to Sukkot are hidden. The task of the student is to find the hidden objects, and either color them in or circle them.

6. Pass around a *lulav* or an *etrog*. The teacher or a student claps hands. Whoever has the object when hands are clapped must say something about the object in a certain amount of time. (For older students, have them name several things associated with the object.)

7. Have students create decorations for the school *sukkah*, the congregational *sukkah*, or the family *sukkah*.

8. Create a doll house sized *sukkah* using a box for photocopy paper as the base. (NSM)

9. Have students lie down in a *sukkah* and look up. Ask: What do you see? Lie down in other places (e.g., under a tree, in the classroom,

under a piece of playground equipment, etc.). Make comparisons. (NSM)

10. Compare an *etrog* and a lemon. After Sukkot, dissect both of these. Decide how they are the same and how they are different. (NSM)

11. Make food from things we harvest (e.g., fruit soup, vegetable soup, fruit salad, or fresh fruits and vegetables). (NSM)

12. Introduce students to the pomegranate. It is a customary *sukkah* decoration in Israel. Consider serving a pomegranate in the *sukkah*. (NSM)

13. Plan a class meal in the *sukkah*.

14. Have children put photos in order showing a *sukkah* being built. (NSM)

15. Don't let used New Year's cards go to waste. Use them to make collages, or save them for decorating the *sukkah*.

16. Help children complete pages 11-15 in *Jewish Preschool/Kindergarten Copy Pak*™ by Nancy Cohen Nowak.

17. Do one or more of the Sukkot art projects in *100+ Jewish Art Projects for Children* by Nina Streisand Sher and Margaret A. Feldman (pages 17 and 18).

Primary

1. Decorate a shoe box and place in it a collection of student-made Sukkot objects — fruit, vegetables, *lulav, etrog,* or even a miniature *sukkah*.

2. Teach students how to make a pretend *lulav* from paper: Roll together several sheets of green 18" x 24" construction paper; tape this together along the roll-side. From one end, make 4 to 5 cuts down the tube approximately 6" deep. Pull out the paper from inside the tube. (NSM)

Resource: *Fast, Clean & Cheap: or Everything the Jewish Teacher (or Parent) Needs to Know about Art* by Simon Kops.

3. Help students to make a pretend *etrog* out of yellow construction paper: Wad up the paper and tape it around with masking tape. Paint the tape and the outside of the "wad" yellow. (NSM)

4. Show students a real *etrog* and *lulav* so they can make comparisons with their pretend ones. Students may use their pretend *lulav* and *etrog* during classroom *hakafot*. (NSM)

5. Teach each student to shake a *lulav*. Practice the *brachot* also. (For blessing, See Appendix, page 250.)

6. Help each student to build a miniature *sukkah*: This can be an elaborate project or it can be done simply. A nice approach is to ask each child to bring in a shoe box. Strips can be cut out in the top and on the sides. Use colored paper or strings of beads to decorate the roof. If desired, put cut-out objects or designs drawn with crayon or markers around the *sukkah*.

7. Draw and cut out shapes of fruits, vegetables, and branches and place them on the windows and the walls, creating the effect of the whole classroom as a *sukkah*.

8. Stuffed vegetables are a traditional Sephardic food served on Sukkot. Make this recipe for Stuffed Pumpkin to serve on a cold day in the *sukkah*: Cut the top off a pumpkin and remove the seeds. Place a layer of ginger snaps on the bottom, followed by a layer of fruit salad. Add another layer of ginger snaps, a layer of fruit salad, and complete with a layer of cookies. Put the top back on, lightly oil the entire outside of the pumpkin, and place it on a stiff cookie sheet covered with aluminum foil. Bake for two (or more) hours at 300 degrees. It's

done when the outside of the pumpkin is soft and the fruit salad is transformed to compote. (NSM)

9. Play a game that deals with both vegetable products and items manufactured in Israel. The first child might say: "I took a trip to Israel and brought back an orange." The second child might then say: "I took a trip to Israel and brought back an orange and an Elite candy bar." Each child must mention every item already enumerated and add one more item to the list.

10. Arrange to have students participate in the building of the congregation's *sukkah*. Try using unique materials. Here are a few suggestions for fashioning booths, both large and small. For the roof, use fiberglass screening. This plastic material can be easily cut with a scissors and taped in place. Use a piece larger than the booth. Or, cut slots in the top of walls and weave threads through slots. Or, use straws or cardboard for the beams. Make furniture — tables, chairs, flower boxes, etc., out of cardboard, folded and taped. Make fruit out of styrofoam balls or obtain tiny fruit from suppliers of dried flowers or a craft materials store. (JB)

11. What goes in the *sukkah*? Give each student a piece of paper. Draw an outline of a *sukkah* on the top half of the page. Below, sketch small objects, such as a *shofar*, fruit, vegetables, a bow and arrows, desk, *menorah*, TV chair, poster, picture, etc. Students color in those items which belong inside a *sukkah* and put an "X" over those which do not belong.

12. Have students observe the changes in the moon, beginning with the first of Tishre (Rosh HaShanah). They could draw the moon's shape on a calendar each night. The moon on Sukkot is full. Use this as an opportunity to discuss the flow of a Jewish month based on the moon's phases. (NSM) Resource: "Moon Watch" in *Original Bulletin Boards on Jewish Themes* by Nachama Skolnick Moskowitz.

13. Place a map of Israel and environs on the wall or draw it on poster board. Briefly describe the map to the class, showing them where Jerusalem and other key cities are located. Then a child is blindfolded and directed to find Jerusalem so that he/she can "go there" to visit the holy city. This activity can be used to remind the children that Sukkot is one of the three Pilgrimage Festivals.

14. Teach the children the basic Sukkot blessings in Hebrew, along with a translation or paraphrase of what the prayers mean. Explain the meaning of each. (For blessings, see Appendix, page 250.)

15. Have students search out examples of good *s'chach*. What is long enough to be placed across a *sukkah*, not too heavy for the roof supports, and allows for seeing the stars through the branches? They could go on a hike to figure this out, look at pictures in books, or visit *sukkot* already built and determine what seems to work well. (NSM)

16. Have a scavenger hunt and make a *sukkah* out of the items found.

17. Make an *etrog* box. Find a box large enough to hold an *etrog*. Decorate it nicely with colored paper, tempura paint, crayons, marking pens, etc., or use mono-prints (see Activity #8c on page 32). Dip the cover and bottom of the box separately. Add lettering if desired. An *etrog* box can also be made of a plain, small box decorated with magazine cut-outs and sprayed with clear lacquer. Fabric scraps are also very colorful. (JB)

18. Make *etrog* marmalade: You will need six slightly used *etrogim*. Quarter, dig out seeds,

and soak overnight in a bowl with water just about covering. The next day, using a food processor, use the chop and stop function, or with a good paring knife, cut up the rind and pulp to the consistency you like. Fast boil the mixture with just enough water to cover for 30 minutes. Then add the same volume of sugar as pulp. Add six cups pulp, six cups sugar, plus a can of apricots (or pineapple) with the syrup. Add a clove or two and fast boil again for as long as it takes for the liquid to form a soft ball on a cold surface. Pour immediately into sterile jars.

19. Preserve the school *etrog* by punching hundreds of holes in it with a nail and fitting the holes with whole cloves. The *etrog,* which will turn brownish, preserved in an attractive covered glass jar, can be used weekly at the synagogue's Havdalah service as *besamim* or loaned weekly to different students for the same purpose. It is said that such *etrogim* may last for over 100 years! (SH)

20. Bring a *lulav* and *etrog* into the classroom for each child to see, smell, touch, and wave. Discuss the feeling and smells evoked by this experience.

21. As a class, visit various *sukkot* in the community, at synagogues, institutions and homes. As a follow-up writing activity, ask the students to prepare a brief essay on "The most interesting *sukkah* I ever saw."

22. Have students interview the synagogue Administrator. Find out what special preparations the synagogue must make in order to celebrate Sukkot. Ask: How long does it take to put up the *sukkah?* How many people are needed? How many fruits and vegetables are used to decorate the *sukkah?* How much *s'chach* is obtained, and where is it from? How is this holiday celebrated differently from the other holidays and festivals?"

23. Select a group of Sukkot objects and assign each student to be one of these objects. Divide the class into small enough groups so that only one of each object is in each group. For example, if you select seven objects and there are 25 students, you can have 3 groups of 6 and one of 7. In the groups, the objects converse with each other, telling each other how they view each other, and how they feel as Sukkot is celebrated. Reassemble the total group and share reactions to this activity.

24. Complete the Instant Lesson *Sukkot.*

25. Do a movement activity related to Sukkot in *Creative Movement for a Song* by JoAnne Tucker (page 24).

26. Do one or more of the Sukkot art projects in *100+ Jewish Art Projects for Children* by Nina Streisand Sher and Margaret A. Feldman (pages 14, 15, 16, 19).

27. Complete pages 6 and 7 in *Jewish Holiday Copy Pak*™ *K-3* by Marji Gold-Vukson.

Intermediate

1. Divide students into groups of 3 to 4. Have them study the requirements for building a *sukkah* (see page 68), then create sketches or model *sukkot* which fit *halachic* requirements according to scale. Ask students to build a *sukkah* which might be found in another era, in another place in the world (consider their natural building materials), or even in students' backyards. (NSM)

2. Have students help put up a *sukkah,* either the one your school or congregation erects or one in someone's backyard (students could be divided among families to help). When done, discuss the materials used, steps involved, and some of the conversations students heard about previous *sukkot* which were constructed. (NSM)

3. Give students ten minutes to see how many words they can make from the phrase "Shemini Atzeret." Scoring is as follows: 3 letter word = 1 point, 4 letters = 2 points, 5 letters = 4 points, 6 letters = 7 points, 7 letters = 10 points.

4. Hand out a sheet to each student that contains a ladder with seven rungs. Next to the ladder, list the seven *Ushpizin* in random order: Joseph, Abraham, David, Isaac, Moses, Jacob, and Aaron. Have students place the seven guests on the ladder in chronological order. Now list in random order: Elisheva, Rachel, Zipporah, Asenat, Bathsheba, Sarah, Rebekah. Have students match the couples.
Answers: Abraham/Sarah, Isaac/Rachel, Jacob/Rebekah, Joseph/Asenat, Moses/Zipporah, Aaron/Elisheva, David/Bathsheva.

5. In the sentences that follow, each contains one word that is related to the holiday of Sukkot. Each word is hidden in the sentence. The task of each student is to find the hidden word. For example:

He nEVEr forgets a face = EVE.
   a. You bet Roger that he could not win. (etrog)
   b. The teacher had a simple solution to the problem. (hadas)
   c. Jacob got stuck in the hall elevator (hallel)
   d. Why must you boo the team? (booth)

6. Have groups of students carefully study the plants which make up a *lulav*. Have them note the shape and smell of the species. Read Leviticus 23:40, and share with students the *midrash* which equates the *lulav/etrog* to different kinds of Jews (see page 68). Can students follow the reasoning of the *midrash*? (NSM)

7. Have students match the items in the two columns.

Sukkah	Myrtle twig
Hadas	A citron
Etrog	Festival of Booths
Aravah	A booth
Sukkot	Palm branch
Lulav	Willow branch

8. Have a contest to see who can come up with the most clever or most humorous Sukkot slogans. Here are some examples:
   a. Join us and eat sukkah-tash.
   b. Jews make waves on Sukkot.
   c. Even Myrtle celebrates Sukkot, so why don't you!
   d. Happy boothday!

9. Ask each student to write one paragraph describing what he/she thinks a *sukkah* should look like. Share some of the descriptions with the class.

10. Create *sukkot* which one might find in different locales — in space, in the wild west, in China, in ancient Greece, in Borneo, in a desert wilderness, on an ice floe, in the distant future, etc. (NSM)

11. Write a haiku for Sukkot. This Japanese form, most often used for nature poetry, has three lines totalling 17 syllables. There are five syllables in the first line, seven in the second, and five in the third. Have the students share their poems with the class and add them to their poetry books.

12. One student volunteers to be the expert. The other students ask questions in an effort to stump "the expert." The person who succeeds in stumping the expert becomes the new expert, and the process is repeated.

13. Divide the class into 3 or 4 teams. Each team is given a sheet of paper with Tishre marked on the top and spaces for each of the days in the month. Working as teams for 10 to 15

minutes, the students must write in the correct spaces where all of the holidays, beginning with Rosh HaShanah and ending with Simchat Torah, belong. At the end of the designated time period, the team with the most correct answers wins.

14. Have the class devise a Sukkot game. Either the class as a whole can create one game, or form smaller groups, each of which creates a game. Then use the game as a review activity for Sukkot and the High Holy Days. The game can also be shared with other classes. If desired, allow students to include any general questions they may wish to add about other holidays.

15. Working in teams, find and circle the words related to the holiday of Sukkot. (High Holy Days and Simchat Torah words may also be used.)

```
A Z C O R H A K A F A H N A E
X C H A G X N B C I R S T S D
A U R C E H V A I N E R O S C
R I N C F A A G L U L A V O U
A Z O N E D A R V N G U V K B
V E A J L A V U W T H I N Z H
A V Q U M S P I I O N S P H E
H R Z A I S T S U K K O T Y C
B R Y U N S C H Y Q U O T H H
K O H E L E T V E R R Y S H A
S P U B C X I O N T E T R O G
R P S T H A A S I F N O Q R T
A A N I Z R Q P I R A B B A H
V L C H A G N Z A R A S T I G
N M Q U P M N S A M E A C H X
```

(Words include: include: Aravah, Chag, HeChag, Etrog, Lulav, Rabbah, HaAsif, Palm, Hakafah, Hadas, Kohelet, Sameach.)

16. The Pilgrims learned the idea of Thanksgiving from the holiday of Sukkot. How do these holidays resemble each other? Does Thanks-giving have the same historical roots as Sukkot?

17. While modeled on the biblical Sukkot, Thanksgiving is different in many ways, even though both holidays can be called *Chag HaHoda'ah*, meaning "Festival of Thanksgiving." Hold a debate on the topic: "Resolved: Thanksgiving is simply an Americanized version of the ancient Jewish festival of Sukkot." Such a debate will help to elucidate the major similarities and differences between Sukkot and Thanksgiving.

18. Have students go to the library and research how Sukkot is celebrated in Israel and in various other countries throughout the world.

19. The Kabbalistic practice of *Ushpizin* symbolically welcomes Abraham, Isaac, Jacob, Joseph, Moses, Aaron, and David to one's *sukkah*. How does this practice reflect the importance of *Hachnasat Orchim* (welcoming of guests) in Jewish life?

20. Ask students to imagine that they were living when the Jews were in the desert after the Exodus. Have them role play wandering through the wilderness of Sinai while living in temporary shelters.

21. Role play the traditional *Ushpizin* guests, as well as some female additions. Have each "guest" discuss the meaning of Sukkot as he/she sees it.

22. Give each of two volunteers a sentence about Sukkot to work into a discussion in front of the class. The rest of the class must identify this. Set a time limit of three minutes. (The two volunteers also try to guess each other's sentence.)

23. Divide into small segments the account of Sukkot in the Bible. Then divide the class into groups of 2 or 3 each. Give the groups 10 to

15 minutes to work out a dramatization of their scene in the story. Then, have each group act out their segment of the Sukkot narrative. If all goes well, this improvisation could become the basis for an assembly presentation.

24. Have a "reporter" interview a Jew living in the Wilderness of Sinai. Give each child a chance to play a role. Afterward, discuss feelings, insights, etc.

25. Divide the class into pairs. Each pair participates at the same time. Student A becomes a *sukkah*, while student B pretends to be a person who has built the *sukkah* and is celebrating Sukkot in that *sukkah*. The *sukkah* speaks to the student. The student listens and speaks to the *sukkah*. Each shares thoughts, impressions, and feelings with the other. A and B then reverse roles and repeat the process. The class reassembles to process the role play.

26. Ask students to close their eyes and to block out all extraneous thoughts. Ask them to try to concentrate on what you will read to them. Read or narrate a description of spending eight days living in a *sukkah* during the harvest season in ancient Israel. Describe the crops, the terrain, the weather. Try to create a mood of being a part of the fall harvest. Then ask the students to open their eyes and react to what has been read.

27. Divide the class into groups of 7 or less. Each student "becomes" one of the following: Abraham, Isaac, Jacob, Sarah, Rachel, Rebekah, Joseph, Moses, Aaron, or David. Keeping these roles in mind, the class visits the school/congregational *sukkah*. Upon returning to the class, the students are divided into *"Ushpizin"* groups in which they describe how they, as these various individuals, felt as they visited the *sukkah*. Let the "guests" speculate about how Sukkot was celebrated in their day.

28. Because they don't wish to waste food, some people no longer put fresh fruits and vegetables in their *sukkah*. Look up Jewish sources that tell what may or must be in a *sukkah* (no foods are required). If the class agrees that to use food is wasteful, brainstorm other things one could hang in a *sukkah* (e.g., rugs, paintings, plastic fruit, gourds, stalks of grain, used New Year's cards, arts and crafts projects, etc.). (NSM)
Resource: *Code of Jewish Law* by Solomon Ganzfried, Chapters 134-137.

29. Do a readers theater performance of "Sukkot — Why Is This House Different?" in *Class Acts: Plays & Skits for Jewish Settings* by Stan J. Beiner (page 33).

30. Complete pages 6 and 7 of *Jewish Holiday Copy Pak*™ *4-6* by Marji Gold-Vukson.

Secondary

1. Hold an open-ended discussion on the subject of Sukkot as it relates to the demands of the modern world: Is full observance of Sukkot a "practical" aim? What happens when business obligations force a person to work on Sukkot? What constitutes a reasonable, attainable form of Sukkot observance for the non-Orthodox Jew today?

2. Divide the class into three groups. Ask each group to examine and summarize for the class one of the following passages related to Sukkot (Leviticus 23:33-44; Deuteronomy 16:13-17, and Deuteronomy 31:10-13). After each group has studied its passage, one representative from each group explains the passage to the rest of the class. Then, ask the entire class to read Nehemiah 8 for a description of how Sukkot was celebrated during the days of the Second Temple. Discuss how this passage reflects the ideas found in the previous three.

3. While Pesach refers back to the Exodus from Egypt and Shavuot to the giving of the Torah at Mount Sinai, Sukkot is linked to the use of booths (i.e., temporary structures) during the 40 years of wandering in the wilderness. Ask: What reasons for celebrating Sukkot would you give to a non-Jewish group?

4. Discuss: What is the connection between Sukkot and nature? Why is Sukkot particularly important to Jews living in an urban environment?

5. Discuss: What implications does Sukkot have for ecology? Whip around the room, asking students to react to the following statement: "Sukkot should be called Jewish Ecology Awareness Week."

6. Have students analyze which of the names for Sukkot they think is the most significant.

7. Research what book of the Tanach is read on Sukkot. Have students state why they think this book (Ecclesiastes) is read.

8. Divide students into six groups. Assign each group one of the passages in the Torah related to Sukkot (Leviticus 23:33-36, 23:39-43; Exodus 23:14-17; Numbers 20:12-39; Deuteronomy 16:13-17, 31:10-13). Have these six groups be prepared to teach others what they learned about Sukkot in the Torah. Then "jigsaw" the groups — re-form them so that at least one member from each of the original groups is with representatives of the other five groups. (If there were three people in each of the six original groups, there will now be three groups of six each.) Ask each person to share with the other five people what they learned about Sukkot from the passage they studied. Have these new groups come to a conclusion about the celebration of Sukkot in biblical days and compare that celebration to today. (NSM)

9. Research why Sukkot was the most important of the three pilgrimage festivals in ancient Israel.

10. Share with the class the different ways of looking at the *Arba'ah Minim*. Create a "personality profile" for four people who exemplify the qualities of each of the four species. Is there any correlation between your results and the four sons/children of the *Haggadah*?

11. Yizkor occurs four times a year (Yom Kippur, end of Sukkot, end of Pesach, and Shavuot). Examine the meaning of the Hebrew word "*Yizkor*" (God will remember). Ask students why they think we have a Memorial Service on special holidays. Have them make a list of good reasons to do so (e.g., we want to remember departed loved ones with whom we have shared these holidays). Ask: How does recalling loved ones at the Memorial Service enhance the meaning of this holy day?

12. On some holidays and festivals, our participation symbolically links us to events in the distant past and creates a symbolic continuum that reaches to the present. Ask students to think of examples of this (e.g., sitting in the *sukkah*, participating in the Passover *Seder*). How does the *mitzvah* of "dwelling in the *sukkah*" reinforce our link with Jews who wandered for 40 years in the Sinai desert? Which is a more convincing link — eating in the *sukkah* or experiencing the Exodus at the Passover *Seder*?

13. Form two concentric circles. The inner circle discusses the relationship between Sukkot and *Tikkun Olam* (repairing the world). Consider such questions as: In what ways does the act of going from a temporary, transient life-style living in temporary shelters to a more permanent life-style in *Eretz Yisrael* remind us of the need to work to bring peace and stability to

the world? The outer circle observes and, afterward, comments on the discussion — the participation, quality of the discussion, intelligence of the students' comments, etc. Next time there is a discussion, have those in the inner circle switch with those in the outer circle.

All-School

1. Since Sukkot commemorates the 40 years of wandering through the wilderness of Sinai, students could take a simulated trip and "visit" some of the places the Israelites visited along the way. Each site can be a brief activity station. Students in the older grades can prepare and run each activity. The first stop can be the Sea of Reeds, followed by a visit to Mount Sinai, where they are presented with the Ten Commandments. Other sites can include Marah, Rephidim, Kadesh Barnea, and the place on the Eastern shore of the Jordan River where Moses gets to see the Promised Land from a distance. Give students a map of the Sinai which can be stamped each time they reach a new destination.

2. Hold a school-wide essay contest on the following theme: What is it that makes each of the *Arba'ah Minim* special and meaningful to you? Select winners by grade level.

Family

1. Organize a family education program for two to four-year-olds (there are two already designed Sukkot programs in *Head Start on Holidays: Jewish Programs for Preschoolers and Their Parents* by Roberta Louis Goodman and Andye Honigman Zell).

2. Ask families that build a *sukkah* to take a picture of it once it is built. Save the pictures, and one month before Sukkot next year, post them on a bulletin board. In this way, families interested in building a *sukkah* can see various options. (NSM)

3. It is believed that one of seven *Ushpizin* symbolically joins each family in their *sukkah* each night. On each night there is a different guest. Encourage families to invite real friends and acquaintances to dine with them in their family *sukkah*. If they don't have a *sukkah*, provide them with instructions on how to build one. In any case, Sukkot is a good time for them to invite guests.

4. Suggest that families take a walking tour of their neighborhood, visiting other *sukkot* and extending a *Chag Sameach* greeting to other Jews in the neighborhood. If the population is spread out, such a tour can be done by car, perhaps with other class members and their families. Arrange to conclude the tour with a *Kiddush* in the *sukkat* at the synagogue or in the Rabbi's *sukkah*.

5. Request that whole families (including, if possible, grandparents) take a walk in a park or visit a nature trail. Sukkot is a reminder of the Jew's sense of rootedness to the land and to the forces of nature. A quiet walk helps to reinforce this idea.

6. Encourage those families that have a *sukkah* to eat some of their meals in it. Pair these families with those who don't have a *sukkah* so they can have the experience of eating in a *sukkah*. Provide words to some songs the children sing in Religious School.

7. Hold a dinner for families of class members in the *sukkah*. Children can teach their parents the meaning of the holiday and the blessings and all can recite them together. Following such a dinner, the children and their parents can participate in a brief Sukkot worship service.

BIBLIOGRAPHY
See pages 268-270.

CHAPTER FIVE
SHEMINI ATZERET AND SIMCHAT TORAH

VOCABULARY

Atzeret: "Ending" or "Conclusion." Refers to either the seventh day of Pesach or the eighth day of Sukkot.

Chatan Beresheet: "Bridegroom of Genesis" is the one who blesses and/or reads the first section of Genesis on Simchat Torah. The use of the word "bridegroom" suggests a covenantal bond, a marriage as it were, between Israel and the Torah, or between Israel and God through God's Law. It is considered a great honor to be asked to be either *Chatan Torah* or *Chatan Beresheet.*

Chatan Torah: "Bridegroom of the Torah" is the one who blesses and/or reads the final section of Deuteronomy on Simchat Torah. See *Chatan Beresheet* immediately above.

Consecration: Reform Judaism introduced the custom of calling all children who are new to the Religious School to the *bimah* on Simchat Torah. They are blessed by the Rabbi and in many synagogues these consecrants are given miniature Torah scrolls and a certificate.

Degel: "Flag." It is customary to give children flags to wave while participating in the seven *hakafot* during the celebration of Simchat Torah. In some synagogues, apples are placed on the flags.

Hakafah/Hakafot: "Circling." For each of the first six days of Sukkot, worshipers walk around — encircle — the sanctuary holding *lulav* and *etrog* and reciting the *Hoshana* prayer. On Hoshana Rabbah, seven processions are made around the synagogue. On Simchat Torah, all of *the Sifre Torah* are taken out of the *Aron HaKodesh* and carried as part of the seven *hakafot.* At the end of each *hakafah* there is singing and dancing on the part of the participants. The *hakafot* are repeated for the morning service on Simchat Torah. *Hakafot* on Simchat Torah originated in the sixteenth century as an effort to endear the Torah to the children.

Kol HaN'arim: "All the Youngsters." The custom has arisen to call up to the Torah an adult male along with all of the pre-Bar Mitzvah age boys who are present. Together, the boys and the adult male pronounce the blessings over the Torah. The participation of the young is encouraged to stimulate interest in and inspire them with love for the Torah and its teachings. They are then blessed with the words from Genesis 48:16 and 20: "Bless the youngsters. In them may my name be recalled, and the names of my fathers, Abraham and Isaac, and may they be teeming multitudes upon the earth."

Maysheev HaRuach u'Moreed HaGashem: "You who cause the wind to blow and the rain to fall . . ." is the key phrase in the Prayer for Rain. Starting on

Shemini Atzeret and concluding on Pesach, the prayer is recited as a part of the week day *Amidah.* It expresses Israel's understandable anxiety about the coming of the seasonal rains, the absence of which spells hunger, thirst, and disease. The Prayer for Rain was postponed until the conclusion of Sukkot so that the rains might not interfere with the celebration of Sukkot.

Shemini Atzeret: "Eighth Day for Concluding." So named because this is the eighth and last day for eating in the *sukkah,* Shemini Atzeret was added to Sukkot during the days of the Second Temple. It was originally an independent two day festival. Simchat Torah, therefore, is historically the second day of the Festival of Atzeret. It is on Shemini Atzeret that the Prayer for Rain is first offered as a part of the *Amidah.*

Simchat Torah: "Torah Joy." Originally the second day of the Festival of Shemini Atzeret, Simchat Torah became a festival in its own right presumably around the ninth century in Babylonia where the annual cycle of reading the Torah prevailed. This was in contrast to the three year (triennial) cycle of reading the Torah that prevailed in Palestine. With the annual completion of the reading of the Torah, a festival marking this important event was created.

BACKGROUND
Shemini Atzeret
While there are no references to Simchat Torah in the Bible, there are two clear references to Shemini Atzeret in the Torah. Leviticus 23:36 reads: "Seven days you shall bring offerings by fire to *Adonai.* On the eighth day, you shall observe a sacred occasion and bring an offering by fire to *Adonai;* it is a solemn gathering: you shall not work at your occupations." The term used for sacred occasion (or holy convocation) is *Mikra Kodesh. Atzeret* is the term used for "solemn gathering."

The second reference is found in Numbers 29:15: "On the eighth day, you shall hold a solemn gathering (*atzeret*); you shall not work at your

occupations." In both biblical passages, it is implied that the eighth day (of Sukkot) is a festival separate unto itself. Furthermore, the Rabbis of the Talmud declare that Shemini Atzeret is a separate festival, unconnected to the previous seven days of Sukkot except that it follows immediately after. In *Sukkah* 48a, the Talmud states *"Shemini regel bifnay atzmo"* — "The eighth [day] is a festival in its own right."

The Mishnah does make one mention of Shemini Atzeret as the "last festival day of the Feast" *(Ta'anit* 1:1). It makes this statement in the context of a discussion regarding when to begin saying the Prayer for Rain. The Hebrew expression used there is *"Yom tov acharon shel heChag"* (the last holy day of the Festival), which thus links Shemini Atzeret, at least in terms of time sequence, to Sukkot.

It may very well be merely an academic question whether Shemini Atzeret is the eighth day of Sukkot or a separate festival which follows immediately after Sukkot. The bulk of evidence, as noted above, points to the latter view. Even though Atzeret originally meant festive or solemn assembly, it came to be understood in the sense of conclusion. Shavuot came to be seen as the Atzeret of Pesach, because it marked the conclusion of the 50 day period of the counting of the Omer. Similarly, Chag HaAtzeret was seen in Talmud as the concluding festival of Sukkot.

A Talmudic discussion (*Sukkah* 55a) contrasts Sukkot and Shemini Atzeret in the context of festival sacrifices. Since Sukkot takes place outside of the home (i.e., in the *sukkah*), by offering 70 bullocks in honor of the nations of the world, its universal aspect is emphasized. Since, on Shemini Atzeret, Jews are concerned only with their own nation, Israel, and its relationship to God, Jews offer only one bullock on this day. This single offering, which represents Israel, is intended to stress the intimate bond between Israel and God. It should be noted, however, that this Talmudic discussion was only academic and symbolic because when it was written the Temple was no longer in existence and animal sacrifice was no longer practiced.

Simchat Torah

Simchat Torah marks the occasion of completing the Torah by reading Deuteronomy 33:1-34:12, and beginning the Torah reading cycle once again with Genesis 1:1-23.

The name Simchat Torah is first mentioned in the *Zohar*, a thirteenth century work of Jewish mysticism. *Song of Songs Rabbah* (81) does mention the custom of having a celebration upon completing the reading of the Torah, but this *midrash* does not mention Simchat Torah by name.

With the completion of the Mishnah in 217 C.E., the Jewish community in Palestine began to decline, and Babylonia gradually became the center of Jewish life. During the next six centuries, a struggle for leadership between Palestine and Babylonia took place. The Jews of Palestine followed a triennial cycle — completing the reading of the Torah every three years. In Babylonia, an annual cycle was followed. During these centuries, there was no celebration of Simchat Torah as such in Palestine. Rather, a festive meal was held at the conclusion of each three year cycle. In Babylonia, the celebration of an annual Simchat Torah festival became customary. Today, the annual cycle of reading the Torah is the accepted norm for almost all Jews.

Simchat Torah has provided each generation of Jews with an opportunity to demonstrate their love for God and the Torah with great rejoicing.

Today in Israel, as well as in most Reform congregations, Shemini Atzeret and Simchat Torah are both celebrated at the same time, on the 23rd day of Tishre. Outside of Israel, Conservative and Orthodox Jews celebrate Shemini Atzeret for two days, calling the second day of Shemini Atzeret, Simchat Torah.

Central Themes

- The theme of Talmud Torah (study, learning) is echoed throughout the celebration of Simchat Torah. The festival is all about concluding and then beginning again the reading of Torah. There is great fanfare and rejoicing associated with this process. In Jerusalem, many streets are closed as Jews dance outside in the neighborhoods carrying the *Sifre Torah* (Torah scrolls) of their synagogue.

- During the years before the break-up of the Soviet Union, Russian Jews lived under great oppression. Unable to obtain prayer books, study materials, or Jewish ritual objects, these Jews nevertheless made Simchat Torah the holiday at which time they publicly affirmed their Jewish identity. Elie Wiesel (*The Jews of Silence*, chapter 5) could find nothing to compare to the joy that he witnessed when he visited Moscow in those years on Simchat Torah.

- In Reform and some Conservative congregations, new students in the Religious/Hebrew School are formally welcomed and consecrated at this time because they, too, are beginning the process of formal study.

- *Tikkun Olam* (Repairing the World/Social Justice) is a theme that pervades all of Jewish life. Neither prayer nor Torah study are ends in themselves. Even though a person may learn something *lishma* (for its own sake), learning is intended to bring us closer to God by motivating us to perform *mitzvot*. Engaging in acts of repairing the world is a way of translating beliefs into action.

- A *Sefer Torah* can be heavy. When a person holds or carries a Torah scroll, the person symbolically feels "*Ol Ha Torah*" (weight/yoke of the Law), the serious responsibility of following the commandments of Torah.

- The term *hakafah* means "circling." The very concept of the *hakafah* is to encircle the congregation thus symbolically including everyone in community. This is to remind us that just as the Torah was given to the entire Jewish people, so, too, Torah is the possession of every Jew, regardless of education or social position. The *hakafot* during a worship service are a symbolic reenactment of the experience of receiving Torah at Mount Sinai.

Simchat Torah Observances

The Torah scrolls are taken from the *Aron HaKodesh* during the Torah service. Respected members of the congregation are given the honor of carrying the scrolls in *hakafot* around the synagogue. During the seven *hakafot,* those who do not carry scrolls wave flags and sing songs. The flags often carry inscriptions such as *Degel Machaneh Yehudah,* meaning "The Flag of the Camp of Judah." In most congregations, there is a great deal of singing and dancing with the Torah scrolls, both inside the synagogue and in the streets surrounding it.

The *Kol HaN'urim* ceremony takes place on Simchat Torah. Two members of the congregation are given the honor of being the *Chatan Torah* and *Chatan Beresheet.* They either read from the Torah or read the Torah blessings, while the Rabbi or *Ba'al Koreh* reads the selections from Deuteronomy and then from Genesis. Youngsters are often called to accompany the "bridegrooms" and to say the Torah blessing with them. They in turn receive a special blessing.

Reform Judaism introduced the custom of Consecration. Children who have just entered Religious School are consecrated on Simchat Torah. They are called to the *bimah* by the Rabbi, blessed, and given miniature Torah scrolls and/or certificates as a memento of this special welcoming ceremony. *Gates of Prayer,* the Reform *Siddur,* offers a beautiful Consecration prayer: "O God, our Creator and our Teacher, bless these children who have come into Your sanctuary with eager minds and warm hearts. This day may they be consecrated to the study of Torah, to lives of loyalty and goodness. Thus will they bring joy to all who love them and honor to the household of Israel. Strengthen them and guide them in all their ways. Blessed is the Eternal, the Teacher of Torah to God's people, Israel" (page 540).

Torah and Haftarah Portions

The Torah Portion for Shemini Atzeret is Deuteronomy 14:22-16:17 and Numbers 29:35-30:1. The selection from Numbers makes specific reference to Shemini Atzeret, while the section from Deuteronomy deals with tithes, the year of release, and the rules about the central sanctuary's role in the celebration of the three Pilgrimage Festivals. This section makes no specific reference to Shemini Atzeret. When Shemini Atzeret and Simchat Torah are celebrated on the same day, these selections are not read.

The *Haftarah* for Shemini Atzeret is I Kings 8:54-66. This is, in effect, a continuation of the *Haftarah* portion for the second day of Sukkot, in which Solomon dedicates the Temple and offers sacrifices to God. The focus of this passage is Solomon's eloquent prayer (verses 56-61).

On Simchat Torah, the last weekly *parashah* called *V'zot HaB'rachah* is read. It consists of Deuteronomy 33:1-34:12, the death of Moses. Then the beginning of *Parashat Beresheet,* consisting of Genesis 1:1-2:3, the creation story, is read. On the Shabbat following Simchat Torah, all of *Parashat Beresheet* (Genesis 1:1-6:8) is read. Numbers 29:35-30:1 is also read. The *Haftarah* for Simchat Torah is Joshua 1:1-18, because it is the beginning of the second section of the Bible, *Nevi'im* (Prophets), and because Deuteronomy concludes with Joshua inheriting the leadership of the Jewish people from Moses.

In Reform congregations and in Israel, the Torah and *Haftarah* readings for Simchat Torah take precedence over those for Shemini Atzeret.

The chart on page 83 represents an overview of Tishre observances.

SCOPE AND SEQUENCE

Grade	Themes/Ideas
Kindergarten	New beginnings, why are they so special?
Grade One	Consecration: a special ceremony to mark a special event in the life of the child.

Observance Dates

Holiday/Festival	Reform/Reconstructionist Congregations & in Israel	Conservative/Orthodox Congregations in the Diaspora
Rosh HaShanah	1-2 Tishre	1-2 Tishre
Yom Kippur	10 Tishre	10 Tishre
Sukkot	15-21 Tishre	15-21 Tishre
2nd Day Sukkot	not observed	16 Tishre
Chol HaMo'ed Sukkot	16-20 Tishre	17-20 Tishre
Hoshana Rabbah	21 Tishre	21 Tishre
Shemini Atzeret	22 Tishre	22 Tishre
Simchat Torah	22 Tishre	23 Tishre

Grade Two   What do we do in the synagogue to celebrate Simchat Torah?

Grade Three   What makes the Torah special to us? How the Torah is written.

Grade Four   Key terms for Shemini Atzeret and Simchat Torah.

Grade Five   Differences between when Conservative and Orthodox Jews observe Shemini Atzeret and Simchat Torah and when Reform Jews and Jews living in Israel observe them (i.e., how the calendar affects changes in religious life).

Grade Six   Is Shemini Atzeret the eighth day of Sukkot or a separate festival? How is Simchat Torah celebrated in Jerusalem?

Grade Seven   Readings from the Torah on Simchat Torah; the concepts of *Chatan Torah* and *Chatan Beresheet*.

Grade Eight   The Origin and development of Shemini Atzeret; the Prayer for Rain.

Grade Nine   Origin and development of Simchat Torah as a post-biblical festival.

Grade Ten   The significance of Shemini Atzeret and Simchat Torah in the past and today.

Grade Eleven   The Torah and *Haftarah* portions for Shemini Atzeret and Simchat Torah.

Grade Twelve   If you had five minutes to tell a non-Jew about Shemini Atzeret and Simchat Torah, what would you say?

ACTIVITIES

Note: Many, if not most, of the Sukkot activities in the previous chapter can also be used for Simchat Torah and Shemini Atzeret. The suggestions that follow are intended as a brief supplement to those activities.

Preschool/Kindergarten

1. Go to the sanctuary and investigate the Torah decorations. How many have *rimmonim* (pomegranate-shaped decorations) on the top? How many have crowns? Which one is the largest? Which ones make sounds? etc. (NSM)

2. Go to the sanctuary. Have children identify sanctuary sounds — the bells on a Torah, the *Aron Kodesh* being opened, someone walking on the *bimah*, a Torah being rolled up, etc. (NSM)

3. Have children dictate prayers for use as part of the Consecration ceremony or for other parts of the Simchat Torah worship service.

4. Create a matching game in which students put pictures of a Torah in order from smallest to largest. Or, do this with Simchat Torah flags. (NSM)

5. Use language about the body to describe things related to Simchat Torah: hands hold the Torah, ears hear the bells, eyes see the decorations, etc. (NSM)

6. Create a set of photos showing in sequence what we do on Simchat Torah (including reading from the end of one Torah and from the beginning of another). Duplicate these on a photocopier and have small groups of students work to put them in order. (NSM)

7. Using white crayon, draw a picture of a Torah on painting paper. Give children paint to "wash" over the picture so that the Torah shows through. (This art technique is called crayon resist.) (NSM)

8. Take pictures of each individual student smiling and holding onto a Torah. Create a bulletin board called "Joy in the Torah!" (NSM)

9. Help children complete pages 16, 17, and 18 in *Jewish Preschool/Kindergarten Copy Pak*™ by Nancy Cohen Nowak.

10. Do a movement activity related to Simchat Torah in *Creative Movement for a Song* by JoAnne Tucker (page 16).

Primary

1. Compare the number of books in the library with the number of Torahs in the sanctuary. Compare the way we house the Torahs and the way we house the books. Explain the difference.

2. Take students to the sanctuary and seat them on the *bimah*. Open the *Aron Kodesh* and have them make observations about what they see; write their words on chart paper. Then, brainstorm a list of things a Torah might say or feel when sitting in the *Aron Kodesh* (either before or after the Ark was opened). Write these down, too. Allow students time to write a "journal entry" as if they were a Torah in the *Aron*. They may use ideas brainstormed by the group. Some may wish to write or dictate a poem. (NSM)

3. Make Simchat Torah flags. Decorate them with insignia of the tribes of Israel, of cities in Israel, with an Israeli flag, with pictures of Israel, or with a personal coat of arms. Use the flags for Simchat Torah worship services.

4. Make a replica of a Torah scroll by using two sticks and some paper. Simulated Hebrew writing can be written on the paper, and the paper then attached to the sticks. In place of simulating Hebrew, passages not containing the name of God can be photocopied from a *Tikkun* and glued onto the paper. A simple Torah cover can be made out of a piece of cloth.

5. This activity is similar to the previous one, but the result is a make-believe "movie." Use a shoe box or a larger box, and clothes pins or dowels for the *Aytz Chayim*. Place holes in the upper and lower parts of the box so that the scroll can be rolled when the box is closed. Make an opening in the front of the box to serve as a "movie screen." Give each student paper (use adding machine tape for a small Torah, butcher paper for a large one). Have them each depict a different important event in the Torah. Collect these pictorial depictions and tape them together in the proper sequence.

On additional sheets of paper, write a one or two sentence narrative about each picture. Place the narrative before or after each picture in the movie. Show the final product at an assembly or worship service.

6. Discuss beginnings and endings, cycles of different kinds, and the concept of joy, which is inherent in Simchat Torah.

7. Divide the class into 2 to 4 teams. Give each team ten minutes to brainstorm reasons why the Torah is meaningful and special. Afterward, discuss and prioritize the list.

8. Have students create a bookmark or post-it note for their *Siddur*, reminding them that it's time to say *"Mayshiv HaRuach u'Moreed HaGashem."* (NSM)

9. Do some practice *hakafot* around the sanctuary. Listen to different music. Which music best expresses the joy of marching with the Torah? (NSM)

10. Simchat Torah literally means, "joy of the Torah." Ask students to talk about what makes them full of joy. The book *Ima on the Bima: My Mommy Is a Rabbi* by Mindy Portnoy has a picture of the congregation being joyful with the Torah. Use the picture as a way to extend your discussion — why are the people so happy? (NSM)

11. Make a truly safe (i.e., no sticks to poke in someone's eye) Simchat Torah flag by following these directions: (NSM)

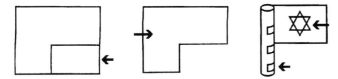

12. Visit the sanctuary. Take a Torah from the Ark and look at it carefully. Discuss how a Torah is written. Invite a *sofer* to speak to the class about writing a Torah. Examine a column of the Torah scroll. Compare it to the same column in a *Tikkun*. Show the students how the scribe makes sure that all lines are exactly the same length. If your students are studying Hebrew, let them look to see if they can recognize any words. If you have a small Torah, give the students an opportunity to hold it. Show the students how to find a passage in the Torah by looking for key phrases, for paragraph endings and for spaces between books of the Torah. Upon returning to the classroom or while sitting in the sanctuary, explore the feelings evoked by this visit.

13. Have students close their eyes and imagine that they are a Torah. Imagine being unrolled and all the people looking at them very intensely. Sit in groups of 3 to 5 and share feelings about the experience with the other members of the group. Then, in the small groups, have students complete the sentences such as the following:
When I was a Torah, I _____.
When everyone was looking at me, I felt

_____ .
When I was a Torah, I thought about

_____ .
Being a Torah, taught me that _____.

Variation: Have students pantomime a Torah by rolling on the floor, stretching out their arms to give the effect of being opened and read, and then rolling again to be closed. Share reactions and feelings with the others in the group.

14. Take students to the sanctuary to "explore" the Torah. Have them think about why we keep it in such a special place (*Aron HaKodesh*), dress it up, and take such good care of it. Allow them to help undress the Torah and look closely at the inside of it. If they know some Hebrew already, see what they can discover in the text. (NSM)

15. Have students complete the Instant Lessons *A Lifetime of Torah* and *Simhat Torah*.

16. Do a Simchat Torah art project in *100+ Jewish Art Projects for Children* by Nina Streisand Sher and Margaret A. Feldman (page 20).

Intermediate

1. Write a class poem. Ask students to respond with a short phrase or a few adjectives to phrases (e.g., What does the Torah mean to you? Describe the joy we Jews feel when the yearly Torah reading cycle is complete and begins again.) When students have finished writing, solicit volunteers to read their responses. Write the lines on the board one at a time as students read them, and you will have a beautiful class poem. Make copies for the students to add to their poetry books.

2. Show students how to find chapter and verse in a *Chumash*. Create a hunt in which students work in groups of 2 or 3 to find out what specific chapters and verses are about. If possible, choose passages which relate to things the class is studying this year, and vary between narratives (e.g., Genesis 1:1) and laws (e.g., Leviticus 23:40). (NSM)

3. Ask students to respond to such questions as: What are the first and last words of the Torah in Hebrew? (*Beresheet* and *Yisrael*); List four "miracles" associated with the wilderness experience (Red Sea splits, manna, water from a rock, quail); How many years did the Israelites wander in the desert? (40); Who was the brother of Moses? (Aaron)

4. Yehudit Yellin has created wonderful pictures of people rejoicing with the Torah. Perhaps someone you know has one of her pictures or posters in his or her home. Find some of these Yellin pictures (or those of another artist) and use them as Simchat Torah discussion starters with students. (NSM)

5. Have students make up Simchat Torah riddles. Some examples:
   a. What movie title mentions this holiday? ("Tora, Tora, Tora")
   b. Where does the Bible speak of baseball? (In the beginning — big inning)
   c. What did Moses do when he had a headache? (He took two tablets)
   d. What did one Torah scroll say as it helped another? (One good turn deserves another)

6. In the following paragraph there are five mistakes. The student's task is to find the errors and write in the correct information:

   In Israel, Shemini Atzeret and Simchat Torah are celebrated on the same day, which is in effect the ninth day of Sukkot. Traditionally, for Jews living outside of Israel, Shemini Atzeret is counted as the eighth day and Simchat Torah as the ninth day of Sukkot. The person who reads the first chapter of Genesis on Simchat Torah is called the *Chatan Torah*. On Sukkot, one *hakafah* is made, while on Simchat Torah, there are eight *hakafot*. The term *"Z'man Simchataynu"* means "Our Festival of Sadness." On Simchat Torah, some congregations hold a Confirmation ceremony.

   (Corrections: The first "ninth" should be eighth; *Chatan Beresheet* for *Chatan Torah*; seven *hakafot* instead of eight; Rejoicing/Happiness instead of Sadness, and Consecration for Confirmation.)

7. Have students write a short essay on the theme "What Simchat Torah Teaches Me." Publish the best essays in the class or school newspaper or in the synagogue bulletin.

8. Examine the *Haftarah* portions for Shemini Atzeret and Simchat Torah. Ask students why they think these passages were selected for these festivals.

9. Show the video *For Out of Zion*, which is about the writing of a Torah scroll. (NSM)

10. Practice Hebrew calligraphy using Torah script. You may wish to invite a local scribe to teach the class how to do this, or use a resource book as a guide. Be sure to have special calligraphy pens or felt-tip markers. (NSM)
Resource: *The First Jewish Catalog* by Richard Siegel, Michael Strassfeld, and Sharon Strassfeld, pp. 184-209.

11. Research the origins of the Torah scrolls which belong to your congregation. How will students get this information? Who will they ask? What records could they search? (Board minutes, articles in the local Jewish newspaper, congregational archives, etc.) (NSM)

12. Interview members of the Worship/Ritual Committee and/or the Rabbi. How are decisions made about the congregation's Simchat Torah celebration? What are the traditions which don't seem to change? What gets discussed every now and then? What different ways of doing things do those being interviewed remember from previous years? (NSM)

13. Prepare a dramatic or artistic service for a congregational Consecration ceremony.

14. To learn about how a *Sefer Torah* is written, visit a scribe or invite a scribe to visit the school. Prepare a list of questions in advance. Be sure the scribe speaks about how long it takes to write a *Sefer Torah*, what happens when a *sofer* makes a mistake, what happens when a mistake is made on a word for God, and what makes a Torah kosher.

15. Discuss why the festival is called Simchat Torah. What makes it such a joyous holiday? Ask: Why do students think it is permissible to take the Torah scrolls out of the synagogue

and dance with them in the streets? What symbolic meaning does that act have?

16. Complete pages 8 and 9 of *Jewish Holiday Copy Pak*™ *4-6* by Marji Gold-Vukson.

Secondary

1. Explore on the Internet the variety of sites which have *Parashat HaShavua* (weekly Torah portion) study guides. Download some of these and compare their differences and similarities. One option is to download 3 to 5 of these and give small groups of students one of the guides to study, deciding what from their reading they would want to share with others. Redivide the students so that representatives from each group are meeting with those from other groups. Allow them time to teach each other what they learned from their on-line *Parashat HaShavua* guides. (NSM)

2. Compare the way Ashkenazic and Sephardic Jews decorate their Torah scrolls. Ask students to speculate why there are differences. See if they can track down some answers.
Resource: *Encyclopaedia Judaica*, "Torah Ornaments," vol. 15, col. 1255ff.

3. Discuss the introduction of new rituals into Judaism, such as the Consecration ceremony. What purpose do they have? Ask students if, in their opinion, it is legitimate to introduce new practices. If so, how should they be incorporated into the corpus of Jewish observance and ritual?

4. Discuss the symbolism of the *hakafah*. Ask: How do *hakafot* symbolize Judaism's sense of inclusiveness rather than exclusiveness?

5. Divide the class into two groups. One group examines Deuteronomy 34 and the second group examines Genesis 1:1-2:4. Give each group 10 to 15 minutes to read and summarize the selection and to prepare a presen-

tation for the other group. Suggest dramatics, narratives, pantomime, etc.

6. Discuss the symbolism of *Chatan Torah* and *Chatan Beresheet*. How do these names symbolize the relationship between God and Israel? What role does "marriage" play in this relationship?

7. Working in pairs, one student becomes *Chatan Torah,* while the second becomes *Chatan Beresheet*. They act out their respective roles, reverse roles, and repeat the process. They then discuss how they feel in each role. After feedback in pairs, the class reassembles to process the exercise.

8. Research and discuss the origins of Simchat Torah. Discuss why this holiday has taken on so much importance even though its origins are clearly post-biblical. Does the post-biblical origin of the holiday diminish its importance in any way?

9. Relate the following to the class: A nearby congregation is closing its doors. You are members of the Board of Directors. You have two Torah Scrolls that you wish to place in the hands of other Jews. What kinds of groups would you select to receive the Torahs?

10. Divide the class into groups and ask each group to come up with 10 words which give the essence of Simchat Torah. After 5 to 10 minutes, compare lists.

11. We speak of *Torah Lishma* (studying for its own sake). There is a joy to learning, but is there a practical side as well? Do we study Torah in order to know Torah, or is there more to it? How might Torah study be connected to *tzedakah* (acts of righteousness and charity) and *Tikkun Olam* (repairing the world)?

12. Pretend the class is the Board of Trustees of the congregation. They are told that they must leave the community in a hurry. They may only take three suitcases of Jewish ceremonial objects and books with them for use by the congregation. Ask: What would you include in these suitcases?

13. Working in pairs, one student becomes Israel and the other a Torah. Each tells how he/she views the other and what each expects of each other. After a few minutes, reverse roles, and repeat the process. Then come together as a class for feedback.

All-School

1. Have each upper grade form its own *minyan* and, with a Torah scroll in each classroom, discuss the meaning of Torah. All classes then form a Torah procession to the sanctuary or social hall. Students say the blessings in unison, then advanced Hebrew students read the portion in each individual *minyan*. Each teacher can give a *D'var Torah* to his or her group, after which all the *minyanim* can join in a huge circle for *hakafot* and songs.

2. Have each class create a simulated Torah. Each class decides what to include and how to put it together. These creative Torah scrolls can then be displayed at the Simchat Torah worship service and carried around the sanctuary along with the congregational *Sifre Torah*. Variation: Do this as a contest, with prizes given to those classes with the most creative and artistic *Sifre Torah*.

3. Using a long roll of heavy paper, the kind that is used for tablecloths, create a school *Sefer Torah*. Assign a *parashah* to each class. In the art room or other central location, each class writes and/or draws a representation of their portion (in order) on the long roll. When all the portions are in, attach a 3' dowel to each end of the "scroll." Students can make a

decorative cover, and the creative Torah can be incorporated into the Simchat Torah service.

Family

1. Send home directions for making an *Aron Kodesh* or a Torah cover for a "toy-size" Torah. Suggest using shoe boxes, fabric, ribbon, glitter, sequins, fabric paint, craft glue, needles and thread, etc. (This can also be done in school with Consecration students and their parents.) (NSM)

2. Invite families to help polish the silver Torah ornaments right before Simchat Torah. (NSM)

3. Organize a family education program for two to four-year-olds (there is an already designed Simchat Torah program in *Head Start on Holidays: Jewish Programs for Preschoolers and Their Parents* by Roberta Louis Goodman and Andye Honigman Zell).

4. Create a family program in which students are helped to make a *wimpel*. Ask families to save

the *wimpels* for their children's use at Bar/Bat Mitzvah. (NSM)
Resource: The program "Exploring Our Jewish Roots Via Wimpel Making," contributed by Debra Cohn-Levine. In *Learning Together: A Sourcebook on Jewish Family Education,* edited by Janice P. Alper, pp.191-199.

5. Encourage families to attend Simchat Torah worship services. Help them get into the spirit of the festival and to feel good about being Jewish.

6. Suggest that families do something special together to celebrate the holiday of Simchat Torah (e.g., go to a different synagogue or take part in a special event). Afterward, share feelings and reactions. It would be especially interesting and educational to attend Simchat Torah worship services at a Lubavitch Hasidic synagogue.

BIBLIOGRAPHY

See Sukkot, pages 268-270.

CHAPTER SIX
CHANUKAH

VOCABULARY

Al HaNissim: This special Chanukah blessing is included in the Grace after Meals and in the Eighteen Benedictions during Chanukah. Meaning "For the Miracles," this thanksgiving prayer recounts the mighty acts of Mattathias and his sons leading up to the rededication of the Temple in Jerusalem.

Antiochus: The name of several Seleucid rulers of Syria during the second and third centuries B.C.E. Antiochus IV, Epiphanes, reigned from 175-163 B.C.E. His repressive, brutal policies and his attempt to impose Hellenism upon the Jews of Judea led to the Hasmonean revolt of 168-165 B.C.E.

Apocrypha: Known as *Sifre HaChitzonim* in Hebrew, these are books which were not included in the canon of the Hebrew Bible, but which are included in the Roman Catholic and Greek Orthodox canon. Written in Hebrew or Aramaic, most of the books of the Apocrypha resemble the *Ketuvim* (the third part of the Hebrew Bible, the Writings). Among the books of the Apocrypha are I and II Maccabees, The Wisdom of Ben Sira (Ecclesiasticus), and Judith.

Chanukah: "Dedication." This holiday commences on the 25th of Kislev and ends on the 1st or 2nd of Tevet — the only Jewish holiday that occurs in two months. It commemorates the rededication of the Temple in Jerusalem in 165 B.C.E. by the Hasmoneans/Maccabees three years after it had been desecrated by Antiochus IV, Epiphanes.

Chanukah Gelt: A Yiddish term meaning Chanukah money; it is called *D'mai Chanukah* in Hebrew. It is customary to give children foil covered chocolates or some small trinket on each night of Chanukah.

Chanukiah: A special *menorah* or candelabra with nine branches, one for each day along with one servant candle. It is used only on Chanukah.

Daniel, The Book of: This book of the Bible, which is part of the *Ketuvim* (Writings), ostensibly is about a series of events during the reign of the Persians. However, many Bible scholars feel that it was written just prior to the Maccabean Revolt and served to rally support for the rebellion against Antiochus.

Haftarah: A section from *Nevi'im* or *Ketuvim* (the Prophets or Writings) read after the Torah portion on Sabbaths, festivals, and fast days. The practice of reading from the second part of Tanach probably originated during the persecutions of Hadrian, when the Jews of Judea were forbidden to read the Torah. (Some say it originated during the reign of Antiochus.) To get around this prohibition, this non-Torah reading which by theme or vocabulary hinted at the Torah portion, was read in its place. After the ban was lifted, the practice of reading this additional section was retained. *Haftarah* means "ending," and is so called because it is read at the end of the Torah service.

Hallel: The *Hallel* consists of Psalms 113-118 and sometimes Psalm 136. It is recited on special occasions, including Chanukah and Sukkot. The word means "praise."

HaNayrot Halalu: "These Lights." This prayer is said or sung each night during Chanukah immediately after the kindling of the first Chanukah candle. The rest of the candles are lit as this praise to God for the miracles of days gone by is recited. (See below, page 96.)

Hannah: Hannah and her seven sons were killed by soldiers of Antiochus Epiphanes because she refused to worship pagan idols (II Maccabees 7).

Hasmoneans: A priestly family from the town of Modin whose patriarch was Mattathias. The origin of the name (*Hashmonaim*, in Hebrew) is unknown. The Hasmoneans led the revolt against Antiochus IV, defeated him after three years of struggle, and then ruled until 63 B.C.E. when Judea became a Roman province.

Hasmonean Scroll: Also known as the Scroll of Antiochus, it was composed around the seventh century C.E. Drawing heavily upon *midrashic* interpretations of the Maccabean struggle, the scroll contains many legends and stories. During the Medieval Period, it served as the chief source of information for Jews about the Maccabean struggle.

Judah Maccabee: One of the five sons of Mattathias who, along with his brothers Jonathan, Simon, John, and Eleazar, led the revolt against Antiochus Epiphanes. The third but best known of the brothers, he was the leader of the uprising and remained at the helm until his death in 160 B.C.E., five years after the rededication of the Temple.

Judith, The Book of: In the Apocrypha, this book tells the story of a beautiful Jewish widow

who cut off the head of the Assyrian commander, Holofernes, after feeding him cheese to make him thirsty and then wine to get him drunk. She thereby saved the Jewish city of Bethulia. The story was probably written during the period of the Hasmoneans. The composition is considered to be fictitious and not historically accurate. It serves as the origin of the custom of eating cheese dishes on Chanukah.

Kislev: The ninth month of the Jewish religious year, it can have 29 or 30 days. Its zodiac sign is Sagittarius. The festival of Chanukah begins on the 25th of Kislev.

Latkes: The Yiddish word for potato pancakes. The Hebrew equivalent is *levivot*. Originally cheese dishes were eaten on Chanukah to commemorate the actions of Judith, a daughter of the Hasmoneans (see The Book of Judith, above). From the custom of eating cheese dishes grew the custom of eating pancakes of all kinds. *Latkes* are also eaten because they are fried in oil symbolizing the miracle of the cruse of oil which burned for eight days when the Temple was rededicated.

Maccabee: A name given to Judah, first leader of the Hasmoneans, and later applied to the entire Hasmonean dynasty. This Hebrew word is usually translated as "hammer," but can also be understood as an acronym of the first letters of *"Mi Kamocha BaAylim Adonai,"* meaning "Who among the mighty is like You, O God?" It may have served as a rallying cry for the Jews in their battle against Antiochus.

I Maccabees: In the Apocrypha, I Maccabees traces the history of the Jewish people from 175 B.C.E. when Antiochus IV, Epiphanes, became King of Syria, until 135 B.C.E., when Simon was killed and his son John Hyrcanus became the leader of Judea. It is generally seen as a reliable historical account of the period, most likely written in the second half of the second century B.C.E. by an admirer of the Maccabees. While it was probably written in Hebrew, only the Greek translation is extant.

II Maccabees: In the Apocrypha, II Maccabees deals with the deeds of Judah Maccabee until 164 B.C.E., the year after the rededication of the Temple. It may be an abridgment of a longer work by the second century Jewish historian, Jason of Cyrene. II Maccabees has a religious rather than a historical aim. It portrays the persecutions of Antiochus in greater detail than I Maccabees and, in effect, seeks to justify the establishment of Chanukah as a Jewish festival. It makes references to God's role in Jewish history, while such references are omitted from I Maccabees.

Ma'oz Tzur: "Rock of Ages" is a Chanukah hymn sung in the synagogue and at home after the kindling of the Chanukah candles. It originated in Germany in the thirteenth century.

Mattathias: (*Matitiyahu* in Hebrew) A priest from the village of Modin, he initiated the revolt against the Syrian Greeks in 168 B.C.E. and, with his five sons, led the battle. He died in 167-166 before the rededication of the Temple (on 25 Kislev, 165 B.C.E.).

Mi Yimalayl: "Who Can Retell," a popular Chanukah song, has the following refrain: "Who can retell the things that befell us, who can count them? In every age a hero or sage came to our aid."

Modin: A village near Lydda (Lod). In the second century B.C.E., it was the home of the Maccabees and the place where the revolt against Antiochus Epiphanes began. Each year, at the beginning of Chanukah, a torch is lit at the tomb of the Maccabees and carried to Jerusalem by runners.

Nes Gadol Hayah Po: "A Great Miracle Happened Here." The word *Po* (here) is substituted for *Sham* (there) on *dreidels* used in Israel, because the miracle of Chanukah occurred in Israel and not in the Diaspora. In Israel, one side of a *dreidel* has a *Pay* instead of a *Shin*.

Nes Gadol Hayah Sham: Means "A Great Miracle Happened There." Each letter on the sides of the *dreidel* refers to one of the four words in this statement. The miracle is, of course, the victory of the Maccabees over the Hellenist Syrians, and the rededication of the Temple in 165 B.C.E.

Seleucids: When Alexander the Great died in 323 B.C.E., his empire was divided among his generals. Ptolomy ruled Egypt and its environs while Seleucus ruled Greater Syria. From then until the Maccabean Revolt in 168 B.C.E., Palestine was sometimes under the control of the Egyptian Greek Ptolomies and sometimes ruled by the Syrian Greek Seleucids. Antiochus Epiphanes and his immediate predecessors were Seleucids.

Sevivon: A four-sided top with a different Hebrew letter on each side. The Hebrew word *sevivon* is derived from the Hebrew root meaning "to turn." In Yiddish, such a top is called a *dreidel*, which is derived from the German word *drehen*, to turn. In the Middle Ages, there were German tops known as *trendels*. The Jewish *dreidel/sevivon* is probably an outgrowth of that top. The letters on the side of the *dreidel* represent Hebrew words meaning "A Great Miracle Happened There" or, in Israel, "A Great Miracle Happened Here." Each of the letters on the side of the *dreidel* also corresponds to a Yiddish word linked to the *dreidel* game: *Nun* for "*nichts*," meaning to take nothing and put nothing; *Gimel* for "*ganz*," meaning to take everything; *Hay* for "*halb*," meaning to take half of the pot; and *Shin* for "*shtellen*," meaning to put into the pot. There are many variations of the *dreidel* game.

Shamash: "Servant." This refers to the ninth — or servant — candle used to light all of the other Chanukah candles each night.

She'ahsah Nissim: "Who made miracles." The second prayer recited when lighting the Chanukah candles is said on all eight nights and speaks of the miracles wrought for our ancestors in ancient times. (See Appendix, page 250, for blessing.)

Shehecheyanu: "The One Who Has Kept Us Alive." This blessing, recited at most new beginnings, is said on the first night of Chanukah. (See Appendix, page 251, for blessing.)

Sufganiyot: An Israeli jelly-filled doughnut. It is eaten on Chanukah because, like the *latke,* it is fried in oil, which is symbolic of the miracle of Chanukah.

BACKGROUND

History

333 B.C.E. Alexander the Great conquered Judea. Now a part of the Greek Empire, the policy of cultural pluralism was applied to the Jews. They were permitted cultural and religious freedom while remaining under the political and economic control of the Greek Empire.

323 B.C.E. With the death of Alexander, his empire was divided among his generals. One section of the empire was centered in Egypt under the control of Ptolemy; another major section of the empire was centered in Syria under the control of Seleucus. Palestine, which was located between these two kingdoms, became a bone of contention.

198 B.C.E. Until this time, Judea had been in the hands of the Ptolemies (Egypt). Now it came under Seleucid (Syria) control. It remained a part of the Seleucid kingdom until the Maccabean revolt.

175 B.C.E. Antiochus IV, Epiphanes, became the ruler of the Seleucid Kingdom. Rather than continue the policies of previous rulers, Antiochus tried to fashion an empire held together by the Greek religion and the Greek way of life. In the process of establishing this common denominator, Antiochus attempted to eliminate all national and religious differences among his subject peoples. He made a special effort to integrate the Jews into his kingdom.

175 B.C.E. Jason, son of Simon II, became High Priest of Judea after offering Antiochus large sums of money. The High Priest was considered to be the head of the Jewish nation. Jason was an assimilationist who sought to incorporate as much of Syrian-Greek Hellenism into Judea as possible. Other elements in Judea, among them the "Hasidim," fiercely defended their Jewishness against all incursions.

171 B.C.E. Jason was dismissed, and Menelaus became the High Priest. The repressive policies of Antiochus continued.

168 B.C.E. Active revolt against Antiochus began with the famous rallying cry of Mattathias: "Whoever is for the Lord, follow me!" For two years, Mattathias and his five sons waged guerrilla warfare against the Syrians. Then, as more and more Jews joined Judah (Mattathias died in 167-166), the Jews pursued a more active military policy and won several decisive battles against the Seleucids. The Hasidim also joined forces with the Hasmoneans.

165 B.C.E. On 25 Kislev, Judah and his forces drove the Greeks out of Jerusalem and rededicated the Temple, which had been intentionally defiled by the

Hellenists. This did not mark a final victory on the part of the Jews, as fighting continued intermittently for more than 20 years.

163 B.C.E. Judah Maccabee obtained internal autonomy for his nation from Antiochus, but continued to fight because he sought full political freedom.

161/160 B.C.E. Judah was killed at Elasa near Beth-Horon. Jonathan became the leader of the Jews. An astute diplomat, Jonathan used unsettled political conditions to Jewish advantage. The Syrian authorities recognized him as both the governor of Judea and its High Priest. This merging of previously separate roles angered the Pharisees who saw in Jonathan's actions a grab for power. From this point on, ill will existed between the Pharisees and the Hasmoneans.

143 B.C.E. Jonathan was murdered and Simon, the last of the five brothers, became the High Priest and ruler of Judea. He succeeded in expelling the Syrian Greeks and establishing an independent kingdom. Simon was murdered by his son-in-law Ptolemy who wanted to succeed him as ruler of Judea. However, his son John Hyrcanus took over and ruled until 105 B.C.E.

104 B.C.E. Alexander Yannai took over as the Hasmonean ruler. His opposition to the Pharisees led to a civil war.

76 B.C.E. With the death of Yannai, his widow, Salome Alexandra (76-67 B.C.E.) became the Hasmonean ruler. It was during her reign that the Pharisees regained a position of religious and political leadership in Jewish life.

63 B.C.E. Judea became a Roman province.

Observance

The Chanukah lights are first mentioned by the Roman Jewish historian Josephus in his book *Antiquities* (12:7): "From that day to this we observe this festival and call it lights."

The Talmud speaks of the *mitzvah* of lighting the Chanukah lights in a prominent place in order to proclaim the "miracle" of Chanukah to the entire world. "Our sages taught: The Chanukah lights should be placed at the door of the house. A person who lives in an upper story should place it in the nearest window to the public thoroughfare. In time of danger, however, it may be placed on the table and that will be sufficient . . . " Rabbi Joshua said: "Women are bound to fulfill the commandment of kindling the lights, for they, too, were involved in that miracle. The lights may be kindled from sunset till the time when all movement comes to an end in the marketplace" (*Shabbat* 21b, 23b).

The Rabbis of the Talmud stressed the miracle of the cruse of oil, rather than the miraculous military victory of the Hasmoneans, for they wished to emphasize the role of divine intervention and minimize the military prowess of the Hasmonean dynasty. A famous passage in the Talmud asks: *"Mai Chanukah?"* — What is Chanukah? In response, the Talmud states: "Our sages taught: Beginning with the twenty-fifth of Kislev, during the days of Chanukah, we neither fast nor mourn. For the idolaters entered the Sanctuary and defiled all the oils in the Sanctuary; and when the power of the Hasmoneans overcame and defeated them, they searched, but found no more than one flask of oil, sealed with the seal of the High Priest, and there was not enough oil in it to last more than one day. But a miracle took place, and they kindled with it for eight days. For future years, therefore, they established these days as days of feasting, praise, and thanksgiving" (*Shabbat* 21b).

How to light the Chanukah lights: On the first night, the first candle is placed in the *chanukiah* on the far right. Each night, an additional candle is added to the left. On the eighth day, the last candle on the far left is added to the other seven. Although candles are added from right to left, they are lit from the left to the right. Each night, therefore, the newest candle is lit first.

The first and second blessings are said every night. *Shehecheyanu* is said on the first night only. (See Appendix, pages 250 and 251, for blessings.)

HaNayrot Halalu is read after the kindling of the newest Chanukah candle. The rest of the lights are kindled as this prayer is being said or sung. The Ashkenazic and Sephardic versions differ somewhat, but the meaning remains essentially the same in both renderings:

"We kindle these lights on account of the miracles, the deliverances, and the wonders which You did work for our ancestors by means of your holy priests. During all of the eight days of Chanukah, these lights are sacred, neither is it permitted us to make any profane use of them; but we are only to look at them, in order that we may give thanks to Your Name for Your miracles, Your deliverance, and Your wonders."

Al HaNissim is read as one of the final blessings of the *Amidah* and is part of the Grace after Meals. It reads:

"We give thanks for the redeeming wonders and the mighty deeds by which, at this season, our people was saved in days of old. In the days of the Hasmoneans, a tyrant arose against our ancestors, determined to make them forget Your Torah, and to turn them away from obedience to Your will. But You were at their side in time of trouble. You gave them strength to struggle and to triumph, that they might serve You in freedom. Through the power of Your spirit, the weak defeated the strong, the few prevailed over the many, and the righteous were triumphant. Then Your children returned to Your House, to purify the sanctuary and kindle its

lights. And they dedicated these days to give thanks and praise to Your great name." (A similar *Al HaNissim* prayer is recited on Purim.)

The *chanukiah* is then placed in a window or in the doorway so that the lighted candles may be viewed from the street. The placement of the *chanukiyah* in the front window can be seen as a statement of Jewish pride and identity.

In addition to these prayers and blessings, there are no other special Chanukah rituals. It is customary to sing various Chanukah songs, but they have no special religious significance. For the enjoyment of all, new melodies and recordings are being produced each year.

Central Themes

- Chanukah was a struggle for freedom of religious practice, the first such (Passover not withstanding) in recorded history. That a subjugated people chose to put their lives on the line and battle a much stronger foe in pursuit of religious freedom and triumphed is the real miracle of Chanukah.

- The events leading up to the Maccabean revolt put in jeopardy the continued religious identity of the Jewish people. Not to fight would have meant an end to Jewish peoplehood. That battle was therefore a fight for Jewish survival.

- Chanukah symbolizes the fight against totalitarianism in all forms. The struggle was waged in a particular context, but its implications are universal — a festival of liberty and freedom. Chanukah celebrates more than the independence of one people; it points toward the right to freedom for all peoples.

- The actions of Antiochus IV represent a classic error committed by non-Jews in their dealings with the Jewish people. He, like many others in the centuries that followed, tried to interfere with the internal life of the Jewish people. He did not realize that Jews had learned to live as a minority element in a dominant non-Jewish culture and that they were prepared to submit to political and economic control for the sake of religious freedom.

- Chanukah affirms the universal truth that the only effective answer to oppression is to fight for and defend the very values and principles which that oppression threatens and tries to suppress.

- Chanukah as a festival of faith affirms the declaration of the prophet Zachariah (5:6): "Not by might, nor by power, but by My spirit, saith the Lord of Hosts." The Maccabean struggle was even more a fight for Judaism than a fight against Hellenism.

- Both Chanukah and Purim celebrate a victory of Jews over larger, more powerful forces.

- In Israel, there is a natural resonance with the victory of the Maccabees in light of the struggle for peace and security in the modern Jewish state.

- The link between Chanukah and Christmas represents an ongoing challenge for North American Jewry. While Chanukah is but a minor festival in the Jewish calendar, Christmas is one of the two main holidays (with Easter) in the Christian calendar. Although Chanukah and Christmas occur at the same time of year, they have virtually nothing else in common. Ironically, of course, had the Maccabees not sustained their commitment to Judaism, the history of the people might have ended then and there. Christianity could not have emerged as it did.

- The story of the oil lasting for eight days may or may not have occurred. If it were merely a legend created to explain why Chanukah lasts eight days, it would not substantially detract from the meaning and importance of the holiday.

SCOPE AND SEQUENCE

Grade	Themes/Ideas
Kindergarten	Stories about Chanukah; basic Chanukah observances in the home.
Grade One	Stories about Chanukah giving of presents — why at this time of year? How do we feel when we receive gifts? How do we feel when we give gifts?
Grade Two	How Chanukah is celebrated in the synagogue; an introduction to the Chanukah story.
Grade Three	A basic Chanukah vocabulary — key terms; introduction to the three blessings.
Grade Four	*Al HaNissim* prayer and review of blessings; how Chanukah is celebrated in Israel.
Grade Five	Chanukah as a religious and a national holiday; Chanukah customs — *gelt, dreidel,* cheese dishes, *latkes,* doughnuts, etc.
Grade Six	Hannah and her seven sons: the event and its implications; the meaning of Chanukah then and now.
Grade Seven	An overview of I and II Maccabees — comparison and contrast of the two sources; The Book of Daniel and Chanukah.
Grade Eight	A critical overview of the Chanukah story — Chanukah in the light of history and politics.
Grade Nine	The origins of Chanukah traditional and non-traditional viewpoints.

Grade Ten   Chanukah and the challenge to Jewish survival — assimilation, anti-Semitism and religious persecution.

Grade Eleven   How Chanukah is treated in Rabbinic literature.

Grade Twelve   A review of the key ideas and themes related to Chanukah; a look at possible reinterpretation of the meaning and significance of Chanukah in the light of modern Israel and the pressures of modern civilization.

ACTIVITIES

Preschool/Kindergarten

1. Place a variety of candles in an empty water table (i.e., no water inside): Chanukah, Shabbat, birthday, dinner, *yahrzeit*. Give children time to explore and engage in free play. (NSM)

2. Cut painting paper in the shape of a *dreidel*. Allow children to paint it as they wish. (NSM)

3. Make a marshmallow *dreidel*. Shape a marshmallow into a square. Cover with frosting all over and put a candy kiss into one end to make a point. Use food coloring to color some of the frosting and for the Hebrew letters. Use red hots for the handle.

4. Make a simple *dreidel*. On a piece of cardboard 2" square, draw lines diagonally so that the lines intersect in the center of the cardboard. In each of the resulting triangles, write one of the letters of the *dreidel* and decorate the space. Take a lollypop stick or a pencil and stick it through the cardboard at the exact center. Put a little glue around the spot where the stick and the cardboard meet to hold it in place.

5. Make a *dreidel* out of a 1/2 gallon milk carton. Fill with *gelt* or other small items. Cover the carton with foil or colored construction paper. This can also be used as a piñata.

6. Use paper plates to make simple Chanukah greeting cards. Glue a paper doily on the plate, then paint and glue on a holiday picture or symbol. Send the cards to shut-ins at care centers and/or hospitals.

7. When making *latkes*, have students watch the "transformation" from the potatoes and other ingredients to the *latke*. When done, have the class dictate to you the steps in making *latkes*; write their words on chart paper. Send home a copy for parents. (NSM)

8. Make a Chanukah mobile using dough art. Mix flour, water, and salt to make clay dough. Use a cookie cutter to cut out the symbols. Paint the symbols and dry them, and put them on hangars. Hang them from a cardboard holder for six packs of soda pop.

9. Experiment with potatoes: use them for *latkes*, potato prints, a *chanukiah* (read *The Odd Potato* by Eileen Sherman or a *Chanukiyah for Dina* by Floreva G. Cohen), grow potato eyes, watch a potato rot. Observe the differences in a potato left on a windowsill, in a refrigerator, in a pan of water, in a dark closet, etc. (NSM)

10. Have students spin like a *dreidel*, light like a *shammash*, etc. (NSM)

11. Have several children make a human *chanukiah*. Discuss what it was like to be a *chanukiah*. Ask the children to value rank which they liked best: being a *dreidel*, a candle, or a *chanukiah*. Have them explain their reasons.

12. Compare a toy top and a *dreidel*. (NSM)

13. Read to the children *Melly's Menorah: A Hanukkah Story* by Amye Rosenberg. When the family's *chanukiah* is lost during a move,

Melly's cookie dough *chanukiah* saves the day. Have children think of other ways the problem could have been solved. Then bake cookie dough *chanukiot*.

Recipe for cookie dough (enough for 3 or 4 students):
Mix 2 eggs, 1/3 cup honey, and 1 tablespoon oil in a bowl. Add 1 tablespoon orange or lemon rind, 1/2 teaspoon salt, and 1 1/2 cups of oatmeal. Mix well. Take small portions of dough and roll into long pieces. On a cookie sheet, shape these into *chanukiot*. Bake 8 to 10 minutes at 400 degrees.

14. Use macaroni shapes to make Chanukah symbols. Spray paint them with silver or gold spray and mount them on tagboard. Or glue macaroni and other bumpy things like beans, plastic, or metal bits in a Chanukah design to a paper plate. Place the plate face down on a larger piece of aluminum foil. Turn the plate to front and press the foil down so that the outline of the objects underneath is revealed. A thin wash of dark colored paint will give the plaque an aged, metallic look.

15. Sitting in a circle, children discuss their favorite Chanukah symbol. Go around, taking turns telling why it is their favorite.

16. Add to the housekeeping or cooking corner: *chanukiot*, candles, *dreidels*, frying pan, brown playdough (for *latkes*), costumes for the Maccabees, etc. (NSM)

17. Ask students to stand with ample room to move around so that they do not bump into each other. Tell them to close their eyes, turn around, and spin about until they get dizzy. While doing this, have them think about what it is like to be a *dreidel*. Tell them to think about how the people spinning them might look from their point of view. How might children see the world about them if they were a *dreidel*? Then gather together and share feel-

ings and thoughts. (Older students can discuss how life can sometimes be symbolically depicted like a *dreidel*: off balance, disoriented, confused, lacking purpose.)

18. Create a matching game in which students have to match up photos of *chanukiot* with the real ones. (NSM)

19. In an area where the children play with clay, add: candles, straws cut in half, sticks, etc., so that they can make pretend *chanukiot*. (NSM)

20. Add golden fabrics and other things to the block area so that students can recreate the Temple that the Maccabees reconquered. (NSM)

21. Put different kinds of candles near the balance scale. See if children can figure out how many Chanukah candles balance a Shabbat candle. (NSM)

22. Demonstrate the various things our bodies do on Chanukah: our hands light the *chanukiah*, hands spin the *dreidel*, eyes see the light, tongue tastes the *latkes*, etc. (NSM)

23. If school meets during Chanukah, use the occasion to introduce language which describes past and future events: Yesterday we lit two candles. Today we light three candles. Tomorrow we will light four candles. (NSM)

24. Observe what happens when a candle is lit. (NSM)

25. Which candle takes longer to burn: Shabbat, Chanukah (different kinds), birthday? Have students predict and then light each of these in a safe place to observe over the course of the session. (NSM)

26. Introduce ordinal numbers, i.e., the *first* candle, the *second* candle, etc. (NSM)

27. Cover a lit candle with a glass jar. What happens? Use this as a time to review or introduce fire safety procedures. If your clothing catches on fire, you need to: stop, drop, roll. This is just like putting a jar over a candle — you deprive the fire of the oxygen it needs to burn. (NSM)

28. Practice putting candles in the *chanukiah* correctly — right to left. Explain that candles are lit left to right. (NSM)

29. One candle, the *shamash*, is "it." His/her eight candles run away and he/she tries to catch them and "light" them. If a "candle" fails to stand still to be lit when caught by the *shamash*, he/she is considered caught and the *shamash* may "light" him or her.

30. Make a snack that looks like a *chanukiah* (for example, nine carrots or cheese strips with grapes on the top). (NSM)

31. Make Chanukah prints using cookie cutters or cut potatoes. (NSM)

32. View and discuss the animated video *Lights: A Hanukah Fable*.

33. Help children complete pages 19-26 in *Jewish Preschool/Kindergarten Copy Pak*™ by Nancy Cohen Nowak.

34. Do one of the movement activities related to Shabbat in *Creative Movement for a Song* by JoAnne Tucker (pages 20, 34, and 36).

Primary

1. Play *Judah Says*, a Chanukah version of *Simon Says*.

2. Sitting in a circle, the first student begins by saying, "I received as a Chanukah gift from Israel a ____. The next and subsequent students begin with the same opening statement, but must list all of the "gifts" already enumerated by the students. Chanukah gifts can be limited to items grown or manufactured in Israel or Chanukah related items.

3. See who can spin the *dreidel* the longest. Begin with groups of 2 to 4, selecting the winner from those groups. Then have the winners engage in a spin-off.

4. If your synagogue has a seven-branched *menorah* on the *bimah*, take the students and a *chanukiah* into the sanctuary. Have them make comparisons between the two. A group of students can research the differences. (NSM)

5. Compare an oil burning *chanukiah* with a candle one. (NSM)

6. Ask students to collect old clothes, scraps of materials, etc., then create a costume based on one of the characters in the Chanukah story. After putting on the homemade costumes, the students act out parts of the Chanukah story.

7. Have a Chanukah party. Invite parents to help and participate. The following preparations might make the party more than just fun and games:
    a. Decorate the room with pictures, drawings, and Chanukah symbols.
    b. Prepare invitations in the form of paper *chanukiot, dreidels,* and six-pointed stars.
    c. Serve potato *latkes* and apple sauce.
    d. Have a grab bag with simple and inexpensive gifts.

8. Make *sufganiyot*. Invite another class in to share the goodies.

9. Make the room as dark as possible and kindle nine lights. Each child closes his/her eyes and thinks of the Chanukah story, of Judah Maccabee, the Temple, a *dreidel*, a *chanukiah*, etc. Students are then directed to think of the brightly burning lights and imagine that they

are Chanukah candles. After a few minutes, divide the class into pairs. Each student shares feelings and thoughts with a partner. After 5 to 10 minutes, the class reassembles and processes the activity.

10. Read to the children *A Great Miracle Happened There: A Chanukah Story* by Karla Kuskin. In this book a boy named Henry shares a Jewish family's Chanukah celebration. His questions and the answers he receives help to explain Chanukah to small children. Afterward, discuss the story. Have children think of other questions Henry might have asked. See who can answer these questions.

11. Play *Chanukah Bingo*. Prepare cards with nine or more squares containing Chanukah symbols and words. Be sure to mix the symbols so that there are different configurations on the bingo cards. To play the game, call the symbols after selecting them from a box or bag. The first person to fill a row wins.

12. Have one child begin a story about Chanukah. Designate other children to continue the story until all have had a turn. Record the story on tape. Act it out and illustrate it.

13. Play one or more of the following *dreidel* games.
    a. *Put and Take: Nun* takes nothing and puts nothing. *Gimel* takes the entire pot. *Hay* takes half of the pot. *Shin* puts in all or half. (Set a time limit. The person with the most coins, buttons, chips, etc., wins.)
    b. *Spin Together:* Assign point values to each letter (*Nun* = 1, *Shin* = 2, *Hay* = 3, *Gimel* = 5). All participants spin their *dreidels* at the same time. After 5 or 10 spins of the *dreidel*, the person with the most points wins.
    c. *Can You Match My Letter?:* The leader spins the *dreidel*. All the students spin their *dreidels*. Those whose letter matches that of the leader remain in the game. The

process is repeated until a winner is selected.
    d. *Call Your Letter:* Students one-by-one call out a letter. If their *dreidel* lands on their letter, they stay in the game. Otherwise, they are out.
    e. *Spin the Same Letter:* Those students who can spin the same letter twice in a row remain in the game. The process is repeated until a winner is found.

14. Play a matching pairs card game. Using 3" x 5" cards, make up sets of matching pairs (e.g, a person and an event, a symbol or ritual object, the meaning of a symbol and its importance). Make about 20 cards — 10 pairs. Make several sets so that the whole class may play at one time in small groups. This game is particularly useful for Chanukah because there are many terms and names to remember.

15. Teach the children the basic Chanukah blessings in Hebrew. Be sure to explain the meaning of each blessing. (See Appendix, page 250, for blessings in Hebrew and English.)

16. Make paper bag puppets. Give each student a paper bag, crayons, a scissors, colored paper, and glue. Each student makes a paper-bag representation of one of the characters in the Chanukah story. Then parts or all of the story can be acted out using the paper bag puppets. Puppets on a more elaborate scale can be made out of a wide range of materials.
    Resource: *Creative Puppetry for Jewish Kids* by Gale Solotar Warshawsky.

17. View and discuss the video *Benjamin and the Miracle of Hanukkah*. Have children imagine they are Benjamin. How did they feel when Judah Maccabee sent them to get the oil for the Temple light? (proud, scared, happy, etc.)

18. Discuss the meaning of freedom and give examples. Let children voice their interpretations of freedom.

19. Have students complete the Instant Lessons *Hannukah — The Story* and *Hanukah — What We Do.*

20. Do one of the movement activities related to Shabbat in *Creative Movement for a Song* by JoAnne Tucker (pages 20, 34, 36).

21. Do one or more of the Chanukah art projects in *100+ Jewish Art Projects for Children* by Nina Streisand Sher and Margaret A. Feldman (pages 22, 23, 25, 27).

22. Complete pages 10, 11, and 12 in *Jewish Holiday Copy Pak*™ *K-3* by Marji Gold-Vukson.

Intermediate

1. Bring to class a variety of *chanukiot* (you might wish to take your class to the synagogue or school gift shop, or you could cut pictures out of Jewish gift catalogs). How are the *chanukiot* the same? different? Study the *halachah* which describes the requirements of a *chanukiah*. Which ones follow the law? Which ones do not? How do students feel about *chanukiot* with Jewish motifs? with secular ones (such as Mickey Mouse)? (NSM) Resource: *Code of Jewish Law* by Solomon Ganzfried, Chapter 139.

2. Make a drip pad to put under a *chanukiah*. This could be a picture which is laminated or a permanent marker drawing on a piece of cork tile (put colored tape around the edges to bind the tile). (NSM)

3. Order *dreidel* making kits from The Dreidelmaker. (NSM) Resource: The Dreidelmaker, Mark Glickman, P.O. Box 1904, Frederick, MD 21702-0904.

4. Give students a Jewish calendar (many Jewish funeral homes or Jewish monument companies have large quantities of these). Have them double check the number of days in the various Jewish holidays: Rosh HaShanah, Yom Kippur, Sukkot, Simchat Torah, Chanukah, Tu B'Shevat, Purim, Pesach, Shavuot, Shabbat. (NSM)

5. Read a statement to students about Chanukah. In their own words, students write a paragraph or two describing what they think the statement means. Follow up with a class discussion about the statement. Some suggested statements:
   a. For a Jew to have a Christmas tree is not only contrary to the spirit of Chanukah, but insulting to Christians.
   b. Jews should put their *chanukiah* by a window where people passing by will see it and enjoy its beauty.

6. Let each student choose one of the following titles and write a short Chanukah story. After they write their stories, these can be typed and bound, shared with the class and with other classes, and added to the synagogue library. Possible titles:
   a. The Chanukah Miracle Man/Woman
   b. I Was a Maccabee
   c. The Mischievous Chanukah Candles
   d. Chanukah in Toyland
   e. The Missing Gimel: Sherlock Cohen to the Rescue

7. Have each student write a letter to Judah Maccabee or to one of the other main characters in the Chanukah story. Have them ask questions of Judah (or the other character) and tell how they feel about the person and what he/she did or said. Read (or ask for volunteers to read) the letters.

8. Have each child relate to classmates, in three or four oral sentences, the characteristics of Judah Maccabee. Follow with a discussion on the similarities and differences between Judah and other Jewish heroes/heroines.

9. Read and discuss *The Christmas Menorahs: How a Town Fought Hate* by Janice Cohn. This book tells the true story of the citizens of the town of Billings, Montana who, after an anti-Semitic incident, all put *chanukiot* in their windows in support of the Jewish community. Afterward, have each student write a thank-you note to the citizens of Billings. Mail the letters to the Billings Gazette, P.O. Box 36300, Billings, MT 59101 or to the Mayor's office, 210 N. 27th St., Billings, MT 59101. (AFM)

10. Make name *chanukiot*. Students write their Hebrew name in a stylized way and use it for a *chanukiah*. A letter that goes below the line can be used as the base. They will need to find a way to locate the nine candles on their name. Give students free reign as to color schemes and media — cut paper, crayola, tempera, etc. When they are completed, mount the *chanukiot* on a bulletin board outside the classroom with a Chanukah greeting from the class. (JB)

11. Do a word search. Find the words related to the holiday of Chanukah. Working in teams, do the following word search and circle the hidden words. The team to complete the word search first wins. (This can also be done individually.)

```
A Z C O R S H A M A S H N A B
X G E L T N N B C I R S T M D
D U R C E A V A N E R O T A C
A N C F R Y G L A T K E O O E
N Z O N E R A R V N G U V Z B
I E A J L O V U W T H I N Z H
E V Q U M T P I I O N S P H A
L R Z A I S T J U D A H X Y N
B R Y U N S C H Y Q U O T H N
D R E I D E L V E R R Y S H A
S Q U B C X I O N T T O R A H
R G S T K I S L E V N O Q R T
A I N I Z R Q P I M S I M O N
V F C F A G N Z A R A S T I G
N T Q U P M N R A M L A C H X
```

(Words to be found: Shamash, Kislev, Hannah, Dreidel, Gelt, Maoz, Gift, Torah, Latke, Judah, Nayrot, Simon, Daniel.)

12. Read I Maccabees to the class before beginning this activity. Students take turns being Judah Maccabee. The others in the class interview Judah. Some questions to help the interviewers start off: In what condition did you find the Temple? What was your reaction when you first saw the Temple? What have you done since you arrived here? How do you feel about things now? What are your hopes for the Jewish people in the years ahead? How do you feel about yourself as a leader of the Jewish people?

13. Write Chanukah headlines. Divide the class into teams of 3 to 5 each. The task of each group is to write one or more headlines to describe the events that they have been studying. The teams can prepare one main headline and several sub-headlines or several main headlines. This can also be handled as a brainstorming activity for the whole class. In the latter case, the teacher writes the suggested headlines on the blackboard and, if desired, the class can decide which they like the best. Humor may definitely play a part in this activity.

14. Have students write a poem and add it to their poetry books. Try a "shape poem." This is a non-hyming poem written in the shape of a symbol, such as a *dreidel*.

15. Write a Chanukah name or object on 3" x 5" cards. Number the cards. Hand out one card to each student and also give each student a blank 3" x 5" card. On the second card, the student makes up a four-line rhyme that corresponds to the name on the other card, then writes the number found on the name card on the rhyme card so that the two numbers correspond. The rhymes are then

read in an effort to match up the rhymes with the names.

16. Interview: Have a "Meet the Press" conference with Judah Maccabee. One child takes the part of Judah; the others become reporters. It will, of course, be necessary for reporters to do some research first in order to know what questions to ask and for Judah, too, so that he can answer correctly.

17. Give each student a sheet containing the Hebrew text (and transliteration if needed) and an English translation of the *Shehecheyanu*. Divide the class into groups of 3 to 4 students each. Each group has 10 minutes to compile a list of possible situations when the *Shehecheyanu* might be said. The groups reassemble and a composite list is made on the board. Then, as a class, discuss the meaning and significance of the blessing.

18. The *mitzvah* of *Hachnasat Orchim* (welcoming of guests /hospitality) is central to Judaism. Discuss how this *mitzvah* can be practiced on Chanukah. What simple ways can students think of to bring sunshine into the lives of others?

19. Have students act out a meeting between Judah Maccabee and Antiochus.

20. Put on Chanukah skits. Divide the Chanukah story into small segments. Then divide the class into groups of 2 or 3 each. Give the children 10 to 15 minutes to work out a dramatization of their scene in the story. Have each group then act out their segment of the Chanukah narrative. If all goes well, this improvisation could become the basis for an assembly presentation.

21. Write scenes from the Chanukah story or that are related to the Chanukah celebration on pieces of paper and put them into a bag. Each student draws a piece of paper and acts out what is written on it for the other students to identify.

22. Do a readers theater of "The Case of the Missing Letter: A Dramatic Reading (see page 110). Or, this can be performed as a play for other classes and parents at an assembly.

23. Ask students to volunteer to be a speaker. Each "volunteer" is given an amusing, Chanukah related topic to speak about for three minutes. It should start out related to the theme, but it may go in any direction whatsoever. The more nonsense that the student says, the funnier it is.

24. On separate index cards, write down questions related to Chanukah. Create enough question cards to equal half the number of students. On separate cards, write answers to each of the questions. Mix the two sets of cards and shuffle several times so they are well mixed. Give out one card to each student. Explain that this is a matching exercise and that some students have questions and others have answers. Have students find their matching cards. When a match is formed, ask the matching students to find seats together. (Tell them not to reveal to the other students what is on their cards.) When all the matching pairs have been seated, have each pair quiz the rest of the class by reading aloud their question and challenging classmates to tell them the answer. (Adapted from *Active Learning: 101 Strategies to Teach Any Subject* by Mel Silberman.)

25. View and discuss the video *In the Month of Kislev*.

26. Play *Hanukkah Board Game*. Discuss the values therein.

27. Complete the Instant Lesson *Mastering the Chanukah Brakhot* by Jane Golub.

28. Do one or more of the Chanukah art projects in *100+ Jewish Art Projects for Children* by Nina Streisand Sher and Margaret A. Feldman (pages 24 and 26).

29. Do a readers theater performance of "Chanukah Visitor" (page 48) or "Star (of Judah) Wars" (page 62) in *Kings and Things: 20 Jewish Plays for Kids 8 to 18* by Meridith Shaw Patera.

30. Complete pages 10, 11, and 12 of *Jewish Holiday Copy Pak™ 4-6* by Marji Gold-Vukson. Have each student make up his/her own activity page. Collect the pages, photocopy them, and bind them as a book for students to take home.

Secondary

1. Provide a Catholic Bible (one with the Apocrypha; you can find one in a library). Have students search and find the Books of Maccabees. Then ask them to find Maccabees in a Tanach. When they can't, explain that the Rabbis who were putting together the Hebrew Bible felt that in their time, Chanukah was too recent in history. They also didn't feel that these books were holy enough to be put into our Bible. But these books were saved in a collection of additional writings called the Apocrypha. (The Book of Judith is also in the Apocrypha; it was probably written during the time of the Hasmoneans.) (NSM)

2. Give students the following paragraph which contains five errors. The task is to locate the mistakes, cross them out, and write in the correct information above each error. If done orally as a team competition, the first team to spot a mistake gets a point, and then that team gets two points for supplying the correct information. If the first team does not have the correct information, the second team is given an opportunity to supply it and score two points.

Ahasuerus was the Syrian-Greek king who ruled over Palestine during the time of the Maccabees. The Greeks took control of the Temple in Tel Aviv and dedicated it to the Greek god Zeus. When Judah and his followers recaptured the Temple, they found a small container of oil which burned for seven days and nights. They called the 25th of Kislev the festival of Chanukah which means "dedication." Each night Jews light Chanukah lights using the *sevivon* candle to light the other candles. Then Jews eat potato pancakes called *sufganiyot*."

(Corrections: Antiochus for Ahasuerus, Jerusalem for Tel Aviv, eight for seven, *shamash* for *sevivon*, and *latkes* for *sufganiyot*.)

3. Give students a list of events related to the holiday of Chanukah. Working individually, they can make a time line (provide them with the necessary dates). Or, they can write the first thing to occur on a blank sheet of paper, draw an arrow, and then write the next episode. In the latter instance, each occurrence is connected by arrows with the direction of the arrow indicating the order of occurrence. This can also be done as a team game. Events might include: the conquest of Judea by Alexander the Great, Judea comes under Syrian control, Antiochus IV becomes ruler of Syria, Greek soldier slain in Modin, rededication of the Temple in Jerusalem, death of Judah, Simon becomes High Priest, Romans take over control of Judea.

4. Three statements are presented together. One statement of the three is incorrect. The student's task is to decide which statement is incorrect and then explain why it is incorrect. In each group of three statements, the incorrect statement is noted here with (F):

The Book of Daniel appears in the Apocrypha. (F)
A dreidel is called a *sevivon* in Hebrew.
Antiochus was a Syrian-Greek king.

Maccabee means "hammer."
Chanukah begins on the 25th of Chesvan. (F)
Al HaNissim means "For the miracles."

Chanukah *gelt* is called *"D'mai Chanukah"* in Hebrew.
We light candles from the left to the right.
We light eight candles on the first night. (F)

We sing *"Maoz Tzur"* on Chanukah.
We sing *"Mi Yimalayl"* on Chanukah.
We sing *"Chad Gadya"* on Chanukah. (F)

5. Have students identify and then discuss the following famous dates in Jewish and world history. If desired, have them construct a time line following the discussion.

   1220 B.C.E.: Jews leave Egypt
   165 B.C.E.:   Maccabean Revolt
   1215 C.E.:   The Magna Carta in England
   1776 C.E.:   The American Revolution
   1789 C.E.:   The French Revolution
   1948 C.E.:   The Establishment of the State of Israel

6. Read a statement to the class. Those students agreeing with the statement go to one side of the room; those disagreeing go to the other. Have each group discuss with those who hold the same view the reasons for their choice. Some suggested statements:
   a. A Jew who has a Christmas tree in his/her home should be publicly criticized.
   b. Public schools should not have Christmas programs or teach Christmas carols.
   c. Jewish children should not sing any Christmas songs in secular school, or participate in any Christmas celebrations.
   d. There should not be a crèche on public or government property.

7. Have a debate on Jewish identity. The Browns are the only Jewish family in a small town, yet, because of their non-Jewish name, they are able to keep their Jewish identity a secret. Chanukah arrives. They wish to light the Chanukah candles, but they have a dilemma: Do they light the *chanukiah* where no one can see it, or do they light it in the front window where it will be in full view of the entire neighborhood and anyone passing by? Form two groups. One group argues for the hidden *chanukiah*, while the second group takes the opposite position. Each group must give cogent reasons for its position. Variation: Divide the class into groups of four students each. Instruct the groups to discuss the Brown's dilemma for 10 minutes and try to reach a consensus. When the groups come together, one representative from each group reports the group's conclusions to the class and the reasons for their decision.

8. Discuss the students' feelings about being exposed at every turn to Christmas — in school, in shops, on the radio. Suggest that students write letters to the editor on this subject. Mail the letters!

9. Chanukah, like Purim, is a minor festival in the Jewish calendar. Ask students why they think that Chanukah is the second most celebrated of all of the Jewish holidays (Passover is first). If Chanukah occurred at a different time of year, do you think it would be celebrated as much?

10. Ask students: What, in your opinion, is the real miracle of Chanukah? Was it the oil lasting for eight days or the courage of a small group of people willing to die for what they believed in? Have them explain their answers.

11. Look carefully at the meaning of the three Chanukah blessings. What are they saying and what values do they reflect?

12. Explain that Jewish art traditionally was centered in ritual objects, because no Jewish community ever knew how long they would be welcome where they were presently living. Why then did Jewish art focus upon objects used for celebration of the various holidays? How do we see this idea reflected in Chanukah art?

13. Judah Leib Gordon, a Zionist leader (1830-1892), made an intriguing statement: "Be a Jew in your tent (i.e., home) and a man in the street." He is suggesting that we do our Jewish "thing" at home, but that we function strictly as secular Jews outside of our home/synagogue context. This view raises some interesting questions. Should we hide our Jewish identity or show it proudly when we are not in our homes? Is there a middle path? Believing as he did, do you think Gordon would have placed his *chanukiah* in the front window of his home? Why would any Jew want to put one in his/her front window? Would placing it there require more courage in a small town than in a large city? Why or why not?

14. On some holidays and festivals, our participation symbolically links us to events in the distant past and creates a continuum to the present. Examine the festival of Chanukah as the first fight for religious freedom. Ask students to imagine that they were living when these events took place. Role play the decision of the Hasmoneans to fight against the Syrian Greeks. Then discuss how the fight for religious freedom needs to be waged in our day and age in the face of pressures from the Christian Right or other extremist groups.

15. Working in pairs, A is Hannah and B one of her sons. The son knows that he and his mother and his brother have a choice of death or submission to idolatry. Each shares feelings with the partner and then reverse roles. Come together as a whole group and process the role plays.

16. Divide the class into groups of 3 to 5 each. Each student in turn completes the following sentences, taking one sentence at a time. After each student in the small groups has completed a sentence, the students in that group may briefly react to what other students say before going on to the next sentence. Some suggested sentences:
    a. I am _____.
    b. When the Christmas season arrives, I as a Jew am concerned about _____.
    c. The group can help me with my concern by _____.
    d. I am going to work on my concern by _____.

17. Divide students into pairs. One becomes A and the other B. Each A becomes a Greek soldier enforcing the edicts of Antiochus and each B becomes an obedient, subservient Jew. Each person acts his/her role to the partner. Pairs reverse roles and repeat the process. Each time, before the actual interaction, the students describe themselves to their partner and how they view the situation. After this interaction has been completed, A becomes a Greek soldier and B, Mattathias. They repeat the process and again reverse roles. Then reassemble as a class and discuss how it felt to be the Greek soldier, the subservient Jew, and Mattathias. Which roles did students like? dislike? Examine the meaning of the term "polarity," looking at opposites in life.

18. Put on the play "Triumph of the Weak" (see page 113) for other classes and/or parents.

19. Complete the Instant Lessons *The December Dilemma: Living in Two Civilizations or Trouble in Short Hills* by Steven Bayar, *The Tannenbaum's Tree* by Yosi Gordon, and *The True Story of Hanukkah* by Joel Lurie Grishaver.

20. Do a readers theater of the play "Chanukah Rap" in *Kings and Things: 20 Jewish Plays for Kids 8 to 18* by Meridith Shaw Patera (page 42). Perform the play for Intermediate level students. Encourage those younger students to make up other "raps" about Chanukah.

All-School

1. Have a school-wide Chanukah Happening. Complete instructions for holding such an event follow.

A CHANUKAH HAPPENING

Rationale

While Purim and Pesach both have a large measure of built-in pageantry as well as educational content, Chanukah usually lacks this "pizzazz." Despite the fact that it is both relevant and significant to the contemporary Jew, Chanukah is often stressed as a response to the Christmas season. A comprehensive learning experience that is also highly enjoyable and involves parents can greatly enrich the Chanukah experience.

Overview

A Chanukah Happening is projected as a school-wide celebration of Chanukah that can run from 1-2 1/2 hours in length. It consists of a series of content-oriented and experiential activities that will enable the students in the Hebrew or Religious School program to reinforce and broaden their knowledge of Chanukah and their enjoyment of the festival. Each class will prepare one activity or several variations of one activity, which will serve as one of the activity stations.

One-quarter to one-third of each class will remain in the room to run the activity while the remainder of the students will participate in the other activities. Students in each class will take turns staffing their class activity.

Each student carries a Chanukah Passport on which will be written their name and class. Inside there will be a listing of all of the activities that comprise A Chanukah Happening. Upon complet-

ing an activity, the student's passport will be stamped, or some other indication given that the activity has been completed.

At the end of the Happening, the school can gather for a brief assembly for the lighting of the Chanukah candles, the singing of Chanukah songs, and for the presentation of Chanukah *gelt* to all participants.

There are various ways to award the *gelt*. Either all students are given a bag of *gelt*, or it is given out in various amounts, depending upon the number of successfully completed activities.

Before You Proceed

This program is designed so that it can be implemented with a minimum of preparation. Each activity can be prepared by the teacher or by the class in one hour or less. Planning for this special program, therefore, should not disrupt the regular school curriculum.

Prior to selecting the activity for your class, it is suggested that one or two 30-minute review sessions be held; this will help the students to decide what aspects of Chanukah they wish to emphasize at their activity station.

Planning the Activities

Each student should have an opportunity to take part in at least six activities during the Chanukah Happening. Each activity must, therefore, be brief, lasting no more than 5 to 6 minutes.

There are three basic types of activities: simple written activities which can be easily corrected, making something, and simple experiential activities. The written activities can be duplicated on a single sheet of paper. The student (or parent) completes the activity, brings the completed sheet to a person supervising the activity, and then the passport is stamped in the appropriate place. Other activities include learning a song, learning a dance, making a *dreidel*, etc.

It should be decided ahead of time which grades to include in this program. In some cases, it may be advisable to group Kindergarten to Grades 3 (or 4) together and Grades 4 (or 5) and up in a second group. In other cases, classes may prepare one activity but with various levels of difficulty. For example, a message in code may contain the key to the code for some students, and instructions to older students to figure out the key to the code before decoding the message. Some activities may have to be modified for non-readers.

Parental Involvement
Parents may accompany their children from activity station to activity station, or assist teachers in supervising the stations. In either case, involvement of parents should be encouraged.

A Selection of Activities
It is suggested that teachers look through the activities above before deciding on an activity for their classes. The following possibilities may also be considered:

1. Hebrew Tracing: The students connect the dots in the order of the Hebrew alphabet.

2. Fill in the Blanks: Information about Chanukah is contained in a medium-length paragraph with 5 to 10 words left blank. The students must correct the paragraph by filling in the missing words. For younger students the missing words can be given at the bottom of the paragraph. Older students must complete the paragraph without a list of words.

3. A Rebus: Use a picture/word puzzle to present key terms or ideas about Chanukah.

4. True-False Questions: Good, easy form of review.

5. *Dreidel*: Play a *dreidel* game.

6. A Map Game: Glue a map of Israel onto cardboard and cover it with contact paper or laminate it. Put holes in the map where Modin, Jerusalem, and other key cities are located. The student sticks a pencil or golf tee through the

hole and identifies the place. The name of each location is written on the back of the map for the "judge" to identify.

7. A Chanukah Jigsaw Puzzle: A picture of something related to Chanukah is mounted on cardboard, laminated, and then cut into pieces. The student must put the puzzle together within a specified time.

8. Card Games: Make up a card game with one of the following: matching a value with an event; matching an event with a person connected to that event, etc.

9. Word Search: Place 10 Chanukah words into a word maze. Students must find at least 5 of the words in order to get their Passport stamped.

10. Who Am I?: Five paragraphs are written on a single sheet of paper. Each paragraph contains the description of a different person connected to the celebration of Chanukah. The student's task is to identify the five people who are described on the sheet.

11. Can You Skip?: A series of letters is presented. Students take every second or third letter to form a message. For example:

O B N L P E S V R G A T O N A Z Y M U W I X O D V N = NER TAMID if every third letter is used.

12. Dancing: Learn an Israeli dance or a Chanukah dance.

13. Chanukah Song: After learning a song, record it on tape, then listen to the recording.

14. Chanukah Time Line: Use 5 to 10 cards, each containing one episode in the Chanukah story. Students must arrange the cards in proper chronological order.

15. Make *latkes* or *sufganiyot*.

16. Put on the play "Chanukah — Behind the Scenes" from *Class Acts: Plays & Skits for Jewish Settings* by Stan J. Beiner (page 43).

Family

1. Organize a family education program for two to four-year-olds (there are three already designed Chanukah programs in *Head Start on Holidays: Jewish Programs for Preschoolers and Their Parents* by Roberta Louis Goodman and Andye Honigman Zell).

2. Send home instructions for the following exercise. Working in pairs, parents and children close their eyes and think of a gift they would like to give to their partner. They present their "gifts" to each other, explaining what the gifts are and why that particular gift was chosen. The gifts may be objects, or experiences, which is to say, either tangible or intangible gifts. The family comes together and each person tells what gift was received. Then they discuss how they felt on giving their gifts and on receiving them. Link this experience to Mother's Day, Father's Day, birthdays, Chanukah, and other gift-giving situations.

3. Suggest that families share feelings about being Jewish, particularly during the Christmas season.

4. Have families make a list of 10 reasons why Judaism is special and why it is important to celebrate our holidays and observe our customs.

5. Encourage families to have a Chanukah party at home. Together, they should plan the party, decorate, cook *latkes,* make applesauce, play *dreidel* games, sing Chanukah songs, light the *chanukiah,* etc.

6. Help families plan a festive meal for the celebration of Chanukah. Suggest that they include at least one dish or dessert item that is eaten on Chanukah, such as *latkes* and/or *sufganiyot*.

7. Invite families to participate in A Chanukah Happening (see above under All-School).

THE CASE OF THE MISSING LETTER: A DRAMATIC READING

Robert Goodman

Note: This skit is appropriate for any age group, including senior citizens.

Cast of Characters
Narrator A
Narrator B
Sherlock Cohen
Chief of Police
Mayor
Mrs. Mayor

(Narrators stand on both sides of the stage, Narrator A at stage left and Narrator B at stage right. The actors stand in the middle of the stage.)

Narrator A: This is the story of the most famous detective in the world, Sherlock Cohen of Brooklyn Yards. You must have heard about how he solved the great Matzah Ball Mystery.

Narrator B: Boy was he ever SOUPER on that case . . . he really used his NOODLE!

Narrator A: You must have also heard about how he solved the great Hamantashen Fake-Out, in which an evil gang substituted prunes for poppy seeds in the *hamantashen*.

Narrator B: Sherlock Cohen had no HALF-BAKED ideas on that case!

Narrator A: Now we come to the famous detective's latest challenge: THE CASE OF THE MISSING LETTER.

Narrator B: It is now the first night of Chanukah. Sherlock is sitting in his office. He is relaxing after having lit his *chanukiah* when the phone rings ....

Sherlock: Cohen, here! What can I do for you?

Chief: Sherlock, this is the Chief of Police. I just received an urgent call from the Mayor. This is a hush-hush matter, so I don't want anything leaking to the newspapers. They will make DREIDEL SOUP out of it! Please call the Mayor right away!

Sherlock: Okay, Chief, I'll get on it. *(Dials.)* Hello, Mr. Mayor, Sherlock Coh-en on the pho-en.

Narrator A: The Chief had told Cohen that Chanukah evening had been quiet and peaceful at the Mayor's house. The family had lit the first candle. Then the children opened their gifts and they ate supper.

Narrator B: After dinner, the children went into the living room to play *dreidel* when tragedy struck. It was an absolute disaster! It was awful . . . .

Mayor: Oh, Sherlock Cohen. Thank you for coming right over. This is terrible — I'm so upset! You know how the *dreidel* has four letters on it: the *Hay*, the *Gimel*, the *Shin*, and the *Nun*. Together they make up the sentence "A Great Miracle Happened There." Here, let my children tell you the rest . . .

Child A: After dinner I went into the living room to play with the *dreidel*. I picked up the *dreidel* and was shocked to see that the *NUN* WAS MISSING!

Child B: Don't you see, Mr. Cohen, the *Nun* was kidnapped At first we were so upset that we didn't know what to do. Then Daddy called the Police Chief.

Mrs. Mayor: That's right, and the Chief called you. We are so glad you could SPIN right over. This case had the Chief going IN CIRCLES.

Sherlock: Tell me, children, when was the last time you saw the *Nun*?

Child C: Before supper, I saw the *Nun*. It was there, like it always is. I really don't understand what happened. We like the *Nun*. Especially since it always comes up when our parents spin.

Sherlock: I have a feeling that the *Nun* was sad. In *dreidel* games, you get everything when you spin the *Gimel* and half when you spin the *Hay*. When you spin a *Shin*, you have to put something in, but with the *Nun*, you don't do anything — you don't put in and you don't take out. Maybe the *Nun* felt . . . ignored.

Mrs. Mayor: I think you're right, Sherlock. But I know you will find our MISSING *NUN*.

Narrator A: So Sherlock Cohen rushed back to his home. He went to his closet where he kept all sorts of disguises and found the one that he wanted.

Narrator B: He dressed up as a *Vav*. The costume fit him perfectly. But he did get a stiff neck from holding his head at an odd angle.

Narrator A: Then Sherlock jumped onto his motorcycle and drove to the post office. He lay down on the floor and played dead.

Narrator B: Well, you can imagine what happened. Two postmen found him and put him in the DEAD LETTER OFFICE. Once he was there, he got up and began to look around. Sure enough, he found the *Nun*, who was very much alive.

Sherlock: Oh, *Nun*, I have been searching for you everywhere. How did you get here?

Nun: I was so sad that I ran away. I decided that I wanted *NUN* of that Chanukah jazz.

Sherlock: You ran away? Shame on you! Do you realize how unhappy you made the Mayor and his family?

Nun: They won't even miss me. In fact, they will be glad that I am gone. Why, every time they spin me, you should hear them groan and complain. I tell you, I was so sad I couldn't stand it any longer.

Narrator A: The *Nun* couldn't decide what to do. She had thought of becoming a Rabbi.

Narrator B: Then the *Nun* thought about going to Hollywood to star in a movie like HIGH NUN.

Narrator A: Then she thought about television; she could play the FLYING NUN.

Narrator B: And so on and so forth.

Sherlock: Boy are you a silly *Nun*! The Mayor and his children miss you. If you don't come back, the Mayor's family will have a miserable, sad, and terrible Chanukah.

Nun: You mean they really want me to come back?!

Sherlock: Maybe you don't realize it, but you are the most important letter of all. You stand for NES, and that means "miracle." It is the first word in the expression, *NES GADOL HAYAH SHAM* — A Great MIRACLE Happened There. Without the word *NES*, the saying doesn't make any sense.

Nun: Wow — I feel better already. Please take me home.

Narrator A: So Sherlock Cohen took the *Nun* home. The *Nun* rode on the motorcycle behind Sherlock, who was still dressed as a *Vav*. To the people on the sidewalk, it looked like a fast "NU!" going by.

Narrator B: Everyone in the Mayor's family was very happy. Sherlock was so happy that he fixed his *dreidel* so that it would always land on the *Nun*.

Narrator A: When people ask the Mayor and his family, WHAT'S NU, they have a simple answer:

Narrator B: NUNthing, NUNthing at all!

Narrator A: And there is also a moral to the story:

Narrator B: When it comes to *dreidels*, they can really SPIN a tale!

(Based on "The Letter That Got Lost" by Daniel Owerbach, which originally appeared in *World Over Magazine*, circa 1950.)

THE TRIUMPH OF THE WEAK
Robert Goodman

Cast of Characters
Narrator
Antiochus
Simon
Jonathan
Judah
Inquisitor
Child A
Child B
Father
Adolf Hitler
1st Member of the Underground
2nd Member of the Underground
3rd Member of the Underground
Gamal Abdul Nassar
Soldier B
Moshe Dayan
Anwar Sadat
Menachem Begin

Introduction: Five events are portrayed, two from the distant past and three from the recent past. In each, the enemy of the Jewish people stands to stage left, while the hero and those who aid him stand to stage right. The Narrator stands at center stage.

Scene One: Antiochus and the Maccabees
Narrator: (*Stage center.*) In our long history, the Jewish people has time and time again, fought to survive. Yet, Israel has had a long and a rich history. As we look back to over two thousand years ago, we can ask: what happened to the powerful Syrian-Greek King, Antiochus, who tried so hard to destroy our people?

Antiochus: (*Stage left.*) I, Antiochus Epiphanes, call my armies to fight the Jews: Yes, my people, the Jews shall soon be destroyed.

Simon: (*Stage right.*) Tell me, brother Judah, how can we fight the mighty Syrian army? Antiochus has a large army that is ready to destroy us. What can we do?

Antiochus: I don't understand those strange Jews. They follow their old fashioned religion. They could become Greeks, and could enjoy our "modern" ideas. How can they worship a God they cannot even see when we offer them the mighty idols of Zeus and Apollo?

Jonathan: (*Stage right.*) Antiochus tried to force us to give up Judaism and become Greeks. We did not do so, and we will never give in. We are Jews and we are proud of it. We must defend ourselves against the enemy.

Antiochus: In no time, Judea will be defeated. We will sweep across the country with ease. We will show those Judeans and all of the people in my empire that no one can stand up against Antiochus and live.

Judah: (*Stage right.*) My brothers — Simon and Jonathan — the time for hiding has ended. Torah will become a symbol of our fight for freedom. It is *our* task to lead our people to victory.

Narrator: (*Center stage.*) Judah and his brothers fought bravely. Fighting first in small groups, and then as an army, they defeated the mighty Syrians. Their courage has inspired people in every age.

ALL SING: "Who Can Retell?"

Scene Two: The Inquisition

Narrator: (*Center stage.*) Over one thousand five hundred years passed. During that time, Jews were dispersed throughout the world. Their Temple was destroyed, and they suffered greatly. But many wonderful things also took place. The synagogue became a place of meeting, study, and prayer. Great leaders such as Rashi, Saadia, and Maimonides inspired Arab, Jew, and Christian alike. Then came the Inquisition. During this time, many Jews became homeless. Some became secret Jews, called Marranos.

Inquisitor: (*Stage left.*) I, the Grand Inquisitor of all Spain, declare on this day in 1492, that all Jews in our land must leave immediately or become Christians. They must give up all Jewish practices or be put to death!

Child A: (*Stage right.*) Father, why do we have to become Christians? I like being Jewish. It's important to me to celebrate the Sabbath and our wonderful Jewish holidays.

Inquisitor: Those Jews are blind to the true path to God. We have shown them the way. Many do not see the light. Our patience is ended. Spain shall be rid of the Jews!

Child B: (*Stage right.*) Father, I do not want to give up my religion. Nothing will make me do it. I would rather die!

Inquisitor: All of Spain will be Christian. We shall spy on the Jews to be sure they become Christian. Anyone practicing Judaism in secret shall be put to death.

Father: (*Stage right.*) Children, Judaism must survive. We cannot let our way of life disappear. We must save our traditions for future generations. We must live as secret Jews, even though we face death if we are found out.

ALL SING: *"Bim, Bam, Bim, Bim, Bim, Bam . . . Shabbat, Shalom . . ."*

Scene Three: Hitler and the Jewish Underground

Narrator: (*Center stage.*) Somehow, the Jews managed to survive. Many fled to other countries; many lived as Marranos — secret Jews. In modern times, Jews were celebrating Chanukah again and were allowed to be free. But the suffering was not ended. The worst monster of them all — Adolf Hitler — was preparing to kill six million Jews.

Hitler: (*Stage left.*) I, Adolf Hitler, the Fuhrer of the Third Reich, shall get rid of all the Jews. Soon the world shall be free of all Jews.

1st Member of Underground: (*Stage right.*) Here we are, a small group of people in the forests of Poland, trying to fight the Nazis. Even though we are small and they are powerful, we will fight.

Hitler: The German people will rule the world. No Jews or Gypsies will bother us. We will make an example of the Jews. No one will stand in our way. We are the master race!

2nd Member of Under-ground: *(Stage right.)* How can Hitler do this to us? He destroyed our synagogues, our stores, our homes. Now he kills thousands of our brothers and sisters each day. Is there no way to stop this madman?

Hitler: No one can stop me now! Soon my brilliant plan for wiping out the Jews will be completed. The whole world will see the superiority of the German people.

3rd Member of Under-ground: *(Stage right.)* We must fight. We must stop Hitler and make sure that this never happens again. We cannot give up!

ALL SING: *"Lo Yisa Goy"*

Scene Four: The Six Day War (1967)

Narrator: *(Center stage.)* Israel won the War of Independence of 1948 and the Sinai campaign of 1956. Now, Israel celebrates her nineteenth birthday and again all of the sur-rounding Arab nations try to destroy her. Hopefully, Israel will win this battle, too.

Nassar: *(Stage left.)* Today, the first of June, 1967, I, Gamal Abdul Nassar, swear to you, my Arab brothers, that by the end of this month we will push those Zionist dogs into the sea.

Soldier A: *(Stage right.)* General Dayan, what are we going to do? Nassar has

blocked the Gulf of Aqaba. He cut off our lifeline to the East.

Nassar: Yes, my friends, the blockade was the first step in my brilliant plan to destroy Israel.

Soldier B: *(Stage right.)* But General Dayan, not only the blockade! The Arabs surround us on three sides. Nassar has two hundred thousand troops along the Gaza Strip. Hussein of Jordan has his army ready to attack us from the East, and Syria's army is also ready to strike from the North.

Nassar: The moment of victory is near. Under me, Egypt, Syria, and Jordan will win over Israel.

Dayan: *(Stage right.)* We are small in num-bers, but we are not afraid! Let them come. We will show them, as we did in 1948 and 1956. No Arab army can destroy the Jewish people.

Narrator: *(Center stage.)* It took only six days for the Israeli army to reach the Suez Canal, and to capture the Golan Heights and Jerusalem. But peace still could not be found. This WAR has only planted the seeds for another war to take place in October 1973.

ALL SING: *"Sim, Sim, Sim, Shalom (3) Tovah, Uvrachah . . . La, La, La . . ."*

Scene Five: The Road to Peace

Narrator: *(Center stage.)* In 1967, it took the Israeli army a few days to win. But there was no peace. On Yom Kippur of 1973, the holiest day of the Jewish year, the Egyptians and the

Syrians attacked Israel. Twenty five hundred Israelis died, but Israel won the war. When the fighting was over, Jews hoped for peace. In November 1977, Egypt's President, Anwar Sadat, visited Prime Minister Menahem Begin in Jerusalem, and took the first step toward peace.

Sadat: *(Stage left.)* In 1973, we almost defeated Israel. Yet, even by surprise, we could not win. When the fighting was over, Israel had boxed in more than fifty thousand of our soldiers. We cannot win any war against Israel. We realize that the best road to take is the road to peace.

Begin: *(Stage right.)* When I became Prime Minister in 1977, I looked back at 29 years of war. When we were not fighting a war, we were getting over one, or getting ready for the next one. We were tired of fighting. We prayed for peace. We decided we had to take big steps to move toward peace with Egypt. Our agents discovered that there was a plot to kill President Sadat. We told him and helped save his life. We reached out to Sadat and to the Egyptian people, and then . . .

Sadat: You, my friend, invited me to visit Jerusalem in November 1977. I accepted, and started the process that led to our treaty of *Shalom*, signed in Washington on March 26, 1979. By visiting Jerusalem, I made many Arab people angry. Peace brings many benefits to my people and to my country. I am pleased. I hope that other Arabs will follow my example.

Begin: For my people, the struggle has also been hard. But we have taken the giant step and we, too, are happy that we did so. Today, Egyptians can visit *Eretz Yisrael* and Jews can see your beautiful country. Let us hope and pray that our neighbors will join us and walk down the path to a deep and lasting peace in the Middle East.

Narrator: *(Center stage.)* Unfortunately, the world is filled with people who put personal gain ahead of the interests of their country. Hopefully, the efforts of Prime Minister Begin and President Anwar Sadat will continue to inspire the desire for peace in the Middle East, and will serve as an example to all who want to live in peace.

ALL SING: *"Hineh Mah Tov u'Mah Nayim Shevet Achim Gam Yachad"*

Narrator: Several decades after the monumental events at Camp David, peace is closer, but still somewhat elusive. A "cool" peace has remained with Egypt. A "warm" peace was established with King Hussein of Jordan. Giant steps toward peace with the Palestinians were also taken, but it could be many years before Arabs and Jews truly learn to live together in peace. It is our hope as Jews that "Nation will not lift up sword against nation; neither will they learn war any more."

BIBLIOGRAPHY

See pages 270-277.

CHAPTER SEVEN

TU B'SHEVAT

VOCABULARY

Aytz/Aytzim: "Tree(s)."

Aytz Chayim: "Tree of Life." The Torah is described in the ritual for the reading of the Torah as "a tree of life to them that hold fast to it." Just as a tree is a source of life and sustenance, likewise the Torah is the source of spiritual life for the Jew.

Bokser: See *Charuv*.

Chamishah Asar B'Shevat: See Tu B'Shevat.

Charuv: "Carob." The fruit of the carob tree may have obtained its name because in both sound and shape it is similar to the Hebrew word *cherev*, meaning "sword." The carob is a food of lowly fare, and accordingly symbolizes humility. The carob fruit is also called "St. John's Bread" because it is connected with the life of John the Baptist. In Yiddish it is called *bokser*, a corruption of the Yiddish *"boihshorn"* meaning "ram's horn" — the long, curved shape of the carob being reminiscent of the *shofar*. Historically, the value of the *bokser* was appreciated as early as the Roman siege of Jerusalem (66-70 C.E.). Because food was scarce, fruit from the carob tree, which did not spoil, was a welcome addition to meager food supplies of the Jews.

Jewish National Fund: See Keren Kayemet L'Yisrael.

Keren Kayemet L'Yisrael: "Jewish National Fund." Founded in 1901 at the Fifth Zionist Congress as the embodiment of a lifelong dream of Hermann Schapira, the J.N.F. was established to acquire and develop land in *Eretz Yisrael* for Jewish settlement. Since then it has played a key role in changing Israel from a desert wasteland into a home for some five million Jews and a place where agricultural experts from all over the world come to learn new and modern farming techniques. In one century, the J.N.F. has planted more than 150 million eucalyptus, cedar, tamarisk, carob, pine, and other trees, changing over 265 square miles of what was once swamp or desert, into arable land. While trees for Israel may be purchased throughout the year, Tu B'Shevat has customarily been the time when trees are sold through the schools. For this reason, there is a special bond between Tu B'Shevat, the Jewish National Fund, and Jewish school children.

Neti'ah Shel Simchah: "Joyous Planting," also known as "Marriage Trees." There is a custom that on joyous occasions, trees would be planted as a part of the celebration. When a boy was born, a cedar was planted and, when a girl was born, a cyprus was planted. Wood from these trees would later be used to fashion the poles for their *chupah*.

Neti'at Aytzim: "Planting of Trees." It is customary to purchase trees through the Jewish National Fund. Individual trees, groves, even forests may be purchased for planting in Israel. Individuals may purchase trees or a class may pool resources to buy one or more trees. When students or tourists visit Israel, it is customary to include a visit to a J.N.F. forest where one may plant trees with their own hands.

Orlah: "Uncircumcized Tree." It is forbidden to eat from a tree that is *orlah*. "When you enter the land and plant any tree for food, you shall regard its fruit as forbidden (literally uncircumcized). Three years it shall be forbidden for you, not to be eaten. In the fourth year, all its fruit shall be set aside for jubilation before *Adonai*; and only in the fifth year may you use its fruit — that its yield to you may be increased" (Leviticus 19:23-25).

Pri Aytz Hadar: The title of a booklet which is read on the eve of Tu B'Shevat containing selections from the Torah, Mishnah, Gemarah, and *Zohar*. This is also the Hebrew designation for an *etrog*. (See Sukkot Vocabulary.)

Rosh HaShanah L'Ilanot: "New Year for Trees." Tu B'Shevat is the agricultural New Year, hence this name.

Seder Layl Tu B'Shevat: The custom of creating a *Seder* for Tu B'Shevat has been recreated in recent years and patterned after a practice in Safed. Similar to the Pesach *Seder*, it includes the drinking of four cups of wine — usually of different types and colors, and with creative interpretations given each. Songs, blessings, the eating of fruit (dried, fresh, and canned), and the sharing of readings about ecological concerns are typical aspects of this *Seder*. Since there is no fixed ritual for Tu B'Shevat, many different forms of ceremony have been developed — some for use by an adult congregation, some for the home, and still others for a school-wide celebration.

Shakayd: "Almond." The Hebrew word comes from the root meaning "watch" or "wake," for the almond tree is the first to awaken from the winter slumber and thus is the hearald of spring. By the 15th of Shevat, the almond trees in Israel are in full bloom.

Shevat: The eleventh month of the calendar, *Shevat* (January/February) has 30 days. Its zodiac sign is Aquarius. The fifteenth of the month is the New Year of the Trees, Tu B'Shevat.

St. John's Bread: See *Charuv*.

Tapuach: "Apple." The apple symbolizes the splendor of nature and of spring love as in Song of Songs 23: "Like an apple tree among the trees of the forest, so is my beloved among the youths. I delight to sit in his shade and his fruit is sweet to my mouth."

T'aynah: "Fig." The fig is a symbol of peace as is understood from the Prophet Micah (4:3-4): "And they shall beat their swords into plowshares and their spears into pruning hooks. Nation shall not take up sword against nation. They shall never again know war. But every man shall sit under his grapevine or fig tree with no one to disturb him."

Tikkun Layl Tu B'Shevat: "Preparation for the Night of Tu B'Shevat." It consists of a special party or gathering in the synagogue or in the *Yeshivah* on the eve of Tu B'Shevat. During this all-night gathering, portions from the Torah, Mishnah, Gemarah, and *Zohar* are read which make reference to the agricultural life of *Eretz Yisrael*. These selections were collected in a small book entitled *Pri Aytz Hadar*, meaning "Goodly Fruit." In Baghdad, among other places in the Oriental world, wealthy Jews would hold feasts during which they would eat more than fifty different kinds of fruits as guests took turns reading from *Pri Aytz Hadar*.

Tu B'Shevat "Fifteenth Day of Shevat." Tu B'Shevat is an abbreviation for "*Chamishah Asar B'Shevat*." Hebrew letters have numerical equivalents. *Tet* is 9 and *Vav* is 6, the combination of the letters adds up to 15. These two letters together can be read as the word "Tu." *Chamishah Asar* is the Hebrew phrase for the number fifteen.

BACKGROUND

In the Bible

While there is no reference to Tu B'Shevat in the Bible, there are a number of biblical selections which have been linked to Tu B'Shevat because of their affinity with what Tu B'Shevat has become. They include the following:

Genesis 1:11-13: "And God said, 'Let the earth sprout vegetation: seed bearing plants, fruit trees of every kind on earth that bear fruit with seed in it.' And it was so. The earth brought forth vegetation: seed bearing plants of every kind, and trees of every kind bearing fruit with the seed in it. And God saw how good this was."

Leviticus 19:23-25: "When you enter the land and plant any tree for food, you shall regard its fruit as uncircumcised (forbidden). Three years it shall be forbidden for you, not to be eaten. In the fourth year all its fruit shall be set aside for jubilation before the Eternal: and only in the fifth year may you use its fruit — that its yield to you may be increased."

Leviticus 26:3-18: "If you follow My laws and faithfully observe My commandments, I will grant your rains in their season, so that the earth shall yield its produce and the trees of the field their fruit."

Deuteronomy 8:7-8: "For the Eternal your God is bringing you into a good land with streams and springs and lakes issuing from plain and hill; a land of wheat and barley, of vines, figs, and pomegranates, a land of olive oil and honey."

Psalm 1:3 speaks of one who has not walked in the counsel of the wicked: "And he shall be like a tree planted by streams of water, that brings forth its fruit in its season, and whose leaf does not wither; and in whatsoever he does, he shall prosper."

Psalm 65:10-12 tells of God's wondrous works which are seen in the splendor of the Land of Israel: "You have remembered the earth, and watered her, greatly enriching her, with the river of God that is full of water . . . . You crown the year with Your goodness and Your paths drop fatness."

Psalm 92:13-16 describes God's blessings in terms of mighty trees: "The righteous shall flourish like the palm tree; they shall grow like a cedar in Lebanon. Planted in the house of the Eternal, they shall flourish in the courts of God. They shall still bring forth fruit in old age; they shall be full of sap and richness; to declare that the Eternal is upright . . . ."

It is believed that Tu B'Shevat may originally have been a folk festival which marked the emergence of spring. At this time of the year, the priests levied the tithes on the fruit trees. The tithes were then sent to the Temple in Jerusalem.

With the destruction of the Second Temple in 70 C.E. and with the dispersion of Jews throughout the Roman Empire, *Eretz Yisrael* (the Land) became almost devoid of *Am Israel* (the Jewish people). Yet, there has been a continuous Jewish bond with *Eretz Yisrael*. Eating the various fruits and nuts which were found in Israel helped to solidify this bond.

Now that the Jewish people once again has a thriving nation in *Eretz Yisrael*, Tu B'Shevat has a renewed significance. Linked to the magnificent accomplishments of the Jewish National Fund, the New Year of the Trees has come to signify the rebirth of the Land and serves as a symbol of hope for the rebirth and renewed strength of peoples everywhere.

Four New Years

The Mishnah makes reference to four different New Years. *Rosh HaShanah* 1:1 states: ". . . the first of Nisan (March/April) is the New Year for kings and festivals; the first of Elul (August/September) is the New Year for the tithing of cattle. Rabbis Elazer and Shimon say that it falls on the first of Tishre. The first of Tishre (September/October) is the New Year for the reckoning of the religious year, of the Sabbatical years (every seven years), and of Jubilee years (every 50 years), as well as the New Year for the planting of trees and vegetables. The first of Shevat (January/February) is the New Year for the (fruit) trees according to the House of Shammai, while the House of Hillel says that it falls on the 15th of Shevat."

The first of Nisan can be considered to be the legal New Year. This was the date around which the reign of Israelite kings was calculated. The dates of each of the festivals of the Jewish year are calculated from the first day of Nisan. Accordingly, Pesach, which occurs on the 15th of Nisan, is the first festival of the year, while Rosh HaShanah takes place on the first day of the seventh month of Tishre — in the exact middle of the year.

The first of Elul is the New Year for tithing. When the Mishnah speaks of cattle, it actually refers to all animals that are counted as part of the tithe. Any animal born before Elul 1st was counted as part of the tithe for that year.

The first of Tishre, the biblical Day of Memorial, became Rosh HaShanah — the beginning of the religious year.

The 15th of Shevat marks the beginning of the fruit crop in Israel. It is the New Year for the fruit trees. This same Mishnah cites two conflicting dates for the New Year of the Trees. The House of Shammai favored Shevat 1st, because Shammai was the spokesperson for the conservative, upper-class Jews who, being able to afford to take good care of their land and their trees, could probably have trees ready to welcome spring early. The House of Hillel, on the other hand, favored Shevat 15th. More liberal and clearly more attuned to the needs of the struggling masses, Hillel believed that the trees belonging to the working class needed those extra 15 days in order to recuperate from the previous year's winter. *Halachah is* according to Hillel.

The Meaning of Tu B'Shevat

The holiday of Tu B'Shevat can be seen on three levels:

1. Historically, it recalls the siege of Jerusalem in the years 66-70 C.E. During the siege, the carob provided sustenance to Jewish fighters who were otherwise able to store only meager quantities of rations.
2. Agriculturally, it is a reminder of the ancient practice of tithing the fruits and is a tangible sign of the physical bond that the people of Israel has with with *Eretz Yisrael.*
3. Religiously or spiritually, the holiday and the trees that are planted serve as a symbol of life and rebirth. The tree weathers all storms yet clings to the soil and tenaciously holds onto life. Similarly, the Jewish people has continued to endure and survive in the face of adversity. Accordingly, trees can be seen as symbolic of the 2000 years of Jewish suffering.

The act of planting a tree represents an investment in the future. When a person plants a tree, he or she declares his belief that there will be a future for children, and that they will reap the fruit of this generation's labor. The famous story from Rabbinic literature about the interaction between the old man and the Roman Emperor is illustrative. This brief story can be presented first as a dramatic reading and then discussed:

THE OLD MAN AND THE EMPEROR

Emperor: What are you doing old man? Why are you planting that tree? You will never live to enjoy the fruits of your labors.

Old Man: I am planting a carob tree.

Emperor: How long will it take before it bears fruit?

Old Man: About ten years.

Emperor: Surely you do not expect to live long enough to enjoy the fruits of this carob tree!

Old Man: When I came here, I found trees planted by those who lived before me. I am simply planting as they did, so that those who come after me will enjoy the fruit of this tree. And thus the chain will not be broken.

Central Themes

• Tu B'Shevat also came to be seen as the Day of judgment for the trees. On this day, it was believed, God decided which trees would flourish and bear fruit, and which would wither and die. This reflects the belief that God is over all creation and exercises direct control over all living things, including humankind, animals, and plants.

• Tu B'Shevat and Ecology: An awareness of the need to preserve the earth and its natural resources has become a priority only in recent decades. For more than 2000 years, it was believed that human beings were not only the final stage of creation, but were created with the express purpose of having dominion over the rest of the earth. Genesis 1:28 states: "Be fertile and increase, fill the earth and master it; rule the fish of the sea, the birds of the sky, and all the living things that creep on the earth." That became the excuse for unbridled use and subsequent depletion of natural resources. With the development of the ecology movement since the 1960s, Jews also find teachings that stress the need to preserve resources. *Bal Tashchit* (do not destroy) became the slogan of the Jewish ecology movement (Deuteronomy 20:19). This passage commanded that even during the heat of battle, one was not permitted to cut down fruit-bearing trees in order to construct battering rams or siege-works. This passage serves as a counterbalance to an otherwise assumed permission to use up the earth's resources at will and for any purpose.

• The principle of *Bal Tashchit* was expanded upon in the Talmud. Gunther Plaut, in his commentary to *The Torah* (p. 1479), states: "They [the Rabbis] ruled that the law against cutting down a fruit tree, by extension, also forbade drawing off its sap for the sake of its destruction, and thus defoliation of such trees would be considered contrary to the spirit of the law. When a tree is cut down, it is as if its pain resounds throughout the world."

• Recognizing the importance of caring for the land, Hermann Schapira, a German mathematician, created the "blue box." These *pushkes* found their way into countless Jewish homes and the coins collected in them went toward the purchase of land and trees in Israel. Out of his idea grew the Jewish National Fund. In the past 100 years, the J.N.F. has planted countless millions of trees throughout Israel in addition to buying enormous tracts of land which it leased to *Kibbutzim* and *Moshavim*. Thanks to its efforts, previously uninhabitable areas in *Eretz Yisrael* were transformed into lush farmland and home sites for thousands of Israelis. It is no accident that a key focus of Tu B'Shevat is the sale of trees through the J.N.F.

• There is a tradition that, at the birth of a girl, a cypress tree is planted, and at the birth of a boy, a cedar tree is planted. When a couple is married, they stand under a *chupah* made of wood from the trees planted at their birth (*Gittin* 57a).

• We learn the following in a *midrash*: "The Holy One led Adam through the Garden of Eden and said, 'I created all My beautiful and glorious works for your sake. Take heed not to corrupt and destroy My world. For if you destroy it, there is no one to make it right after you'" (*Ecclesiastes Rabbah* 7:13).

• Trees and the Messiah: In a *Midrashic* collection, *Avot D'Rabbi Natan*, we read: "Rabbi Yochanan ben Zakkai was accustomed to say: 'If you were planting a seedling and you were told that the

Messiah has come, first plant the seedling and then go and greet him.'"

- A blessing for a Tree: Once, a woman was traveling in the desert. She was hungry, tired, and thirsty when she came upon a tree. She rested under its shade, ate of its fruit, and drank of the spring water that flowed beside it. As she was about to continue her journey, she said, "Tree, how shall I bless you? Shall I say, 'May your shade be pleasant?' It is already so. Shall I say, 'May your fruit be sweet?' It is sweet already. Shall I say, 'May a stream of water flow next to your branches?' A stream of water already flows beside you. Therefore I say, 'May it be God's will that all of the shoots taken from you shall be just like you'" (*Ta'anit* 5b-6a)

- The Theme of Renewal: Tu B'Shevat serves as a reminder that the cycle of life and nature is an ongoing process. Israel's winters are relatively mild, but they are nevertheless very cold at times. Toward the end of the month of Shevat, we see the first sign of spring: the blossoming of the almond tree (*shakayd*). Little by little, other signs of spring soon appear. During the month of Adar, which follows Shevat, the green of spring appears in abundance. Winter is past.

- Noah's task was not merely to sustain the various animal species, but to ensure their survival as well. He was to work on behalf of nature in the same way that one tries to preserve one's own well-being. Genesis 7:3 states: " . . . to keep seed alive upon all the earth," suggesting that Noah was also to preserve various species of plants and trees.

Why Trees?
There are many practical reasons why trees are planted and, in particular, why trees have been so important to the growth and development of *Eretz Yisrael*. Some of these reasons are as following:
1. Trees serve as windbreakers to halt the spread of desert sands.
2. Trees help to drain swamps, such as in the Hulah Valley in the Galilee.
3. Trees help to bring productivity to the soil.
4. Trees help to prevent erosion.
5. Trees provide wood for construction.
6. Trees provide fruit for eating.
7. Trees provide shade.
8. Trees help to improve the climate of the country.
9. Trees provide a haven for nesting birds.

Celebrating Tu B'Shevat
Different places in Israel experience great variations in the length and severity of winter. Tel Aviv may occasionally get as cold as 40 degrees Fahrenheit on a winter morning. In Jerusalem, winters are also relatively mild, occasionally reaching into the low 30s. Yet, once every few years, a bit of snow falls. Regardless of the climate of the various places in which Jews reside throughout the world, Jewish holidays are celebrated with respect to the climate of Israel. Consequently, while it may still be bitter cold and snowing in Canada, Northern Europe, and the upper United States, spring officially begins for us when the almond trees blossom in Israel around mid-January. By the 15th day of the month of Shevat, then, which occurs between mid-January and mid-February, Jews celebrate the New Year of the Trees. Tu B'Shevat is regarded as a minor festival or a semi-holiday for liturgical purposes. No penitential prayers are recited on Tu B'Shevat, nor is fasting permitted.

In addition to eating carob and planting trees on Tu B'Shevat, there are other customs and practices associated with this festival. Among Ashkenazic Jews, particularly those in Europe, Tu B'Shevat was an occasion for eating 15 different kinds of fruit, with preference given to those varieties which can be found in *Eretz Yisrael*. Psalms 104 and 120-134, the Psalms of Ascension, and special liturgical poems were read.

Among Sephardic Jews, there are a series of special customs as well as a distinctive terminology which draws heavily upon the Ladino language — a blend of Spanish and Hebrew. Tu B'Shevat is called "*Frutas*," meaning Festival of Fruits. It is also known as "*Rosasana del Arbores*," or Rosh

HaShanah of the Trees. Special poems called *"complas"* are sung. Children are given small bags filled with nuts. These have their names embroidered on them and are worn as festive pendants around their necks.

Among some Sephardic Jews, a *"Tikkun Layl Tu B'Shevat"* takes place. This consists of a special party or gathering in the synagogue on the eve of Tu B'Shevat. During the all-night gathering, a special booklet known as *Pri Aytz Hadar* is read.

In recent years, the Tu B'Shevat *Seder* has become very popular. Modeled after the Pesach *Seder*, it consists of a creative ritual that is geared to Tu B'Shevat.

In Israel, it is customary for school children to visit a nearby Jewish National Fund Forest and plant trees there. In recent years, the J.N.F. established the Children's Forest in the Galilee, which honors Israeli children and Diaspora children and hallows the memory of more than 1,000,000 children who died in the Holocaust.

SCOPE AND SEQUENCE

Grade	Themes/Ideas
Kindergarten	The miracle of planting, and the growth that follows. This is the New Year of the Trees, when trees bloom again.
Grade One	Planting and growth as an act of partnership between people and God; special Tu B'Shevat fruits: almond, carob, fig, etc.
Grade Two	Tu B'Shevat stories: "The Old Man and the Emperor," etc.
Grade Three	Why are trees important to us? Why do we have a new year for the trees?
Grade Four	Tu B'Shevat terminology — key terms and phrases.
Grade Five	What is the special relationship between the Jewish National Fund and Tu B'Shevat? Why is the J.N.F. so important to Israel?
Grade Six	Tu B'Shevat as one of four different Jewish New Years.
Grade Seven	Tu B'Shevat in the Bible and in Rabbinic literature.
Grade Eight	The origin and development of Tu B'Shevat as a minor festival in the Jewish calendar.
Grade Nine	Preparing and then leading a *Seder* for Tu B'Shevat for part or all of the school.
Grade Ten	The meaning of Tu B'Shevat; underlying themes; Tu B'Shevat and its relation to ecological concerns.
Grade Eleven	Special Tu B'Shevat customs among Ashkenazic and Sephardic Jews.
Grade Twelve	Summary and recapitulation. Symbolism inherent in Tu B'Shevat, including the ideas of rebirth and fertility.

ACTIVITIES

Preschool/Kindergarten

1. Compare the taste and smell of different fruits and nuts. Children can rate their enjoyment of each by using a smiley-face chart. (NSM)

2. Place fruit segments into small, opaque boxes (do not use 35mm film canisters; they have a chemical residue children shouldn't inhale). Have children match the smell with actual fruit. (NSM)

3. Take a field trip to visit a carpenter who can talk with children about different kinds of wood and what he/she does with each to make objects. (NSM)

4. In an art center, provide a variety of wood items for use in creating a project. (NSM)

5. Make a greenhouse. Line aluminum foil broiler trays with 3 to 4 thicknesses of wet paper toweling. Push the towels down into the contours of the tray. Lay seeds taken from various fruits and vegetables in the "furrows." Cover the tray with plastic food wrap and tape shut. (Try grape seeds; they grow well.) (NSM)

6. Make a terrarium. Take the label off a clear plastic soda bottle. Cut the bottom off the bottle (you want to leave a lower container 2"-3" high). Fill the lower container with small stones and dirt. Plant small seedlings, then add water. Place the top part of the bottle back over the bottom. Be sure the cap is screwed on. Open the bottle and mist, if needed. (NSM)

7. Make a list of the things we get from trees. (NSM)

8. Visit a grocery store and buy only things which grow on trees. (NSM)

9. Invite grandparents to class. (Ask those children whose grandparents do not live in the community to "adopt" another elderly adult for the session.) Read to the group *Pearl Plants a Tree* by Jane Breskin Zalben. Pearl is inspired by a tree planted by her grandfather to plant her own. Together with her grandfather, she plants a tree in the yard, imagining the day when she will show it to her grandchildren. Talk about the story with the group, then have a tree planting ceremony. Make a plaque for the tree, telling who planted it and on what date. (AFM)

10. Add different wood toys to your toy area. (NSM)

11. Put away any puzzles that are made of plastic. Use just wooden and cardboard puzzles.

Discuss the attributes and connection to Tu B'Shevat. (NSM)

12. Have students sand wood smooth. (For easier handling, glue sandpaper to wooden blocks.) (NSM)

13. Fill a "feelie bag" with fruit and nuts. See what students can identify by touch. (You might have two of each fruit — one in the bag and one displayed on a table — so that students can make visual comparisons as they are reaching into the bag.) (NSM)

14. Buy two or three of several varieties of oranges and apples. Have students examine them for comparison and sort the fruit. How are they the same? How different? (NSM)

15. Cover baby food containers with opaque Contact paper. Fill the containers so that pairs have the same kind and quantity of nuts inside. Have students shake the containers and try to find the matching sounds. They can check their matches by opening the containers or looking at a self-checking mark on the bottom. (NSM)

16. Compare pictures of trees at different seasons. You might cut seasonal trees from travel magazines, glue them on paper, and have students sort them into winter, spring, summer, and fall. (A parent can help with this activity.) (NSM)

17. Compare fruits using rulers, scales, etc. Use a balance scale for students to see how many nuts will balance out one piece of fruit. (NSM)

18. Arrange fruit from smallest to largest. (NSM)

19. Have students open oranges and count the number of sections. Are there the same number of sections in each orange? (NSM)

20. Place celery in a glass with food coloring and watch to see how trees drink water. (NSM)

21. Make snacks in the spirit of Tu B'Shevat: trees (broccoli) and dip, ants (raisins) on a log (peanut butter in celery), sticks (pretzels), nuts and raisins, any fruit, or a birthday cake for the trees. (NSM)

22. Glue sawdust or wood chips onto construction paper in a free-form design. (NSM)

23. Make a handprint tree. (NSM)

24. Plan a class birthday party for the trees. What would be appropriate activities? What food might be served? (NSM)

25. Pantomime growing as a tree. (NSM)

26. Have each student adopt a tree otuside your school. Have them sketch it, make a bird feeder for its branches, water it, etc. Observe the tree by lying under it, from a window, from the side, etc. (NSM)

27. Help children complete pages 27 and 28 in *Jewish Preschool/Kindergarten Copy Pak*™ by Nancy Cohen Nowak.

28. Do one or two of the Tu B'Shevat art projects described in *100+ Jewish Art Projects for Children* by Nina Streisand Sher and Margaret A. Feldman (pages 28 and 29).

29. Do the movement activity on page 45 of *Creative Movement for a Song* by JoAnne Tucker. This is based on "The Planting Song" from the album *Growin'*, Volume II by Kol B'seder.

30. Do some of the Tu B'Shevat activites on pages 80-83 of *The Jewish Preschool Teachers Handbook* by Sandy Furfine Wolf and Nancy Cohen Nowak.

Primary

1. Assign each student the name of a tree. (Several students will be assigned the same tree.) A student or the teacher improvises a narrative about planting trees in Israel or about a visit to Israel. When a particular tree is mentioned in the story, those students who are assigned that tree stand up, say the name of their tree in Hebrew or English, and then sit down.

2. Place a large number of peanuts, dried beans, or seeds in a bowl or a jar. The student who guesses the correct number or who is closest to the right number is the winner.

3. Force a branch of a tree to leaf. On a tree, find a live branch that is well covered with buds. Cut it off. Crush 2" to 3" at the cut end with a hammer. Soak the entire branch overnight in warm (not hot) water. Remove the branch from water. Set just the crushed end in a jar or can of warm water, then cover it entirely with a sheet of plastic and keep it in a dark place. Mist daily. When the buds begin to open, bring the branch into the light. (NSM)

4. Provide small groups of children with travel brochures and postcards of Israel. Ask them to find the ones with trees. Have children see what can they learn about Israel and the importance of trees by studying the pictures. (NSM)

5. Compare dried fruit with their fresh counterparts. (NSM)

6. Make bark or leaf rubbings. Students can go into a wooded area near the school to do this. See if other students can find a tree which matches individual rubbings. (NSM)

7. Create pictures using seeds and/or nuts. (NSM)

8. Make food for the birds. Roll a pine cone in peanut butter and bird seed. Hang the bird feeder in a tree. (NSM)

9. Fill a cigar box with dirt. Paste or draw an Israeli scene on the inside lid. Stick twigs in the dirt for the foreground. Add a toothpick bridge. Sprinkle with grass seed and moisten the dirt, or plant flower seeds and watch it grow.

10. Scoop out the inside of a large potato. Leave plenty of potato on the side and on the bottom. Pin buttons on the two front sides for eyes and push wood matches or toothpicks into the bottom for feet. Place wet cotton inside the potato and put either mustard seed or grass seed on it. Water every day, and soon Mr. Potato will be growing.

11. Collect pictures of trees, farming implements, fruit, planting time, farm buildings, animals, and anything else that might be linked to nature or farm life in Israel. Have each student make a Tu B'Shevat scrapbook.

12. Make terrariums in class. Cover the bottom of widemouthed mayonnaise or peanut butter jars with 1" of sand. Pat down. Then sprinkle in 2" of potting soil and yard dirt mixed. Insert plants into holes made with fingertips. Gently pat soil around roots. Use colorful stones to create a pattern inside the jar. Spray plants with water from a spray bottle, then secure a piece of plastic wrap over the top of the jar with a string or a rubber band. Plants will create their own moisture and will not need watering for about three months. The finished products make wonderful classroom displays and gifts.

13. Read to the class *A Prayer for the Earth: The Story of Naamah, Noah's Wife* by Sandy Eisenberg Sasso. Before the flood, Naamah was asked to save a sample of each plant on earth. Afterward, the plants must be returned to the earth. Discuss with the children what they can do to care for the earth. As a class, carry out some of their ideas.

14. Bring in (or have students bring in) various fruits to taste, especially those mentioned in the Bible — figs, pomegranates, dates, grapes, etc.

15. Each student takes a paper bag and draws or paints a tree on it. Have each student select a tree that is somehow in keeping with that student's character or personality. After making their tree masks, students go around the room, introducing themselves to each other, saying something like: "I am Chaim, an oak tree, because I feel that I am big and strong." Follow these introductions with a discussion about the importance of trees in our lives. Teach the children the names of their trees in Hebrew.

16. Using a number of different crayons, students cover an entire sheet of plain white or light-colored paper. Then they cover this multi-colored sheet with a black crayon until the sheet is entirely black. At this point, they take a sharp object such as a stick pen, knife, nail file, or scissors, and draw a still life Tu B'Shevat picture. The black crayon will come off and the bright colors will sparkle through with a lovely picture.

17. Plant parsley to harvest at Pesach. Note: Parsley takes a very long time to germinate. You might add an herb such as basil to the seed mixture so that something comes up a bit earlier. Use the following technique to encourage faster parsley seed growth: Place parsley seeds in a saucer or low-sided dish. Cover with warm water and let it sit overnight. Then, put the saucer in the freezer until the water is frozen solid. Remove the saucer and allow the ice to thaw. Plant immediately into pots. (NSM)

18. Ask each student to bring for "show and tell" something that is either grown or manufactured in Israel. The items can include clothing, books, religious articles, foods, etc. Try to encourage

the students to find something that is grown in Israel, such as *bokser*, a Jaffa orange, pomegranate, or pomelo.

19. Create a list of why trees are important. (NSM)

20. Transplant seedlings in class. Take care of them until you can plant the tree(s) outside. (NSM)

21. Have children work at an art center, making paper chains of green and brown strips that are long enough to wear around the shoulders. Then have them choose what kind of tree they want to be, and also the proper color of the blossom or fruit of their tree. Staple to the chain a number of colored paper circles to represent the fruit or blossoms. Children attend the tree planting ceremony dressed as trees and present a little poem or thought. (EB)

22. Make a class tree puzzle. You will need: very large pieces of butcher paper, scissors, pencil, felt pens, glue, crayons, and/or paint. Decide how large a space your finished project will fit (perhaps a door, bulletin board, or classroom wall). If necessary, glue pieces of butcher paper together to make it wider. Using a black felt pen, the teacher should draw a large tree with many branches (no leaves). Make it interesting, with a gnarled trunk and twisted branches. Write "Tu Bishevat" in double outline letters, and the Hebrew year. Now you are ready to make the pieces. With a pencil, outline in jigsaw puzzle style, enough pieces for the number of students in the class (no limit). Give each child one piece (it is better if students do not see the tree as a whole before they begin). Let each decorate his/her piece, using imagination and any desired media. To complete the project, have the children fit their pieces together as they hang up the tree. (JM)

23. Make mobiles from plastic lids. You will need: a variety of plastic can lids from products of various sizes, seed envelope covers, flower and fruit clippings. Cut fruit and flowers from paper and glue to lids or, using felt markers, have students paint their own fruit and flowers. Decorate both sides. Punch a hole in the top and bottom of each lid with a nail. Tie lids one to the other with string and attach to a cord stretched across the room. (JB)

24. Make a sponge garden. Soak a natural sponge in water. Squeeze most of the water out and center it in a bowl. Sprinkle with grass seeds or other seeds. Keep moist and in a few days you will have your crop. Or, fill a pot to within 1/2" with soil. Plant apple, orange, pear, and grapefruit seeds in the same pot. Keep the soil damp. When plants appear, move the pot to a sunny place. Water each day. (JB)

25. Do the movement activity on page 45 of *Creative Movement for a Song* by JoAnne Tucker. This is based on "The Planting Song" from the album *Growin'*, Volume II, by Kol B'seder.

26. Do one or two Tu B'Shevat art projects described in *100+ Jewish Art Projects for Children* by Nina Streisand Sher and Margaret A. Feldman (pages 32 and 33).

27. Complete pages 13 and 14 in *Jewish Holiday Copy Pak™ K-3* by Marji Gold-Vukson.

Intermediate

1. Research the implications of the vast destruction of the trees of the rainforests. What action might students take to preserve these forests? (NSM)

2. Pass out the following paragraph which contains five errors. The student's task is to locate the mistakes, cross them out, and write in the correct information above each error. If done orally as a team competition, the first team to spot a mistake gets a point, and then gets two points for supplying the correct information. If the first team does not have the correct infor-

mation, the second team is given an opportunity to supply it and score two points.

Tu B'Shevat is one of four New Years. It occurs on the 15th of the month of Elul. It is also called Rosh Chodesh L'Ilanot. On Tu B'Shevat, we eat *bokser* fruit which is called *cherev* in Hebrew. In Israel, even though Tu B'Shevat occurs in either January or February, it marks the first signs of summer. Tu B'Shevat helps Jews to feel close to the land of Israel by helping Jews to remember many of the things that grow in *Eretz Yisrael*. This feeling of closeness is strengthened by buying trees from the Jewish Federation.

(Corrections: Shevat for Elul; HaShanah for Chodesh; *charuv* for *cherev*; spring for summer, and Jewish National Fund for Jewish Federation.)

3. Have students make up limericks about trees, both humorous and serious. Be sure to add these to their poetry books.

4. Give students ten minutes to see how many words they can make from the term "Tu B'Shevat." Scoring is as follows: 3 letter word = 1 point, 4 letters = 2 points, 5 letters = 4 points, 6 letters = 7 points, 7 letters = 10 points.

5. Give each student three pieces of paper. On each piece of paper, the student writes one question to be asked to the rest of the class. Collect the questions use them for a class quiz game or written quiz.

6. Ask students to reorder the words in the correct order in the following quotations about nature and trees:
   a. planted as shall river the waters tree be it by a of, forth season that fruit brings its its in = "it shall be as a tree planted by the river of waters, that brings forth its fruit in its season."

   b. represents courage tree beauty strength the and cedar palm the = "The cedar represents strength and courage, the palm tree beauty."

7. Have students make up Tu B'Shevat riddles. Here are a few for starters:
   a. Why is Chamishah Asar B'Shevat sometimes dangerous? (Because it is also called "To be shot")
   b. Why does the carob put you in a fighting mood? (Because it's called a "bokser")
   c. Why do dogs get confused on Tu B'Shevat? (Because they are always barking up the wrong tree)
   d. Why has the Jewish National Fund been so important to Israel? (Because it helps Israel to get to the "root" of its problems)

8. Working in groups of 3 to 5 students, each student completes the following statement: I feel that I am most like a (kind of tree) because ____. Students may, if they choose, react to the statements of any of the others in their group. Then each student assumes the "personality" of the tree he or she selected.

9. Find pictures, newspaper and magazine articles, articles from the synagogue bulletin, photocopies of pertinent materials from textbooks, original essays and art work which deal with trees, spring, and/or the holiday of Tu B'Shevat. If the class is particularly successful in gathering materials, the display can be placed at the entrance to the school or in the hall. Jewish National Fund materials are particularly good for bulletin boards and displays.

10. View and discuss the video *Grandpa's Tree*, in which an American Jewish students locates the tree his grandfather planted in Israel many years before. Afterward, collect money as a class to purchase trees through the Jewish National Fund in honor of grandparents.

11. As a class or in small groups, students create an original learning activity for review and reinforcement. Then use the game is used as a review activity. The fall holidays and Chanukah can also be reviewed through the game. Have an open house for parents and play the game with them.

12. Prepare a special edition of a class newspaper devoted to the holiday of Tu B'Shevat and looking forward to spring. Students can write about how the holiday is celebrated, its underlying themes, descriptions of home celebrations, etc. Articles about forthcoming holidays such as Purim, Pesach, and Yom HaAtzma'ut can also be included.

13. It is traditional to feed the birds on Shabbat Shirah. To make a bird feeder, you will need: empty plastic milk containers (gallon size) and a cutting tool. Cut an opening with an X-Acto blade. Fill the bottom with plaster of paris, or place a saucer in the bottom. Suspend from the handle or from the neck of the bottle. Birds like to eat bird seed, cereal grains, sunflower seeds, cookies, etc. (JB)

14. There are many different ways of observing Tu B'Shevat. Have students think about what they might do on Tu B'Shevat. How can they make the day different from any other day? Discuss in large or small groups.

15. Form small groups. Ask each group to examine and summarize for the class one of the passages related to trees or nature in the Bible (see page 119 for a listing of the passages).

16. Analyze and discuss the following statement from *Pirke Avot* (3:22): "When our deeds exceed our learning, we are like trees whose branches are few, but whose roots are many, so that even if all the winds of the world blow against them, they would be unable to move them."

17. Read and discuss *Listen to the Trees* by Molly Cone. Afterward, go over the quotations from the Torah and Rabbinic sources found in the book. Have students make up original sayings about the Jewish connection to the natural world and the importance of taking care of the earth.

18. Investigate the organization known as Neot Kedumim. What does the name mean? What does this organization do? How are the efforts of Neot Kedumim related to Tu B'Shevat? (AFM)
Resource: American Friends of Neot Kedumim, Steinfeld Rd., Halcott Center, NY 12430.

19. Discuss how the activities of the Jewish National Fund are related to Tu B'Shevat. Examine J.N.F. Tu B'Shevat material for the current year and from previous years. Investigate some of the multi-faceted Jewish National Fund projects in Israel to see how this organization is linked to nature and the land of Israel. Explore tree planting, land reclamation, road building, establishing new settlements, establishing special forests, *Pitchat Shalom*, etc.
Resource: Jewish National Fund, 42 East 69th St., New York, NY 10021.

20. Hold a debate on the following topic. Resolved: Planting trees in Israel is as important as giving dollars for human services.

21. Hold a class Tu B'Shevat *Seder*. Through the *Seder*, children and their parents will become familiar with the teachings and ideals of Tu B'Shevat in a special manner. Children can teach their parents the important ideas which they have already learned. Use an existing *Seder* or create an original one. Compare the Tu B'Shevat *Seder* to the Pesach *Seder*.
Resource: *A Seder for Tu B'Shevat* by Harlene Appelman and Jane Shapiro.

22. Seat the class in a circle and start telling a Tu B'Shevat story. Speak for 15-20 seconds and

stop. Go around the circle giving each student 15 seconds to continue the story. Record the story on audio or videotape and play it back for the class to see.

23. Shomrei Adamah is an organization that develops programs and publications that inspire environmental awareness and practice among Jews. Among their other offerings are note cards with nature designs on the cover. Order these and show them to students. Then have students design their own notecards on 8 1/2" x 11" paper folded twice. Decide on the best card and run them off on the synagogue copier. Provide several of the cards to each of the students in the class. (AFM)
Resource: Shomrei Adamah, 50 W. 17th St., 7th floor, New York, NY 10011.

24. Use the short dramatic reading, "The Old Man and the Emperor" (see page 120). Divide the class into groups of two, with one student playing the Emperor and the other, the old man. All pairs work at the same time. Each pair role plays the dialogue between the Emperor and the old man. They reverse roles and repeat the scene. Then, remaining in pairs, the students discuss how they felt in each role. After a few minutes, the students reassemble and process the activity.

25. Do one or two of the Tu B'Shevat art projects described in *100+ Jewish Art Projects for Children* by Nina Streisand Sher and Margaret A. Feldman (pages 30 and 31).

26. Complete pages 13 and 14 in *Jewish Holiday Copy Pak™ 4-6* by Marji Gold-Vukson.

Secondary
1. Let older students take the lead in organizing the food drive (see All-School, below).

2. Have students discuss the following statement from Deuteronomy and analyze its signifi-cance: "When in your war against a city you have to besiege it a long time in order to capture it, you must not destroy its trees, wielding the ax against them. You may eat of them, but you must not cut them down. Are trees of the field human to withdraw before you under siege?" (20:19) Compare this quotation with Genesis 1:28. Discuss how one statement counterbalances the other. Ask: Which one do you think has been the guiding "principle" over the centuries? Do you agree with this rationale? In what ways can *Bal Tashchit* serve as the theme for the modern ecology movement? Why do you think it is necessary to shift emphasis from the Genesis 1:28 quote to the Deuteronomy 20:19 phrase? What will be the consequences if we continue the status quo?

3. *Tikkun Olam* (repairing the world) is normally thought of in terms of economic, social, and political activism. Discuss: How would the concept of *Bal Tashchit* fit in with the concept of *Tikkun Olam*? How does this serve to broaden the framework in which *Tikkun Olam* is understood?

4. It is believed by some that the *menorah*, the symbol of Jewish life, was originally patterned after the olive tree, which can live for thousands of years and produce fruit throughout the life of the tree. Have students discuss and explain this possible connection.

5. In the Torah service, we read: "It is a tree of life to those who grasp it, and whoever holds on to it is happy. Its ways are pleasant and all its paths are peaceful" (Proverbs 3:17-18). Discuss: In this quotation, why and how is the Torah (and all of Jewish life for that matter) compared to a tree?

6. Discuss Tu B'shevat as a symbol of the process of renewal in nature.

7. *Guarding the Garden* is a musical play about Judaism and the environment which "stars" Lilith, Eve, Adam, and God and *Shechinah*. Listen to and discuss some of the songs on the audiotape of this play. Have students create their own songs about the environment. Resource: *Guarding the Garden: A Journey from Eden to the Edge* (audiocassette).

8. Have small groups of students make up a song about Tu B'Shevat for younger children. Each group sings their song to the rest of the class. All decide for what age group the song is appropriate. Then the small group goes into the classes of children of that age to perform it. (AFM)

9. Devise three questions on the subject of ecology (e.g., How is the environment being endangered? What can the government do? What can Jewish groups such as our class do?). Set up chairs in a fishbowl configuration (two concentric circles). Have the students count off by 1, 2, and 3. Ask the members of group 1 to occupy the discussion-circle seats, while the other groups sit in the outer-circle seats. Ask your first question. Allow up to ten minutes for discussion. Invite a student to act as facilitator or facilitate yourself. Next, ask group 2 to sit in the inner circle, replacing group 1 members who now sit in the outer circle. Ask group 2 if they would like to make any brief comments about the first discussion, and then segue into the second discussion topic. Follow the same procedure with members of group 3. When all three questions have been discussed, come together as one discussion group. Ask students for their reflections on the entire discussion. (Adapted from *Active Learning: 101 Strategies to Teach Any Subject* by Mel Silberman.)

10. Discuss: How did Noah help preserve the world? What more might he have done? How do I/you/we help to preserve the environment? What more might be done?

All-School

1. Have each class research the appearance and characteristics of one kind of tree that is mentioned in the Bible. Class members then draw a floor to ceiling replica of the tree and paste it onto the classroom door, along with a chapter and verse reference from the Bible. (PT)

2. To reinforce the idea that we do not take God's gifts for granted, have the students and/or the youth group organize a food drive. Have each student bring one can or one paper product to Religious School each week, then donate the food to a local food pantry. Having a food drive on and around Tu B'Shevat is fitting for two reasons: (1) it reinforces the link between trees and food, and (2) it helps students remember that the poor and needy cannot wait until the follow Thanksgiving to Christmas period for more food. Giving to others on this occasion encourages students not to take God's gifts for granted.

3. Plan and hold a school-wide Tu B'Shevat *Seder.* Resource: *Seder Tu Bishevat: The Festival of Trees* by Adam Fisher.

4. Organize a school-wide drive for trees through the Jewish National Fund. As an aid in promoting the drive, obtain from J.N.F. posters of the *Sheva Minim* (Seven Species), as well as posters depicting various types of trees commonly found in Israel. These can be laminated and used from year to year.

5. This group participation activity is geared to younger children. (It can also be used at a family education program.) The participants are divided into groups and assigned a word related to Tu B'Shevat. When its word or phrase is read (see "The Narrative," page 132), a group responds to the word with the

appropriate sounds: every time the word "TREES" or "TREE" is read, that group says, "bark bark bark"; every time the word "TU B'SHEVAT" is read, that group says, "bang bang bang" (because it sounds like "to be shot"); every time the word "PLANT," "PLANTED," "TO PLANT," or "PLANT-ING" is read, that group says, "dig dig dig"; everytime the word "ISRAEL" is read, that group says, "Shalom, Shalom"; every time the word "WINTER" is read, that group says, "yucko, yucko." When the word "SPRING" is read, all groups say, "hooray, hooray" and when the phrase "NEW YEAR" is read, everyone says *Shanah Tovah, Shanah Tovah.*"

The Narrative

The 15th of the Hebrew month is known as TU B'SHEVAT. It is the NEW YEAR of the TREES. It is the time when WINTER ends in ISRAEL and farmers begin to PLANT TREES. In ISRAEL, SPRING will come very soon. In North America we still have a lot of WINTER left. According to our calendar, there are two months left to WINTER. The calendar says that WINTER ends in late March, and, most of the time, it really does. Sometimes we even have snow in April. In ISRAEL, things are very different. The WINTER is much shorter and much milder than in America. The holiday of TU B'SHEVAT is a way of telling Jews in ISRAEL that SPRING is around the corner.

What is TU B'SHEVAT like in ISRAEL? It is called the NEW YEAR of the TREES even though it is still WINTER, because at that time, children and adults go out to the countryside and to the Jewish National Fund forests to PLANT TREES. Millions and millions of TREES have been PLANTED in ISRAEL by the J.N.F. We, too, can PLANT TREES in ISRAEL by buying TREES here in _____ (*insert name of your city*). We receive a TREE certificate from the Jewish National Fund which says that we PLANTED a tree in Israel. TU B'SHEVAT is also the birthday of all of the TREES in the world. Since we do not know exactly when each TREE started to grow, we celebrate TU B'SHEVAT as the birthday of all TREES. What better time than TU B'SHEVAT to PLANT new TREES? Even here in North America, we can PLANT some things indoors. That will help us to remember that WINTER will be over before we know it, and once again SPRING will be here.

Family

1. Suggest that families plan a festive meal for the celebration of Tu B'Shevat. They should include at least one dish or dessert item that is eaten on Tu B'Shevat. Have them go through Jewish cookbooks to find out interesting things to do with carob.

2. Encourage families to visit a Sephardic congregation to see how the celebration of Tu B'Shevat is different from that of Ashkenazic groups.

3. Suggest that families pretend they are living in a ghetto in Europe in the Middle Ages. Since conditions are probably very confined, what might you do in place of planting trees in your yard? As a family, they discuss what preparations need to be made for the forthcoming celebration of the holiday of Tu B'Shevat. Or, they might imagine they are living in Jerusalem. What would they plan to do on Tu B'Shevat there?

4. Organize a family education program for two to four-year-olds (there are three already designed Tu B'Shevat programs in *Head Start on Holidays: Jewish Programs for Preschoolers and Their Parents* by Roberta Louis Goodman and Andye Honigman Zell).

5. Have a family Tu B'Shevat *Seder.* Resource: *A Seder for Tu B'Shevat* by Harlene Appelman and Jane Shapiro.

BIBLIOGRAPHY
See pages 277-278.

CHAPTER EIGHT
PURIM

VOCABULARY

Adar: The 12th month of the Jewish year, corresponding to February-March, its zodiac sign is Pisces. Adar has 29 days in an ordinary year and 30 days during a leap year. Adar 7th is the traditional date of the birth and death of Moses. Adar 13th is the Fast of Esther, Adar 14th is Purim, and Adar 15th is Shushan Purim.

Adar Sheni: In leap years, a second month of Adar is added to the calendar. This happens seven times every 19 years (see "About the Calendar" in the Chapter on Rosh Chodesh, page 243). The Fast of Esther, Purim, and Shushan Purim are celebrated in Adar Sheni.

Adloyada: Literally, "Until He Did Not Know." Because of the great victory by the Jews over Haman and, because the path to victory began at a "banquet of wine" (Esther 5:6), getting drunk was permitted, even encouraged, on Purim. Rava, a Talmud sage, stating that a person should imbibe until he cannot distinguish (*adloyada*) between "cursed be Haman" and "blessed is Mordecai" (*Megillah* 7b). This Hebrew word also refers to the Purim carnival and to the celebration that takes place in the streets of Israel during Purim.

Ahashuerus: The King of Persia who married Esther in the Book of Esther. Though not certain of his identification, many scholars identify him with Xerxes I (486-465 B.C.E.)

Al HaNissim: "For the Miracles" is a prayer read on Purim as one of the final blessings of the *Amidah* and as part of the Grace after Meals. A different version of this prayer is recited on Chanukah.

Bigtan and Teresh: The two eunuchs of King Ahashuerus who plotted to kill the king, but who were discovered by Mordecai (Esther 2:21-23).

Esther: The central character and heroine of the Book of Esther. The name probably derives from the Persian goddess Ishtar. It is through her intervention that the Jews of the Persian kingdom were saved from destruction. Her Hebrew name was Hadassah.

Hadassah: The Hebrew name for Esther. Esther 2:7 reads: "He [Mordecai] was foster father to Hadassah, that is Esther, his uncle's daughter, for she had neither father nor mother."

Haman: The vizier of Ahasuerus who plotted to exterminate the Jews. He was hanged on the gallows that he built to hang Mordecai. An Agagite, Haman was seen as a descendant of Amalek, a traditional enemy of the Israelites. This ancestry may have been attributed to him to reinforce the evil nature of the man.

Hamantashen: Originally called *Mohn Taschen,* a German term meaning "poppy seed pockets." In the course of time, these triangular-shaped pockets of dough came to be filled with either poppy seeds, prunes, cheese, or other fruits. Because the phrase *"mohn taschen"* sounded like *"hamantashen"* meaning Haman's pockets, the latter name came into use. The triangular shape was also a reminder of the three-cornered hat supposedly worn by Haman. Another explanation links the three corners to the three Patriarchs: Abraham, Isaac, and Jacob. In Israel, *hamantashen* are called *Oznay Haman,* meaning "Haman's ears." Not only does a *hamantashen* resemble the shape of an ear, but it was sometimes the practice to cut off the ears of criminals before hanging. Because Haman was hung, the term *Oznay Haman* came into use.

Krobetz: Hebrew acrostic for the expression "The voice of rejoicing and salvation is in the tents of the righteous . . ." (Psalm II 8:15). The term refers to the hymns sung on Purim.

Masechot: "Masks." Generally speaking, masquerading is prohibited in Jewish Law. This is an extension of the prohibition of Deuteronomy 22:5: "Neither shall a man wear the garments of a woman." However, because of the joyous nature of Purim, an exception was made by the Rabbis. Since the fifteenth century, masquerading has become a prominent part of the modern Purim celebration.

Matanot L'Evyonim: "Gifts to the Needy." It is a custom to send baskets of food to those in need so that they, too, can enjoy the holiday.

Megillat Esther: "The Scroll of Esther" is one of the five *Megillot* (Ruth, Song of Songs, Lamentations, Ecclesiastes, and Esther). It contains the story of the salvation and deliverance of the Jews of the Persian Empire. It was written around the year 330 B.C.E. When the word *Megillah* is used without mentioning a specific scroll, it refers to the Scroll of Esther because, until about 250 C.E., the Scroll of Esther was the only scroll (aside from the Torah) read in the synagogue. *Megillat Esther* is read on *erev* Purim and on Purim Morning.

Mishloach Manot: "Sending of Gifts" is a custom that derives from the scroll of Esther. Mordecai, in recording the events leading up to the deliverance of the Jews of Persia, wrote that the 14th and 15th of Adar were to be observed ". . . as days of feasting and merrymaking and as an occasion for sending gifts to one another and gifts to the poor" (Esther 9:22). These gifts are usually Purim delicacies, such as homemade *hamantashen,* salted almonds, wine, grapes, and sums of money should the recipients be in need.

Mordecai: The cousin of Esther who served as her foster father because her parents were no longer living. Mordecai and Esther were the heroes of the Purim saga. He uncovered plots against the life of King Ahashuerus and against the Jews of Persia. After saving the king's life, he persuaded Esther to intercede with the king on behalf of her people. The name may be related to the Persian god Marduk.

Pur: "Lot." Haman cast "lots" *(purim)* to determine the day and month on which the Jews would be destroyed. The day Haman chose, the 14th of Adar, "had been transformed for them from one of grief and mourning to one of festive joy" (Esther 9:22).

Purim Katan: "Small Purim." It refers to the minor festival that occurs on I Adar 14 in a leap year. In leap years, Purim itself is celebrated on the 14th day of Adar Sheni.

Purim-Shpiel: "Purim Play" in Yiddish, the *shpiel* has come to be an important part of the folklore of Purim. Originating at least five centuries ago, the *Purim-shpiel* is usually a humorous, satirical, even biting spoof on anyone and everything. It can range from a retelling of the Purim story, to a simple burlesque, to an elaborate spoof of Rabbis and religious leaders. The Purim players are called *Purim-shpielers.* It was also customary for one person in a community to become the Purim "Rabbi," who served in mock dignity from the new moon of Adar until the eve of Purim.

Ra'ashan: "Noisemaker" in Hebrew, the *ra'ashan* often goes by its Yiddish name *gragger*, which, in turn, comes from the Polish word "to rattle." Because Haman is described as a descendant of Agag, the King of the Amatekites, and a traditional enemy of Israel (Exodus 17), it became customary to make noise to blot out the name of this Amalekite. The stamping of feet along with all sorts of noisemakers and rattles are used in the synagogue during the reading of the *Megillah*. In addition to making noise, one may also shout "Cursed be Haman/*Arur Haman*" and "May his name be wiped out/*Yimach Sh'mo*."

Seudah: A festive meal. It has become customary to have a festive meal at home at the conclusion of Purim . . . as well as in conjunction with joyful life cycle events, festivals, and the completion of the study of a tractate of the Talmud.

Shabbat Zachor: "Sabbath of Remembrance," is the Sabbath preceding Purim. In addition to the regular weekly Torah reading, Deuteronomy 25:17-19 is read. It states: "Remember what Amalek did to you by the way as you came forth out of Egypt . . ."

Shushan: The capital of Persia in the Book of Esther, possibly the city of Susa. Shushan is, according to tradition, the burial place of Mordecai and Esther.

Shushan Purim: A semi-holiday that falls on Adar 15, the day after Purim. It recalls the tradition that the Jews who lived in Shushan continued the fight against their enemies on the 14th of Adar and, therefore, celebrated their victory one day later. It is celebrated on that date in cities which have been walled since the time of Joshua, such as Jerusalem.

Special Purims: These are anniversaries of deliverance celebrated by individuals, families, or communities throughout the world. For example, on 28 Adar, the Jews in Cairo observe a special Purim in commemoration of their deliverance, some 450

years ago, from the hands of Pasha Ahmed Shitann. The 20th of Adar marks the rescue of Frankfort Jewry in 1616.

Ta'anit Esther: "Fast of Esther," occurs on the 13th of Adar, the day before Purim. One fasts from the morning until after the reading of the *Megillah* in commemoration of the message that Esther sent to Mordecai after he asked her to intercede with King Ahashuerus: "Go, assemble all the Jews who live in Shushan, and fast in my behalf; do not eat or drink for three days, day or night" (Esther 4:16).

Vashti: The Queen of Persia, wife of Ahashuerus. She was expelled from the king's court before he married Esther.

Zeresh: The wife of Haman.

BACKGROUND

The Purim Story
The Purim story is the Book of Esther, which is a part of the *Ketuvim* or Writings (also called the Hagiographa), the third section of Tanach. An outline of the Purim story follows:
King Ahashuerus dethrones Queen Vashti.
Esther is crowned queen after winning a beauty contest.
Mordecai uncovers a plot to kill the king and reports it.
Mordecai refuses to bow before Haman.
Haman seeks to destroy the Jews after his run-in with Mordecai.
Mordecai appeals to Esther to save her people.
Esther approaches King Ahashuerus and invites him and Haman to a banquet.
Mordecai is honored for having saved the king's life.
Esther entertains the king and Haman, and invites them to a second banquet.
Esther pleads for her people at the second banquet. She accuses Haman.
The king grants Esther's request and condemns Haman to die on the gallows which he built for the Jews.

The Jews defend themselves throughout Persia.
The holiday of Purim is established.
Mordecai advances to a position of importance.

Central Themes

• Esther 3:8 is a classic statement of anti-Semitism, perhaps the first such written anywhere. It reads: "Haman then said to King Ahashuerus, 'There is a certain people, scattered and dispersed among the other peoples in all the provinces of your realm, whose laws are different from those of any other people and who do not obey the king's laws; and it is not in Your Majesty's interest to tolerate them.'" Haman tells the king that, because the Jews are different, they must be suspect. He then lies to compound the felony, for indeed the Jews did follow the laws of the land. Unfortunately, this type of reasoning has, again and again throughout Jewish history, been the unwarranted rationale for the persecution of Jews.

• The word God is not mentioned in the entire Book of Esther. This omission exists in spite of the fact that throughout the Bible, God's intervention is ever present. Mordecai does, however, make an indirect reference to God when he speaks with Esther about intervening with the king: ". . . if you keep silent in this crisis, relief and deliverance will come to the Jews from another quarter, while you and your father's house will perish. And who knows, perhaps you have attained to royal position for just such a crisis" (Esther 4:13-14). In other words, not only does Mordecai suggest that God might indeed play an active role in resolving the crisis, but further suggests that Esther's becoming queen may have been the work of God, Who was preparing for the day when the Jewish people would face crisis. Another explanation for the absence of the name of God is that since the book was written in scroll form and sent to Jews throughout Persia, the name of God was omitted in case the scroll was desecrated in any way.

• Whether the events related in the book are factual or not, the Book of Esther is more truthful than many so-called historical works.

Unfortunately, the story has been repeated throughout Jewish history on many occasions, but without the benefit of a hero or heroine. The Book of Esther thus serves as an allegory describing the life and lot of the Jewish people in an alien and hostile world.

• Purim has become the symbolic name for Jewish deliverance. When a community of Jews was saved from a terrible fate, it would celebrate its days of deliverance each year by establishing a special Purim for that community.

• Purim teaches the idea of *K'lal Yisrael* — all Jews must stick together as a "community of Israel." In times of crisis no one is free from the obligation to help out. A key teaching of Judaism is *"Kol Yisrael Arayvin Zeh BaZeh"* — Every Jew is responsible for every other Jew. This value is certainly evident in Mordecai's charge to Esther (4:13-14).

• Purim stresses the idea of *tzedakah* through the practice of *Mishloach Manot*. While *tzedakah* is practiced all year long, the Jew is specifically reminded on Purim of a responsibility to those less fortunate.

• Unlike many other more serious, even somber observances on the Jewish calendar, Purim serves as a catharsis, a relief from the stresses of life. It is a time for party and carnival, for masquerade and "cutting loose." It lends a sense of balance and perspective to life.

• The role of chance, or what appears to be chance, in the Book of Esther testifies to how God works in mysterious ways. Is every stage of the Purim story mere happenstance, or might it actually be part of the divine plan to save the Jews from destruction? Consider:
By pure chance, Esther was chosen to be queen.
By pure chance, Mordecai overheard the conspiracy against the king.
By pure chance, the king slept badly one night so that he ordered the royal chronicle to be read to him.

By pure chance, Ahashuerus came across the record of Mordecai's meritorious service.
By pure chance, Haman entered just as the king was thinking of how to reward Mordecai.
By pure chance, the king was in a receptive mood when Esther came to call.
By pure chance, Harbonah the chamberlain broke in at a critical moment to report that Haman had already erected the gallows.

Fact or Fiction

Some scholars question the historical accuracy and the authenticity of the Purim story. In examining the evidence pro and con, it is important to keep in mind that the significance of the message may far outweigh the question of the historical accuracy of the account.

The following facts bolster the claim that the Book of Esther is a work of romantic fiction and not a true story:

1. No Persian king ever had a wife named either Vashti or Esther.
2. No man by the name of Haman was ever a vizier for a Persian king.
3. Ahashuerus could not have married Esther because a king was only permitted to marry into one of the seven leading families of Persia, and none of those families was Jewish.
4. The name Esther bears a striking resemblance to the name of the Persian goddess Ishtar, while Mordecai resembles the name of the Persian god Marduk.
5. If Mordecai were expelled from Jerusalem with Jeconiah, King of Judah in 597 B.C.E., and the Purim events take place in the third year of the reign of Ahashuerus (Esther 2:6), which can be no earlier than the year 482 B.C.E., Mordecai would be at least 115 years old, when he left Jerusalem.

On the other hand, there is some evidence which points to the authenticity of the story. The following points demonstrate at least that the author was intimately familiar with life in Persia:

1. Many names, institutions, and descriptions in the Book of Esther agree with non-Jewish sources. Tablets containing the name Mordecai have been found, but it is not known if they refer to this Mordecai.
2. Esther illustrates the ancient Persian practice of dissimulation — concealing her true identity in order to preserve her life. (Mordecai had urged Esther to conceal her Jewish identity.) Later in the story, after the king gave the Jews permission to defend themselves, many non-Jews pretended to be Jews until the fighting ended: "And many of the people of the land professed to be Jews for the fear of the Jews had fallen upon them" (Esther 8:17). Dissimulation is also in evidence in Arab countries today, where there exists a struggle between Shiite and Suni Moslems; often one will pretend to be the other.
3. Aramaic was a language used in the Persian Empire. The Book of Esther contains some words in Aramaic, thereby indicating a fairly late date for the book.
4. It was known that the kings of Persia often relied on foreigners as their closest advisors, for it was felt that while native Persians might be caught between loyalty to the king and to his family, foreigners were totally dependent upon the king. In this context, it is not surprising that Haman and Mordecai were able to rise to high positions.

Each person must decide whether to treat the Book of Esther as a true story or as a work of fiction. In the process of reaching this decision, however, one should remember that the significance of the message may outweigh the question of historical accuracy.

Purim Foods

Many customs related to eating special foods have developed around Purim. The most famous Purim food is *hamantashen*, which is also known as *Oznay Haman*, meaning "Haman's ears." In addition to eating *hamantashen* filled with poppy seeds, fruit, cheese, or jellies, other foods are also traditional for Purim:

A special Purim *challah,* known as *keylitsh* in Russian, is sometimes made. This *challah* is oversized and extensively braided. The braids on the *challah* are intended to remind people of the rope used to hang Haman.

Kreplach is customarily eaten whenever beating takes place: before Yom Kippur when men have themselves flogged, on Hoshana Rabbah when the willow branches are beaten, and on Purim when Haman is beaten. The *kreplach* consist of triangular pouches of dough filled with chopped meat. They are eaten as a separate dish or served in soup.

Bean dishes are also eaten. They include salted beans boiled in their jackets, and chick-peas boiled and seasoned with salt and pepper. This is meant to remind us that Esther would not eat anything at the court of King Ahashuerus that was not kosher, so she mainly ate peas and beans. A similar idea is expressed regarding Daniel and his friends (Daniel 1:12).

Among Sephardic Jews, it is a custom to wrap pastry dough around a decorated hard-boiled egg to create the shape of a Purim character or an animal. After baking, these artistic creations *(Folares)* are displayed with pride and eaten with delight.

Highlights of the Liturgy

Very few modifications in the liturgy are made for Purim morning. Three blessings precede the reading of the *Megillah:* over the reading of the *Megillah, Sheh Asah Nissim,* and *Shehecheyanu.* (See Appendix, pages 252 and 253, for blessings.)

The Megillah is usually chanted by the Cantor. The first two chapters are relatively calm. The noisemaking begins with the opening verse of chapter three when Haman's name is read for the first time.

The *Al HaNissim* prayer is read as a part of the *Amidah* and the Grace after Meals. Two versions of the prayer are found in the *Siddur:* one for Chanukah and one for Purim. The Purim version reads as follows: "We give thanks for the redeeming wonders and mighty deeds by which, at this

season, our people was saved in days of old. In the days of Mordecai and Esther, the wicked Haman arose in Persia, plotting the destruction of all the Jews. He planned to destroy them in a single day, the thirteenth of Adar, and to permit the plunder of their possessions. But through Your great mercy, his plan was thwarted, his scheme frustrated. We therefore thank and bless You, O great and gracious God!"

After the reading of the *Megillah,* a blessing which is taken from the Talmud is chanted: "Blessed are You, *Adonai* our God, Sovereign of the universe, who has contended for us and defended our cause, avenging us by bringing retribution on all our enemies. Blessed are You, O God and Redeemer, who delivers Your people Israel from all their adversaries" *(Megillah* 21b).

SCOPE AND SEQUENCE

Grade	Themes/ideas
Kindergarten	Stories about Purim.
Grade One	Getting ready for Purim at home. Stories about Purim.
Grade Two	Purim in the synagogue.
Grade Three	Blessings before reading the *Megillah.*
Grade Four	Review of blessings before reading the *Megillah.* Basic Purim vocabulary.
Grade Five	Expansion of Purim vocabulary. *Al HaNissim* prayer and review of blessings.
Grade Six	A careful look at the Purim story. Preparation of an original Purim presentation.
Grade Seven	Examination of the Book of Esther. A look at customs originating with

the Book of Esther, and special
Purims.

Grade Eight   Purim foods and other special
customs.
What happened to God in the book
of Esther?
A look at the role of chance and
purpose in the story.

Grade Nine   Purim — fact or fiction: evidence
for and against the historical
accuracy of the Book of Esther.

Grade Ten   The meaning of Purim for the
contemporary Jew.

Grade Eleven   A review of the customs and
activities related to the celebration
of Purim.

Grade Twelve   An examination of Purim in the
context of the history of anti-
Semitism.
What lessons of history can be
learned from the Purim story?

ACTIVITIES

Preschool/Kindergarten

1. Show students a *Megillah* and a Torah scroll.
    Have them tell what is the same and what is
    different about the two. List their ideas on
    chart paper. (NSM)

2. Make a sorting game with shapes of a *Megillah*
    and a Torah. Have students put the correct
    shapes into piles. (NSM)

3. Help students make sock puppets of the
    characters in the Purim story. Then have them
    act out all or parts of the story using their
    puppets.
    Resource: *Creative Puppetry for Jewish Kids* by
    Gale Solotar Warshawsky.

4. Read the Purim story, pausing at Haman's
    name for students to make noise with their
    *gragge*rs. Teach students to stop their noise
    when the teacher's hand is raised. (NSM)

5. Make masks out of stockings. Sew bits of
    wool, felt, fabric, etc., onto an old nylon
    stocking with bits of colorful thread.

6. Have several *graggers* available that make
    different noises. With children's eyes closed,
    the teacher makes a sound with one *gragger*
    then another. Children identify whether the
    sounds are alike or different. (NSM)

7. Sort *graggers* according to characteristics and
    then regroup them. For example, first sort
    according to color and then sort according to
    size. (NSM)

8. Take apart a *gragger* and see how it words. (Be
    careful doing this; the edges can be sharp.)
    (NSM)

9. Make a learning center in which students
    arrange pictures of *graggers*, *Megillot*, or
    hamantashen from smallest to largest, or vice
    versa. (NSM)

10. Create a picture recipe of *hamantashen*. Help
    children follow it as they bake. (NSM)

11. Draw "lots" for something in your class, just
    as Haman drew lots. (NSM)

12. Show students puppets of the Purim characters.
    Have the puppets talk to the students. The
    students could tell each character what his or
    her actions are in the story, then the puppets
    carry them out. The puppets can become part
    of the housekeeping area or reside in a puppet
    center. (NSM)

13. Turn your housekeeping area into ancient
    Persia. First, look at books with Persian motifs,

and then provide appropriate materials. Create a palace, turrets, ornamental gates, and a throne. Place costume materials in the area as well. (NSM)

14. Think about items you can add to the block area to stimulate the building of the city of Shushan. (NSM)

15. Use scarves for rhythmic movement while dancing to Persian-type music. Consider using "Scheherezade." (NSM)

16. Make a *gragger*. Provide a variety of containers, noisy fillings, and decorations. Let the children be creative! One unusual idea is to use dried gourds left over from Sukkot (feel free to cut one open to see what makes the noise). (NSM)

17. Read to the children *A Costume for Noah* by Susan Remick Topek. Ask them to think of some things they could do if their own Purim costume wasn't ready ready on time.

18. Ideas for snack and classroom *Seudat* Purim: *hamantashen*; Queen Esther Salad (cottage cheese face, sliced pineapple crown with colored sprinkles for jewels, raisin eyes, etc.); Purim masks (rice cakes with peanut butter and garnishes to make the faces). (NSM)

19. Provide students with an outline of Esther's shape. Let children create "the most beautiful" dress for her, using paint, glitter, sequins, etc. (NSM)

20. Do some of the activities on pages 84-89 of *The Jewish Preschool Teachers Handbook* by Sandy Furfine Wolf and Nancy Cohen Nowak.

21. Help children complete pages 29, 30, 31, and 32 in *Jewish Preschool/Kindergarten Copy Pak*™ by Nancy Cohen Nowak.

22. Do one or more of the Purim art projects in *100+ Jewish Art Projects for Children* by Nina

Streisand Sher and Margaret A. Feldman (pages 60, 61, 62).

Primary

1. Draw or adapt a picture in which one or more objects related to Purim are hidden. Students must find the hidden objects.

2. Put each of the following statements on a card and ask the students to put the cards in the correct order. (Make picture cards for those children who are not yet able to read.)
   a. Esther is crowned Queen after winning a beauty contest.
   b. Haman seeks to destroy the Jews after his run-in with Mordecai.
   c. Esther invites the king and Haman to a banquet.
   d. Mordecai is honored by the king for having saved the king's life.
   e. Jews defend themselves throughout Persia.

3. Teach children the Purim blessings in Hebrew and explain the meaning of each. (See Appendix for blessings, pages 252 and 253.)

4. Make crowns for Esther: Cut a headband of poster board and spray it gold. Place it face down on table. Cut 8 to 10 strips, 8" long and 3/4" wide. Spray these also. Place the gold side down along edge of headband and tape strips in place. Bend each small strip toward you exactly in half. Tape or staple the headband together. Bring all small strips together with staple. Top with a 1" styrofoam ball covered with gold tissue, sequins, or glitter. For a glamorous arrangement, make a veil out of one yard of organdy. Catch it between embroidery hoops. (ML)

5. Ask students to collect old clothes, scraps of materials, etc., and create a costume that reflects one of the characters in the Purim story. After putting on the homemade costumes, the students act out parts of the

Purim story. As an extra bonus, they may wear the costumes for the Purim carnival.

6. One student is "It" and gives the class a clue as to his/her identity as one of the characters in the Purim story. The other students guess who it is. If one clue is not sufficient, "It" gives another clue. The person guessing the student's identity becomes "It."

7. Have each student dictate to an adult the story of Purim in his/her own words. Make the stories into *Megillah* shapes. Allow students to illustrate their stories. (NSM)

8. If the weather is nice, transform the playground into Shushan. Provide children with crowns, horses, "tea-time" materials, capes, etc., so that they can recreate parts of the Purim story on their own, without teacher direction. (NSM)

9. Have children personalize the values of the people behind the Purim story. For example, when were they like Esther — helping others? (A good source to help stimulate this discussion is *A Purim Album* by Audrey Friedman Marcus and Raymond A. Zwerin.) (NSM)

10. Tell or read the story of Purim. Stop along the way and have students see if they can remember what comes next. (NSM)

11. Make *hamantashen* or cookies to deliver to a center for the homeless. Discuss with students the *mitzvah* of *Matanot L'Evyonim* (giving gifts to poor people). (NSM)

12. If you know of anyone with a collection of fine Purim artworks (e.g., *Megillot, graggers,* pictures) invite him or her to show the items to the students. (NSM)

13. Use strawberry baskets, or paper plates folded, gathered, and decorated for *Shalach Manot.* Bake or buy *hamentashen* or cookies and arrange these in the baskets. Have students prepare a Purim skit or puppet show and visit a nursing home. After the skit, have students distribute the *Shalach Manot,* sing Purim songs, and socialize with the residents. (They can also deliver treats to synagogue staff and/or parents.)

14. Make a Purim *Megillah* using an opaque projector. Follow this procedure: All must first know the Purim story. Assign each student a scene to illustrate on a piece of 9" x 12" construction paper. Join the completed drawings together and fasten each end to a dowel rod. One student pulls the drawings across the stage of the opaque projector as a narrator relates the story. Or, use the drawings as you would if they were slides. Place one drawing down at a time as the story unfolds. (JB)

15. Do a readers theater version of "A Purim Reading for Children" (see page 147) at an assembly for other students and/or parents.

16. Make *graggers* out of Pringle potato chip cartons, cardboard mailing tubes, any small paper carton with a pencil or dowel poked through it, or paper plates folded in half and stapled together. Fill with dried beans, peas, pebbles, or marbles. Decorate all *graggers* with Purim motifs. Make a double "Hopper" out of pieces of wood 6" x 1" x 1/4". Hold both in your hand. Hold one still, while the other bangs against it. (JB)

17. Introduce young children to Purim via a magic carpet. Seat children in a circle. Ask them to close their eyes and feel their bodies resting on the floor. Then have each child cut out a circle around him/her (imaginatively of course) and take them by your narrative, out of the window, above the rooftops, soaring high in the sky to the city of Shushan. There, from their perch, they can see proud Mordecai sitting on a white horse, being led by Haman

through the street where happy Jews are yelling, rejoicing, and dancing, Esther the Queen and Ahashuerus the King sit proudly and happily on their beautifully bedecked thrones. (BR)

18. For centuries, it was common practice for someone to become the "Purim Rabbi" for a day or two around the time of Purim. Select a student to be the class Purim Rabbi. Also select from among the students the Purim teacher, Cantor, principal, etc.

19. Ask a parent, principal, the Rabbi, or another teacher to dress up as Mordecai or Esther. He/she comes to the class pretending to be that person. The class interviews the character, asking questions related to the events in the person's life and his/her accomplishments.

20. Make a big *Megillah* out of butcher paper. Have groups of students break through the paper at various times and enact the scenes of the Purim story. (OM)

21. Have students complete the Instant Lessons *Purim — The Story* by Debra Markovic, *Purim — What We Do,* and *Purim Megillah*.

22. Perform the play "Purim Customs" from *Class Acts: Plays & Skits for Jewish Settings* by Stan J. Beiner (page 54). Invite parents and/or other classes to the performance.

23. Do one or more of the Shabbat art projects in *100+ Jewish Art Projects for Children* by Nina Streisand Sher and Margaret A. Feldman (pages 34, 37, 39, 41).

Intermediate

1. Ask the students to create newspaper headlines to describe the various events in the Purim story. Put the headlines together and you will have an outline of the Purim story.

2. Write key Purim words on the blackboard. Let students write at least one four line poem using a minimum of two of the holiday terms. The poem may be serious, silly, or somewhere in between. Be sure to have students put the poems in their poetry books.

3. Encourage students to write an "I Urge Telegram." Each student writes a telegram in 15 words or less to one of the main characters in the Purim story. Hints to students: Write to Haman expressing anger at his becoming a role model for anti-Semites, to Esther asking her to be brave, to Mordecai in appreciation of his courage and wisdom, or to Vashti concerning her refusal to dance before the court. Read or ask for volunteers to read the telegrams to the class.

4. Have students print the name "Haman" on their shoes in pencil. Every time Haman's name is mentioned, they stomp their feet. If the name is still visible after the *Megillah* reading, the students didn't stomp hard enough! (JB)

5. Ask students to keep a diary as Esther fighting Haman or as Mordecai working quietly to save his people. They can respond in their entries to the very real threat posed by Haman to the survival of the Jewish people.

6. Divide students into groups of 3. Give each group a week's worth of newspapers and several news magazines. Ask them to search and find examples of prejudice against others, much like the prejudice Haman had against the Jews. Esther stood up against Haman. Discuss what could be done in each of the reported instances to stop the prejudice? (NSM)

7. Ask students to put themselves in the place of Esther or Mordecai or Ahasuerus. Have them write a brief essay entitled: If I were _____,

then I would _____. This assignment can serve as the trigger for an excellent discussion.

8. Read *Esther's Story* by Diane Wolkstein, which tells the Purim story from Esther's point of view. Students can rewrite the story from the point of view of one of the other characters, then compile the stories into a class book.

9. Form a circle. Each child states "Purim is _____" and completes the statement with a feeling or mood or characteristic of Purim. Variation: The first student completes the sentence with a word beginning with A, the second student with a word beginning with B, and so on (skipping Q and X).

10. Read statements from the Book of Esther and see who can guess the identity of the speaker.

11. Play a lively Purim quiz game. On a series of 8 1/2" x 11" sheets, write four words or phrases, three of which refer to Purim. Form two or three teams and give each a *gragger*. The teams decide which word or phrase doesn't belong, then use their *gragger* to signal that they are finished with the assignment. The first team to make a noise gets to guess first. If the guess is correct, the team gets 2 points; if not, the next team to make a noise with a *gragger* gets to guess.

12. Make personal Purim masks. You will need heavy duty aluminum foil, masking tape, newspaper. Have students work in pairs. For each pair, cut two 12" x 16" sheets of heavy duty aluminum foil. One student of the pair places the foil over the other student's face and molds it to the face while the other holds the aluminum in place. Press the foil gently over the nose, eyes, mouth, chin, and sides of the face. Punch holes where the nose is to allow the person to breathe. Place a few strips of masking tape up and down over the face. Carefully lift off the mask. Place crushed news-

papers under the mask to support it. Cut 30 to 40 newspaper strips 1" x 10". Place in a pail of water for 10 minutes. Take out one strip at a time and glue gently to mask, first horizontally, then vertically for four layers of strips. Let dry. Tape several strips inside, too. The last step is to paint the mask a flesh color. Paint the eyebrows and mouth. For Ahasuerus, add a mustache and a crown. Conclude the project with an exhibit of masks. (JB)

13. Search through daily or weekly cartoons in the newspaper and collect those cartoons that can be open-ended when the dialogue is whited out. Divide the class into small groups and give each group the same cartoon. The task of each group is to write a dialogue for the cartoon that is related to Purim. The groups share their results with the class.

14. One student stands and begins to retell the story of Purim. After 30 seconds, say "Stop!" The student sits down and the student on his/her right stands and continues the story for another 30 seconds. This continues until everyone has had a chance to speak. Record the story on audio or videotape and play it back to the class. Variation: Use this as a Purim carnival activity. Children can be "guests" on WPUR radio.

15. Let each student make a puppet. Here are several kinds to choose from:

Pencil Puppets: You will need octagonal shaped wooden pencils, poster board, paints, glue, a table for the "stage," actors. Follow this procedure: Draw and cut out of cardboard a front view and a back view of one of the Purim characters, each 1/2" longer than the pencil and 1 1/2" to 2" wide. Glue the back cutout to the pencil, allowing the pencil to extend 1/2" below the cutout. Staple back cutout to front cutout. Your pencil figure will thus acquire a roundness. Now on with the play! Grip "player" with thumb and index fingers. The puppet manipulators (students) rest their forearms on a table as they move figures around. "Walk" the figure off the table when leaving a scene. The class sits around the table and becomes the audience. For a Purim play, write an original script, present the *Megillah,* modernize the Purim story. (JB)

Broomstick Puppets: These are easy to make and easy to manipulate. Decorate the straw part of brooms as puppets, using construction paper, fabric scraps, etc. Manipulate with the handles. (JB)

Styrofoam Puppets: Core a 4" to 6" styrofoam ball like an apple, halfway through the ball. Insert a piece of small tube about 1 1/2" long, such as the ones you get inside wrapping paper. Let the tube hang out of the ball about 3/4" to attach dress later. Glue the tube to the ball if necessary. Now, take scraps of styrofoam and roughly shape two ears and a nose. Pin on at the right place. Tear (don't cut) tissue paper of various colors into small pieces about 1" x 1 1/2". Wallpaper the tissue onto the ball (all over) for skin, using thin white glue or acrylic medium. (Put the ball on top of a pop bottle while you are doing this.) While this is drying, mix skin color out of acrylic paint, 2 tbs. white per puppet, some yellow ochre or a tiny bit of brown, some red, and some yellow. Paint the skin. Make eyes, eyebrows, and mouth out of tissue or paint them on. Now wallpaper the features onto the face. Use yarn for hair and stick it on with white glue and, if necessary, pins. For younger children, make the clothes in advance. Older students can make their own. Use a basic pattern like a dress with sleeves cut out of it. Sew it up, leaving openings at the top and bottom. Decorate with colorful braid, sequins, etc. Run some glue around the protruding cardboard (the neck). Attach the top opening of the dress to the cardboard sleeve. Cut four hands from the pattern. Glue two together on each side of the

sleeve of the dress. (This gives you a back and front to the hand, which is similar to a mitten.) Sandwich the end of the dress sleeve so it all hangs together. Puppets can have long or short noses, three cornered hats, moustaches, *kipot,* or whatever. (ML)

16. Have students magine they are a specific Purim object and depict it through the medium of pantomime. Other students guess what the object is.

17. Divide the Purim story into small segments. Then form groups of 2 or 3 each. Give the students 10 to 15 minutes to work out a dramatization of their scene in the story. Have each group then act out their segment of the Purim narrative. If all goes well, this improvisation could become the basis for an assembly presentation.

18. Divide the class into pairs. One person of each pair is a reporter, while the second person becomes Haman, Mordecai, or Esther. The reporter interviews the personality. Then the students reverse roles and the second student serves as the reporter. Come back to the group as a whole to process the role play.

19. Perform or do as a readers theater "The Story of Purim: A Slightly Fractured Version" (see page 148).

20. Give the characters in the Purim story modern names, such as Mordecai Schwartz, Esther Levy, Haman Tashen, Ahasuerus Brown, Vashti Clothes, etc., and have the students act out parts of the Purim story in a contemporary setting. The funnier they make the story, the better.

21. Complete the Instant Lessons *Two Mitzvot of Giving* and *Our Purim Problem.*

22. Perform or do a readers theater version of the play "I Dream of Purim" from *Kings and*

Things: 20 Jewish Plays for Kids 8 to 18 by Meridith Shaw Patera (page 80).

23. Do one or more of the Shabbat art projects in *100+ Jewish Art Projects for Children* by Nina Streisand Sher and Margaret A. Feldman (pages 35 and 36).

Secondary

1. Have students write a Purim parody magazine. Include riddles, take-offs, and "commentaries." For ideas, consult *Sh'ma's* annual Purim issue and/or check the Internet.

2. The message of Purim has been relevant throughout the ages. Describe the context in which the following people, who were Hamans with a different name, lived, and what harm they brought to the Jewish people:
   a. Antiochus (vs. Maccabees, 165 B.C.E.)
   b. Torquemada (Grand Inquisitor, Spain, 1492 C.E.)
   c. Pharaoh (Egypt, c. 1220 B.C.E., possibly Ramses)
   d. Czar Nicholas I (early nineteenth century Russia)
   e. Hitler (twentieth century Germany)
   f. Saddam Hussein (Leader of Iran late twentieth century)

3. Divide the class into several groups. Ask each group to examine and summarize for the class one of the passages related to Purim from the Book of Esther.

4. Discuss: Do you think that Haman serves as the "role model" for the anti-Semite? Despite being, in all likelihood, a fictitious character, does he create a mold into which many persecutors of Israel have shaped themselves?

5. Investigate the preparations a person makes for the reading of the *Megillah*. What kind of trope is used? Is it different from that of the Torah or *Haftarah*? What other special preparations for Purim are made in the synagogue?

6. In small groups, have students brainstorm the concepts, ideas, rituals, and customs that are unique to Purim. Based on the ideas the groups come up with, have them think of ways to make the Purim celebration more meaningful to teenagers.

7. God is never mentioned in the Book of Esther. Discuss the implications of this. Does it mean that God is not present in the Purim story? Might it mean that God sometimes works in mysterious ways? Some people believe that the entire course of events in the story follow a predetermined divine plan, which is to say, God set into motion a sequence of events starting with the selection of Esther and leading up to the death of Haman. Ask students their opinions on this.

8. Purim is a time to enjoy great humor. Divide students into groups to develop any of the following for famous Jews: (1) answering machine messages (e.g., Joseph: "Hi, this is Joseph. I never dreamed you'd call. I'm probably in conference with the Pharaoh right now. Leave your message after the beep."); e-mail addresses (e.g., Judah Maccabee: 8NITES, Sarah: MOM@90, Elijah: W8-4-YN, or Albert Einstein E=MC2); and/or Purim home pages for the Web. (NSM)

9. Encourage students to do a Purim *shpiel* which pokes fun at something as a sub-text (teachers, an event in the news, etc.). (NSM)

10. Arthur Waskow has stated, "That Purim is a gigantic joke on anti-Semitism (represented by the recoil of Haman's hatred on his own head) has been apparent for many centuries" (*Seasons of Our Joy: A Handbook of Jewish Festivals*, page 126). Discuss what Waskow means by a "joke on anti-Semitism." Ask students to research other historical examples of this. (NSM)

11. *Tzedakah* is an ongoing responsibility for Jews. We are taught to give on a weekly basis and on

the occasion of all festivals. *Mishloach Manot* (sending of portions of food) is a custom practiced on Purim. Often, these small food packages are sent to friends as an expression of caring and friendship. *Matanot L'Evyonim* (gifts to the poor) could take the form of bringing food baskets to needy families. Have a congregational food collection, or work through a local food pantry and then bring generous boxes or baskets of food to needy families in your area. These gifts need not be limited to Jewish families. The *mitzvot* of giving applies to all people.

12. Because Purim is a post-biblical holiday, it is technically not a *Yom Tov* (i.e., a Holy Day), but rather a festive occasion. Ask: In light of this, is Purim less important than other special days in the Jewish calendar? Have students explain their reasoning

13. It is *a mitzvah* for Jews to redeem captives (*Pidyon Shevuyim*). Discuss whether or not students think the king's decree against the Jews of Persia in effect made them "captives." Was Esther actually fulfilling the *mitzvah* of *Pidyon Shevuyim*?

14. In the midst of one of his lengthy parties, King Ahashuerus ordered Vasti to dance in a seductive manner in front of the guests. She refused, and lost her position as queen as a result. For standing up to her husband, Vashti is viewed by some as one of history's first feminists. Ask: Do you agree or disagree with this assessment? Does Vashti deserve praise or criticism for her actions?

15. Provide each volunteer speaker with a potentially amusing, Purim-related topic to speak about for three minutes. The speech should start out related to the theme, but it may go in any direction whatsoever. The more nonsense the student says, the funnier it can be.

16. Ask each student to speak of a personal "Haman" whom they know or once knew. If they do not know such a person, imagine what a contemporary Haman would be like. How would they cope with such a person?

17. Debate: The *hamentashen* is a more important Jewish symbol than the *latke* or the *matzah*. (RAZ)

All-School

1. In addition to the usual fun booths (ring toss, hit Haman, cast lots, refreshments, etc.), add an educational component to the Purim carnival. Some ideas: Students find the mistakes in a one paragraph summary of the Purim story; sequence cards with a segment of the Purim story on each; teachers or parents dress up as Mordecai, Haman, Esther, and Ahashuerus and roam around the carnival with 3 or 4 questions on cards which might be asked of him/her. Each student is permitted to approach these characters and to ask one question. If the question is one of the 3 or 4 that the character is carrying, the student receives a bonus prize ticket; otherwise, no ticket. (For additional ideas, see the other activities in this chapter.)

Family

1. Urge parents to take their children to a different synagogue on Purim morning when the *Megillah* is read a second time. Afterward, compare and contrast the observance to that of your home congregation.

2. Suggest that families plan a festive meal for the celebration of Purim. They can bake two or three varieties of *hamantashen* and look through Jewish cookbooks to find unusual Jewish dishes to serve.

3. Organize a family education program for two to four-year-olds (there are three already designed Purim programs in *Head Start on Holidays: Jewish Programs for Preschoolers and*

Their Parents by Roberta Louis Goodman and Andye Honigman Zell).

4. Do a name exchange, trading names and addresses of families in your school or class. Ask each family to deliver a basket of *Mishloach Manot* to the name they received. (NSM)

5. To raise money for a favorite *tzedakah* cause, have a Purim auction. Ask families to donate *Mishloach Manot* baskets which may be auctioned-off. (Or, ask local Jewish "celebrities" to donate baskets for auction.) (NSM)

6. Ask each family to make up a series of questions related to the celebration of Purim and then survey the members of their immediate family and other relatives. They can record the responses and summarize the findings at the next family holiday celebration.

7. Suggest that families discuss Purim and decide what each member would like to donate to a needy family. They then bring *Shalach Manot* to family, friends, hospitals, and old age facilities.

A PURIM READING FOR CHILDREN

Robert Goodman

Cast of Characters
Reader 1
Reader 2

Reader 1: Happy Purim to you! May this be a very happy Purim for everyone. Every year when Purim comes, we look forward to the costumes, the reading of the *Megillah,* and eating the delicious *hamentashen.* But the best part of Purim is the story itself.

Reader 2: Once there was a king in Persia. His name was Ahasuerus (Ah-hah-shoe-air-us). And there was a very bad man who wanted the king to do bad things. The name of this man was Haman.

Reader 1: But there was a brave and wise man who saw how wicked Haman was. That good man was Mordecai the Jew. Mordecai told his cousin, the beautiful Queen Esther, about Haman's plan to kill the Jews of Persia. Esther risked her life in order to tell the king about Haman's plot.

Reader 2: It was the law that a person could only come before the king if he asked the person to be there. The queen knew this, but she also knew that she had to do something or she and her people would die. She must have been very frightened!

Reader 1: O God, help us when we are afraid! May we always remember that You are with us. Help us to understand that if we work hard to do the right thing, we can make our world better for everyone. Give us the strength and courage, O God, to work for a better world.

Reader 2: Had Haman been able to carry out his evil plan, Esther might have escaped death because she was the queen. But the Jews were her people and she felt that she had to risk her life to save her people. She knew that it was wrong to think only about herself.

Reader 1: O God, help us to remember that whatever we have comes from You.

Help us to remember that we use our talents and abilities best when we share them with others. Keep us from being selfish, so that we can always be kind and considerate to other people.

Reader 2: What would we do without brave men and women like Mordecai and Esther? Who would help God to make this a better world? We understood, O God, that with Your help, we can do special things to bring happiness and Shalom to others. We count on Your love and support.

Reader 1: We remember that many times in our long history, wicked people have tried to destroy us. Again and again You came to our aid. We thank You for Your love and caring. When we come together to celebrate the Shabbat or a holiday such as Purim, we remember our special bond with You, O God.

Reader 2: Purim is also a time when we can laugh and be silly. When we hear Haman's name, we can make all kinds of noise, and even boo Haman. We can dress up in costumes and look as ridiculous as we want. It is the one time in the year when anything goes, when we don't have to be serious. It's lots of fun!

Reader 1: We have learned some of the serious lessons of Purim. Now we are ready for some of its fun. Let us now enjoy the wonderful story of Purim.

THE STORY OF PURIM: A SLIGHTLY FRACTURED VERSION

Robert Goodman

Cast of Characters
Narrator 1
Narrator 2
King
Vashti
Haman
Mordecai
Esther
Guard

Narrator 1: Good evening ladies and gentlemen, and children of all ages. Welcome to the Kingdom of PERSIA. Have we got a story for you! We will make a BIG MEGILLAH of it. Before we begin with our story, let me introduce our cast of characters. And believe me, they are characters!

King: I am King Ahashuerus. I am the King of Persia, a land you now know as the countries of Iran and Iraq. Iran is right next to the country of I WALKED. My palace is located in the city of SHOESHINE where all the shoes look great. Actually it is called SHUSHAN.

Vashti: I am Queen Vashti. Actually I am not in this story for very long because I don't like the way the King bosses me around. I get no respect around here!

Haman: HAMAN's the name; hatred's the game. I am the Prime Minister of Persia. I am the bad guy in this story. When you see me, you bow down to me; and don't call me: HEY MAN!

Mordecai: I am Mordecai. I am the uncle of Esther. I play an important part in this story. I do not like HAMAN and will not bow down to him.

Esther: I am Esther. Mordecai is my uncle. I am your normal everyday beautiful woman who just happens to become queen. Otherwise my life is boring! Ha ha!

Guard: I am the King's guard. My first name is "OH." When the King wants me, he calls out my name: OH GUARD. I do my best to protect the King.

Narrator 2: And now to our story! Remember, every time you hear the name HAMAN, shake the noisemaker. Let's try it! Good.
One day, the King said to Queen Vashti . . .

King: Vashti, I am having this big party for many important people in my kingdom. I want you to come and do your famous belly dance for my guests.

Vashti: Your kingship, sir: Before I became Queen, I had a wicked wiggle and could do a dynamite belly dance. But now that I am Queen, it is not right for me to act that way. I am sorry, but I must refuse.

King: Vashti, you are fired!

Narrator 1: And so the King invited all of the beautiful young ladies of his kingdom to come to the city of Shushan where he held a beauty contest. Young Esther was the most beautiful and was chosen to be his new queen.

Narrator 2: This is a pretty complicated story, so please listen carefully. To make matters a bit less confusing, we are going to leave out the part about Mordecai uncovering a plot to kill the king and Haman leading Mordecai around Shushan on the king's horse.

Narrator 1: Let me tell you a little bit about Mordecai and Esther. Mordecai was a leader of the Jews of Shushan and a very well respected man. After Esther's parents died, she lived with her Uncle Mordecai. Now Esther had a real Hebrew name. It was HADASSAH. She wanted to be called O.R.T., but they did not have a local chapter in Shushan. King Ahashuerus did not know that Esther was Jewish.

Narrator 2: Now we meet the bad guy in this story! His name is HAMAN! The king made him the Prime Minister of all of Persia. Wherever he went, people would bow down to HAMAN, because he was so important.

Haman: I like being a big shot. Being Prime Minister is good stuff! Everyone bows down to me and makes me feel very important. Oh, here is Mordecai. I know that he is well known in these parts.

Mordecai: Good day, Mr. Prime Minister. How are you today?

Haman: Now wait a minute Mordecai! You are supposed to bow down to me. Why do you not bow down before HAMAN, the one and only?

Mordecai: I am sorry, Sir. As a Jew, I can only bow down before God. I treat you with respect, but I will not bow down before you.

Haman: *(Very angry and walking away.)* That man makes me very angry. He says he won't bow down to me because he is a Jew. Then, I know what I am going to do: I am going to kill Mordecai . . . and all the other Jews as well.

Narrator 1: So HAMAN decided to kill Mordecai and all the Jews of Persia. He went to the king and tricked the king into going along with his evil plan. He was so angry at Mordecai that he was very willing to lie about the Jewish people in order to get even with Mordecai.

Haman: Good day, O King. I come to you very upset about some of your subjects, who live all over your kingdom. There is a people in your land whose laws and customs are different from everybody else. Not only are they different, but they do NOT follow your laws, O King, I think they should all be killed!

King: Their behavior does not please me one bit, HAMAN. Your suggestion to hang them on the gallows is a good idea. So it shall be. Your request is granted

Narrator 2: When Mordecai heard what had happened, he put on rags and sackcloth and covered his body with ashes. All over Persia, Jews heard that wicked HAMAN wanted to kill them. They were very sad and very worried.

Narrator 1: But then Mordecai had an idea. He thought of a way that perhaps — just maybe — the Jews of Persia could be saved from HAMAN'S wicked plan. He went to see his niece Esther and told her what she had to do. He knew that she had to be very brave in order to save her people.

Mordecai: You realize, Esther, that the King does NOT know that you are a Jew.

Esther: If he did, I do not think he would have agreed to HAMAN'S terrible plan.

Mordecai: You are probably right Esther. The king may have agreed to the plan of HAMAN without understanding it or paying much attention to what he said. You must go before the king and ask him to spare you and your People.

Esther: But, dear Uncle — a person who comes before the king without an invitation can be put to death. If I do as you ask, I could be put to death.

Mordecai: I realize that, but you must take that chance. You are our only hope!

Esther: I will do what you ask. Pray for me, and in three days, I will go to the king.

Narrator 2: After three days, Esther put on a beautiful dress and went to see the king. She stood in the courtyard and waited for him to see her.

King: Good morning, Queen Esther. Please come in to my court and be with me. What brings you to my court this fine morning? Please tell me what you would like!

Esther: Oh King, I would like to invite you and HAMAN to come to a banquet this evening. I would be very honored if you would attend.

King: We will delighted to be with you this evening.

Narrator 1: And so that evening, King Ahashuerus and HAMAN came to Esther's wonderful banquet. It was a delicious meal with lots of fine wine. During the banquet, the king spoke to Esther:

King: Tell me, Esther, what can I give you? You may have anything — even half of my kingdom.

Esther: I ask only that you, O King — and HAMAN — return tomorrow night.

King: We will be delighted to return tomorrow evening, Queen Esther.

Narrator: Well, HAMAN was very happy about being invited to a second banquet given by the queen. He did not know that he was in for a big surprise.

Esther: Welcome, O King, to my quarters once again. I am so pleased that you and HAMAN could join me again this evening. I hope you enjoyed last night.

King: Esther dear, it was wonderful. Tell me, my queen, what may I give you? I will give you anything — even half of my kingdom.

Esther: Oh King, if I have found favor in your sight, please let my life be spared. Please let me and my people live.

King: I don't understand. I would never hurt you. Tell me how your life is in danger.

Esther: I am a Jew. On the 13th of Adar, all of my people are to be put to death because an evil man decided that I and my people are bad.

Haman: Oops, I think I am in heap big trouble. When I decided to get rid of Mordecai, I didn't realize that I would also have to kill the queen. I don't like this at all!

King: Oh Esther, who would do such a terrible thing to you?

Esther: (*Pointing at Haman.*) It is that man, the prime minister — HAMAN.

Guard: (*Rushes in.*) Oh King, I just learned that HAMAN built gallows to hang Mordecai and all the Jews.

King: Oh Guard, take HAMAN away, and hang him on the gallows that he built for Mordecai and the other Jews.

Narrator: And so Esther, Mordecai, and all the Jews of Persia were saved by Esther's bravery. Wicked HAMAN was hanged, and Mordecai became the new Prime Minister of Persia. And the Jews of Persia lived again in peace.

BIBLIOGRAPHY

See pages 278-279.

CHAPTER NINE

PESACH

VOCABULARY

Adir Hu: "God Is Mighty" or "God of Might" is a hymn sung at the end of the *Seder* service. Composed by an unknown poet, it consists of eight stanzas of eight lines each. The hymn speaks of how God's might and power brought freedom to the Israelites and offers the hope of freedom for all people living in servitude.

Afikoman: Greek for "Dessert." A portion of the middle of the three *matzot* on the *Seder* plate, it is hidden by the person leading the *Seder*, and redeemed after the meal from the children who have searched for and found it. It is the last morsel eaten on the *Seder* night.

Arami Oved Anochi: "My father was a fugitive Aramaean" (Deuteronomy 26:5). The verse continues: " . . . He went down to Egypt with meager numbers and sojourned there; but there he became a great and very populous nation." The Passover *Haggadah* includes this verse to reinforce the idea that despite humble beginnings, even subjugation, the Jews became a great and free people.

Arba'ah Banim: Literally "Four Sons." The *Haggadah* labels four types of Jewish youngsters based on how each approaches the story of the Exodus. The wise one asks about Pesach and wants to learn (Deuteronomy 6:20). The wicked one contends that the observance of Pesach does not pertain to him (Exodus 12:26). The simple person is bewildered by the celebration of Pesach and asks

what it is all about (Exodus 13:14). The ignorant person is unable to ask even the simplest questions related to Pesach and must be taught on the simplest level (Exodus 13:8).

Arba Kosot: "Four cups" of wine are served during the *Seder*, two before the meal and two during the concluding portion of the *Seder* service.

Arba Kushiyot: "Four Questions." Posed by the youngest child able to read or recite questions, this comes early in the *Seder* immediately after *Ha Lachma*, which opens the *Magid*, the fifth section of the *Seder* service. If there are no children present, an adult may ask the questions. The leader responds with a complex answer that includes: a brief historical account of the liberation of the Jews from Egypt, evidence of God's protection of Israel since the deliverance, and some of the rules of Pesach observance.

Barayech: Meaning "Bless," this is the thirteenth part of the *Seder* Service, and consists of the Grace after Meals with special Pesach additions.

Baytzah: "Egg." Usually roasted, an egg is one of the symbols on the *Seder* plate. It may be a substitute for the festival sacrifice (*Chagigah*), which was offered on Pesach in the Temple. The egg may also be a symbol of springtime and the rebirth of a people. Eating the egg in salt water may derive from the fact that this was a freeman's dish in ancient times.

Bedikat Chamaytz: "Search for Leaven." After having thoroughly cleaned one's home, a search for leaven takes place on the evening before Pesach. So as not to make this a vain search, a few crumbs are conspicuously placed, searched for by candlelight, and when "found," swept onto a wooden spoon with a feather. Once these last crumbs are burned, any other *chamaytz* in the house is considered to be just dust.

Bi'ur Chamaytz: "Burning of *Chamaytz.*" By 10:00 A.M. on the morning of *erev* Pesach, all *chamaytz* which has not been sold is burned.

Chad Gadya: "An Only Kid," is a folk song which concludes the *Seder* service. Intended for the entertainment of the children, it consists of ten stanzas written in the form of a nursery rhyme using Aramaic rather than Hebrew. Some people regard it as an allegorical song that speaks of the eventual destruction of all tyrants and oppressors.

Chag HaAviv: "Festival of Spring," is one of the four names of Pesach. This is the end of the rainy season in Israel.

Chag HaMatzot: "Festival of the Unleavened Bread," is one of the four names given to Pesach (Leviticus 23:6).

Chag HaPesach: "Festival of Passover," is one of the four names given to Pesach. The word *"pesach"* is of uncertain origin. It may mean to "pass over," as the Angel of Death passed over the homes of the Hebrews, or it may refer to the lamb offered in sacrifice on the holiday, or it may refer to an ancient nomadic festival.

Chamaytz: "Sour" or "Leavened." No leavening agent may be used or owned during Pesach. *Chamaytz* is symbolically sold to a non-Jew before Pesach and then bought back after the festival is concluded.

Charoset: One of the symbols on the *Seder* plate, it is a combination of apples, nuts, cinnamon, and wine. This sweet mixture symbolizes the mortar used by the Israelites to make bricks for the building projects ordered by Pharaoh. It is used to sweeten the bitter herbs.

Chazeret: "Bitter Herb," is one of the symbols on the *Seder* plate. *Chazeret* can be any vegetable with a bitter taste — cucumber, watercress, radish, endive, etc. Numbers 9:11 speaks of eating the Paschal lamb "with unleavened bread and bitter herbs (*m'rorim*)." Since bitter herbs is in the plural, *chazeret* is used in addition to *maror.* While most Seder trays have a compartment for *chazeret,* its use is considered optional.

Chol HaMo'ed Pesach: "The intermediary days of Pesach." Of the eight days of Pesach, the third, fourth, fifth, and sixth days are considered intermediary. Chol HaMo'ed Pesach and Sukkot are semi-holidays, observed with special prayers. However, one may treat these days as any weekday with only minor restrictions. In Jerusalem, and among liberal Jews, Pesach is celebrated for seven days.

Echad Mi Yodea: "Who Knows One?" is a cumulative riddle that is sung at the conclusion of the *Seder* service. Using the format of questions and answers, basic Jewish beliefs and traditions are conveyed in the thirteen stanzas. Each number has a special meaning: 13 attributes of God, 12 tribes of Israel, 11 stars in Joseph's dream, 10 Commandments, 9 months of pregnancy, 8 days for *Brit Milah,* 7 days in a week, 6 sections in Mishnah, 5 books in Torah, 4 Matriarchs, 3 Patriarchs, 2 tablets of the Covenant, and One God.

Eliyahu HaNavi: "The Prophet Elijah." This ninth century B.C.E. prophet who took on the evil Ahab and Jezebel as described in I Kings, according to tradition, did not die, but ascended to heaven in a firey chariot. He remains among us testing the hospitality and generousity of people, protecting children, helping the poor, and primed to announce the coming of the Messiah. Opening the door for Elijah during the *Seder* symbolizes hope in that time of redemption. A fifth cup of wine is on the *Seder* table for Elijah. Should he arrive, he will answer all difficult questions . . . including, are there to be four or five cups of wine at the *Seder*.

Eser Makot: "Ten Plagues" were inflicted upon Egypt (Exodus 7:14 - 12:36) because Pharaoh refused to let the Hebrew leave his country. The plagues were: 1) waters of the Nile turned to blood; 2) infestation of frogs; 3) lice; 4) swarms of insects; 5) a pestilence affecting livestock; 6) boils; 7) hail and fire; 8) locusts; 9) three days of darkness; 10) the death of the firstborn of man and beast. A drop is removed from the wine cup upon mention of each plague.

Haggadah: "Telling" or "Narrative." This book contains the rituals for the observance of the *Seder*, including the stories, songs, and prayers. *Magid*, which is the fifth section of the *Seder* service, comes from the same Hebrew root.

Ha Lachma: "This Is the Bread," is a prayer in Aramaic which marks the beginning of the *Magid* section of the *Seder* service. Holding half of the middle *matzah* from the stack of three, the leader announces: "This is the bread of affliction, the poor bread, which our ancestors ate in the land of Egypt . . ." Dating back some 2000 years, this prayer goes on to invite the needy to join in the *Seder*, and it concludes with an expression of hope for all people: "This year we celebrate here. Next year in the land of Israel. Now we are all still slaves. Next year may we all be free."

Hallel: The *Hallel* consists of Psalms in praise of God. Psalms 113-118 are recited on the first two days of Pesach and serve as the fourteenth section in the *Seder* service. During the last six days of Pesach, the first 11 verses of both Psalm 115 and 116 are omitted. The *Chatzi-Hallel* is said on these days because of a tradition which states that God stopped the angels from singing praises when they saw the Egyptians drowning in the sea — a reflec-

tion of Jewish sensitivity toward the suffering of others.

Isru Chag: Meaning "Bind a Festival," this term comes from Psalm 118:27 which states: ". . . hold onto the festival even as it departs." Thus, the day following Pesach, Shavuot, and Sukkot is Isru Chag. It is a minor festival for liturgical purposes.

Kadaysh: "Sanctify." This is the first section in the *Seder* service, the recitation of the Passover *Kiddush* and the drinking of the first of four cups of wine.

K'arah: The Passover *Seder* plate.

Karpas: "Green Vegetable," is one of the symbols on the *Seder* plate. While parsley is the usual *karpas*, lettuce or celery may also be used. *Karpas* symbolizes the green of spring and the spirit of hope for the future. It also recalls the meager food available to the Hebrews living as slaves in Egypt. (See Appendix, page 253, for blessing.)

Kittel: A white robe, usually made of linen, that is worn on Rosh HaShanah, Yom Kippur, and Pesach. The *kittel is* worn on Pesach to symbolize the release from bondage and slavery and the beginning of a life of freedom. It is also worn by a groom, and serves as a burial shroud.

Koraych: Hillel "Sandwich," is the tenth section of the *Seder* service. So named because of the custom of Hillel to place *maror* on *matzah* and eat as a sandwich. The source of the practice is Numbers 9:11: "They shall eat it (i.e., the paschal lamb) with *matzah* and *maror*."

Koso Shel Eliyahu: The "Cup of Elijah" is set aside for the Prophet's arrival at the *Seder*.

Lechem Mishneh: "Double Portion of Bread," refers to the double portion of manna collected by the Israelites in the wilderness before the Shabbat to last for two days (Exodus 16:22). It also is the term used to refer to two of the three pieces of *matzah* on the *Seder* plate.

Lechem Oni: "Bread for the Poor," refers to the *matzah* which was the bread eaten by those living in a state of stress and hardship. The third of the three *matzot* on the *Seder* plate is called *Lechem Oni.*

Magid: From the same Hebrew root as *Haggadah,* this is the section that tells the Pesach story. It begins with the *Ha Lachma* prayer and the Four Questions.

Ma Nishtanah: Meaning "What is different," this is a name for and also the first two words of the Four Questions.

Ma'ot Chitim: Literally "Money for Wheat," this is a special fund which provides even the poorest Jew with *matzah,* wine, and the other essentials for a festive celebration of Pesach. Thus all can celebrate Pesach in dignity. This fund is in addition to regular *tzedakah* gifts made throughout the year.

Maror: The bitter herb, usually horseradish root, which symbolizes the bitterness of slavery. (See Appendix, page 253, for blessing.)

Matzah/Matzot: Unleavened bread made from flour and water, quickly kneaded, and then rapidly baked so that no fermentation takes place during the baking. *Matzah* is also the term for the eighth section of the *Seder* service consisting of reciting the grace for the *matzah,* then the breaking of the upper *matzah* and distributing pieces to the participants at the *Seder.* (See Appendix, page 253, for blessing.)

Matzah Ashira: Literally "Rich *Matzah,*" it is made with wine, oil, honey, and eggs instead of with just flour and water. The Talmud (*Pesachim* 36a) states that, since this kind of *matzah* does not conform with the idea of *matzah* as "bread of affliction" *(Lechem Oni)*, it may not be used for the celebration of Passover.

Matzah Sh'murah: Literally "Guarded *Matzah,*" it is made from wheat that is watched carefully from harvest to baking so that it is not exposed to moisture or excessive heat. Once mixed with water, the batter must be kneaded, rolled, and baked within an 18 minute time period. It is considered by some the most desirable *matzah* to use during Pesach.

M'chirat Chamaytz: "The Selling of *Chamaytz.*" Since one must not own *chamaytz* during Pesach, it sold for the duration of Pesach, and then repurchased. While the transaction is technically a sale, it is really a "legal fiction." The Rabbi draws up a bill of sale for the *chamaytz,* temporarily transfering ownership to a non-Jew.

Motzi: "The Blessing over Bread" is the seventh section of the Pesach *Seder.* At the *Seder* it is said over a piece of the upper *matzah* immediately followed by the blessing for eating *matzah.* (See Appendix, page 253, for blessing.)

Nirtzah: "May it be Acceptable," is the fifteenth and final section of the *Seder* service. The *Seder* is concluded with the hope that all of the prayers recited will be acceptable to God, and with the final words *l'Shanah HaBa'ah Birushalayim* — Next Year in Jerusalem.

Nisan: The first month of the Jewish year, corresponding to March/April, it has 30 days, and its zodiac sign is Aries. In ancient times, Nisan 1 was the New Year for dating the years of a king's reign. The 15th is the first day of Pesach.

Pesach: The actual meaning of this word is in doubt. It may mean to pass over (as did the Angel of Death), or to skip (like a young lamb), or it may mean a young lamb (the sacrifice in the Temple), or it may have its origin in an ancient nomadic festival. Pesach is called Passover in English.

Pesach Shayni: "Second Pesach." Sometimes called *Pesach Katan* ("Small Pesach"), this was for someone unable to offer the Pesach sacrifice in Nisan due to travel, illness, or ritual defilement. In accordance with Numbers 9:9-13, such a person may celebrate *Pesach Shayni* on the 14th of Iyar, a month after Pesach.

Rachatzah: Washing, is the sixth section of the *Seder* service, consists of washing one's hands accompanied by the customary blessing. (See Appendix, page 253, for blessing.)

Seder: Meaning "Order," it refers to the order of the *Seder* service on the first night(s) of Pesach. The *Seder* is traditionally divided into 15 sections, each of which has a name.

Sefirat HaOmer: "The counting of the *Omer*." An *Omer* was a measure of barley brought in ancient Israel to the Temple on the first day of Pesach as a thanksgiving offering. Leviticus 23:15-16 commands: "From . . . the day that you bring the sheaf (*omer*) of wave offering, you shall keep count until seven full weeks have elapsed: you shall count 50 days, until the day after the seventh week (Shavuot); then you shall bring an offering of new grain to *Adonai*." The Counting of the *Omer* is a part of the daily evening service from the day after Pesach until Shavuot. This provides a link between Pesach and Shavuot.

Shabbat HaGadol: "The Great Sabbath" precedes Pesach and is so called because the *Haftarah* for that day is Malachi 3:24, which ends with the words: "Lo, I will send the prophet Elijah to you before the coming of the awesome great day of *Adonai*." Traditionally, the Rabbi's sermon is devoted to the rules and dietary laws pertaining to Pesach.

Shalosh Matzot: "Three *Matzot*" are placed on the *Seder* plate, two are the *Lechem Mishneh,* and one the *Lechem Oni.*

Shalosh Regalim: "The Three Pilgrimage Festivals." On Pesach, Shavuot, and Sukkot, Israelites journeyed on foot to Jerusalem to offer sacrifices at the Temple in accord with Deuteronomy 16:16-17.

Shir HaShirim: "Song of Songs," one of the five *Megillot,* is read on Shabbat Chol HaMo'ed Pesach, the Shabbat in the middle of Pesach. *Shir HaShirim,* described as a love song between God (the bridegroom) and Israel (the bride), is read on Pesach to symbolize the courtship between Israel and God which began with the Exodus and continued with the wedding at Mount Sinai, when Israel accepted the Torah.

Shulchan Oraych: Literally, the "Table is Ready." This is the term for the eleventh section of the *Seder* service, eating the Passover meal. Four sections of the *Seder* service remain to be completed after the conclusion of the meal.

Ta'anit B'chorim: "The Fast of the Firstborn." On *erev* Pesach in Egypt, the firstborn of the Egyptian were slain, while the Hebrews were spared. In memory of that deliverance from the tenth plague, it is a custom for first born sons to fast all day until the *Seder*. To obviate the fast, it is customary to finish a tractate of Talmud that morning so as to celebrate with a *siyyum* — a celebratory snack.

Tefillat Tal: "Prayer for Dew" is recited at the Musaf service on the first day of Pesach. It was composed by Eleazar Kalir in the tenth century and takes the form of a reverse acrostic which asks for dew to freshen the soil of Israel.

Tzafun: "Hidden." This is the twelfth section of the *Seder* service. It consists of eating the *Afikoman* which had been hidden then found by a child. No other food may eaten after the *Afikoman.*

Urchatz: Literally, "And Wash." This second section of the *Seder* service consists of washing one's hands without saying the customary blessing.

Yachatz: This fourth section of the *Seder* service consists of breaking the middle *matzah* and putting half away to be hidden for the *Afikoman.*

Yizkor: The memorial service that takes place on the last day of Pesach, Sukkot, Shavuot, and on Yom Kippur.

Z'man Chayrutaynu: "The Season of Our Freedom." This is one of the names for the festival of Pesach. The Israelites were slaves in Egypt, and then during this season became a free people.

Z'roa: The roasted "Shankbone" is one of the symbols on the *Seder* plate. It represents the paschal offering that was brought to the Temple in Jerusalem. It can also be seen as a symbolic representation of God's "outstretched helping hand."

BACKGROUND

The story of the Exodus from Egypt is found in the first half of the Book of Exodus with chapters 12 and 13 serving as the focal point of the historical narrative.

Leviticus 23:5-8 contains the biblical injunctions to celebrate the Festival of Pesach: "in the first month, on the fourteenth day of the month, at twilight, there shall be a passover offering (Pesach) to the Lord, and on the fifteenth day of that month is the Lord's Feast of Unleavened Bread (Chag HaMatzot). You shall eat unleavened bread for seven days. The first day shall be for you a sacred occasion: you shall not work at your occupations. Seven days you shall make offerings by fire to *Adonai*. The seventh day shall be a sacred occasion: you shall not work at your occupations."

Efforts to probe the origins of the Jewish holidays are in no way intended to denigrate the importance or the meaning of the festivals. Rather, they help to demonstrate the genius of the Jewish people who drew from their environment, transforming what might have begun as a pagan idea or practice into something with universal and timeless significance.

According to such scholars as Hayyim Schauss and Theodor Gaster, the modern festival of Pesach is a combination of a shepherd's festival and an agricultural festival. Leviticus 23 reinforces that idea.

It is possible that a Pesach festival had its earliest stirrings among semi-nomads who thousands of years ago wandered the desert and the semi-arid environs around Palestine. Nisan was the month when sheep most often gave birth. These nomads came to observe a festival at the time of the full moon. Just before nightfall, a sheep or goat was sacrificed. The animal was then roasted, and the family ate a hasty meal so that all of the animal would be eaten by daybreak. No bones of this sacrificial animal could be broken. Tent posts were daubed with the blood of the slain animal as an antidote to plagues, misfortune, and illness. The original meaning of the Hebrew word "*pesach*" is lost. The interpretation signifying "skip over" or "pass over" was later given to the word.

Perhaps the Feast of Unleavened Bread was a six or seven day festival marking the beginning of the spring harvest period that was celebrated by the farmers of Canaan. It was started with the cutting of the barley and the offering of the first sheaf of the newly cut barley to the priest as a sacrifice to God. The elimination of *chamaytz* may have originally been precautionary so as not to infect the new incoming crop. Or, it may have been a way of propitiating the priests and God so as to assure health and bounty.

As Judaism moved away from being agriculturally based, new interpretations and new customs were added to the Pesach ritual so that Jews living all over the world and in all ages could meaningfully celebrate Pesach. The prototype *Haggadah* finds its way into the Mishnah as Tractate *Pesachin*. By the end of the Talmudic period, its form and much of its content were as they are today. It must have been widely accepted, because the *Haggadah* was included in the very first prayer book of Rav Amram in the eighth century, as well as in the prayer book of Saadia Gaon in Babylonia (tenth century). Somewhere around the twelfth century, it began to be copied as a separate book. It attracted many commentaries, and became the favorite subject of Jewish artists who found the subject liberating. Illuminated *Haggadot* were especially prevalent in the sixteenth and seventeenth centuries in Prague, Amsterdam, and Venice, among other important cities. A magnificent Sephardic *Haggadah* made its way from Spain eastward in the fifteenth century and is named after the city which claimed it — *The Sarajevo Haggadah*. Today, the making of *Haggadot* is without end. The artistry and commentaries continue to delight and amaze. Often such works are not only used at the *Seder* table, they become treasured possessions.

Central Themes

- The four names for Pesach reflect four aspects of this festival:

  Chag HaPesach is linked with the account of the tenth plague when God passed over the homes of the Israelites, and with the Pesach offering that was brought to the Temple in Jerusalem.

  Chag HaMatzot, The Festival of Unleavened Bread, is an outgrowth of an early agricultural festival and reflects the centrality of *matzah* in the celebration of Pesach.

  Chag HaAviv, The Festival of Spring, reflects the seasonal significance of Pesach.

  Z'man Chayrutaynu, The Season of Our Freedom, marks the attainment of freedom from bondage by the ancient Israelites.

- Pesach can be viewed as a time of release, accompanied by a positive achievement. This theme is seen on three levels. On a seasonal plane, there is the release of the earth from the grip of winter, and the time of the reaping of the grain. The grain is harvested by people, but could not have been grown without God's help. On a historical plane, there is the release of the Children of Israel from the grip of Egypt, and the birth of the Jewish nation in Covenant with God. On a universal plane, Pesach symbolizes the hoped for release of all people from physical and spiritual bondage, and the ability of all to live in dignity.

- While Pesach was at first an agricultural festival, through the centuries it became a festival of freedom and deliverance. This gradual shift took place in response to the growing numbers of Jews living outside of *Eretz Yisrael* and to the reality of the end of the biblical period and the beginning of the Rabbinic era. Change brought added new symbolism, concepts, and dimensions to the festival.

- Pesach marks the emergence of Israel as a nation and as a people, freely accepting Torah as its constitution, and as the basis for Jewish life. Until Sinai, God made covenants with individual Jews; this time it was with *Am Yisrael,* the entire Jewish People.

- By participating in the *Seder*, one symbolically and vicariously relives the Exodus from Egypt. Around the festive table, past and present merge, and the future is promising. In a certain sense, the *Seder* ritual is a reflection of Deuteronomy 29:13-14, which speaks of just such time-lessness: "I make this covenant . . . not with you alone, but with those who are standing here with us this day before *Adonai* our God and with those who are not (yet) with us here this day."

- The *Seder* is abundant in symbolism. Each aspect and item in the service can be interpreted on many levels, leading to ever newer interpretations which further enrich the meaning of the Festival. On such innovation took place in the late 1970s and the early 1980s. The Matzah of Hope was added to remind us of the plight of Soviet Jews who were then virtual prisoners in their country. While many Jews from the FSU have subsequently found a home in Israel, America, and elsewhere, we can still set aside a Matzah of Hope for people everywhere who are victims of political, economic, and religious oppression. It is our hope as Jews that all people everywhere will soon live in freedom.

- The *Haggadah* is a masterpiece of pedagogy. It uses many effective and affective learning techniques, employing the Socratic method of questions and answers, storytelling, show and tell, song, play, food as stimulus and as reward, suspense (will Elijah appear?), pathos (plagues), and more. It is especially structured to involve children meaningfully and to hold their interest by carefully integrating activities for them. These include: a child reciting the Four Questions, the singing of familiar melodies throughout the service, the search for the *Afikoman*, and the question and answer approach during the *Magid* section of the *Seder* service.

• The origins of Pesach reflect Judaism's ongoing process of development and change. Two ancient pagan festivals, the semi-nomadic one-day Pesach festival and the seven-day Canaanite *Matzah* grain festival are mixed together in the blender of Judaism. It is interesting to trace to references to Chag HaPesach and Chag HaMatzot in the Torah. Sometimes they occur together, and at other times, Passover is described as one or the other. Time and again throughout Jewish history, ancient customs have been adapted for inclusion within the framework of Jewish life. In the process the meaning and significance of these practices, ideas, and customs were radically transformed and given a

spiritual dimension. This brief explanation can serve as a backdrop for a discussion about how Judaism changes and develops in our day.

Order of the Passover Seder
There are 15 parts to the *Seder* service. Some are very short, and one, the *Magid*, is extremely long. For the order of the *Seder*, see below on this page.

Highlights of the Liturgy
For the first Day of Pesach, there are two Torah readings. First, Exodus 12:21-51 is a description the last of the ten plagues, the events leading up to the Exodus, and some of the basic laws regarding the Passover offering. The second portion, the *Maftir*, is Numbers 28:19-25, which describes in detail the Pesach offerings to be brought to the sanctuary.

The *Haftarah* is Joshua 5:2-6:1, which describes how Joshua gathers the Israelites at Gilgal; circumcizes all males who had been born after the Exodus; and, while still encamped at Gilgal, offers the Passover sacrifice.

On the Second Day, two Torahs are again taken from the Ark. First, Leviticus 22:26-23:44, con-

Name		Description
1	KADAYSH	Recite the *Kiddush* over the day. All drink the first of the four cups of wine.
2	URCHATZ	Wash the hands without reciting a blessing.
3	KARPAS	The celery is dipped in salt water, blessed, and eaten.
4	YACHATZ	Break the middle *matzah*, putting half away for the *Afikoman*.
5	MAGID	Tell the story of the Exodus and sing praises to God over the second cup of wine.
6	RACHATZAH	Wash the hands with the customary blessing (*Al Netilat Yadayim*).
7	MOTZI	Recite the blessing over bread using a piece of the upper *matzah*.
8	MATZAH	Recite blessing over the *matzah*, break and distribute the upper *matzah*.
9	MAROR	Eat the bitter herbs dipped in *charoset*.
10	KORAYCH	Eat the *maror* and *matzah* in a sandwich.
11	SHULCHAN ORAYCH	Serve the Pesach meal.
12	TZAFUN	Eat a piece of the *Afikoman*, after which no other food may be eaten.
13	BARAYCH	Say the Grace after Meals.
14	HALLEL	Chant the *Hallel* (Psalms 113-118).
15	NIRTZAH	End the *Seder* with a prayer for the acceptance of the service.

tains instructions regarding the celebration of the major festivals of the Jewish year with specific reference to the bringing of the Omer. The *Maftir* is the same as for the first day.

The *Haftarah* is II Kings 23:1-9 and 21-25, which describes the Pesach celebrated by King Josiah around the year 621 B.C.E. when the Book of Deuteronomy was "discovered" in the Temple and read to the people.

The counting of the *Omer* begins on the Second Day of Pesach. Leviticus 23:15-16 is read each evening during the Counting of the *Omer*: "From the day after the Sabbath [i.e., Pesach], the day that you bring the sheaf of wave offering, you shall keep count until seven full weeks have elapsed: You shall count 50 days, until the day after the seventh week; then you shall bring an offering of new grain to *Adonai*." This passage is followed by: Blessed are You, *Adonai* our God, Sovereign of the World, who has hallowed us by Your commandments, and has commanded us concerning the Counting of the *Omer*." Then: "This is the _____ day of the *Omer*."

Because this seven week period is full of sad memories for the Jewish people, weddings are permitted only on Lag B'Omer, Rosh Chodesh Iyar, and Sivan, and recently Yom HaAtzma'ut and Yom Yerushalayim. A Yizkor service is held on the last day of Pesach.

The liturgy for the Shabbat that falls on Chol HaMo'ed Pesach essentially follows that of a regular Shabbat with the addition of a passage related to Pesach in the *Amidah*. The Torah portion is Exodus 33:12-34:26, about the Pilgrimage Festivals and ending with the command to eat unleavened bread. The *Maftir* is identical to that for the first two days of Pesach. The *Haftarah* is Ezekiel 37:1-14, the famous vision of the valley of dry bones. At the conclusion of the morning service, Song of Songs is read. It speaks of the love between a young man and young woman and has been likened to the covenantal relationship between God and Israel. The love song, whether it be understood literally or allegorically, is well suited for the spring. It speaks of the winter being past, the rain gone, and flowers upon the earth. Hope, too, springs eternal.

Passover Foods

Removing all leaven *(chamaytz)* from the home is part of making a home *Kasher l'Pesach* — Kosher for Pesach. In addition to removing any leavened foods, all utensils which came into contact with *chamaytz* may not be used during Pesach or on the day preceding Pesach. Two special sets of utensils, flatware, and dishes are used for Pesach: one for *milchig* (dairy) dishes and one for *fleishig* (meat) dishes.

All cooking, food preparation, and eating surfaces are scoured and usually covered for the duration of Pesach. The refrigerator is likewise cleaned to remove all traces of *chamaytz*. The care and the extent that Pesach preparations are made depends on the fervor with which a person celebrates Pesach. Some people do not prepare the home for Pesach, but refrain from eating anything that is *chamaytz*, while others meticulously follow all of the rules and regulations.

Many foods are labeled *Kasher l'Pesach*. Each year the Union of Orthodox Jewish Congregations of America publishes a directory of Passover products that are recognized by them as *Kasher l'Pesach*. In the choice of foods, there is also a wide range of observance.

In addition to bread products containing leaven, there are a few other foods which are not eaten on Pesach. The basic rule is that any product that is fermented or can cause fermentation may not be eaten, including five grains: wheat, rye, barley, oats, and spelt. Any food or drink that is made from one of these grains or which contains one of these grains, even in very small quantity, is considered *chamaytz*.

Ashkenazic Jews follow the custom of not eating rice, corn, peanuts, or other vegetables in the pea family, treating them as *chamaytz*, because these products swell when cooked and so resemble a leavening process. Neither the grains nor any of the flours or oils made from them may be used. Sephardic tradition allows these products to be eaten.

Matzah is an unleavened bread made from water and flour of any of the five major grains which have been carefully tended from harvest through the baking process to make certain that they have no leaven in them.

SCOPE AND SEQUENCE

Grade	Themes/ideas
Kindergarten	Stories about Pesach. A first look at the *Seder* service.
Grade One	Stories about Pesach. What children can do to help their families prepare for the family *Seder*.
Grade Two	A basic *Seder* service: a look at some of the key sections, such as the "Four Questions" and "The Four Sons."
Grade Three	Preparing and leading a *Seder* for students in Kindergarten through Grade 3. The main *Seder* symbols and their significance.
Grade Four	The Pesach vocabulary related to the *Seder*. How Pesach is celebrated in Israel.
Grade Five	Pesach customs and practices apart from the *Seder* service.
Grade Six	The Order of the *Seder*. Review of Pesach vocabulary.
Grade Seven	Pesach as it is described in the Bible. A close look at Leviticus 23:5-9. An overview of the events leading up to the Exodus as portrayed in the book of Exodus.
Grade Eight	The Meaning of Pesach, its significance for contemporary Jewry. Writing and leading a creative *Seder* entitled "Passover Old and New."
Grade Nine	The origin and development of Pesach.
Grade Ten	Review of Pesach vocabulary, the origin of Pesach, and its significance for modern Jewry.
Grade Eleven	The mechanics of having a *Kasher l'Pesach* home and the rationale for it.
Grade Twelve	Exploring new symbolism and new ideas to add to the many varied interpretations of Pesach and its symbols.

ACTIVITIES

Preschool/Kindergarten

1. Before Pesach have a "tasting party." Compare the taste of *matzah* with other kinds of crackers and/or bread. (NSM)

2. Help children make a *Seder* plate. Children decorate a paper plate with pictures of items used on the *Seder* plate. Variation: Cut the likenesses out of colored paper, glue them on the plate and decorate it.

3. Work with sand and water to mold bricks. (You'll need to warn parents that you're going to be playing with wet sand in the sandbox). Let the bricks dry. Compare these bricks with bricks of mud baked slowly in an oven. (NSM)

4. Bring a commercially made brick into the classroom. Make observations and comparisons concerning its size, shape, and weight. Mark the water line in a tub of water. What will happen if you put in a brick? Put the brick in and check the line. Take it out and remeasure. (NSM)

5. Use a balance scale. How much *matzah* does it take to balance out an amount of *charoset*? (NSM)

6. Have each child illustrate a scene from the Passover events. Then mix up the pictures and take turns sequencing them. You might have children use clothespins to hang the pictures in order on a clothesline.

7. Do paintings with some items from the *Seder* table: hard boiled egg, parsley, *matzah*. Provide paint and paper and let children roll or make prints with the items. (NSM)

8. Make up stories about the children in your class as slaves in Egypt. For example, "Jamie was in charge of carrying the water. She took the water to the adults making the bricks, etc." (NSM)

9. Have each student make a picture book of the Four Questions so he/she can use the pictures as reading clues. Ask some parents to search magazines for pictures. These can be placed in a pile from which students may choose. (The first page might have a picture of the night sky. When children see it, they'll know to ask, "Why is this night different?" Another page might have a picture of bread and of *matzah*, etc.). (NSM)

10. To the housekeeping area add: costumes for Egyptian life, *matzah*, a *Seder* plate, sandals, a staff (like that of Moses), a feather and candle, several *Haggadot*, etc. (NSM)

11. Let students make their own salt water recipe. Provide carrots, celery, and parsley to dip in and taste. (NSM)

12. View and discuss the video *Passover at Bubbe's*. Ask: How did the puppets help Bubbe prepare for her *Seder*?

13. Little ones can learn about the Exodus story by playing *Follow the Leader* and *I'm Going on a Trip to _____*.

14. Think of an object, symbol, person, or custom related to Pesach. The children try to guess what that something is. The child who guesses successfully then thinks of something for the others to guess.

15. Read to the children *A Taste for Noah* by Susan Remick Topek. Ask children how they handle it when they don't like a specific holiday food.

16. Pass around a "feelie bag" filled with items related to Pesach. Students must reach in the bag and guess what each object is. After everyone has had a chance to feel the contents of the bag, pass around each object. The child who is holding an object when the teacher claps, must tell something about it.

17. Hide some crackers in the room and provide students with a spoon, candle, and feather for searching out the *chamaytz*.

18. Kindergarten students can complete the Instant Lesson *Seder Symbols and Their Stories* by Debra Markovic and Lisa Rauchwerger.

19. Help children complete pages 33-39 in *Jewish Preschool/Kindergarten Copy Pak™* by Nancy Cohen Nowak.

20. Do one of the movement activities related to Shabbat in *Creative Movement for a Song* by JoAnne Tucker (pages 20, 28, 32, 44).

21. Complete some of the activities in *The Jewish Perschool Teachers Handbook* by Sandy Furfine Wolf and Nancy Cohen Nowak (pages 89-95).

22. Do a Pesach art projects in *100+ Jewish Art Projects for Children* by Nina Streisand Sher and Margaret A. Feldman (page 42).

Primary
1. Each student makes a take-home kit for Pesach — a decorated shoebox or other small box with a collection of hand-made Pesach objects

placed inside it. These can include a *matzah* cover, a *Seder* plate, *Kiddush* cup, a creative *Haggadah*, etc.

2. Taste the foods on the *Seder* table. Discuss what each tastes like and what it is supposed to remind us of. (NSM)

3. Ask a parent, principal, the Rabbi, or another teacher to come to class dressed as Moses, Aaron, Miriam, or Nachshon. The class interviews the person, asking questions related to the events in his/her life and his/her accomplishments.

4. If the school is in session when tables are being set for a school or synagogue *Seder*, take the class to look at the tables. What is on them? What is still missing? (NSM)

5. Have a (Jewish) construction worker come to class to show his/her tools and compare his/her work to life in Egypt. Talk about choosing to work and being a slave. (NSM)

6. Let children make paintings using finger paints or chocolate pudding, then make Pesach cards out of their art work. Or, use vaseline and water paint to make a paint resist. In the latter case, children draw their picture on white paper with vaseline. (Don't cover the whole paper with the vaseline, just use it on the outline and some fill-in.) They then paint over each object drawn in vaseline with water paint, using either a brush or a finger. In order to get a beaded effect in the finished picture, they should use more water than paint. Let the pictures set on a level surface in order to dry so that the beads don't run. Send the cards to friends and family members, as well as to Jews in the hospital and elderly members of the congregation.

7. Take a field trip to a grocery store and see what is kosher for Pesach. (NSM)

8. Work in small groups to see what happens when water is added to yeast. Use a magnifying glass. Add some flour to the yeast and water mixture, make a dough, and observe it. Also, add some flour to water (no yeast), make a dough, and observe it. Roll both dough mixtures out thinly, cover them, and keep them in a warm spot for 15 to 20 minutes. Make observations. Then, bake both mixtures. Analyze what yeast does to dough. (NSM)

9. Make a "television show" about Pesach. Have each child depict a different scene on an 8 1/2" x 11" sheet of paper. When they are finished, have them write or dictate a one sentence description of each picture on a blank sheet of paper. Then attach the sheets together, putting the appropriate description right before each picture. Put a dowel at each end of the connected sheets. Cut out the front of a large box, and you will have a television set. The story of Pesach can then be viewed by turning the dowel and showing one picture at a time.

10. Cut up two *Haggadot* and cut off the page numbers at the bottom. Glue the pages onto construction paper. (By using two *Haggadot*, when you glue them onto paper, you'll have one of each side of the paper.) Have a small group of children work together to try and put the *Haggadah* together in order based on what they know of the order of the *Seder*. They can check their work by looking at a *Haggadah* that hasn't been cut apart. (NSM)

11. Take two photos of each child. Have each child cut out his/her body in both pictures. The child uses one photo in a scene he/she draws that shows himself/herself as a slave and the other in a scene that shows himself/herself in the Exodus from Egypt. (These can be done as individual pictures or in a class mural.) (NSM)

12. Read to the children *Mrs. Katz and Tush* by Patricia Polacco. Have children act out scenes from the story, then discuss it.

13. When children return to school after Pesach, discuss their home *Seder*. Share stories. (NSM)

14. Have children match cards which have one question from "Who Knows One?" to cards with the answers.

15. Have class members collect favorite recipes from home and put them together in a class or school Pesach cookbook.

16. Bring to class several different *Seder* plates. Have children analyze them to figure out what is the same and what is different about the various plates. Discuss what the plates are used for. (NSM)

17. Have students make the bowls out of clay for dipping parsley. Adorn them with a word or symbol and glaze.

18. Each student traces a doll figure and pastes it onto a cardboard cut out. Then he/she draws four different faces (the same size as the head of the cardboard doll) to represent the Four Sons. Mount the head on cardboard and cut tabs (as for paper dolls) to attach the heads to the cardboard doll. Have a dialogue between the dolls. Have students create faces for other types of people besides the intelligent, wicked, simple individual, and the one who doesn't know how to ask. Ask them to suggest ways to add these characters to the liturgy. (JB)

19. Bake *matzah* and make *charoset in* class. Try recipes for *charoset* from different countries.

20. Make *matzah* covers in any of the following ways:
    a. Simple Embroidery: Draw the design in pencil on a piece of cloth. Plan the stitches to be used. Choose one or more of the following: line stitch, chain stitch, criss-cross stitch, running stitch, or loop stitch. Using colored yarns, embroider the *matzah* cover.
    b. Applique: Use colored felt. Sew the pieces of felt to a piece of cloth with a chain stitch. Do not use glue.
    c. Vinegar Egg Temperas: Add 1/4 spoonful of vinegar to the white of one egg. Add one brushful to tempera paint. Stir, then paint on cloth. Put the design face down on a board. Cover with a wet cloth and iron.

21. Form a circle and begin telling a Pesach story. Speak for 15 to 20 seconds and stop. Each student takes a turn continuing the story for 15 seconds. Record the story on audio or videotape and play it back for the class.

22. Students close their eyes. Pass one or more Pesach objects from person to person. Students touch and smell each object as it comes around. They open their eyes, discuss what they were thinking and feeling and what thoughts or memories, if any, these objects evoked. (This can also be done with eyes open.)

23. Have students complete the Instant Lessons *Passover — The Story* and *Passover — What We Do.*

24. Perform the play "Seder Time" from *Class Acts: Plays & Skits for Jewish Settings* by Stan J. Beiner (page 59). Invite parents and/or other classes to the performance.

25. Complete the activity pages related to Pesach in *Jewish Holiday Copy Pak™ K-3* by Marji Gold-Vukson (pages 18, 19, and 20).

26. Do one or more of the Shabbat art projects in *100+ Jewish Art Projects for Children* by Nina Streisand Sher and Margaret A. Feldman (pages 44, 45, 48).

Intermediate

1. In small groups, have students make a dictionary of Pesach vocabulary (see pages 153-158.).

Have a contest for the cover of the dictionary. Reproduce the dictionary and send it home to parents.

2. Share with students the illustrations in some beautiful *Haggadot* from different eras, then have them make illustrations for a contemporary *Haggadah*.
   Resource: *Haggadah and History* by Yosef Hayim Yerushalmi.

3. Have students compare the language and art work of various versions of the Four Children/Sons in different *Haggadot*. Or, do the same with the Ten Plagues. (NSM)

4. After studying the treatment of the Four Children in different *Haggadot*, divide students into small groups to see if they can create their own examples of Four Children. What would the Four Children (wise, wicked, simple, doesn't know how to ask) be like if involved with a specific sport? If part of the current Israeli government? If living in poverty? Groups can pick their own thematic area and create pictures or use words to describe these children. (NSM)

5. Have students match the items in column one and column two:

Charoset	Something leavened, like bread
Afikoman	Pesach Song
Haggadah	*Matzah* that is hidden
Elijah	Bitter herbs
Maror	Promises made by God
4 cups of wine	Nuts, apples, cinnamon, wine
Matzah	*Seder* Ceremonies and story
Seder	Unleavened bread
Chamaytz	Passover dinner and ceremonies
Chad Gadya	Open door for him

6. Have students pretend they are Moses discovering his mission, confronting Pharaoh, leading the Israelites out of Egypt, and then providing leadership to them during the wandering in the Wilderness of Sinai. Then have them write out a brief diary reflecting their thoughts as they deal with Moses' critical role in the events related to the festival of Pesach.

7. Have students work in pairs to find as many references to freedom or redemption as possible in the *Haggadah* (each pair should have the same version). Give each pair small post-it notes and ask them to flag each instance. Count the number of references and compare answers between groups. Students can also search out important numbers in the *Haggadah* (e.g., 3, 4, 10, 13). (NSM)

8. Ask each student to bring one object from home that relates to the holiday of Pesach (e.g., a ritual object, a book about Pesach, a *Haggadah*, photographs, a CD or audiotape, etc.). The student then writes a one paragraph description of his/her item. As a class, create a museum display of the objects and invite other classes to come and see it. Be sure to end the display prior to the onset of Pesach so that the ritual objects can be used at home!

9. Have the class (or classes) prepare for a Religious School or Hebrew School *Seder* by writing a different kind of *Seder* service, one that uses both the traditional prayer and a contemporary equivalent. Suggest they make use of creative prose, poetry, music, and the like.

10. Help students make a bulletin board about Pesach. Ask the librarian for help in finding pictures, newspaper and magazine articles, articles from the synagogue bulletin, photocopies of pertinent materials, original essays, and art work that relate to the holiday of Pesach. Local secular newspapers often carry articles about Pesach or about Pesach foods around the time of the holiday.

11. As a class, devise a survey that tests the knowledge of their non-Jewish friends about the holiday of Pesach. Tabulate the results during the following session. Then design a public relations campaign aimed at educating the public about Passover. (AFM)

12. In small groups of 3 to 4 students, study Exodus 12:14-27 and 12:43-51. Have each group create two lists: (1) how Pesach was to be celebrated at the time of the Exodus, and (2) what seems similar to what they observe today in their own homes or at the synagogue. (NSM)

13. Ask each student to think about three people, living or dead, that he/she might want to invite to a *Seder*. Give them a worksheet for each invitee, stating: To _____ . You are Invited To Our *Seder*. We are inviting you because _____ . We would like you to bring along _____ . We think you will enjoy _____ . (NSM)

14. Divide the Pesach story into small segments. Then form small groups of 2 or 3 students each. Give the students 10-15 minutes to work out a dramatization of their scene in the story. Have each group then act out their segment of the Pesach narrative. Invite parents and/or other classes to see the final product.

15. View and discuss the video *The Animated Haggadah*.

16. Have each student make a list of things that God has done for him/her. Then have them make the list into a poem and add it to their poetry book. Variation: Have them write an essay on whether or not they would consider it enough *(dayenu)* if God had done only some of the things on their list.

17. One student volunteers to be the expert. The other students ask the "expert" questions in an effort to stump him/her. The person who succeeds in stumping the expert becomes the new expert, and the process is repeated.

18. Read to the students, or let them take turns reading aloud, *Matzah Ball: A Passover Story* by Mindy Avra Portnoy. Ask students to talk about times they have been embarrassed in front of their friends by not being able to eat certain foods during Passover. How did they handle it? Ask them to describe situations in which they have wished for an Elijah to rescue them.

19. Have each student interview two older people about their childhood Pesach memories. You may wish to develop interview questions to guide this, including: memories of helping to clean the house and change the dishes for Pesach, *bedikat chamaytz*, cooking, the *Seder*, etc. Turn the interviews into a book of Pesach Memories. (NSM)

20. Reproduce a chart for students to fill in. Include a place for students to write in the famous Jewish people, Jewish foods, Jewish symbols, and Jewish places connected with Pesach and other holidays they have studied to date.

21. As a review or reinforcement activity, devise a list of tasks related to the holiday of Pesach. Put each task on one card. Give out the cards to the students. Each student must follow the instructions on his/her card. If the activities are brief, make up several sets of ten cards each. Divide the class into groups of ten or less and give each student in each group one card. Each group sits in a circle and all function at the same time.

22. Four is a key number in the celebration of Pesach. Have students see how many fours they can find in the *Haggadah*. (Four questions, four cups of wine, four sons, four

mothers of Israel, four promises of redemption)

23. On a sheet of construction paper, each child creates a Pesach coat of arms. On it, he/she writes the name of the holiday, then draws Pesach-related ritual objects, slogans, general Jewish symbols, etc., that meaningfully represent the holiday.

24. Have students make a list of 20 things they love to do (use a smaller amount for younger children). Students code the lists by putting an X next to those things they could not do if they were a slave. Discuss how it would feel not to be able to do things they like to do. How many things would need to be taken away from them before they would rebel?

25. View and discuss the video *My Exodus*.

26. Brainstorm the qualities of leaders. Have students rank these in importance, then check the qualities which Moses possessed. Put up signs around the room, each with the name of a Jewish leader (Moses, Herzl, Deborah, Ruth, etc.). Students go to the person that best demonstrates the qualities of leadership they brainstormed. Have them explain the reasons for their choices.

27. Select a group of Pesach objects and assign each student to be one of these objects. Form groups small enough so that only one of each object is in each group. In the groups, the "objects" converse, telling each other how they view each other, and how they feel as Pesach is being celebrated. Reassemble the total group and share reactions to this activity.

28. Divide the class into two groups of task-masters and slaves. Have the taskmasters boss the slaves and then reverse roles. Discuss how students felt in each role. What similar situ-

ations do they encounter in their own lives in terms of family, friends, school, etc.?

29. Have students role play the Four Children in different situations, then decide which of the four they are most like, which they would like to have as a friend, which they would want to work with on an assignment. Have them defend their choices.

30. Complete The Instant Lesson *Mastering The Four Questions*.

31. Play *The Seder Game* in *Holiday Game Pak* by Bonnie Berman and Laura Glatstein.

32. Perform or do a readers theater version of the play "The Magician" from *Kings and Things: 20 Jewish Plays for Kids 8 to 18* by Meridith Shaw Patera (page 93).

33. Complete the activity pages related to Pesach in *Jewish Holiday Copy Pak™ 4-6* by Marji Gold-Vukson (pages 17, 18, 19).

34. Do one or more of the Shabbat art projects in *100+ Jewish Art Projects for Children* by Nina Streisand Sher and Margaret A. Feldman (pages 43, 46, 47).

Secondary

1. Form small groups. Ask each group to examine and summarize for the class one of the passages in the Torah related to Pesach (see page 160). You may deal mainly with the first half of the book of Exodus, but also select various legalistic portions related to Exodus found in other parts of the Torah.

2. The celebration of Pesach teaches us about the departure from slavery in Egypt to a life of freedom. Shavuot celebrates the giving of the Torah to Israel. In what ways are these two

festivals two sides of the same coin? (Note: The key is the connection between freedom and responsibility.)

3. Ask: Why, other than the lighting of Shabbat candles, is the Passover *Seder* the most widely observed ritual in Jewish life? What makes it so special and appealing?

4. Each student writes down what he/she considers to be the 10 most essential words related to Pesach. In pairs, they converse using *only* these words. First, each partner speaks for two minutes, using only the ten words on the list, and then partners may converse using both lists of words. Discuss the activity.

5. Divide students into groups of 3. Give each group a *Haggadah* to work with (better yet, give every student in the group a copy to use during this exercise). Make sure that students also have access to different *Haggadot* and other resources about Pesach. First, have each group member describe what they remember happening at the *Sedarim* he/she has been to in recent years. Then, ask each group to go though the *Haggadah* as if they were planning a *Seder* and determine what they would omit and what would they want to add in. (Note: This is an excellent exercise for Grade 12 students to do, as they think about Jewish issues in college.) (NSM)

6. There are great Pesach treasures on the Internet. Have your students search them out, either using the Search feature of their Browser, or check out: http://www.jewishfamily.com or http://virtual.co.il/(NSM)

7. Have students compare the language and art work of various versions of the Four Children/Sons in different *Haggadot*. Or, do the same with the Ten Plagues. (See the Bibliography, starting on page 280, for a listing of a number of *Haggadot*.) (NSM)

8. Examine the four names for Pesach. Discuss why each is an appropriate name for the holiday: (1) Chag HaAviv (The Festival of Spring), (2) Chag HaMatzot (The Festival of Unleavened Bread), (3) Z'man Chayrutaynu (Season of Our Freedom) and (4) Chag HaPesach (The Festival of Passing Over).

9. The following statement appears in the *Haggadah*: "This year we celebrate here. Next year in the land of Israel. Now we are all still in bonds. Next year may all be free." Have students write a paragraph describing what they think this statement means. Then, as a class, discuss the statements.

10. Israel Zangwill, a famous English Jewish author, stated: "On Passover, Jews eat history." Discuss the meaning and implications of this powerful statement.

11. *Ma'ot Chitim* (which literally means "Money for Wheat") is the term used for programs to help those in need to celebrate Pesach with joy and in dignity. Organize a school-wide *Ma'ot Chitim* program or participate in a community-wide program that is already in existence. Discuss the importance of *tzedakah* and the phrase "Every Jew is responsible for every other Jew" in the context of the *Ma'ot Chitim* program.

12. A Yizkor service is held at the end of Pesach. Have students write memorial prayers for loved ones, friends, or famous Jews who have died recently, and/or for Holocaust victims who have no one left to remember or mourn them. (AFM)

13. Ask: Why do we open the door for Elijah? The most common answers are: to demonstrate that the stranger is welcome to share Passover with us and in order to perform the *mitzvah* of *Hachnasat Orchim* (hospitality). There is a second, very somber meaning as

well: that Jews have nothing to hide on Passover or at any other time. During the late Middle Ages, anti-Semites accused Jews of killing Christian children in order to make Passover wine. Read segments of the powerful novella *The Rabbi of Bachrach* by Heinrich Heine, which places this cruel theme in the context of early nineteenth century Germany.

14. Discuss with the students how, in recent years, a number of special additions have been made to the *Seder*, such as a special fourth *matzah* to honor Soviet Jewry used at Pesach in the years before Jews were allowed to emigrate from there, a special prayer to memorialize victims of the Holocaust or to recount the heroism shown in the Warsaw Ghetto, a prayer for the rescue of Jews in Ethiopia, and a special fifth cup of wine to bless Israel's independence. Also, the local Jewish newspaper in Denver carried a special *Seder* reading relating to pride in one's Jewish identity. Examine carefully the reasons for some of these additions. Then have students create their own modern addition to the *Haggadah*. They can write four questions about our lives and our world, other types of sons/daughters who live in our world, ten (or more) evils that plague our society and ways to eliminate these. They can include some contemporary music by such artists as Debbie Friedman. (RAZ)

15. View and discuss the video *Passover Seder*. Talk about the various techniques used in this video. What was the role of Elie Wiesel? Have students write a script for their own video on the subject of the *Seder* and then actually make it.

16. Have students react to the following statement: "Flowers blossom in the spring; people blossom when they are free."

17. Examine the meaning and the symbolism of such songs as *"Echad Mi Yodea," "Chad Gadya,"* and *"Dayenu."* Make an effort to determine what each stanza refers to.

18. Discuss the varied Jewish ritual art that was and is a part of Jewish life wherever Jews have resided. Why did Jews focus their attention on such objects instead of on building large buildings or painting portraits of famous Jews? What Passover ritual objects reflect this preference? (The *Haggadah*, the *Seder* plate, the *matzah* cover, the Cup of Elijah, etc.)

19. Ask: Is the *Haggadah* an ongoing "work in progress"? Why have there been thousands of different editions of the *Haggadah* printed in the last several hundred years?

20. When everyone is comfortable, do the following guided imagery: "Close your eyes. I want you to imagine that you are in the desert after the Exodus from Egypt. Moses has gone up the mountain, and you and the others are waiting for his return. Soon there is a buzz among the crowd. 'It's Moses,' they are saying." Continue your instructions, painting a word picture of Moses relating his experiences to the assembled throng and telling them about the gift of Torah. The students listen carefully and try to feel what it is like to be a part of the experience being described — in effect, to be standing at Sinai. After you complete the description, the students open their eyes and discuss how they felt and what they learned.

21. Have students complete the Instant Lesson *Fifteen Steps to Freedom*.

22. Perform or do a readers theater version of the play "The Passover of Hope" from *Kings and Things: 20 Jewish Plays for Kids 8 to 18* by Meridith Shaw Patera (page 99).

All-School

1. Organize "A Pesach Happening" for Grades 4 and up (see immediately below for some ideas).

A PESACH HAPPENING

Note: This school-wide activity is intended to serve in addition to, or in place of, the typical Model *Seder* program. For additional activities, see above.

Overview

"A Pesach Happening" lasts for approximately two hours. After spending 15 minutes in their regular classroom, each class goes together from station to station where they will participate in a learning, doing, or experiential activity related to Pesach. Parents may participate along with their children and can also help teachers staff the stations.

Time Frame

Eight activity stations are suggested here (adjust this number based on the number of students involved). It is important that the timing at each station be carefully coordinated. In this plan, classes remain at each activity station for 12 minutes, with 3 minutes allocated for movement from station to station,

Activity Stations

1. Sing Pesach Songs: *"Echad Mi Yodea," "Chad Gadya," "Adir Hu,"* etc.
2. Decipher the Code: Participants decipher a statement containing in code the four names for Pesach, and discuss the significance of each name. Younger students can be told the code key, while older students can figure it out.
3. Role Play: Four students are chosen to be sons/daughters. The facilitator writes four brief statements in the form of personality profiles, each one representing a modern son/daughter. After the four students role play their parts, the group discusses other sons and daughters for our age.

4. Questions and Answers: As a parallel to the traditionally asked four questions, each participant may ask one question about Passover, which is answered by the facilitator.
5. The *Seder* Plate: Display a *Seder* plate and the items that belong on it. Students must explain the significance of each item. For younger children, provide a handout in the form of a matching activity. In the left column, list the items on the plate and in the right column, the explanations for each of the symbols.
6. Pesach in the Bible: Give out a list of biblical quotations related to Pesach and have participants find the key ideas each contains.
7. The Order of the *Seder*: Each group that comes to the station sorts in the correct order a set of cards, each of which has written on it one step in the order of the *Seder*. The facilitator times the team and at the end of the session, members of the group with the shortest time wins a prize.
8. Evils in Our Society: Each participant describes one evil that brings hurt, pain, or suffering to our society.

Family

1. Organize a family education program for two to four-year-olds (there are three already designed Passover programs in *Head Start on Holidays: Jewish Programs for Preschoolers and Their Parents* by Roberta Louis Goodman and Andye Honigman Zell).

2. Send home some sentences for families to complete as they sit around the dinner table. Some suggested sentences:
   I like Pesach because _____.
   Pesach is special to me because _____.
   The person in the *Haggadah* I feel closest to is _____.
   On Pesach I wish our family would _____.

3. Suggest that families attend a second *Seder* that is different from their own first night *Seder*. Afterward, they can compare and

contrast the two experiences. Each member of the family tells what he/she liked and disliked about each *Seder.*

4. It has been said that the *Seder* is not only a reliving of the Exodus from Egypt, but is also a carefully planned educational experience for the entire family, particularly for the children. Ask families to react to this statement. Do individual family members agree or disagree with it? Why? Have them talk about the ways the *Seder* is a successful educational experience.

5. Suggest that families research all sorts of delicious Pesach dishes. In this way, they can become acquainted with the wide range of delicious and different Pesach foods. The whole family can then help to make some of the dishes.

6. Help families to make a family *Haggadah* for use at their *Seder.* All the children in the family, as well as the parents, can contribute readings, a rendering of the Passover story, poetry, art, etc. Let the whole family have a voice in deciding who will read which sections.

7. Send home a sheet asking parents to pass along a great idea used during their *Seder* that involves young children. Compile the answers and send these home to all the families a week or two before Pesach. (NSM)

BIBLIOGRAPHY

See pages 280-285.

CHAPTER TEN
YOM HASHOAH

VOCABULARY

Chal'lay HaShoah: "Victims of the Holocaust."

Har HaZikaron: "Mount of Remembrance," is the site of the Yad VaShem Holocaust Memorial in Jerusalem. It is not far from Mt. Herzl, where Theodor Herzl is buried.

Har Tziyon: "Mount Zion," is a hill in Jerusalem opposite Har HaBayit (the Temple Mount). While the burial place of King David is not certain, tradition ascribes it to this location. Mt. Zion also has a Holocaust museum.

Kibbutz Lochamay HaGetaot: "*Kibbutz* of the Ghetto Fighters," which is located along the Mediterranean coast near Haifa. It was founded in 1949 by survivors of the Polish and Lithuanian ghettos who fought in the resistance against the Nazis. The *kibbutz* is dedicated to the memory of the six million Jews who died in the Holocaust. Located at the *kibbutz* is a very large Holocaust museum and memorial.

Kibbutz Yad Mordecai: "Kibbutz of the Memorial to Mordecai" was founded in 1943, and is located south of Ashkelon near the Gaza Strip. It is named after the commander of the Warsaw Ghetto uprising, Mordecai Anielewicz, and a statue of him has been erected at the *kibbutz*. This was the site of fierce fighting and a crucial battle against Egyptian invaders in May, 1948. A mock-up of that battle-

field may be visited. This is the site of a Holocaust museum.

Kol Yisrael Arayvim Zeh BaZeh: "All Jews are responsible for one another." Jews feel a bond with other Jews, wherever they live in the world, and are responsible for each other's welfare and safety.

Nisan: The first month of the Jewish year, it corresponds to March/April, has 30 days, and its zodiac sign is Aries. In the Torah it is referred to as Aviv, the month of spring. Pesach falls on the 15th of Nisan and Yom HaShoah on the 27th.

Shoah: Usually translated "Holocaust," but can also be translated as "destruction," "ruin," "catastrophe."

Ya'ar Shaysh Milyon: "The Forest of the Six Million," is a large forest planted by the Jewish National Fund on both sides of the Jerusalem-Tel Aviv corridor. The six million evergreens here serve as a memorial to the six million Jewish martyrs who died at the hands of the Nazis. The Jewish communities of France, Poland, Czechoslovakia, and Belgium suggested its creation to help keep alive the memory of the six million. There are 19 sections, each one representing a different European Jewish community.

Yad VaShem: "A Memorial and a Name." Yad VaShem is located about ten miles outside of

Jerusalem on Har HaZikaron. It is the site of Israel's most famous Holocaust museum and memorial, as well as a center for Holocaust research. There is a stark, low slung building made of rough concrete which has the names of concentration camps inscribed on the floor and an eternal flame burning. Yad VaShem also includes a museum building, a lecture hall, a synagogue dedicated to the memory of the thousands of European synagogues destroyed during the Holocaust, a Children's Pavilion (which shows the pictures and announces the names of the one million children killed by the Nazis), and an outdoor memorial called Valley of the Fallen. A well stocked library contains letters, books, and documents related to the Holocaust, as well as individual records of the dead who have been given "memorial citizenship" in Israel.

Yom HaShoah: "Holocaust Memorial Day," is the official day of mourning and memorial for the victims of the Holocaust. The Israeli Kenesset designated the 27th day of Nisan, because on that date in 1943 (April 19th), the Warsaw Ghetto uprising began.

BACKGROUND

Central Themes
It is beyond the purview here to deal with the Holocaust in depth. In addition to the vocabulary of key terms and useful strategies, the following few points can serve as the basis for discussion, as well as for personal introspection.

• The Hebrew word for Holocaust is *Shoah —* *shin, alef, hey*. It has been said that the letter *shin* is pronounced *shhh* and reminds us to be silent. After all, what can one say in the face of such horror? The *alef* is a silent letter and makes no sound at all. And the *hey* is the sound of breathing — a reminder that despite the silence of others in the face of Jewish suffering, and despite the silence that the horror inflicts on the Jewish psyche, we are still alive and breathing.

• In spite of continual persecution, Jews have never abandoned hope for the future. Optimism seems to be an indelible part of the Jewish psyche. Although there may have been ample reason for abandoning hope at times, Jews have steadfastly refused to do so, believing that the future will bring better days and that one day the Messiah or the Messianic Age will arrive.

• Judaism is a family-centered religion. The *Shoah* caused the tragic destruction of millions of Jewish families. Judaism affirms life. The *Shoah* destroyed life. Judaism affirms human dignity, civil liberties, economic opportunity, religious freedom, education, strong communities. The *Shoah* tore away at all of this. It destroyed a way of life.

• Although many Jews went to their death without resistance, there were thousands of Jews who fought against hopeless odds, never giving up. The heroes and heroines of the Warsaw Ghetto and of the Resistance Movements in nearly every country in Europe can be compared to the Maccabees.

• Many false accusations against the Jews set the stage for the *Shoah*. Jews were accused of being leaders of a capitalist plot to conquer the world. Jews were also accused of fomenting a Communist plan for world domination. Jews were labeled as members of an inferior race, pariahs, and worse, in a campaign of anti-Semitic propaganda which knew no bounds. In a word, Jews became scapegoats for many failings and problems which in no way were related to them.

• It was not enough that the Nazis robbed the Jews of their possessions and their lives; they also attempted to rob them of their dignity.

• In the last analysis, many Jews believe that they cannot rely on anyone to guarantee their survival. During World War II, the leading democracies of Europe as well as the United States pretended not to know what was happening at Auschwitz, Dachau, Buchenwald, and the other death camps. Some say that the aftermath of the 1973 Yom Kippur War brought back remembrances of that World War II feeling of being alone.

- There are very few Holocaust survivors left. Soon there will be none. Jews face the task of keeping the memory of the *Shoah* alive even after there are no more eye witnesses to the horrors of that era. Various films as well as Holocaust "projects," have sought to capture on audiocassette, film, and videotape the stories of some of the last survivors. The depth and breadth of the *Shoah* may have no parallel. Yet, there have been and will no doubt continue to be horrible acts of mass murder in our day that bear resemblance to the some of atrocities of the *Shoah*. Many believe that it is the sacred task of the Jewish People to make sure that there will never again will be another such genocide by speaking out and against any such occurrences.

- The events of the *Shoah* affected the faith of many. To some Jews, the God of the Patriarchs and Matriarchs, the God who controlled and directed history, was dead. Some Jews asked if God had abandoned them — had been in eclipse — during the Holocaust. They wondered why God seemed to be silent throughout the nightmare. The Holocaust raises profound religious questions, among them the issue of theodicy: Why do the innocent suffer? Why is there seemingly little correlation between how we live our lives and what befalls us? Why do bad things happen to good people? How one responds to these questions can serve as the underpinning of one's belief system.

- One of the most neglected aspects of the *Shoah* and the observance of Yom HaShoah is the role played by the *Chasidei Umot HaOlam* (Righteous Gentiles). Harold Schulweis, in his book *For Those Who Can't Believe*, devotes 14 pages to stories of some of the tens of thousands of non-Jews who risked their lives to save Jews (pp. 145-158). It is important to focus on the fact that these people had nothing to gain (except

their humanity), and everything to lose by taking such enormous risks to save Jews. They understood the meaning of the Talmudic dictum that to save one life is as if to save the entire world.

ACTIVITIES

Note: Because Yom HaShoah is a serious, somber day, and because of its recent origins, there are fewer activities in this chapter than in other chapters. For obvious reasons, most of the the activities herein are for Intermediate and Secondary students.

Preschool/Kindergarten

1. As an introduction to the Holocaust, read to the children the book *As Big As An Egg: A Story about Giving* by Rachel Sandman. The story tells of hard times in Russia during World War II without ever mentioning the Holocaust or Nazis.

Primary

1. Read to younger primary children the book *The Tattooed Torah* by Marvell Ginsburg, and to the older ones, *Child of the Warsaw Ghetto* by David Adler.

2. Seat the children in a circle. Explain that things happen to us that make us sad and that sometimes we do things that we are unhappy about. While it is not good to think about these sad things all of the time, it can be helpful to remember them from time to time so that we will be able to avoid them in the future. Remembering sad things sometimes helps us to make happy things happen later on. Ask each child to complete the following sentence: "One sad thing that I remember is _____." After everyone has had a chance, let the children react to each other's recollections. add your comments if you so desire.

Intermediate

1. Read, discuss, and look at the photographs in the book *Tell Them We Remember: The Story of the Holocaust* by Susan Bachman. Through

identity cards, students follow the lives of several young Holocaust victims and see how they fared.

2. For Yom HaShoah, visit a nearby Jewish cemetery and hold a brief memorial service there. There might be things to do to beautify the Jewish cemetery. Discuss how these activities would fall under the *mitzvah* of *Kavod HaMayt* (respect for the dead). Resource: *Teaching Mitzvot: Concepts, Values, and Activities* by Bruce Kadden and Barbara Binder Kadden, p. 46.

3. During the Holocaust, Jews were forced to wear the yellow star. Since that time, Jews have worn the Star of David with pride. Invite an artist who makes jewelry to guide students in the making of personal Stars of David. (NSM)

4. Offer several resources for students to use to research quotations about the Holocaust. Working alone or in pairs, have students pick a quotation that could be used on a bookmark. Design bookmarks by putting the quote on a large rectangular shape drawn with a word processing program; include appropriate clip art. Print with a color printer and insert in Holocaust books in the library for others to use. (NSM)

5. Have students research any stamps issued by the Postal Service in memory of the Holocaust. (Invite in a stamp collector, check the Internet, or ask at the Post Office). Discuss the criteria for new stamps. Ask students to develop a stamp which might be accepted by the Postal Service for the Holocaust. Create a display in the synagogue. (NSM)

6. Offer students collections of writing on the Holocaust. Include poetry, works of children, literature, and general quotations. Working in groups of three, have students choose a read-ing they would like to share with others in a memorial service. Then, have the class choose the setting they would like for their memorial (in the sanctuary? outside? with *yahrzeit* candles or without? with parents or another class? reading names of family members who perished? etc.). Hold the service in the manner that the students decide. (NSM)

7. Brainstorm the themes of Yom HaShoah. Write the list of themes on the blackboard. Then give each student 10 or so minutes to write a prayer related to Yom HaShoah and reflecting one of its themes. Add the prayers to the students' prayer books. Use some or all of them at a Yom HaShoah observance.

8. Choose musical and Cantorial selections for a Yom HaShoah memorial Service (e.g., *"Ani Ma'amin," "Ayl Mahlay Rachamim,"* Yiddish songs of the partisans, *"Oseh Shalom,"* etc.). What else might be fitting? (RAZ)

9. Give students a list of events that occurred leading up to and during the Holocaust. Working individually, they make a time line. Then, as a class, discuss the major occurrences related to the *Shoah*.

10. Make a master sheet with as many stars or slashes as possible. Photocopy the sheet, making enough copies to have six million stars/slashes so that students can get an idea of the magnitude of the number. Hang the copies around the room. Darken the room and have a service. Give those who wish to speak a chance to say how they feel at the end of the service.

11. Find out if your synagogue (or another synagogue or a Jewish museum in your community) has a Torah scroll rescued from the Holocaust. Ask the Rabbi, or someone else who knows, about the history of this particular scroll. Read the *Yanov Torah* by Erwin Herman and Agnes Herman, about a Holocaust Torah.

How does the story of the Holocaust Torah in your synagogue/community compare with that of the Yanov Torah? (NSM)

12. Display a map of Israel and the surrounding areas. Point out and describe places identified with the Holocaust (e.g., Mount Zion, Kibbutz Lochamay HaGetaot, Kibbutz Yad Mordecai, Yad VaShem).

13. Invite a Holocaust survivor to class to share his/her experiences with you. Have students prepare a list of questions to ask in advance of the visit.

14. Write for information from Survivors of the Shoah Visual History Foundation, the organization begun by Steven Spielberg to gather 50,000 oral histories: P.O. Box 3168, Los Angeles, CA 90078. Find out who the interviewers are in your community. Invite one of them to class to tell about the progress of the project, the training an interviewer receives, and what he/she has learned and experienced by meeting with survivors. (AFM)

15. Help students construct a model of the Warsaw Ghetto. Read descriptions of the heroic resistance of the ghetto fighters.

16. With students, make a list of reasons why it is important to observe Yom HaShaoah. Have students rank the reasons in order of importance to them, placing a 1 next to the most important reason, a 2 for the second in importance, etc. Then, after they have ranked the reasons, form small groups and discuss their choices and the reasons they made them.

17. View and discuss the video *The Journey of Butterfly*. The poetry from the book *I Never Saw Another Butterfly* has been set to music and accompanies the drawings in this video. Afterward, have students write their own poems about the Holocaust and add them to their poetry books.

18. Complete page 24 in *Jewish Holiday Copy Pak*™ *4-6* by Marji Gold-Vukson.

Secondary

1. Ask around and locate copies of past program books of Yom HaShoah observances in your community, synagogue, or organization. Give these to groups of students to analyze (e.g., how would they categorize the ways we publically remember the 6,000,000 Jews who died?). Have students develop such a program for the community. (NSM)

2. Read some of the accounts in *Young People Speak: Surviving the Holocaust in Hungary*, edited by Andrew Handler and Susan V. Michael. The stories therein are about living in the ghetto, avoiding being caught and deported, and adjusting to a life in hiding or under an assumed name.

3. Share with students both volumes of *Maus* by Art Spiegelman. In these cartoon books, the Nazis are portrayed as cats and the Jews as mice. (There is also a CD-ROM, *The Complete Maus: A Survivor's Tale*, that would be of interest to students.) Then have students make up their own cartoons about the Holocaust.

4. Obtain archival photos of the Holocaust (from posters, photo sets, books, etc.). Ask students to decide what they might choose for a photo exhibit appropriate for teens in observance of Yom HaShoah. Ask them to explain their choices. Why did they pass over certain photos and choose others instead? What captions would they provide? Titles? What else would they want to add to the exhibit? (You may be able to mount a mini-exhibit using your school's bulletin boards. Be aware of the effect of some photos on young children in your school; you could shift the assignment to an exhibit appropriate for upper elementary school students. Discuss how this would change choices and labels.) (NSM)

5. View and discuss the video *One Survivor Remembers*, a first person account by Gerda Weissman Klein, who was a teenager when the Nazis invaded her home town in Poland.

6. Look at pictures of concentration camps. Discuss what it might have been like to be a prisoner in such a place. Read excerpts from *Night* by Elie Wiesel.

7. Discuss: What will you tell your children about the Holocaust? Do we have a responsibility to make them aware of it so that they can work to ensure that there will never be a recurrence? Or, should we keep silent so as not to disturb them?

8. Musically inclined students can research music created to memorialize the Holocaust. Are there composers who are more prolific in this area than others? What themes seem to be chosen for the music? Which music might students choose for their own memorial service? A group of students might learn some of the music to play or sing for a performance. A Cantor or other music specialist can help students with this research. (NSM)

9. There are people who claim that the Holocaust was a fabrication and a hoax. Ask: How would you react to such a person? How would you refute such a person's contentions? Resource: *Denying History: Who Says the Holocaust Never Happened & Why Do They Say It?* by Michael Shermer and Alex Grobman; *Denying the Holocaust: The Growing Assault on Truth and Memory* by Deborah E. Lipstadt.

10. Some say that the *Shoah* occurred so that the State of Israel could come into being. Ask: What do you think of linking these two events in this manner? If one links the two events theologically, one raises some troublesome religious issues. For example: Why did six million have to die in order for Israel to come into being? Wouldn't one or two million have been sufficient? If you were in a boxcar on the way to Auschwitz and told that you were to die to make possible a modern State of Israel, what would your reaction be? (In discussing this cause-effect connection, it might help to note that after World War II, many countries were at least superficially sympathetic to the plight of the Jews and more willing to support the establishment of a Jewish Homeland. One can make a case for saying that the tragic events of the Holocaust may have quickened the process of creating a Jewish state, but these events did not bring about the establishment of the State of Israel.)

11. Have students react to the following: Are Jews ever going to be free from being the victims of irrational anger, hatred, and prejudice? Will anti-Semites always invent the ammunition they need?

12. What are our responsibilities vis-a-vis not allowing the world to forget the lessons of the Holocaust? How can we carry out this responsibility?

13. Have students investigate the fact that the United States in World War II knew about the death camps and did not act specifically to stop the extermination. Resource: *The Abandonment of the Jews: America and the Holocaust 1941-1945* by David S. Wyman.

14. View and discuss the video *Schindler's List*. Give students ample time to "process" the video and to deal with the emotions that it evokes. Answer whatever questions they might have about the factuality of the film, and then examine its significance. Harold M. Schulweis (*For Those Who Can't Believe*, p. 157) says that the film has become the defining symbol of the Holocaust "not because of its artistry alone, but because it enables the viewer to

enter the dark cavern without feeling that there is no exit. Memory of the Holocaust is a sacred act that elicits a double mandate: to expose the depth of evil, and to raise goodness from the dust of amnesia." Discuss this powerful statement.

15. Leviticus 19:34 states: "The stranger who resides with you shall be to you as one of your citizens; you shall love him as yourself, for you were strangers in the land of Egypt." There are similar statements in the *Haggadah*. How would you connect this idea to the Jewish task of keeping alive the memory of the Holocaust and working to ensure that it will never occur again?

16. Take a class trip to the U.S. Holocaust Museum in Washington, D.C. If that is not possible, visit the Holocaust memorial nearest to you. Many large and medium-sized cities have Holocaust museums and/or memorials.

17. Prepare a dramatic presentation using excerpts from such books as *The Diary of Anne Frank, I Never Saw Another Butterfly,* etc.

18. Investigate some of the tens of thousands of non-Jews, Christians, and non-believers who risked their lives to save Jews. It is important to focus on the fact that these individuals had nothing to gain and everything to lose by taking such enormous risks. They understood the meaning of the expression: "The person who saves one life is as if that person saved the entire world." Write to the Jewish Foundation for the Righteous for information on their aid to rescuers who are in financial need: 165 East 56th Street, New York, NY 10022. Have students raise funds for this worthy cause through bake sales, car washes, etc., and send the money they raise along with letters of appreciation to the rescuers through the Foundation.
Resources: *Rescuers: Portraits of Moral Courage*

in the Holocaust by Gay Block and Malka Drucker; the video *Weapons of the Spirit*.

19. Listen to the traditional rendition of *"Ani Ma'amin"* and several contemporary versions on cassette tapes or CDs. Compare the various versions. Which is the most unusual? The most moving?
Resources: *Ani Ma-Amin* by Debbie Friedman; *Hineni* by Sam Glazer; *Life's a Lesson* by Ben Sidran.

20. Complete the mini-course *The Holocaust: A Study in Values* by Raymond A. Zwerin, Audrey Friedman Marcus, and Leonard Kramish.

21. Involve students in *Gestapo: A Learning Experience about the Holocaust* by Raymond A. Zwerin, Audrey Friedman Marcus, and Leonard Kramish. Afterward, do some of the additional activities suggested in the Leader Guide.

22. Since the end of World War II, Swiss banks have hoarded gold and monies rightfully belonging to Jews. Many of those Jews are now dead. Ask: To what organizations should this money be given? (RAZ)

All-school

1. On paper, draw a 3" high outline of a *yahrzeit* candle. Run off enough copies to send 5 to 7 copies home with students in every grade from Grade 4 up. Ask each student to find out if any of his/her family perished in the Holocaust, and, if so, to write the name of each person who died on one of the candles, along with the relationship to the student. When the candles are brought back to school, post them on a bulletin board labeled, "Yom HaShoah — Remembering the 6,000,000." (NSM)
Resource: *Original Bulletin Boards on Jewish Themes* by Nachama Skolnik Moskowitz, pp. 118-119.

Family

1. Encourage families to attend a Yom HaShoah Memorial Service and to talk about the experience afterward.

2. Suggest that families make up a series of questions related to Yom HaShoah and the Holocaust and survey friends and members of their immediate family. They can record the responses and summarize the findings when the family is next together.

BIBLIOGRAPHY

See pages 285-294.

CHAPTER ELEVEN

YOM HAZIKARON - REMEMBRANCE DAY

BACKGROUND

The Fourth of Iyar, the day before Yom HaAtzma'ut (Israel Independence Day) is a solemn day of memorial in Israel. Throughout the land there are civil, military, and religious ceremonies to honor the memory of those who died in the War of Independence (1948), The Suez Campaign (1956), the Six Day War (1967), the Yom Kippur War (1973), as well as all others who gave their lives to preserve Israel.

Memorial Day in Israel has taken on a very different tone from Memorial Day in the U.S. Many Americans pay more attention to the parades than to the remembering of fallen heroes. What makes Israel different is its size. When the number of soldiers who died in the various wars are looked at in proportion to the Jewish population of Israel, it casts a different light. One example will suffice — 2500 Israelis died in the Yom Kippur War, which occurred over a very short period of time. During the nearly ten years that the U.S. spent in Vietnam, approximately 50,000 Americans died. Comparing these numbers in proportion to the population of the U.S. and Israel, Israel's losses in 1973 were as if 150,000-200,000 Americans died in the Gulf War. What makes Israel's losses even more poignant is the fact that virtually everyone in Israel was either related to or knew a person killed in that war and in other wars. No family, no town, no *kibbutz* was left untouched. Such is the price that Israel has paid in order to remain a free and independent nation.

Observance

The ceremonies begin at sunset and conclude the next evening with a blast of sirens throughout Israel as the stars appear in the sky to mark the beginning of Yom HaAtzma'ut. Memorial candles are lit in military camps, at schools, in synagogues, and in public places. Flags fly at half-mast. Soldiers and former soldiers serve as guards of honor at the various memorial sites throughout the country and at military cemeteries. On Yom HaZikaron, theaters are closed, as are schools and government-run broadcast facilities. During the morning of Yom HaZikaron, there is a period of two minutes of silence throughout the country. Special prayers for this day include Psalms 9 and 144.

In many cities in the Diaspora, Israelis living abroad gather to present tribute in the form of readings, songs, prayers, and remembrances.

ACTIVITIES

Intermediate/Secondary

1. Read the beginning of Psalm 9 and Psalm 144. Why do students think these Psalms were singled out to read on Yom HaZikaron?

2. Discuss: What effect does Yom HaZikaron taking place the day before Yom HaAtzma'ut have upon the tenor and tone of the celebration of Yom HaAtzma'ut?

3. Examine guidebooks for Israel. Read the description of the military cemetery at Mount

Herzl where Theodor Herzl and other Israeli leaders are buried. One part of the cemetery contains memorial markers for young sailors who died during the War of Independence. Their stones/markers are arranged in the shape of a ship. This is both dramatic and poignant. Have students design a memorial for the cemetery honoring those who gave their lives for the survival of Israel. (If you plan a congregational trip to Israel or a Confirmation class trip, be sure to include a visit to the cemetery on Mount Herzl.)

4. Discuss: Do you think that Israel takes its freedom and independence for granted? What is the connection between Yom HaZikaron and Yom HaAtzma'ut?

5. Discuss: How does the breaking of the glass at a wedding symbolize the relationship/connection between Yom HaZikaron and Yom HaAtzma'ut? (Both remind us that just as joy, happiness, and freedom are a part of life, so are sadness and loss.)

BIBLIOGRAPHY

See Bibliography for Yom HaAtzma'ut, pages 295-303.

CHAPTER TWELVE
YOM HAATZMA'UT

VOCABULARY

Am Yisrael: The Jewish people.

Canaan: The name of *Eretz Yisrael* when it was inhabited by the Canaanites. Most of those early tribes were driven out or absorbed during the period of the Israelite judges and kings.

Chalutzim: "Pioneers." The *chalutzim* were largely responsible for transforming *Eretz Yisrael* from a semi-arid land to a land that could support a large, thriving population. *Chalutzim* began to arrive in Israel with the onset of the First Aliyah in 1882.

Eretz Yisrael: "Land of Israel." There are a number of names which are used to refer to Israel, including: Palestine, Israel, Canaan, Judea, Zion. The term now means the geographical area of the State of Israel.

Hatikvah: "The Hope," is the national anthem of Israel. In 1878, it was written as a poem by Naphtali Herz Imber and later was set to music by Samuel Cohen. The melody is based on a Moldavian-Rumanian folk song.

Herzl, Theodor: (1860-1904) The father of political Zionism. He was the driving force who helped to transform the Zionist idea from a dream to a reality. Raised as a non-observant Jew, Herzl was compelled to confront his Jewishness when he covered the Dreyfus trial in 1894 as a correspondent for the *Vienna New Free Press*. Shocked by the implications of the trial and the blatant anti-Semitism it exposed, Herzl took action. He began to solicit the moral support of world leaders. In 1896, he wrote *The Jewish State*, in which he argued that Jews need a land of their own because they are not safe under anyone else's rule. In 1897, he brought together some 200 Jewish leaders in Basle, Switzerland, for the First Zionist Congress. Herzl was the organizational genius who set political Zionism into high gear. The fruits of his labors were realized when Israel became a state on May 14, 1948.

Iyar: The second month of the calendar, corresponding to April/May, it has 29 days, and its zodiac sign is Taurus. Israel Independence Day (Yom HaAtzma'ut) is on the 5th of Iyar and Lag B'Omer is on the 18th of Iyar.

Judah/Judea: After the death of King Solomon, the 10 northern tribes formed a separate kingdom which they called Israel. It broke away from the southern kingdom of Judah. In 721 B.C.E., the Assyrians defeated Israel, sending its inhabitants (the 10 lost tribes of Israel) into exile. In 586 B.C.E., Judah was destroyed along with its capital, Jerusalem, by the Babylonian king, Nebuchadnezzar. In 536 B.C.E., Cyrus the Persian defeated the Babylonians and permitted Jews to return to Jerusalem. In the second century B.C.E., a Greek assault on the spiritual and political life of the region was repelled, but the Romans who followed in their wake dominated the area and renamed it Judea. Its inhabitants became Judeans, from which the name Jew derives.

Magen David: "Shield of David." A hexagram or six-pointed star made by inverting two equilateral triangles over one another. It was used for both decorative and magical purposes by Jews and non-Jews in ancient times, and later by Christians during the Middle Ages. Around the seventeenth century, the *Magen David* became a specifically Jewish symbol. It was taken over by the Zionist movement and later became a part of the national flag of Israel. The Magen David Adom ("Red Shield of David") is the Israeli Red Cross. It was founded in 1930.

Medinat Yisrael: "The State of Israel." The official name of the nation. The term *medinah* means "nation," as well as "state."

Milchemet HaAtzma'ut: "The War of Independence" began on May 14, 1948, the day Israel became a nation. The actual fighting began in earnest at the time of the United Nations partition vote on November 29, 1947. In 1949, a series of Armistice agreements ended the fighting, but did not bring about recognition of Israel by the Arab countries which were fighting against her. Another name for this war is *Milchemet Shichrur,* which means "War of Liberation."

Palestine: This term was used by the British and the Turks to describe the area now known as the Hashamite Kingdom of Jordan and the State of Israel. The name derives from the Philistines, a seafaring people who settled along the Judean coast and were a main adversary of the Israelites until defeated by King David. The name Philistia was used by the Romans as the name of a province. The name Palestine Liberation Organization was adopted by Arabs hoping through terror to drive the Jews out of Israel. With the peace accords signed in 1993, the Palestine Authority was given control over territory populated mostly by Arabs.

Tziyon: "Zion." A poetic term for *Eretz Yisrael* as well as the name of a hill in Jerusalem (Har Tziyon/Mount Zion). *Tziyon* is a synonym for Israel.

Tziyoni: "Zionist." A person who is a supporter of Israel and the Zionist movement. Politically and ideologically, one who avows that Israel should be the residence of all Jews.

Tziyonut: "Zionism." Coined by Nathan Birnbaum in 1890, the term refers to the movement whose goal is the return of the Jewish people to the land of Israel. There are many definitions for Zionism just as there are many different Zionist groups. Each of these groups functions under the umbrella of the World Zionist Organization (W.Z.O.) whose founder was Theodor Herzl. Labor Zionism, Political Zionism, Cultural Zionism, Religious Zionism are all variations of the Zionist Movement, and each has its own history, leaders, and ideology.

Yisrael: "Israel," which in Hebrew connotes wrestling with God. In Genesis, the Patriarch Jacob, wrestling with a stranger, exacts a blessing for his victory: "Your name shall no longer be Jacob, but Israel, for you have wrestled with beings divine and human and have prevailed" (Genesis 32:29).

Yom HaAtzma'ut: Israel Independence Day — the 5th of Iyar. On May 14, 1948, 5 Iyar 5708, Israel became a nation.

BACKGROUND

Chronology

1882	Beginning of First Aliyah (24,000 Jews in Israel).
1894	Herzl covers trial of Captain Alfred Dreyfus.
1895	47,000 Jews in Palestine.
1896	Herzl publishes *The Jewish State.*
1897	First Zionist Congress held in Basle, Switzerland.
1901	Fifth Zionist Congress establishes Jewish National Fund. Uganda crisis.
1903	End of the First Aliyah.

1904 Death of Theodor Herzl.
1905 Beginning of the Second Aliyah.
1913 85,000 Jews in Palestine.
1914 Beginning of World War I.
      End of Second Aliyah.
1917 British government issues the Balfour Declaration.
1918 British drive out Turkey from Palestine and take over.
1920 British Mandate begins.
      Large scale Arab riots.
1921 Arab riots and terrorism continue.
1922 League of Nations approves the British Mandate over Palestine.
1925 Hebrew University opened on Mt. Scopus.
1929 Large scale Arab riots (133 Jews die).
1931 174,600 Jews in Palestine.
1936-
1939 Large scale Arab riots and terrorism.
1939 British White Paper limits Jewish immigration.
      449,500 Jews in Palestine.
1939-
1945 World War II; Jewish Brigade fights alongside the British.
1945-
1948 Active, often violent, struggle by the Jews of Palestine against the British.
      "Illegal" Jewish immigrants placed in Detention Camps on Cyprus by the British.
1947 United Nations votes on November 29th to create a Jewish state in Palestine by approving the Partition Plan.
1948 Israel officially becomes a nation on May 14th (5 Iyar).
      Mass immigration of Jews from Arab lands to Israel begins.
      758,700 Jews living in Israel
1949 Cease-fire signed ending War of Independence.
      Israel becomes a member of the United Nations.
      The First Knesset opens with David Ben Gurion as Prime Minister and Chaim Weizmann as President.

1950 "The Law of Return" is passed by the Knesset, giving all Jews the right to live in, and be citizens of, Israel.
      "Operation Magic Carpet" brings more than 50,000 Jews to Israel by air from Yemen.
1951 "Operation Ezra and Nehemiah" brings 123,500 to Israel by air from Iraq.
      1,404,400 Jews living in Israel.
1956 Israel victorious over Egypt in the Sinai Campaign.
1960 Adolph Eichmann, Nazi war criminal, captured in Argentina.
1961 1,982,700 Jews living in Israel.
      Eichmann executed in Israel after a lengthy trial.
1963 Israel begins archaeological excavations at Masada.
1966 S.Y. Agnon and Nelly Sachs share Nobel Literature Prize.
1967 Israel fights Six Day War against Egypt, Syria, and Jordan capturing Gaza Strip, Golan Heights, West Bank, and East Jerusalem.
      2,383,600 Jews living in Israel.
1972 2,723,000 Jews living in Israel.
1973 Yom Kippur War against Egypt and Syria; 2500 Israelis die.
1976 Israeli commandos rescue 110 hostages after the P.L.O. hijacks an Air France plane to Entebbe, Uganda, July 4th.
1977 President Anwar Sadat of Egypt visits Jerusalem for peace talks with Prime Minister Menahem Begin of Israel.
1978 Begin and Sadat share Nobel Peace Prize.
1979 Prime Minister Begin, President Sadat, and President Carter finalize Camp David peace treaty March 26th.
1981 President Sadat murdered by Arab fanatics.
1982 Remainder of Sinai given to Egypt by Israel.
      Israel invades Lebanon to rid Lebanon of P.L.O. and Syrian presence.
      3,400,000 Jews living in Israel

1984   National unity government (Likud and Labor) formed after elections.

"Operation Moses," immigration of 15,000 Jews from Ethiopia.

1985   Free Trade Agreement signed with United States.

1987   Widespread violence (Intifada) starts in Israeli-administered areas.

1988   Likud (Yitzhak Shamir) government in power following elections.

1989   Four-point peace initiative proposed by Israel.

Start of mass immigration of Jews from former Soviet Union.

1991   Israel attacked by Iraqi Scud missiles during Gulf War.

Peace conference convened in Madrid.

"Operation Solomon," airlift of 15,000 Jews from Ethiopia.

1992   Diplomatic relations established with China and India.

New government headed by Yitzhak Rabin of Labor party.

1993   Declaration of Principles on Interim Self-Government Arrangements for the Palestinians signed by Israel and P.L.O., as representative of the Palestinian people.

1994   Implementation of Palestinian self-government in Gaza Strip and Jericho area.

Full diplomatic relations with the Holy See.

Morocco and Tunisia interest offices set up.

Israel-Jordan Peace Treaty signed.

Rabin, Peres, Arafat awarded Nobel Peace Prize.

1995   Broadened Palestinian self-government implemented in West Bank and Gaza Strip; Palestinian Council elected.

Prime Minister Rabin assassinated at peace rally.

Shimon Peres becomes Prime Minister.

1996   Fundamentalist Arab terrorism against Israel escalates.

Operation Grapes of Wrath, retaliation for Hezbollah terrorists' attacks on northern Israel.

Trade representation offices set up in Oman and Qatar.

Likud forms government after Knesset elections. Benjamin Netanyahu is Prime Minister.

A Capsule List of Israelis & Zionists

Ahad Ha'am (1856-1927): Hebrew essayist and Zionist leader, the leading exponent of cultural Zionism.

Bar Ilan, Meir (1880-1949): Leader of the Religious Zionists; Bar-Ilan University is named for him.

Begin, Menahem (1913-1992): Prime Minister of Israel 1977-1984; leader of the Likud Party from 1948-1977; active leader of resistance against the British; recipient of the Nobel Peace Prize.

Ben-Gurion, David (1886-1973): Israel's first Prime Minister; the George Washington of the country; thought by many to be the most important Zionist leader of the twentieth century.

Ben-Tzvi, Yitzhak (1884-1963): Second President of Israel 1952-1963; Zionist leader.

Ben-Yehuda, Eliezer (1858-1922): Instrumental in transforming Hebrew into a spoken language; the first man to use Hebrew as a spoken language in *Eretz Yisrael;* prepared a massive dictionary of the Hebrew language; founded the Hebrew Language Council.

Bialik, Chaim Nachman (1873-1934): Great modern Hebrew poet, essayist, scholar, publisher of Hebrew writings.

Bluwstein, Rachel (1890-1931): Poet of her people.

Borochov, Dov Ber (1881-1917): Founder and leading thinker of Labor Zionism; leading socialist thinker with a major influence on the *kibbutz* movement.

Dayan, Moshe (1915-1982): Soldier and politician; army chief of staff during the victorious Sinai Campaign of 1956; held various government posts between 1959 and 1982.

Eshkol, Levi (1895-1969): Zionist leader and statesman; Prime Minister 1963-1969; a founder of *kibbutz* Degania Bet (1920).

Gordon, Aharon David (1856-1922): Important Zionist leader of the Second Aliyah (1904-1914); advocate of the "religion of labor" and an inspiration to fellow *chalutzim*.

Herzl, Theodor (1860-1904): Father of Political Zionism; author of *The Jewish State;* organizer of the World Zionist Movement.

Hess, Moses (1812-1875): One of the early Zionist thinkers; author of *Rome and Jerusalem* (1860).

Jabotinsky, Zev Vladimir (1880-1940): A Zionist leader; founder of Revisionist Zionism; an activist/extremist on behalf of Zionist causes; founder of the Betar movement and ideological father of the Herut Party.

Kook, Rav Abraham Isaac HaCohen (1865-1935): Chief Rabbi of Palestine 1921-1935; a leading thinker and leader of the Religious Zionists; showed that Zionism and traditional Jewish thinking could be compatible.

Meir, Golda (1898-1978): Israel's first Ambassador to Moscow 1948-1949; Foreign Minister 1956-1965; Prime Minister 1969-1974; great Zionist leader and world political figure.

Netanyahu, Benjamin (1949-): Leader of the Likud Party; elected Prime Minister 1996.

Nordau, Max (1849-1923): Philosopher, intellectual giant, and Zionist leader; the elder statesman of Zionism from the time of Herzl's death (1904) until 1923.

Peres, Shimon (1923-): Key figure in the Labor Party; served in the Knesset since 1948; held various government posts between 1948 and 1977; leader of the opposition Labor Party during the Begin government. Acting Prime Minister (1995-1996) following the assassination of Yitzhak Rabin; recipient of the Nobel Peace Prize.

Pinsker, Leon Judah Leib (1821-1891): Early Zionist thinker and writer; author of *Auto-Emancipation: An Appeal to His People by a Russian Jew;* leader of the "Lovers of Zion" (*Hovavay Tzion*) movement until his death.

Rabin, Yitzhak (1922-1995): Important military leader and Israeli Chief of Staff during the Six Day War of 1967; Ambassador to the U.S. 1968-1973; Prime Minister of Israel 1973-1977 and 1993-1995; assassinated 1995; recipient of the Nobel Peace Prize.

Schapira, Hermann (1840-1898): Early Zionist leader and father of the Jewish National Fund; great mathematician; attended the First Zionist Congress.

Sharett, Moshe (1894-1965): Father of the Israeli Foreign Service; Prime Minister 1954-1955; Zionist leader and statesman, holder of many important posts.

Sharon, Ariel (1928-): Soldier and politician; scored military victories in 1967 and 1973 campaigns, and engineered the Israeli invasion of Lebanon in 1982; held various posts in the Begin and Netanyahu governments.

Shazar, Zalman (1899-1974): Third President of Israel 1963-1974; writer, journalist, and Zionist politician; well known as a scholar.

Sokolow, Nahum (1859-1936): Prolific Hebrew writer; pioneer in modern Hebrew journalism; president of the World Zionist Organization.

Szold, Henrietta (1860-1945): Founder of Hadassah; founder of Youth Aliyah; active in Zionist politics and Zionist affairs; the first woman to be elected to the Executive of the Jewish Agency.

Ussishkin, Abraham Menahem Mendel (1863-1941): President of the Jewish National Fund 1923-1941; a Zionist leader throughout his life.

Weizmann, Chaim (1874-1952): Scientist and statesman; largely responsible for the issuance of the Balfour Declaration by Britain (1917); served as president of the World Zionist Organization for 21 years; a Zionist leader all his life; first President of Israel 1948-1952.

Central Themes
* Israel is the heart of the Jewish People: Mordecai Kaplan described Judaism as a wheel, with Israel as the hub and the various Diaspora communities as the spokes. Without the hub, the wheel cannot function. For World Jewry, Israel is a great source of religious, cultural, and educational inspiration. It is the only place in the world where Jews set the norm for a society.

* The existence of Israel is essential to the survival of the Jewish people. When the Second Temple was destroyed in 70 C.E., Israel ceased to exist as a political entity. At that point, Israel was transformed into a spiritual ideal. For the Jews living during the past 1900 years, Israel was as focal as in the days of the Second Commonwealth. Remembering Zion suffused the religious and cultural life of the Jew. In 1948, Israel once again became a political reality. Israel's survival, many believe, is linked to the survival of World Jewry.

* Israel is the refuge for the Jewish people. Israel is virtually the only place in the world to which Jews can flee from oppression and persecution and be welcomed. Other countries may temporarily permit an influx of Jews, but there is nowhere else in the world where an unlimited number of Jews are certain to be received with open arms and granted instant citizenship.

* While anti-Semites often raise the question of dual loyalty, it is, in reality, only a theoretical problem. On few occasions have the interests of Israel and the United States been fundamentally different. Jews in North America are no different from any other religious or ethnic group which feels free to lobby and push for programs that respond to its needs and best interests.

* While the political landscape of the Middle East has changed radically during the past several decades, Israel remains the only reliable ally of the United States in the Middle East. It is still the only remaining democracy in the region, and the only country which has consistently supported the United States since 1948, and vice versa.

* Israel has improved the image of the Jew in the world, while at the same time helping Jews throughout the world to strengthen their self-image. Because of Israel's positive, forceful, and assertive role in the world arena, and because of Israel's military successes, the image of eternal victim and wanderer has begun to fade. Moreover, Israel as the people's ancestral home gives Jews a sense of rootedness and a bond with their past.

* Jewish life is not monolithic. The various Jewish life-styles found in Israel reinforce the concept of Jewish pluralism. As the locus for the ingathering of the exiles, Israel is home to the many and diverse Jewish sub-cultural groups.

* Israel seems to be judged differently from other nations. One set of standards seems to be in place for other nations, while Israel has to answer to a higher standard. The world seems unwilling to allow Israel its character flaws or failings. Israel's actions are the focus of other people's microscope. The blessing in all of this is that it has caused the people of Israel to examine their deeds and actions closely as well.

- Throughout Jewish history, the ideal spot on earth to be buried is in Jerusalem on the Mount of Olives. When that is not possible, a small bag of earth from that place is put in the casket at the time of burial. In this way, a Jew who is buried in the Diaspora still rests on the soil of the Holy Land.

- So often a beleaguered people, Jews have had to learn to rely on one another for safety and protection. In the Middle Ages, Jews would be captured by brigands and held for ransom. The community would raise the funds necessary to redeem and free those held captive. Several examples of the *mitzvah* of *Pidyon Shevuyim* (Redemption of the Captive) are:

  a. July 4, 1976: Elite Israeli Paratroopers flew 2500 miles over hostile territory to the airport in Entebbe, Uganda, where they rescued over 100 Jews held hostage by Arab terrorists. There were Americans among the hostages.

  b. From its inception in 1948, Israel opened its doors to welcome Jewish victims of oppression. Because of a tremendous influx of refugees from Arab lands, the Jewish population of Israel doubled from 750,000 to 1,500,000 in its first five years of statehood. These refugees were truly rescued by the Jews of Israel. Jewish communities throughout the world lent financial support.

Israel and Yom HaAtzma'ut

There is a great difference between teaching about Israel and teaching about and celebrating Yom HaAtzma'ut. The Land of Israel and the Jewish people have been inextricably intertwined for nearly 4000 years. The State of Israel has been a part of our history for just a few decades. It is not possible to teach our involvement with the Land of Israel in just a few weeks, but one can touch upon a few ideas related to the State of Israel in a short time frame so as to prepare students for the celebration of Yom HaAtzma'ut. The centrality of Israel in the life of the Jew cannot be stressed too

strongly because, while physically distant from North America, Israel is integral to Jewish life here. Celebrating Yom HaAtzma'ut helps remind the student of that.

ACTIVITIES

Note: Yom HaAtzma'ut provides a wonderful opportunity to have an Israel culture day with Israeli foods, Israeli music, Israeli dancing, and a few enjoyable learning activities. Many of the activities listed below can be also used as part of an Israel Celebration. (See page 197 for an example of such a program.)

Preschool/Kindergarten

1. Put an Israeli store in your housekeeping area. Use boxes of food from Israel. (NSM)

2. Place pieces of fruits we find in Israel (e.g., oranges, dates, figs, peaches, bananas) in small opaque containers. (Note: Do not use used 35mm film containers; they have chemical residue.) Poke a hole in the top to allow the smell to come through. Have students smell real fruits and match them up with the smells they get from the containers. Open them to check the students' accuracy. (This can be an activity center). (NSM)

3. Compare the seeds of a fig with the seeds of an orange. (Dissect them; you can even show what happens when you cut them horizontally or vertically.) (NSM)

4. Think of an object, symbol, person, or custom related to Yom HaAtzma'ut, or to Israel in general. The students try to guess what that something is. The person who guesses successfully then thinks of something for the others to guess.

5. Divide the class into groups of 10 or less and have each group sit in a circle. One person in each group starts by saying, "I packed my trunk for *Eretz Yisrael* and in it I put _____."

Each person adds one more item to the list and each person must try to repeat all of the items put into the trunk so far.

6. Cut a Hebrew newspaper into picture size paper (most Jewish bookstores carry Israeli newspapers). Provide cut up Israeli oranges and paint. Have students print on the newspaper with the oranges and decorate with paint. (NSM)

7. One student leaves the room and the others select a word, phrase, or person related to Israel. The student returns and is allowed five questions including how, when, and why to identify the mystery word or phrase.

8. Read to the children the book *And Shira Imagined* by Giora Carmi, which presents a young child's first view of Israel. Black and white drawings of Israeli sites contrast with full-color images of Shira's thoughts. Make a photocopy for each child of one of the black and white drawings, and have the child color them in. Then make a display with captions of all the drawings.

9. Create a deck of cards with Hebrew and English words. Shuffle the cards. Have students sort the cards into two piles: one of English words and one of Hebrew. (NSM)

10. Create a Hebrew activity center. Include Hebrew rubber stamps (check Jewish book stores for these), stickers, newspapers, magazines, tourist booklets, etc.). Have paper, scissors and glue for students to create pictures. (NSM)

11. Begin a story by saying: "Once there was a child who went to Israel." Each child then may add one sentence to what has already been said. The class story can be recorded on a tape recorder and played back to the class.

12. Compare an Israeli flag with the flag of this country. (NSM)

13. Gather actual or hand drawn Israeli flags of different sizes. Have students sort them from the largest to the smallest. (NSM)

14. Create a matching game in which students match Hebrew letters (e.g., an *alef* with an *alef*). (NSM)

15. Give students a variety of pictures or postcards of both Israel and your own city and/or famous places in your country. Have students work together to sort them into piles according to the place (i.e., your city in one pile and Israel in another).

16. View and discuss an age appropriate video on Israel. The *Shalom Sesame* segments would be ideal (see Bibliography, page 299 for a listing of these and other videos). Talk about life in Israel as compared to the students' lives in this country. (NSM)

17. Put birthday candles in a jar, one candle per year of existence (e.g., in 1996 you would have had 220 candles in a jar for the United States). Put candles in another jar representing the age of Israel. Talk about the quantity difference. (NSM)

18. Complete some of the activities in *The Jewish Preschool Teachers Handbook* by Sandy Furfine Wolf and Nancy Cohen Nowak (pages 95-98).

19. Help children complete page 40 in *Jewish Preschool/Kindergarten Copy Pak*™ by Nancy Cohen Nowak.

20. Do a Yom HaAtzma'ut art project in *100+ Jewish Art Projects for Children* by Nina Streisand Sher and Margaret A. Feldman (page 50).

Primary

1. Mount pictures related to the holiday of Yom HaAtzma'ut or Israel in general on pieces of cardboard. Laminate the pictures and then cut each picture into puzzle pieces with a jigsaw. Divide the class into groups of 3 to 5 students. Each group receives the same or a different picture. The group to put its picture together first wins. Give the winning group special responsiblities related to your unit on Israel.

2. Point out that archaeology is the Israeli national hobby. Use a heavy cardboard box or a sandbox as the archaeological site. Students take turns "digging" for artifacts. Students explain what they find to the rest of the class. The teacher and students together figure out what each artifact is.

3. Make a collage. Gather lots of magazine pictures, letters and words, photographs, packaged punch-out gold letters, etc. Students paste them layer upon layer in a thoughtful, creative way onto a piece of 8" x 10" cardboard, then paint on two or three layers of Damar Varnish over the entire surface, letting each layer dry between coats. Frame in an inexpensive frame. These make wonderful gifts for Mother's Day or Father's Day.

4. To learn about major cities in Israel, try an Israel Cake Walk. On a sheet of paper or on the floor, draw a large outline map of Israel, big enough for a group of children to march on. Write in the major cities. Place slips with the cities written on them in a box. Each player takes a position on a city as the music begins. Players walk around until the music stops. The leader reads one of the slips, and the person standing on the spot called wins. Repeat, of course. Add to the learning process by having students describe the city. This same activity may be done with personalities, resources, or historical sites as well. (PM)

5. Make a mosaic design. Cut tiny squares of different colored construction paper. Students can make pictures and designs similar to mosaics by pasting the squares on posterboard with white glue. To help students get into the spirit of the project, show them pictures of Israeli mosaics. Cereal, beans, and macaroni are other good materials for mosaics. You can also make an interesting map of Israel out of any of these materials. Vary the textures and colors, then shellac for protection.

6. Have students make posters for Yom HaAtzma'ut. Use regular size or large size colored paper for backing. They can cut out objects, decorate them, and paste them on the colored paper. Hebrew or English lettering can also be cut out and pasted on the colored paper.

7. Each student brings a Jewish object or artifact from home which is special to that individual and/or his/her family and which originated in Israel. Students tell each other why the precious objects are special. Create a traveling museum made up of these objects.

8. Divide students into groups of 2 or 3. Provide each group with pictures or postcards of people in Israel. Have them analyze the pictures for one or more of the following: what people do in Israel, what the climate is like there, what is the same or different about Israel and your city, etc. You might give students a chart to fill in which helps them draw out their comparisons. (NSM)

9. Play or sing "*Hatikvah,*" and identify it as Israel's national anthem (or special song). Then have students listen to your country's national anthem. What comparisons can students make? (NSM)

10. Read to the children the book *Chicken Man* by Michelle Edwards, about a man who works in the *lul* (chicken coop) on a *kibbutz*. Discuss

what life is like on a *kibbutz*. Ask: Would you like to live on a *kibbutz*? Why or why not? With the class, build a model *kibbutz*.

11. Order posters and materials of Israel from the Israel Consulate. (Some travel agencies can also provide these.) Have students help to put the posters up. Discuss the scenes. (NSM)

12. Create a Hebrew writing center. Have students trace, copy, or rub letters of the Hebrew alphabet. (Use colored glue to make the letters of the alphabet on 3" x 5" cards; allow the glue to dry. Students can place paper over these and rub the pattern with crayon or pencil.) (NSM)

13. Invite a teenager or adult who has visited Israel to come to the class and talk about the trip and what they learned about Israel. Encourage the person to bring along objects and/or pictures. (NSM)

14. Hang a large topographical map of Israel on the bulletin board or over the blackboard. Then give out outline maps to each of the students for them to color in one part at a time. Briefly discuss the importance of each area as the students color it in.

15. Find some parents willing to research and come in to your classroom dressed as Golda Meir, Theodor Herzl, Ben-Gurion, Eliezer Ben-Yehuda, etc. The characters should be prepared to talk about their lives and then take questions from students. (NSM)

16. Cut a variety of pictures of Israel from travel brochures and magazines (about 10 to 15 different ones). Glue the pictures onto posterboard. Then, count items which are alike, recording them on cards, (e.g., 5 pictures of the *Kotel*, 6 street signs with Hebrew, 3 T-shirts with Hebrew). Have students search the pictures to find the numbers of items you identified. (NSM)

17. Eat an Israeli breakfast — diced cucumber/tomato salad, yogurt, cheese, bread (Italian style), or pita.

18. Complete some of the creative activites in *Imagine . . . Exploring Israel: Creative Drawing Adventures* by Marji Gold-Vukson.

19. Complete some of the pages in *Israel Copy Pak™ K-3* by Fran Borovetz.

20. Do one or more of the Yom HaAtzma'ut art projects in *100+ Jewish Art Projects for Children* by Nina Streisand Sher and Margaret A. Feldman (pages 49, 51).

21. Perform the play "Abraham and the Promised Land" from *Class Acts: Plays & Skits for Jewish Settings* by Stan J. Beiner. Invite parents and/or other classes to the performance.

Intermediate

1. One student volunteers to be the expert. The other students ask the "expert" questions about Israel in an effort to stump the expert. The person who succeeds in stumping the expert becomes the new expert, and the process is repeated.

2. Students sometimes lose track of the fact that the bond between American Jews and Israel is spiritual, cultural, and religious, as well as political. Form small groups. Give each student a copy of the *Siddur* that is used in your congregation. (Point out that Israel refers to Israel the land (*Eretz Yisrael*) and Israel the people (*Am Yisrael*). In a specified amount of time, the teams find as many references to Israel as possible in the *Siddur* (e.g., *Sh'ma, Tzur Yisrael, V'Shamru, R'tzay, Sim Shalom, Shalom Rav, Kaddish*, etc.). As the teams report their findings, list the references on the blackboard. Then come together as a whole group and discuss the refererences.

3. Have students write an "I Urge Telegram" to key Israeli figures, reflecting their views on Israel-Diaspora relations, Israel-Arab relations, peace, etc.

4. Invite stamp collectors to bring in their Israeli stamps to class, especially those stamps that depict various Jewish holidays. From the library, obtain books about Jewish stamps. Students may also look through a recent stamp catalogue, reading the descriptions of Israeli stamps, in order to determine which stamps deal with the holidays and festivals.

5. Divide the class into pairs. One person of each pair is a reporter while the second person becomes Menahem Begin, David Ben-Gurion, Golda Meir, Theodor Herzl, or another famous Israeli or Zionist. The reporter interviews the personality. Then the students reverse roles and the second student serves as the reporter. Come back together as a class and process the activity.

6. Put words pertaining to Yom HaAtzma'ut and Israel on the blackboard. Ask students to write a poem or song at least four lines long using a minimum of two of the terms. If writing a song, use the tune from "Sing Along Song" on the tape *Especially Wonderful Days*, or make up new verses in English or Hebrew for "*Hatikvah.*" Have students put the poem or song in their poetry books.

7. Have students take turns reading aloud some of the stories in *Next Year in Jerusalem: 3000 Years of Jewish Stories* by Howard Schwartz. Afterward, have them make up their own stories about Jerusalem and Israel.

8. Have students find pictures, newspaper and magazine articles, articles from the synagogue bulletin, photocopies of relevant materials, original essays, and art work that deal with the holiday of Yom HaAtzma'ut and the State of Israel. They can write to El Al Airlines, the Israel Consulate, Jewish National Fund, etc., for materials. Together, make an attractive and educational bulletin board display for school or classroom.

9. Give students a list of events related to the history of Israel since 1948 (see Chronology, page 182). Working individually, students make a time line. Display the time line in the classroom or the hallway.

10. Give students a narrative or story about Israel to read. Their assignment is to write a brief essay entitled "If I were living in Israel, I would ____ ." The intention is for the student to put himself/herself in the place of the main character of the story or the leading figure in the narrative and to speculate what he/she would do as that person. This can serve as the trigger for an excellent discussion.

11. Collect articles and photos of Israel from the newspaper. Put Israel current events on your class agenda. Help students understand the peace process. (NSM)

12. Have students honor famous Zionists (see page 184) by making commemorative plates out of plaster of paris (purchase in craft or hobby shop). After doing the necessary research on the individual they choose, students can create their own designs.

13. Use Israeli stamps to decorate rice cans, note paper boxes, and other sturdy containers to be used as pencil holders, pin boxes, stamp holders, jewelry boxes, etc. Glue the stamps onto the container (overlap the edges). Dry at least 24 hours, then seal with varnish.

14. Make and taste felafel, hummus, tehina, and other Middle Eastern specialties. If desired, have a sale of the food after Religious School for parents and other children. Donate the proceeds to a *tzedakah* project in Israel.

15. Divide the class into groups of 3 to 5 students, and ask each group to write slogans that reflect the key values and ideals reflected by the modern State of Israel. Groups then share their slogans with the rest of the class.

16. Invite a speaker from the Jewish Federation to speak about how the money raised from the community is apportioned. Prepare a list of questions in advance. During the next session, the class becomes the Board of the Jewish Federation, with each student representing a different agency or community organization. The task of the Board is to weigh local needs against monetary support of Israel, and to decide what percentage of the money raised by the Federation will go to each.

17. Do some map activities (NSM):
    a. Hang a large topographical map of Israel at the front of the classroom. Then give outline maps to each of the students to color in one part at a time. Briefly discuss the importance of each area as students color it in.
    b. Give students a map of Israel and the surrounding areas. Students must locate the places on the map that are connected to Yom HaAtzma'ut or Israel in general. Have them make a statement about the significance of each place in no more than one sentence.
    c. In groups, have students study maps of Israel's changes over time. What can they learn from the maps? Have students research why the changes occurred. Resource: *Atlas of Jewish History* by Martin Gilbert.

18. Form groups. Give each group a Hebrew newspaper. Have them look through the paper and figure out what sections are in it (news, poetry, classifieds, weather, etc). How does it compare with an English paper? (Note: Students who don't know Hebrew could still do this exercise just based on the format of the sections.) (NSM)

19. Choose age appropriate videos on Israel from among those listed on pages 299ff. View and discuss one or more of them.

20. Do "A Dramatic Reading for Two Groups" on page 195. This can be used for an assembly or for a family worship service. Have students pantomime scenes from Israel at various points throughout the reading.

21. Have students complete the *Passport to Israel Lessons* by Sharon Lerner. This set consists of eight Instant Lessons: The Judean Desert, Tel Aviv, The Negev, The Coast, Ha-Ir Ha-Atikah, The Galilee, Modern Jerusalem, and Haifa. Students receive a passport which is stamped each time they complete a lesson.

22. Perform the play "This Is Your Life, Israel" from *Kings and Things: 20 Jewish Plays for Kids 8 to 18* by Meridith Shaw Patera (page 114). Invite parents and/or other classes to the performance.

23. Complete some of the pages in *Israel Copy Pak*™ *4-6* by Fran Borovetz.

24. Complete page 23 in *Jewish Holiday Copy Pak*™ *4-6* by Marji Gold-Vukson.

25. Do a Yom HaAtzma'ut art projects in *100+ Jewish Art Projects for Children* by Nina Streisand Sher and Margaret A. Feldman (page 50).

Secondary
1. Discuss such questions as the following:
    a. At this stage in Jewish history, could Judaism survive without Israel? Could Israel survive without the Diaspora?
    b. Is dual loyalty a problem for American Jewry? If so, how?

c. Why has world Jewry been so consistent in its support for Israel over the past decades?

d. Why does the United States need Israel? What are the publicly stated reasons and what are the reasons that are left unstated?

e. Why is Israel important to North American Jewry?

f. Why is North American Jewry important to Israel?

g. To what extent does Israel need North American support?

h. Do Jews living outside of Israel have the right to try to influence the policies of the government of Israel?

i. Do American political leaders have the right to try to influence the policies of the government of Israel?

j. Do Israeli leaders have the right to try to influence the decisions and policies of the U.S. or Canadian government?

k. What, in your opinion, are the highlights of Israel's accomplishments since 1948? If you had to pick one event above all others as the most significant, which would you choose?

2. Create a mini-Israeli film festival. Your local video store might have the following: *Exodus*, *Raid on Entebbe*, and *Golda*. (NSM)

3. Invite to class a person in your community who was in Israel during its founding years. Study the time period with your class and prepare them to ask the visitor meaningful questions.

4. Examine the concept of *Pidyon Shevuyim* (redemption of the captive). Israel, as the spiritual center of Jewish life, accepts Jews from all over the world and works to help them get reestablished. Israel also tries to save Jews held "captive" in other lands (see the rescue at Entebbe, Operation Magic Carpet, Operation Moses, and Operation Ali Baba in

the Chronolgy, page 182). What Jewish value does this best exemplify? (*Pidyon Shavuyim*) By living this value, how does Israel appear in the eyes of other nations and peoples?

5. Have students prepare a creative worship service in honor of Israel's birthday.

6. Israel appears to be judged differently from any other country in the world. Especially has this been so in the press and in the United Nations. Discuss possible reasons for this and what can be done about it.

7. Yom HaAtzma'ut and Yom HaShoah are modern additions to the Jewish calendar. They commemorate pivotal events in the history of the Jewish people. Discuss: Are these observances as important as Chanukah and Purim? Are the rituals that are developing around these holidays as significant as rituals used for the older holidays and festivals? As the generation of survivors disappears along with the generation of the founders, will the relevance of these new observances retain their meaningfulness and their power?

8. Divide the class into several groups. Ask each group to examine and summarize for the class one of the biblical passages related to Israel, noting whether the passage refers to Israel the land or Israel the people (e.g., Numbers 23: 5-9).

9. Discuss the role of *tzedakah* in the relationship between the Jews in the Diaspora and Israel. How has world Jewry's *tzedakah* helped Israel become a powerful and influential nation on the world scene?

10. The *Brit Ahavah* relationship between North American Jewry and Israel is complex. There exists a mutual interdependence that is often not clearly recognizable, yet it is there. Divide the class into two groups, one representing the

Jews of Israel and the other representing the North American Jewish community. Each group must formulate a list of reasons why it is important to the other. After 10 or so minutes, the two groups come together, with each group sitting separate from the other. Their task is to negotiate a *Brit Ahavah* between Israel and North American Jewry. The covenant may take a simple form, such as the following:

We the Jews of Israel and the United States/Canada recognize the value and importance of Jewish life in both North America and Israel, and hereby affirm the following:
a.   The Jews of Israel agree to do the following with regard to the Jews of North America (students fill in).
b.   The Jews of North America agree to do the following with regard to the Jews of Israel (students fill in).

Discuss the covenants. Which ones seem workable, and which do not? Which is the most creative? Which is the most balanced?

11. Discuss the *mitzvah* of *Ahavat Tzion* (Love of Zion) and discuss why the State of Israel should matter to us today. Consider ways students and their families can carry out the obligation this *mitzvah* poses.
Resource: "Ahavat Tziyon: Zionism and Israel," in *It's a Mitzvah! Step-by-Step to Jewish Living* by Bradley Shavit Artson.

12. Choose age appropriate videos on Israel from among those listed on pages 299ff. View and discuss one or more of them.

13. Using Israeli symbols and foods, have students create a brief Israel Independence Day *Seder*. (The United Jewish Appeal published such a *Seder* a number of years ago.) Include Israeli music. Students can lead the *Seder* in the classrooms of younger students.

14. Complete one or more of the Instant Lessons *Neighbors in a Crowded House* by Yosi Gordon, *One Has to Make Peace with One's Enemies — Not with One's Friends* by Justin David, and *Peace in Jericho: An Instant Lesson with an Archaeological Perspective* by Steve Fine.

15. Perform the play "That's Incredible" from *Kings and Things: 20 Jewish Plays for Kids 8 to 18* by Meridith Shaw Patera (page 106). Invite parents and/or other classes to the performance.

16. Listen to and learn some of the songs, and do some of the suggested activities, in *Shirah B'Tiyul: A Musical Israel Curriculum* by Lori L. Abramson and Joel K. Abramson. Ten geographic areas are introduced by the songs. Holidays are among the many topics explored.

17. Do the dance *midrash* "Land of Milk and Honey" from *Torah in Motion: Creating Dance Midrash* by JoAnne Tucker and Susan Freeman (page 218). Afterward, students can create movement activities about Israel and teach them to younger students.

All-School
1.   Plan a "Walk through Israel." Participants go along a set route (inside or outside, depending on the weather), visiting important places in Israel along the way. Individual classes can prepare each site or activity station. Variation: Plan a "Walk through Jerusalem."

2.   Have an Israel Celebration for the entire congregation (for ideas, see page 197). You will need to start planning this many months in advance. This is a good opportunity to involve parents.

3.   Plan a Yom HaAtzma'ut assembly, with each class responsible for a short presentation (e.g., a skit, an Israeli dance, an "interview with a famous Israeli personality," etc.). At the conclu-

sion, sing *"Hatikvah"* and serve felafel to all. (FWM)

Family

1. Suggest that family members share objects and memories related to Israel as they sit around the dinner table. If they have traveled to Israel, they can look at their photographs after the meal.

2. Arrange for families to attend a community Yom HaAtzma'ut celebration or Walkathon together. This is a special opportunity for Jews to gather on a joyous occasion. If no such celebration is planned, families can get together and, with your help, arrange an observance for the families with children in the school.

A DRAMATIC READING FOR TWO GROUPS

Robert Goodman

Group A: Nearly 4000 years ago, God made a very special promise to Abraham, the father of the Jewish people.

Group B: "Go forth from your native land and from your father's house to the land that I will show you."

Group A: God continued saying: "And I will make of you a great nation, and I will bless you; I will make your name great and you shall be a blessing."

Group B: When Abraham and Sarah came to the land of Israel, God said to them: "I will give this land to you and your children and to all future generations. Later God told Abraham that one day there would be many, many Jews in the world. God said:

Group A: "Look toward the sky and count the stars if you can. That is how many sons and daughters of Abraham there will be.

Group B: In the centuries that followed, there were many great leaders of Israel. There were the Patriarchs of Israel: Abraham, Isaac, and Jacob.

Group A: There were the Matriarchs of Israel: Sarah, Rebecca, Rachel, and Leah.

Group B: There was Joseph, Moses, and later Joshua, who led the Israelites back into the Promised Land.

Group A: There were the brave judges of Israel: Deborah, Gideon, and Samson, and there were the early kings of Israel: Saul, David, and Solomon.

Group B: Later came the prophets of Israel: Amos, Micah, Isaiah, and Jeremiah.

Group A: Then for centuries, Jews were forced to live all over the world. During those hard times, Jews prayed to be able to live in *Eretz Yisrael,* but only a few thousand were able to do so.

Group B: About 100 or so years ago, a man named Theodor Herzl decided that prayers were not enough, and he did something very important.

Group A: Herzl started the modern Zionist Movement in 1896. He got people thinking about a modern state of Israel, a place where Jews from all over the world could live in freedom.

Group B: At first, people called his idea a dream, but he convinced many to work with him to make the dream come true. Theodor Herzl died at the age of 44, but his dream did not die with him. Others carried on where he left off.

Group A: Let us tell you a little bit about this special place known as *Eretz Yisrael*.

Group B: It is a land filled with dry valleys and rugged hills, a land with a bitter salt sea and sweet running streams.

Group A: Our ancestors loved to till the soil and plant the fields. They gathered their harvests and thanked God for all of their blessings.

Group B: As the rain fell from the heavens, they saw the deserts come alive with flowers and plants. They saw new life appear before their eyes.

Group A: Our ancestors loved this Homeland. Even when they were living far away, it always filled their minds and hearts.

Group B: And when our ancestors returned to the land, they were filled with joy. They worked hard to bring new life to places in which nothing had grown before.

Group A: With love and hard work, modern-day Jews brought new life to the land. All over Israel settlements appeared.

Group B: Roads were built; villages and *kibbutzim* established. Cities appeared as if overnight.

Group A: Many of the people in the surrounding countries did not want to have a Jewish state there.

Group B: Modern-day Jews have had to fight many wars to protect their lives, even though they want only to live in peace.

Group A: Jews in Israel and all over the world hope that there will be peace and sharing in the years to come, and an end to war.

Group B: Not many years ago, Arab and Jewish children wrote poems about peace for a book called *My Shalom, My Peace*. Tali Shurey wrote a poem called "The Paint Box."

Group A: In it she talks about the colors in her paint box — cool and bright, without the red for wounds and blood, and without the black for orphaned children, and without the white for the face of the dead.

Group B: Full of joyful orange and tree leaf green and sky blue and dream-filled pink.

Group A: And with her colors, she painted a picture of peace.

Group B: Let us pray for peace for Israel, and for everyone in the world.

Groups A & B: And let us all say "*Shalom Chaverim.*"

AN ISRAEL CELEBRATION

Created by Robert Goodman

Rationale

The goal of an Israel Celebration is to provide a framework within which Jewish schools, synagogues as a whole, and Jewish organizations, ranging from youth groups to senior citizen groups, can plan and carry out an interesting, enjoyable, and satisfying program for Yom HaAtzma'ut. Within this framework, the individual group or organization has a wide range of choices of activities to include in its celebration. The goals of such a celebration are simple, yet important:

To celebrate Yom HaAtzma'ut joyfully.

To engender a feeling of closeness to, and identification with, Israel.

To enrich knowledge and understanding of Israel's struggle for survival.

Overview

An Israel Clebration offers a simple framework with an almost unlimited number of built-in programming possibilities.

For the sake of discussion, let us say that a synagogue is planning such a program. The Planning Committee decides who is going to be involved. It might be just the Religious School, or it could be the men's club, the women's organization, Youth Group. Each auxiliary could in fact be responsible for 2 or 3 activities. Once the scope and breadth of the program has been determined, small groups of 5 or 6 people are put in charge of each activity, most of which can be prepared quickly and with ease. During the day of the Israel Celebration, the people who operate each activity take turns managing the activity station. In this way, the organizers can also have an opportunity to participate in the program.

In planning the individual activities, it may be desirable in some cases to prepare 2 or 3 parallel versions for various age groups — one for young children, one for older children, and one for adults. If an activity station has a message in code, for example, one version would have the message to be decoded along with the key to the code, while a second version would ask the participants to figure out the code.

How An Israel Celebration Works

This program may last for one hour, two hours, or even a full day. It consists of a series of concurrent activities. There may be 2 or 3 activities, or there may be 15, depending on the size and nature of your group.

As they arrive, give participants a single 8 1/2" x 11" sheet of colored paper folded in half. Print on the front cover the words "YOUR ISRAEL CELEBRATION PASSPORT." On the inside, print a listing of the activities and a place for credit and/or score for having completed each activity. The entire program can be portrayed as a trip through Israel, and each activity given an Israeli place name.

The inside of the passport might look something like this:

LOCATION	NAME OF ACTIVITY
Jerusalem (Room 1)	"An Archaeological Dig"
Tel Aviv (Room 7)	"Films Galore"
Haifa (Main Hall)	"Food Fair/The Deli Lamah"
Eilat (Room 9)	"Sing a Song"
Safed (Main Hall)	"Famous Israelis"

CREDIT FOR COMPLETION ____
SCORE ____

With passport in hand, participants go from activity to activity, selecting those which interest them the most. Some can be set up in classrooms while others can be in a central hall. Similarly, all of the activities can be in individual rooms or the entire program can be set up in one large room.

Participants receive a "credit" on their passports when they complete an activity. This can take the form of a signature or a special stamp. Participants can also receive a score based on how well they have performed in that activity. This is optional. If an activity involves checking a person's knowledge on a subject (see Information Quiz) or skill activities (see Card Games, Word Games, and Messages in Code), answers should be available for participants to score themselves. For example, if an information quiz is printed on a single sheet of paper, the answers can be given on the other side or upside down at the bottom of the page. Participants may then keep their worksheets and take them home, along with the passport. In this way, the learning component becomes painless and non-threatening.

General Activities

1. Next Year in Jerusalem. Write a poem, parable, allegory, dialogue, or draw a picture about Jerusalem or any other aspect of Israel that catches your fancy.

2. Make Up Your Own Poem. Give the participants line 1 and ask them to write three more lines or give them lines 1 and 3 and ask them to compose lines 2 and 4. The poems can either be serious or humorous.

3. Make Your Own Israeli Flag. Sew an Israeli flag using pre-cut pieces of material, and threaded needles. Participants sew together the flag and staple it to a dowel. The participants' passports are stamped, and each gets to keep the flag he or she made. Or, follow the same procedure using heavy colored paper or oak tag.

4. Make Your Own Coat of Arms. Using emblems of the 12 tribes or of the various cities in Israel, participants make a personal coat of arms. These can be mounted on oak tag.

5. Make Your Own Bookmark. This can be done quickly and simply using construction paper, crayons, sequins, rick-rack, stickers, etc., and clear Contact paper to cover.

Music and Dance

1. Being in Step with Israel. Participants enter a room and dance one or more Israeli dances.

2. Learn an Israeli Dance. Participants are taught an Israeli dance (about 10 people at one time).

3. Sing a Hebrew Song. Choose 3 or 4 Hebrew songs. One song is recorded on a cassette. Participants enter the room and sit down alongside a tape recorder. Different songs are recorded on the various tape recorders. Each person receives a card with the words in Hebrew and in English transliteration to accompany the tape. He or she listens to the song, practices it, and sings it to one of the people running the activity in order to get the passport stamped.

Videos and Feelings

1. Short Videos: Excellent short videos related to Israel can be borrowed at little or no cost from such organizations as: the Israeli Consulate, the Israel Government Tourist Agency, your local Jewish Federation, the Israeli Aliyah Center, and the Anti-Defamation League. Other sources for videos on Israel (though not free) are listed in the Bibliography (see pages 299ff.).

2. Show a Video and React To It: Show a short video on Israel that is both informative and evokes feelings. After participants have seen the film, give them an "Opinionaire" to help them to respond to the video. They might be asked to react to five statements using a Likert Scale: Strongly Agree, Agree, Undecided, Disagree, or Strongly Disagree. The completed opinionaires are submitted (without names) and credit is given. The results can be tabulated later. Some suggested statements include:

    a. This film makes me proud to be a Jew.
    b. This film helps me identify with Israel.
    c. Israel is vital to Jewish survival.

3. Sentence Completions: Show a short video or play an audiotape or CD. Ask the participants to complete about 5 sentences which, like the

Opinionaire above, help them to think through what they have just experienced. Point out that there is no wrong answer. Participants are to write down what first comes to mind.

Role Playing and Group Interaction

Note: When doing these activities, make it clear that the participants are *not* being tested. They will then will feel less inhibited about participating actively. Videotape these activities and show them later to the participants.

1. Be a Famous Israeli: Give 5 to 10 people at a time role profiles of different Israelis. They read over their profile and then introduce themselves to the other "Israelis." They discuss briefly how they see Israel today, or some other predetermined topic, and then their passports are stamped.

2. Two Israelis Meet: As participants enter a room, they are paired with another person and each is given a role profile. Each person then introduces himself/ herself to a partner. They discuss some predetermined question and then get their passport stamped.

3. A Trip through Israel: Sitting in a circle, approximately 10 people take turns narrating "their" trip through Israel. An activity leader starts off the narration (presenting either a serious or a humorous context). Each participant then adds either a sentence or a short paragraph to the story.

4. If I Were Going to Israel: With about 10 participants, each person states an item he/she would take on a trip to Israel; however, the participant must repeat all of the previously mentioned items. This can be done as an elimination game, or as simply a fun activity.

5. What Would You Say If . . . . : Using a group of 5 to 10 people, the activity leader has a series of humorous questions. He/she alternates the questions while going around the circle. Each person must come up with some kind of a response.

6. An Israeli Radio Station: Using a microphone, several speakers, and an amplifier, a "radio station" can be set up. Brief scripts can be given to participants, each of whom reads one as a "guest announcer." The person gets credit for being an announcer. The radio program can be broadcast throughout the celebration area.

For Young Children

Note: Many of the other activities also are suitable for young children, but the following are particularly good for the preschool or primary grades.

1. Put the Tag on Jerusalem: Based on *Pin the Tail on the Donkey*, the child is blindfolded and must locate Jerusalem (which can be pointed out beforehand) on a wall map of Israel. The map can be mounted on the wall, and either a pin or masking tape can be used by the child as a marker.

2. An Israel Coin Toss: Use a board with different size openings (one for each coin used). Give the child several coins to throw through the openings. A picture of the coin can be placed above each opening. There can be openings of different size to correspond to the coins of Israel.

3. Rebus: Use a picture puzzle to present a message or idea.

4. Puzzles: Take either a map of Israel or a picture of a place in Israel and mount it on heavy cardboard or wood. Then make pieces with a jigsaw. The child must put the puzzle together.

5. Archaeological Dig: Fill a sandbox with sand and place miniature replicas of artifacts and/or

sherds amidst the sand. The amateur archaeologists dig for the artifacts.

6. A Treasure Map: Children follow the numbers to make a picture of something related to Israel.

7. Find the Hidden Objects: In a picture, Israel-related objects are hidden. The children must locate them and color them in.

Map Games

1. Identification Game: Laminate a map of Israel or Jerusalem onto heavy cardboard. Make holes where key cities or locations are found. The student sticks a pencil or a golf tee through the hole and identifies the location. The activity leader checks the accuracy of the responses by seeing if the name corresponds with the name that is written on the back side of the map.

2. Outline Map: With a large map of the Middle East clearly visible, give the participants an outline map and ask them to fill in:
   a. Countries surrounding Israel.
   b. Designated spots within Israel (cities, Masada, etc.)

3. Puzzle Map: Put together a puzzle to reconstitute a map of Israel.

Information Quizzes

Note: The answers to these quizzes can be typed upside down, so that the participant has to turn the paper around to read the answers. Completing the questions brings "credit"!

1. Identify the Pictures: Show a series of pictures or slides depicting various aspects of Israel or places in Israel. Each participant has a sheet of paper numbered 1 to 10. The participant identifies the picture, or has 10 multiple choice questions, and (hopefully) selects the right answer to each question.

2. Which Is Correct?: Give multiple choice questions or present groups of three statements. One statement of each three is correct. The aim is to identify the correct statement in each group, or to find the right answer to each question.

3. How Much Hebrew Do You Know? Using commonly used Hebrew words or phrases, such as *Eretz Yisrael, Chutzpah, Knesset,* etc., ask the participant to match a Hebrew term with either a definition or a statement that corresponds to it (e.g., A stately place, You really have a lot of nerve, "meet market"). Humor is definitely called for!

4. Order the Events: Participants put in correct chronological order 5 to 10 famous events and/or leaders.

5. To Jerusalem with Love: Questions about Jerusalem on a game board where flags serve as stepping stones. History in game form!

6. Fill in the Blanks: Give information about Israel in a paragraph, leaving out 10 words. The participant selects from 10 to 12 words given at the bottom of the paragraph and fills in the appropriate words.

7. The Detective Game: A paragraph about Israel contains 5 mistakes. The participant must locate and circle the errors. If desired, have them make corrections.

8. True False Questions (Call it Fact or Fiction): Give 10 statements about modern Israel calling for a T or F answer.

9. Who Am I?: Give the participant a sheet of paper with brief descriptions of five famous Israelis. He/she must identify each person.

Card Games

1. Israel Sort: Arrange three pockets labeled Person, Place, and Thing. Give each participant 10 cards to place in the correct pocket. (Good for younger children.)

2. Matching Pairs: The participant is given 10 cards and has to make them into 5 pairs. Examples:
    a. A Person in a Category: Prime Minister/Menahem Begin
    b. First Name/Family Name: David/Ben-Gurion
    c. Event/Name: Weizmann/Balfour Declaration
    d. Event/Date: War of Attrition/ 1968-1970
    e. Event/Concept: Six-Day War/Reunification of Jerusalem.
    f. A Stamp/An Event: Match the event portrayed on a postage stamp with either a picture of a stamp or a stamp mounted on a card.

3. Israel or Not: Out of 10 cards, a participant must pick those cards which have something to do with Israel. (Good for young children.)

4. Poke and Pull: A series of pictures of things about Israel. At the bottom of each card are choices. The participant marks the word or phrase that correctly describes the picture.

5. Jerusalem of Gold: The participant sits before a pictorial map of Jerusalem. He/she has five cards depicting places in Jerusalem and must locate these places on the map, placing the cards in the correct places on the map.

Word Games and Messages in Code

Note: The key to a code can either be supplied or the participant can be asked to "decipher" the code.

1. Build a Pyramid with Consonants: The words that follow are supplied with vowels. The participant fills in the consonants:

_ A I _ A
_ A _ A _ A
_ I _ _ U _ _
A _ _ _ E _ O _
_ E _ U _ A _ E _

A city in Israel (Haifa)
An "up and up" place (Masada)
A collective farm (*kibbutz*)
A city near Gaza (Ashkelon)
The capital of Israel (Jerusalem)

2. How Many Words Can You Make?: Using JERUSALEM or ERETZ YISRAEL, ask participants to make as many words as they can from the word or phrase. Any word they make that relates to Israel counts as five words.

3. Messages in Code: Take Israel-related messages and put them in a simple code. Some "codes" include:
    a. Move each letter back one: ANX is BOY.
    b. Move each letter forward by one: CPZ is BOY.
    c. Assign each letter a number value: A=1, B=2, 2-15-25=BOY.
    d. For a message in Hebrew, use the number value of each letter such as Aleph = 1, Yod = 10, Tav = 400, etc.

4. Can You Skip?: Present a series of letters. The participant must take every second or third letter to form a message. For example, every third letter in the following string equals NER TAMID: OBNLPESVRGATONAZYMUWIXODVN.

5. Scrambled Words: Individual words are presented with the letters scrambled. Several can be put together to form a message such as ECAPE LIWL ONSO VARIER, which equals PEACE WILL SOON ARRIVE.

6. Word Search: In the maze of letters that appear, participants seek out 10 words related to Israel.

7. A Name Game: A name is hidden in a sentence. The letters of the name are in the sentence in correct order but hidden: Example: A Beginning is always difficult (Begin).

8. Israel Anagrams: Participants complete each sentence. Each letter of each answer goes in a numbered space. When the letters are filled in, a message results.

Exhibits, Displays, and Sales

1. Israeli Stamps: These make a beautiful and interesting display. First day covers, stamps, and postcards can also be sold.

2. Food Fair: Sell food to be eaten at the Celebration. In addition, sell imported packaged and canned foods from Israel.

3. Judaica Shop: Sell gift items from Israel.

4. Photography Exhibit: A display of photographs taken in Israel, along with posters, can add much to the spirit and atmosphere of the program.

5. Exhibit Art Work: Works by Israeli artists can be exhibited and/or sold. Art work done by children can also be displayed.

6. Entertainment Center: For people who don't wish to participate actively in the program, live or video entertainment can be provided, perhaps using the format of an Israeli coffee house. Dance groups, singers, and dramatic readings can also be utilized.

A Final Note: An Israel Celebration offers the opportunity to culminate a week of Yom HaAtzma'ut celebration with a truly delightful and meaningful program — one which you can shape and design. It provides something for everyone, and leaves all who participate with a good feeling of *Ahavat Yisrael* (Love of Israel). If your Celebration helps to strengthen the bond between world Jewry and Israel, then your efforts will have been a great success.

BIBLIOGRAPHY

See pages 295-303.

CHAPTER THIRTEEN
LAG B'OMER

VOCABULARY

Bar Kochba: "Son of a Star." Bar Kochba led the revolt of the Jews against Rome from 132-135 C.E. Rabbi Akiba regarded him as "king messiah." Bar Kochba managed to drive the Romans out of Judea, and established a revolutionary regime, minting coins which were inscribed "for the freedom of Jerusalem." The Romans launched a counterattack, finally defeating Bar Kochba at Betar in 135 C.E.

Bayt HaMikdash: The Temple in Jerusalem. A temple or synagogue is called *Bayt Knesset*, but The (First and Second) Temple in Jerusalem is designated by the name *Bayt HaMikdash* — "The House of Holiness." The First Temple was built by King Solomon around the year 950 B.C.E. and destroyed by Nebuchadnezzar in 586 B.C.E. The Second Temple (according to tradition) was rebuilt under the guidance of Haggai and Zechariah and was completed around 518 B.C.E. Some say it was built a century later. It was expanded and redone by Herod in the first century B.C.E. The Romans destroyed it in 70 C.E.

Chalakah: "Portion or Smooth." The word used for the ceremony of giving a first haircut to three-year-olds at Mount Meron on Lag B'Omer.

Iyar: The second month of the Jewish year corresponds to May/June. It has 29 days and its zodiac sign is Taurus. Yom HaAtzma'ut (Israel Independence Day) falls on the 5th of Iyar and Lag B'Omer on the 18th of Iyar.

Lag: Means "thirty-three." The letter *lamed* has a numerical equivalent of 30 and the *gimel* is three.

Lag B'Omer: The "thirty-third day of *Omer*." Lag B'Omer is the name given to the thirty-third day in the Counting of the *Omer*, 17 days before Shavuot. Lag B'Omer falls on the 18th day of Iyar, which is usually in May.

Omer: A measure of barley brought to the Temple as an offering on the first day of Pesach. Fifty days were counted from the beginning of Pesach until Shavuot was celebrated.

Rabbi Akiba: Akiba was a great scholar, patriot, and martyr. He was born around 50 C.E. and died in 135 C.E. at the hands of the Romans. Akiba was an enthusiastic supporter of Bar Kochba and his war against Rome. He was arrested by the Romans for teaching Torah, tortured and executed by burning at Caesaria. A plague broke out among his followers during the period of the Counting of the *Omer*. It ended suddenly on Lag B'Omer.

Sefirah: "Counting." This refers to the 50 day counting period from Pesach to Shavuot.

Sefirat HaOmer: "Counting of the *Omer*." Leviticus 23:15-16 states: "From . . . the day you bring the sheaf of wave offering, you shall keep count until seven full weeks have elapsed: you shall count 50 days, until the day after the seventh week; then you shall bring an offering of new grain to *Adonai*." The ritual of the Counting of the *Omer* is a part of every evening service from Pesach until Shavuot.

Shimon bar Yochai: A leading scholar and pupil of Rabbi Akiba, Shimon bar Yochai opposed the Romans. He was sentenced to death, but managed to elude capture. He and his son Eleazar lived in a cave for 13 years. The authorship of the *Zohar*, the key work of Kabbalah, is attributed to bar Yochai. His tomb is located at the foot of Mount Meron in the Galilee. Meron is the scene of mass celebrations on Lag B'Omer (see Customs below).

Zohar: "Splendor." The *Zohar* is the major work of Jewish mysticism. It was attributed to Rabbi Shimon bar Yochai, but was probably written by Moses de Leon in Spain in the thirteenth century. It is written in Aramaic in the form of a commentary on the Torah. It contains a vivid, imaginative, symbolic examination of God and human beings and their mystical relationship.

BACKGROUND

The origins of Lag B'Omer are obscure. It has no roots in the Bible whatsoever. In all likelihood, it was originally an ancient pagan festival that included superstitious beliefs and woodland lore. When Judaism made it into a minor festival, it linked the 18th of Iyar with important events in Jewish history.

Just as Tishah B'av has become the day when many tragic events in the history of the Jewish people supposedly occurred, Lag B'Omer has become the "traditional" date for joyous events. These include the following:

1. Bar Kochba and Rabbi Akiba led an uprising against Rome from 132-135 C.E. Talmudic and *Midrashic* sources indicate that a fearsome plague hit the disciples of Rabbi Akiba, killing (according to various sources) 12,000 to 24,000 people. This plague, which broke out right around Pesach, suddenly ceased on the 18th of Iyar, giving rise to great rejoicing.

2. During this war against Rome, the Romans, in an effort to wipe out all opposition, forbade the Jews from studying Torah. Rabbi Shimon bar Yochai and his son hid in a cave for 13 years. There they studied in secret. Many of bar Yochai's pupils came to visit their hermit teacher. They would dress as hunters and would carry bows and arrows with them. They were armed because there was always the possibility that they would have to confront Roman soldiers on their way to or from the visit. Another explanation: *keshet* is the Hebrew word for bow and for rainbow. According to a tradition, out of respect for Rabbi Shimon bar Yochai, a rainbow did not appear in the sky during the 13 years that he and his son were in hiding.

3. Shimon bar Yochai asked his disciples not to mourn him when he died, but rather to make the anniversary of his death a day of rejoicing. He died on Lag B'Omer at Mount Meron in the Galilee. It is also said that he was born on that day.

4. It is said that manna first fell in the desert on Lag B'Omer.

5. It should be noted that the *Omer* period was a time when Jewish suffering seemed to be particularly intense. Massacres of Jews during the First Crusade (1096 C.E.) occurred during the period. The Cossack pogroms led by Bogdan Chmielnitzki in Poland in 1648 also took place during this season.

6. Lag B'Omer gradually evolved into a joyous holiday, a welcome respite from the austerity and restrictions of the *Omer* period.

Customs/Observance

Lag B'Omer is known as Scholars' Day because of its happy connections with Rabbi Akiba and Rabbi Shimon bar Yochai.

The *Omer* period is traditionally a time of austerity because of the many tragic events that are believed to have occurred then during the Roman occupation of Judea. As a result of the prevailing mood of sorrow and mourning, no marriages take place during this period except on Rosh Chodesh Iyar and Sivan and on Lag B'Omer. Some Rabbis permit marriages after Lag B'Omer; some wait until the three days prior to Shavuot to permit marriages.

In Israel, Hasidic Jews visit the grave of Rabbi Shimon bar Yochai at the foot of Mount Meron near the city of Safed in the Galilee. On Lag B'Omer, thousands of people come to the *Bayt Midrash* which is located at Meron. There they light candles and engage in singing and dancing, as was bar Yochai's wish. At midnight, a huge bonfire is lit. At dawn, little boys who have reached the age of three are brought forward to receive their first haircut.

The Sephardim permit shaving and haircuts only on the thirty-fourth day of the *Sefirah* — the day after Lag B'Omer.

Lag B'Omer is primarily a children's holiday and a family holiday. It is customary to hold family or school picnics on this day. Children are given bows and arrows in memory of the students of Shimon bar Yochai who came to his cave dressed as hunters. Among some congregations, a Lag B'Omer picnic serves as a joyful end to the Religious School year.

Schools in Israel are let out for the day. At night, in some years, huge bonfires using old tires are lit throughout the country. Potatoes are roasted.

ACTIVITIES

Note: As a joyous spring festival, Lag B'Omer is most commonly celebrated by a picnic and games. The picnic is often occasioned by the conclusion of the Religious School or Hebrew School year. Because of when it falls in the religious calendar, very little time is usually devoted to the study of Lag B'Omer. Accordingly, only a few strategies are listed below. For additional strategies, consult the chapter on Shavuot. Very few textbooks or other classroom materials contain information on Lag B'Omer, and no storybooks seem to be available. For this reason, the Bibliography is very small.

Preschool/Kindergarten

1. Hide a picture of a cave somewhere in the classroom. The students must find the cave where Rabbi Shimon bar Yochai is hiding.

2. Prepare five cardboard squares, each at least one foot square. On each, place a picture of a symbol, person, or activity related to Lag B'Omer. The students stand 5' to 6' away and try to throw coins on the five squares. When a coin lands on one of the five squares, the student has to say something about the symbol depicted on that square. Healthy treats can be given as prizes for correct responses and accurate coin tossing.

Primary

1. A parent, principal, the Rabbi, or another teacher dresses up as Bar Kochba and comes to class pretending to be that person. The class interviews Bar Kochba, asking questions related to the events in his life and his accomplishments.

2. Design a maze geared to the holiday of Lag B'Omer. The student has to take a trip through "holidayland," visiting 4 to 5 sites related to the holiday of Lag B'Omer. The starting point can be Pesach, then to Yom HaShoah, then to Yom HaAtzma'ut, then to Lag B'Omer, and finally to Shavuot. Number the items.

3. Bring a real bow and arrows to class. Using these props, tell the story of Rabbi Shimon bar Yochai. Be sure to refer to the bow and arrows.

4. Since Lag B'Omer is a time when we honor teachers, have students pair off and write (or draw) the characteristics they have found in their favorite teachers.

5. Give each student a paper bag, crayons, a scissors, colored paper, and glue. Using these materials, each makes a paper bag representation of one of the characters in the Lag B'Omer

story (e.g, Rabbi Akiba, Rabbi Shimon bar Yochai, Bar Kochba, Rabbi Judah, Roman soldiers, Zealots.). Then have the class act out parts (or all) of the story using the paper bag puppets.

6. Do the Lag B'Omer art project in *100+ Jewish Art Projects for Children* by Nina Streisand Sher and Margaret A. Feldman (page 52).

Intermediate

1. Have students match the items in the two columns:

a. Iyar	1.	Hid in a cave
b. Lag	2.	A mystical book
c. Bar Kochba	3.	A Hebrew month
d. *Sefirah*	4.	Thirty-three
e. *Zohar*	5.	Counting
f. Bar Yochai	6.	Leader of a revolt

2. Have students keep a diary as Rabbi Shimon bar Yochai, who spent 13 years living in a cave while hiding from the Romans. Encourage them to describe how it feels to be hiding from the Romans and teaching students in secret.

3. Give students a list of events related to the holiday of Lag B'Omer. Working individually, they make either a calendar time line or connect events by arrows. Include the holidays of Pesach, Yom HaShoah, Yom HaAtzma'ut, Lag B'Omer, and Shavuot. Each occurrence is connected by arrows with the direction of the arrow indicating the order of occurrence.

4. Present groups of three statements together to the students. One of the statements in each group of three is incorrect. Students must decide which statement is incorrect and then explain why in the space that follows. The false answer in each group is indicated here by (F):

    Lag B'Omer takes place in the month of Nisan. (F)

Lag B'Omer means 33rd day in the counting of the *Omer*.
Lag B'Omer occurs 17 days before Shavuot.

Bar Kochba was a great Jewish general.
Akiba was a Rabbi who hid in a cave for 13 years. (F)
The Second Temple was destroyed 70 C.E.

Rabbi Akiba was a great Rabbi.
Rabbi Shimon bar Yochai is buried near Mount Meron.
It is said that the *Zohar* was written by Rabbi Akiba. (F)

5. Write Lag B'Omer slogans. Either in small groups or individually, have students create a motto or slogan to reflect the events surrounding the holiday of Lag B'Omer. Using burlap or felt, make banners with the slogans emblazoned on them.

6. Play *Twenty Questions*. One student leaves the room. The class thinks of a name or term related to Lag B'Omer. The student returns and can ask only questions which elicit a yes or no response. The student who guesses in the least number of guesses is the class winner.

7. Have students design and create an *Omer* Calendar. Make room for seven weeks plus one extra day on the calendar. Number the days of the *Omer* period. Mark in Pesach, Lag B'Omer, Shavuot, Yom HaAtzma'ut, Yom HaShoah, and Rosh Chodesh (twice).

8. Make Lag B'Omer posters. Use regular size or large size colored paper for backing. Cut out objects, decorate them, and paste them on the colored paper. Hebrew or English lettering can also be cut out and pasted on the colored paper.

9. Have students create a stamp to commemorate the heroism of Rabbi Akiba, Bar Kochba, and/or Rabbi Shimon bar Yochai. First, of course, they will need to research the lives and

accomplishments of these individuals. Display the finished products and have students explain the reasons for their choice of design and motif.

10. Ask students to close their eyes and to block out all extraneous thoughts as you read to them a description of the life of either Rabbi Shimon bar Yochai or Bar Kochba. Have them concentrate intently on the reading. Then ask them to open their eyes and react to what has been read.

Secondary

1. Give a quiz on Lag B'Omer. Here are a few suggested questions:

   How many days are there between the first day of Pesach and the first day of Shavuot? (50 days)

   What are these days called? (*Sefirah* or Counting the *Omer* Days)

   What does Lag B'Omer mean? (Thirty-third day of Counting the *Omer*)

   Why are weddings held only on Rosh Chodesh, Lag B'Omer, and Israel Independence Day, but not on other days between Pesach and Shavuot? (This is a period of sadness and mourning)

   How were Pesach and Shavuot related to each other in terms of the agricultural cycle of Palestine? (They mark the beginning and the ending of the spring harvest period)

2. The Committee on Jewish Law and Standards of the Rabbinical Assembly (Conservative) has adopted a policy allowing marriages during the *Sefirah* if the wedding is not accompanied by dancing, singing, and music. Ask: How important to a Jewish wedding ceremony are dancing, singing, and music? What would the ceremony be like without any of these? Would you personally want to be married without them? Why or why not? (AFM)

3. Discuss the following:
   a. Why is it customary to go on a picnic on Lag B'Omer?
   b. What is the reason Lag B'Omer is known as Scholars' Day?
   c. What historical events took place during the *Omer* period?
   d. What is the significance and symbolism of the bow and arrows for Lag B'Omer?
   e. Why are no weddings permitted during the period of the counting of the *Omer* except on Lag B'Omer and Rosh Chodesh?
   f. How is the importance of Torah study emphasized in the celebration of this holiday? Is the right to study Torah still of central importance to Judaism? What risks did Shimon bar Yohai and his son take in order to be able to study and teach Torah?

4. Jewish history is filled with a great deal of sadness and tragedy. Yet, somehow, the Jewish People has managed to survive and thrive. Ask: In what ways does the celebration of Lag B'Omer serve as a reminder of the need to maintain a balance between painful memories and joyous celebration? Is the "traditional" mourning period at this time of year necessary, or would you prefer some modification of the limitations on weddings and joyous celebrations during the period of the Counting of the *Omer*?

5. Post signs in three corners of the room, each with one of the following responses on it:

   Go along with the Roman edict and give up study of the Torah.

   Try to rally the people to fight the Romans.

   Go into hiding to be able to continue to study and teach.

   Have students imagine they are Rabbi Shimon bar Yochai. The Romans have issued an edict forbidding study of Torah under penalty of death. Have each student go to the sign which represents what they would do. In the three groups, students discuss their reasons for making that choice. Reconvene the class as a whole and process learnings, insights, etc.

6. Divide the class into pairs. One student in each pair becomes Akiba and the other Bar Kochba. They describe to each other the struggle against Rome, the former from a religious perspective and the latter from a military, political viewpoint. After a few minutes, they reverse roles. Then the class reassembles and explores their reactions to both famous Jewish leaders.

All-School
1. As a school, celebrate Lag B'Omer with a picnic. Offer free Lag B'Omer haircuts!

2. Initiate a Maccabiah Sports Festival as part of the Lag B'Omer celebration.

Family
1. Invite families to take part in the congregation's Lag B'Omer picnic.

2. Organize a family education program for two to four-year-olds (there is an already designed Lag B'Omer program in *Head Start on*

Holidays: Jewish Programs for Preschoolers and Their Parents by Roberta Louis Goodman and Andye Honigman Zell).

3. Suggest that family members talk about the heroism of Rabbi Akiba, Bar Kochba, and Shimon bar Yochai around the dinner table. Decide together what makes each hero special and important. Discuss how each family member can become more like these heroes. Explore what makes each person special and important.

4. In ancient times, the *yahrzeit* of a great person was often turned into a holiday. Lag B'Omer is celebrated in honor of Shimon bar Yochai, who is said to have died on the 18th of Iyar. Suggest that each family decide on a great person they wish to honor. Find out the date of that person's *yahrzeit*. Design holiday observances and celebrations in honor of the person and carry them out on the appropriate date. Have each student report to his/her class which great person their family chose and why, and what they did to honor that person. (AFM)

BIBLIOGRAPHY
See page 303.

CHAPTER FOURTEEN

YOM YERUSHALAYIM

BACKGROUND

Yom Yerushalayim is the latest addition to the Jewish holiday calendar. It marks the liberation and reunification of Jerusalem after the Six Day War.

In 1967, escalating Arab terrorist raids across the Egyptian and Jordanian borders, as well as ongoing Syrian artillery bombardment and sniper attacks from the Golan Heights on Jewish settlements in the Galilee, were followed by a massive Arab military build-up. In May of that year, Egypt moved troops into the Sinai Desert and ordered the United Nations peacekeeping forces to evacuate. Egypt then blockaded the Straits of Tiran, effectively cutting off Israeli shipping from arriving from the Far East or leaving from Eilat. When Egypt entered into military alliance with Jordan and Syria, Israel was left with little choice. On Monday, June 5, 1967, a pre-emptive strike was launched. On that fateful morning, with pinpoint accuracy, the Israeli air force destroyed most of the Egyptian and Syrian air force while those planes were still on the ground. With the air war over in a matter of hours, Israel launched simultaneous attacks against Egyptian tanks in the Sinai (the largest tank battle in history) and against Syrian forces in the Golan Heights. Though warned to stay out of the fray, Jordan soon joined the other Arab forces and Israel was forced to engage her in a battle for Jerusalem.

By the end of the six days of fighting, Israel had captured the Sinai (driving the Egyptian army well into Egyptian territory even to the very gateway to Cairo), the Gaza Strip, the West Bank of the Jordan River, the Golan Heights, and all of Jerusalem. The most difficult fighting took place in Jerusalem. There, in an effort not to harm Jewish, Christian, or Moslem holy places, Israeli soldiers fought street to street and door to door, avoiding the use of heavy artillery. Finally, near the end of the third day of the battle, on Wednesday, Iyar 28th/June 7th, all of the city was in Israeli hands — united once again. At that time, Israel made commitments that the city would never again be divided, that all holy places would be guarded, and the faithful of each religion would be given access to worship at those places. These commitments have been kept at much cost.

Centrality of Jerusalem to Jews

The connection of *Am Yisrael* to *Eretz Yisrael* and its capital is historical, religious, and emotional.

On the historical level, from the day that King David purchased Jerusalem from the Jebusites some 3000 years ago and made it his capital, there has been an ongoing Jewish presence in the city. Through the centuries, the numbers of Jews living in the city has varied — sometimes there were few, as after the Roman conquest of Bar Kochba. At other times, large numbers of Jews made this Holy City bustle with commerce and pulsate with Jewish activity. But regardless of the numbers living there, the tie was always maintained — ownership was always guarded.

On the religious level, there is not a day that has gone by in these past several millenia in which Jerusalem was not mentioned by countless Jews the world over. In reciting daily prayers, Israel and Jerusalem are prayed for, and the desire for peace in the Land has been a constant of the Jewish people. Every day, after every meal eaten by Jews on every continent, petitionary prayers for a Jerusalem rebuilt and restored have been spoken. Every *Seder* ends with the hope that next year we will be in Jerusalem. Life cycle events, such as the wedding ceremony, call upon the very streets of Jerusalem to rejoice with bride and groom. And even at a funeral, a sack of dirt from Jerusalem is placed in the casket as a way of connecting those who have lived and died in the Diaspora with the land of our ancestors.

On the emotional level, Jerusalem has been the focus of Jewish eyes, mind, and heart. Synagogues throughout the world are oriented toward our Holy City. Those in the west face eastward, while those east of Jerusalem face westward. On synagogue walls, as well as on the walls of individual homes, it is common to see a decorated wall hanging called a *Mizrach* (meaning "east") beckoning attention toward Jerusalem. There is a teaching that an ideal Jerusalem — *Yerushalayim shel ma'alah* (Jerusalem on high) — serves as the model for what the earthly city can and should become. This Jerusalem on high has also been thought of as the ideal, or the heaven, to which one might aspire. And, in the end of days — in the days of the Messiah — tradition rooted in folklore holds out the promise that resurrection of the righteous will take place on the Mount of Olives in Jerusalem.

Thus, in the history and the heart, in the prayers and blessings, in the celebrations and observances, in the mind and soul, in the psyche and in the collective subconscious of the Jewish people . . . Jerusalem!

Observance

Yom Yerushalayim is a day of special prayers (especially *Hallel*, a collection of joyous Psalms) and a celebration of the beauty, special nature, and centrality of Jerusalem to the Jewish people. Yom Yerushalayim, occuring as it does on Iyar 28, comes amidst the rush of holidays in May/June — Yom HaAtzma'ut, Lag B'Omer, and Shavuot.

ACTIVITIES

Note: Many of the activities found in Chapter 12, Yom HaAtzma'ut, are also appropriate for Yom Yerushalayim.

Preschool/Kindergarten
1. View and discuss the video *Jerusalem*, a segment of the Shalom Sesame Street series. Afterward, have children draw pictures of sites in Jerusalem and talk about what makes this beautiful city so special to Jews.

Primary
1. Complete the Instant Lesson *Seven Weeks of Remembrance*.

2. Invite someone from the congregation or community who has visited Jerusalem to speak about the experience and what it meant to him/her and to share their videos and/or photo albums.

3. Read and discuss the mini-magazines *Our Jerusalem*. Complete some of the classroom activities contained therein.

Intermediate
1. Give students copies of the *Siddur*. In small groups, have them find as many references as possible to Jerusalem (and Israel).

2. The bond between Jews and Israel is deeply rooted. When Theodor Herzl suggested Uganda as a temporary Jewish home, Jewish leaders quickly vetoed the idea because Israel and only Israel is the home of the Jewish People. Have students complete sentences to elicit feelings about Israel and Jerusalem. Some suggestions for sentences:
   One thing I have learned about Jerusalem is
   _____.

   One word that describes Jerusalem to me is
   _____.

   When I think about Jerusalem, I think about
   _____.

Jerusalem makes me feel proud because ____. When I see pictures or videos of Jerusalem I feel ____.

3. Give each student a mini-biography of a famous Israeli, someone either presently living or previously influential (Ben-Gurion, Golda Meir, etc.). With each student playing the role of an Israeli leader past or present, discuss the prospects for peace in the Middle East and how to reach that goal.

4. Introduce students to Jerusalem through *Jerusalem 3000: The CD-ROM*. Divide the class into four groups, each of which takes one of the narrated tours of the city — modern Jerusalem, Jewish Jerusalem, Christian Jerusalem, or Moslem Jerusalem. Each group then reports on what they learned to the group as a whole.

Secondary

1. Of the many *midrashic* references to Jerusalem, there are several that extol her beauty, e.g., "When God divided up the beauty in the world, nine parts were given to Jerusalem and one part to the rest of the world." Discuss what this statement really means. Ask students who have been to Israel to share their feelings about Jerusalem and Israel with the class. Ask them what it is that gives Jerusalem its mystique and its striking beauty. Do they think that its unique role in Jewish life enhances our perception of Jerusalem's beauty and splendor?

2. View and discuss *Jerusalem: Between Heaven & Earth*, consisting of three videos. *Part I: City of History* is an in-depth look at the city's fascinating history through the eyes of academics and native citizens. *Part II: City of Religion* depicts the spiritual importance of Jerusalem to the world's three major faiths. *Part III: City of Peace* deals with the hopes and dreams of Jerusalem's inhabitants, as well as some recently established bi-cultural projects

that sensitize both Jews and Palestinians to each other's needs.

3. Debate the following statement: Be it resolved that Israel should not split off any part of Jerusalem to the Palestinians for the sake of permanent peace.

4. Listen to and sing the song *"Yerushalayim Shel Zahav"* on the audiocassette *Shirah B'Tiyul* by Lori L. Abramson and Joel K. Abramson. Engage in some of the discussions and activities suggested in the accompanying curriculum.

Family

1. Suggest that families read S.Y. Agnon's tale *"Ma'aseh Ha'ez"* (The Tale of the Goat), in which a goat enters a cave and magically enters into the Holy Land.

2. Remind families about the custom of inserting written prayers into the cracks of the Western Wall in Jerusalem. Recently, Bezek, the Israeli telephone company, announced that it would receive and place faxed messages into the Wall. The charge for this service is the same as for an ordinary fax. Families can discuss whether sending prayers via fax affects in any negative way the seriousness or spiritual aspect of a prayer. What might God's reaction be to a faxed message? Family members can write prayers to fax to Bezek. If they actually want to fax their prayers, the direct dial number is (011)972-2-661-2222. (AFM)

All-school

1. Set up a number of activity stations that highlight key places in Jerusalem and prepare a brief booklet describing the places to be visited in Jerusalem. Give each student a tour booklet before they begin their "visit." Some suggestions for stations:

a. The *Kotel* (the Western Wall): Have a simulated Wall and have the children participate in a brief prayer service while standing in front of the *Kotel*. The Rabbi or Cantor can serve as the guide at this station.

b. The Knesset: A *Chaver* (Member) of the Knesset welcomes the students and tells them about how the Knesset functions and what kinds of decisions it makes. Have pictures/posters of the Knesset as a backdrop to the activity station. The *Chaver* can present an issue to them, and ask them to vote on the issue in order to help him/her to vote the "right" way.

c. Mount Herzl: Theodor Herzl magically reappears at this station to tell his story, and how his dream became a reality. He tells the students what it feels like to see his dream come true.

d. The Kennedy Memorial and the J.N.F. forest that surrounds it: Students learn a bit about the role of the Jewish National Fund, and how Jews in the Diaspora have contributed to the growth, development, and security of Israel.

e. An *Ulpan* (Intensive Hebrew Class): For 5 to 10 minutes, the students become part of an *Ivrit B'Ivrit* (Hebrew taught in Hebrew) learning experience. They learn about the *Ulpan* where people from different countries come together and learn to speak Hebrew.

f. Visit the religious centers of the Reform and Conservative movements in Jerusalem. Visit a *Yeshivah* in the Old City.

BIBLIOGRAPHY

See Yom HaAtzma'ut, pages 295-303.

CHAPTER FIFTEEN

SHAVUOT

VOCABULARY

Akdamut: "Introduction" in Aramaic. The *Akdamut* is a hymn attributed to Rabbi Meir ben Isaac Nahorai of Orleans in southern France. It was written in the eleventh century. Ninety verses long, this is perhaps the best known liturgical poem in the *Siddur*. It is recited just before the Torah reading on the first day of Shavuot. The first part of the poem describes the majesty and glory of God who created heaven and earth. The second part of the poem takes the form of a dialogue between Israel (a constant victim of persecution) and those who seek to convince Israel to give up the faith that she retains with such tenacity. The poem concludes with a lavish description of the hoped for messianic era.

Aseret HaDibrot: Literally, "The Ten Statements," but usually translated as the "Ten Commandments." They appear twice in the Torah, in Exodus 20:2-14 and in Deuteronomy 5:6-18. Tradition teaches that the Ten Commandments were given to Moses on Mount Sinai and served as the basis for Torah legislation and all Jewish law. *Aseret HaDibrot* are also known as the Decalogue, from the Greek meaning "ten words."

Atzeret: "Cessation" or "Solemn Assembly." The Rabbis of the Talmud viewed Shavuot as the conclusion of Pesach and therefore referred to Shavuot as the solemn assembly of cessation. They drew a parallel with Shavuot and Shemini Atzeret, at the end of Sukkot.

Chag HaBikurim: "Festival of the First Fruits." Deuteronomy 26:1-11 commands the owner of land in Israel to take the first ripe fruits of the harvest to the Temple in Jerusalem. The first fruit offerings were limited to the seven species (Deuteronomy 8:8): wheat, barley, vines, figs, pomegranates, olive oil, and honey. These first fruits (*bikurim*) were to be brought to the Temple from Shavuot until Sukkot. Numbers 28:26 explicitly links the first fruits and Shavuot: "On the day of the first fruits, your Feast of Weeks, when you bring an offering of new grain to *Adonai*, you shall observe a sacred occasion."

Chag HaKatzir: "The Festival of the Harvest." Shavuot is observed when the first fruits of the wheat harvest are offered as a sacrifice. To celebrate the harvest, Israelites brought two loaves of bread from the newly harvested wheat. This name derives from Exodus 23:16 which states: " . . . and the Festival of the Harvest, of the first fruits of your work, of what you sow in the field."

Chag HaShavuot: "The Festival of Weeks." Seven weeks are counted from the second day of Pesach until Shavuot. Shavuot is therefore seven weeks of seven days plus one day after the first day of Pesach. It is celebrated on the sixth and seventh days of the month of Sivan.

Confirmation: Students completing the upper grade of their Religious School take part in the ceremony of Confirmation. The Confirmation ceremony is linked to this holiday because Shavuot represents the time when Israel confirmed its faith and its commitment to Judaism by accepting the Torah Law and by forging a covenant with God.

Isru Chag: "Bind a Festival." The term is given to the day following a festival and is considered to be a minor festival for liturgical purposes. The expression is taken from Psalm 118:27 which states: "Hold onto the festival, even as it departs. Isru Chag, which occurs on the day after the festivals of Shavuot, Sukkot, and Pesach, in effect, extends each festival by one day.

Megillat Ruth: "Scroll (or Book) of Ruth," which is read as a prelude to the afternoon service on Shavuot. The story takes place against the backdrop of the barley harvest. It relates how a Moabite woman came to embrace the faith of Israel and throw in her lot with the Jewish people. The Book of Ruth reflects two important themes of Shavuot: the ingathering of the harvest, and the acceptance of the Torah by a non-Jew. According to biblical tradition, Ruth was an ancestor of King David. According to a tradition mentioned in the Talmud, David was born and died on the festival of Shavuot. Ruth demonstrates her loyalty to the Torah by becoming a Jew. Such a story is fitting for the festival of Shavuot which is dedicated to the centrality of the Torah.

Pentecost: A Greek word meaning "Holiday of 50 Days." This name is applied to Shavuot because it occurs 50 days after the first day of Pesach. There is also a Christian holiday by the name of Pentecost. The Jewish Pentecost is the anniversary of the establishment of the Jewish people, when Israel became a nation. Similarly, the Christian Pentecost is the anniversary of the time when the Holy Spirit descended upon the disciples of Jesus, thereby making it the anniversary of the establishment of the Catholic Church. It is possible that the idea of having a Pentecost holiday was borrowed from Judaism by Christianity.

Sefirat HaOmer: "Counting of the *Omer*." An *omer* was a measure of barley brought to the Temple on the first day of Pesach as a thanksgiving offering. Leviticus 23:15-16 states: "From . . . the day that you bring the sheaf of wave offering, you shall keep count until seven full weeks have elapsed: you shall count 50 days, until the day after the seventh week; then you shall bring an offering of new grain to *Adonai*." This grain offering is therefore made on Shavuot. The ceremony of the Counting of the *Omer* during the Ma'ariv service each day serves as a link between Pesach and Shavuot.

Shalosh Regalim: "Three Pilgrimage Festivals." On Pesach, Shavuot, and Sukkot, Israelites journeyed on foot to Jerusalem to offer sacrifices at the Temple according to the injunction in Deuteronomy 16:16-17. Because the journey to Jerusalem was long and difficult for most Jews, it took on the character of a pilgrimage.

Shavuot: "Weeks." The Festival of Weeks occurs 49 days (a week of weeks) after the second day of Pesach. Shavuot takes place on the sixth and seventh days of Sivan.

Sh'loshet Y'may Hagbalah: "Three Days of Setting Bounds." The three days immediately preceding Shavuot are seen as days of preparation for the Festival of Shavuot. From Rosh Chodesh Sivan, all of the semi-mourning restrictions of the *Omer* period are dropped in anticipation of the forthcoming Shavuot festival. The three day period reflects back on the instructions given by God to Moses before the Revelation at Sinai: "Go to the people . . . Let them be ready for the third day; for on the third day God will come down, in the sight of all the people, on Mount Sinai" (Exodus 19:10-11). On *Sh'loshet Y'may Hagbalah*, Lag B'Omer, and Rosh Chodesh, marriages are permitted during the *Omer* period.

Sivan: The third month of the Jewish year. It has 30 days and its zodiac sign is Gemini, the twins.

Sivan coincides with the months May/ June. Shavuot takes place on the 6th and 7th of Sivan.

Tikkun Layl Shavuot: "Preparation for Shavuot," spending the first night of Shavuot in the study of selections from the Bible, Talmud, *Zohar,* the *Siddur,* and *piyyutim.* After the evening meal on *erev* Shavuot, the studying begins. An anthology, also called *Tikkun Layl Shavuot,* is generally used for the night of study. Other sections from sacred literature may also be used.

Whitsun Day: A corruption of the term White Sunday. Whitsun Day is another name for Pentecost among Christians. It was customary to deck churches with wreathes and flowers. In the synagogue, lilies were used to symbolize the "lily of the valley" in Song of Songs that was symbolically taken to be Israel.

Yatziv Pitgam: "True Is the Word" in Aramaic. On the second day of Shavuot, just before the reading of the *Haftarah,* the *piyyut* (liturgical poem) *Yatziv Pitgam* is read. While this 15 line poem contains no reference to Shavuot, it serves as a prayer for the welfare of the Jewish people. It may be seen as the counterpart to the *Akdamut,* which is recited on the first day of Shavuot. Authorship is generally attributed to Rabbenu Tam (1100-1171), grandson of Rashi.

Z'man Matan Torataynu: "Season of the Giving of Our Torah." According to tradition, Shavuot is the day when Israel accepted the Torah.

BACKGROUND

The biblical names for the holiday are Chag HaKatzir (Exodus 23:16), Chag Shavuot (Exodus 34:22; Deuteronomy 16:10), and Yom HaBikkurim (Numbers 28:26). Clearly, Torah references are to a harvest festival when the farmers would make pilgrimage to Jerusalem to offer a tithe of their first fruits/first barley grains to the Temple. Before the building of the First Temple,

which was completed around 950 B.C.E. by King Solomon, Shavuot was probably not celebrated.

In the Talmud, the festival takes on two additional names. One is Atzeret (*Rosh HaShanah* 1), which is the same name as is linked to the day after Sukkot. By association this could indicate that the Rabbis viewed Shavuot as the end of Pesach, or at least the end of a significant period of observance.

The second name is Z'man Matan Torataynu, which is based on the Rabbinic tendency of tying every festival to an historic event. They justified this connection between Shavuot and receiving Torah on an interpretation of Exodus 19:1 which states: "On the third new moon after the Israelites had gone forth from the land of Egypt, on that very day, they entered the wilderness of Sinai." If, as Rashi points out, the Israelites arrived at the foot of Mount Sinai on the first day of Sivan, which was the third month after the Exodus (but not a full three months after the Exodus), then the identification of Shavuot with the events surrounding the giving of the Torah at Sinai is plausible. The earliest reference to Shavuot as Z'man Matan Torataynu is in the Talmud (*Pesachim* 68b). By forging the link between the giving of the Law at Mount Sinai and Shavuot, the Rabbis were able to lend greater significance to the festival.

Throughout history, there have been different traditions as to when the festival is to be observed. Some communities observe the 50th day after the end of Pesach, some chose to begin counting from the Sabbath after Pesach. Others fixed their calendar so that the festival would always fall on a Sunday. However, the sixth (in Israel and among liberal Jews) plus the seventh (among traditional Jews in the Diaspora) of Sivan are now the customary dates of observance.

Of the three Pilgrimage Festivals, Shavuot was the most difficult for the farmers in ancient Israel because it fell in the middle of the growing season. Making a pilgrimage to Jerusalem was easiest at Sukkot because the fall harvest was completed. Going to Jerusalem at Pesach was possible because the work load was not yet great.

The book of Jubilees in the Apocrypha states that Shavuot is celebrated to commemorate the pact between God and Noah, promising that there would be no general flood in the future. Each year, according to Jubilees, this pact is renewed on Shavuot.

Central Themes

• Shavuot, as the anniversary of the giving of the Torah at Mount Sinai, is, in effect, the birthday of the covenant concluded between God and the Jewish people.

• Shavuot serves to highlight the centrality of the Torah in Jewish life. Torah is the foundation upon which all of Judaism rests. It has enabled the Jewish people to survive and prosper despite continual persecution.

• The giving of the Torah and accepting it were both important. A spirit of collaboration can be seen in the cooperative acts of offering and accepting. The Law issues from God, but its fulfillment lies with Israel. Similarly, inspiration comes from God, but aspiration stems from the people.

• The material harvest is paralleled by the spiritual harvest. The people were enjoined to bring an offering (to the Tabernacle/Temple) of two loaves of bread (Leviticus 23:17). The festival is thus symbolically tied to the giving of the Law in that the two loaves take the shape of the two tablets of the Law.

• In Shavuot, we see the relationship between God and people, not as one of boss and servant, but rather as mutually dependent partners in a joint enterprise of ongoing, continuous creation. Creative acts are not single, separate actions, but are linked together in an ongoing process of creative endeavor.

• The act of carrying the Torah around the sanctuary, of encircling the congregation during a *hakafah*, reminds us that Torah was received by all the people and is the possession of every Jew, regardless of education or social position. When *hakafot* are made during a worship service, the experience at Mount Sinai is symbolically reenacted.

Highlights of the Liturgy

Unlike Pesach and Sukkot, there is no distinctive ceremony that marks the celebration of Shavuot in the synagogue. In many congregations, it is customary to decorate the sanctuary with flowers and plants in honor of the festival and as a remembrance of the agricultural origins of Shavuot.

The Book of Ruth is read as a prelude to the afternoon service on the first day of Shavuot. The story of Ruth and Boaz takes place during the spring, at the time of the barley harvest, and is a fitting selection for Shavuot.

The *Akdamut* is read on the first day of Shavuot before the reading of the Torah. On the second day of Shavuot, another *piyyut* called *Yatziv Pitgam* is read. Both liturgical poems are written in Aramaic.

Torah and Haftarah

For the first day of Shavuot, Exodus 19 and 20 are read from one Torah. This describes the giving of Torah at Mount Sinai. A second Torah is then used to read the *Maftir*, which consists of Numbers 28:26-31. This begins with, "On the day of the first fruits, your Feast of Weeks, when you bring an offering of new grain to *Adonai*, you shall observe a sacred occasion." It continues with a description of the various offerings and sacrifices that are to be made on Shavuot.

Haftarah for the first day of Shavuot is Ezekiel 1:1-28 and 3:12. Chapter 1 describes a vision Ezekiel had concerning the conquest of Jerusalem. Out of the fire, heavenly creatures appear which reflect the glory of God and bring hope to Jews living in Babylonian Exile. Ezekiel 3:12 ends the portion on a high note: "Then a spirit carried me away, and behind me I heard a great roaring sound: Blessed is the Presence of God, in this place."

The Torah portion for the second day of Shavuot is Deuteronomy 15:19-16:17, which contains a series of laws relating to Israel including: tithes for the Temple, rules for the release of debts every seventh year, setting aside food for the poor, the release of slaves every seventh year, and rules regarding the three Pilgrimage Festivals. Deuteronomy 16:9-12 deals specifically with Shavuot. The *Maftir* is the same as on the first day of Shavuot.

Haftarah for the second day of Shavuot is Habakkuk 2:20-3:19, which is often called the "Prayer of Habakkuk." This contains a vivid, poetic depiction of God as if a mighty warrior. While almost nothing is known about Habakkuk the man, the context of his writing reflects the time of the Assyrian exile (eighth century B.C.E.).

Customs

In Eastern Europe, children aged 3 to 5 were often introduced to their *Yeshivah* on Shavuot. Children were given cakes, honey, and candy on the first day so that they would associate Torah study with sweetness and joy.

The custom most commonly associated with Shavuot is the ceremony of Confirmation. The festival of Shavuot, because of its association with the giving of Torah, has been linked with the study of Torah. The ceremony of Confirmation was introduced by Reform Judaism in the early part of the nineteenth century in Europe and was brought to the United States about mid-century. Confirmation originally took place at the end of the eighth year of Religious School, but it has since been moved to the end of the ninth or tenth year (and occasionally later). In this ceremony, the now maturing student "confirms" a commitment to Judaism and to Jewish life. While boys and girls are considered to be spiritual adults by age 13, they are better prepared at age 16 and 17 to make the kind of emotional and intellectual commitment to Judaism that Confirmation implies.

The ceremony of Confirmation is almost universally practiced in Reform, Reconstructionist, and Conservative synagogues. It has also been introduced in some Orthodox congregations.

There is a custom to bake a special *challah* (round or elongated) for Shavuot. An elaborate braid in the shape of a ladder is placed on the top of the bread to symbolize the giving of the Torah at Mount Sinai. The reason for the design is that the Hebrew word for ladder *(sulam)* and the Hebrew word for Sinai have the same numerical letter value (130). Hence, the symbolic association.

Triangular-shaped *kreplach* (dumplings) are served on Shavuot to reflect the three Patriarchs of Israel (Abraham, Isaac, Jacob), the three categories of Jews (Israelites, Kohanim, Levites), and the three sections of Tanach (Torah, *Nevi'im, Ketuvim*). These dumplings are filled with either meat or cheese.

Cheese products are customarily eaten on Shavuot. The origin of this custom is somewhat unclear. Some people eat two cheese blintzes on Shavuot to remember the two tablets of the Law. One explanation cites Song of Songs 4:11 which states: "honey and milk under your lips." This links the sweetness of Torah with the sweet combination of milk and honey. A second explanation is based on Exodus 23:19: "The choice of first fruits of your soil you shall bring to the house of . . . your God. You shall not boil a kid in its mother's milk." From this is extrapolated the idea that first a dairy dish is to be served as the main meal on Shavuot, followed by a meat dish at a later meal.

Some synagogues decorate the sanctuary with greenery as well as flowers. In the Talmud (*Rosh HaShanah* 1b), it is stated that Shavuot is the judgment day for fruit trees. This statement may have served as the basis for the custom of bringing greenery into the synagogue. A recent custom is for congregation members on the day(s) before Shavuot to plant flowers around the synagogue.

In Israel, especially on *kibbutzim* and *moshavim*, members dress in white and ride on carts filled with the late spring harvest.

SCOPE AND SEQUENCE

Grade	Themes/ideas
Kindergarten	Stories about Shavuot; decorating the sanctuary with flowers and branches.
Grade One	Getting ready for Shavuot at home: Preparing cheese dishes.
Grade Two	Shavuot as a Pilgrimage Festival. The significance of *hakafot*.
Grade Three	The account of the giving of the Law at Mount Sinai. The giving and accepting of the Torah.
Grade Four	Shavuot as it reflects the centrality of the Torah in Jewish life. The relationship between God and the Jewish people.
Grade Five	Shavuot vocabulary. A look at Moses the lawgiver.
Grade Six	Confirmation and the meaning of Shavuot. A comparison of Confirmation and Bar/Bat Mitzvah.
Grade Seven	Origins of Shavuot: Examination of the link between Shavuot and the Giving of the Law at Mount Sinai.
Grade Eight	Torah and *Haftarah* portions read on Shavuot.
Grade Nine	Special Shavuot customs and their origins.
Grade Ten	The meaning of Shavuot in the light of the multifaceted interpretations of the festival. Writing creative prayers for inclusion in the Confirmation ceremony.
Grade Eleven	Examination of *Akdamut* and *Yatziv Pitgam*.
Grade Twelve	Review and recapitulation. What new themes or ideas might you wish to bring to the celebration of Shavuot?

ACTIVITIES

Preschool/Kindergarten

1. Shavuot comes at the end of one grain harvest and the beginning of another. Bring in a variety of whole grains for students to investigate. They can look at these with a magnifying glass, sort mixed grains, sprout grains, listen to opaque containers with different grains and match sounds, match grains with pictures in books, etc. (NSM)

2. We eat dairy foods on Shavuot. Show students how milk is the basis of other dairy foods. Shake sweet cream and make butter; use on bread or crackers for a snack. Make ice cream or yogurt. (NSM)

3. Using two sticks and some paper, make a miniature Torah. Write simulated Hebrew on the paper, then attach the paper to the sticks. (In place of the simulated Hebrew, passages from a *Tikkun* can be photocopied and glued onto the paper.) Children can make a simple Torah cover out of a piece of cloth and a little glue.

4. If your synagogue has a representation of the Ten Commandments in the sanctuary, take your students on a field trip to see them. Practice counting to ten. Discuss the importance of the Ten Commandments. (NSM)

5. Make and/or eat cheese blintzes. Ask students why the shapes might remind us of something to do with Shavuot. (Two of them together look a little like the two tablets of the Ten Commandments.) (NSM)

6. Make a round or elongated *challah* with a special braid in the shape of a ladder and/or *kreplach* in class (see page 217, for a rationale).

7. Using finger paints or chocolate pudding, have children write the numbers of the Ten Commandments, then cut these out in the shape of tablets. Display the products around the school or classroom.

8. Help children complete pages 41, 42, and 45 in *Jewish Preschool/Kindergarten Copy Pak*™ by Nancy Cohen Nowak.

9. Do a movement activity related to Shavuot in *Creative Movement for a Song* by JoAnne Tucker (page 18).

10. Do one or more of the Shabbat art projects in *100+ Jewish Art Projects for Children* by Nina Streisand Sher and Margaret A. Feldman (pages 54 and 57).

11. Perform the play "Torah, Torah, Torah" in *Class Acts: Plays & Skits for Jewish Settings* by Stan J. Beiner (page 5).

12. Complete some of the activities in *The Jewish Preschool Teachers Handbook* by Sandy Furfine Wolf and Nancy Cohen Nowak (pages 98-101).

Primary

1. Go on a field trip to a farmer's market or supermarket. Have the class purchase a variety of fruits. Back in the classroom, make a couple of large, lovely fruit baskets which may decorate the sanctuary during Shavuot. Immediately after the holiday, donate the baskets to a soup kitchen or center for the homeless. (NSM)

2. Do a planting project immediately before Shavuot. Transplant flowers from flats into pots to donate to a nursing home, or begin work in a garden which students can tend over the summer. (NSM)

3. Make tissue paper flowers. Use them to create flower garlands and have students arrange them in baskets. Have a *Shalosh Regalim* parade with students wearing the garlands and carrying the baskets. (NSM)

4. Make a class cookbook of dairy recipes in honor of Shavuot. (NSM)

5. Draw or adapt a picture of a sanctuary in a synagogue that contains one or more mistakes. The task of the student is to find the mistakes in the picture and cross them out.

6. Take a picture of each individual student. Cut out the faces and have students draw a body and "desert clothing" for themselves. Have a group of students create on mural paper a picture of a mountain (they can use the description of Mount Sinai in Exodus 19 to guide their illustration). Place each of the student figures around the bottom of the mountain. Label the board, "We All Stood at Sinai." (NSM)

7. Roll out a 20' length of mural paper and mark it into 10 sections of 2' each. Glue onto each section a large print version of one of the Ten Commandments (one commandment per section). Then give students lots of newspapers, glue, and scissors. Working in pairs, have them search the magazines for modern examples of people either following or breaking each of the commandments. Glue the corresponding articles onto the correct section. (NSM)

8. Read *The 11th Commandment: Wisdom from our Children* by "The Children of America." Afterward, brainstorm with the children to come up with an 11th commandment. Areas covered by children in the book that you

might suggest to the class: living with others, living with the earth, living with family, living with yourself, living with God.

9. Using a variety of media, have students illustrate the story of Ruth. If desired, create a scroll to be read on the holiday. Or, draw the illustrations on transparencies and pull them across the stage of an overhead projector.

10. Using scrap plexiglass cut into squares, make "stained glass" that depicts the giving of the Law. Put crayon on it. Using tempera paint and glue will produce a stained glass look.

11. Make a Shavuot mural/collage using various media, including pictures from magazines, fabric, and other scrap materials.

12. Using large butcher paper or a long piece of fabric held at each end, roll students up one at a time so they get the feeling of being a Torah. Share feelings afterwards. Include a discussion of the traditional notion that each of us writes a Torah scroll during our life.

13. One student leaves the room and the others select a word or phrase related to Shavuot. The student returns and is allowed five how, when, and why questions to identify the mystery word or phrase.

14. Have each child do a silent role play of a commandment while the other children guess which one it is.

15. Read and discuss some of the stories in *Who Knows Ten?: Children's Tales of the Ten Commandments* by Molly Cone.

16. Complete some of the activities in *The Ten Commandments* by Nancy Karkowsky.

17. Have students complete the Instant Lessons *A Lifetime of Torah*, and *The Ten Commandments* by Marci Fox.

18. Do one or more of the Shavuot art projects in *100+ Jewish Art Projects for Children* by Nina Streisand Sher and Margaret A. Feldman (pages 53, 55, 56).

19. Complete the pages on Shavuot in *Jewish Holiday Copy Pak™ K-3* by Marji Gold-Vukson (pages 22 and 23).

Intermediate

1. Provide small groups of students each with a calendar (many Jewish funeral homes have complimentary calendars for the community). Have students read Leviticus 23:15-16 and use their calendars to count from Pesach according to the words of the biblical passage. Did they reach the day indicated on their calendar as Shavuot? Share with students some of the Rabbinic controversy around when one starts counting toward Shavuot. How was it resolved according to our calendar? (NSM)

2. Read some of the *midrashim* describing the giving of the Torah at Sinai. Provide large mural paper and art supplies for groups of students to illustrate different stories. (NSM)

3. As Moses on Mount Sinai, have students write out a brief diary reflecting Moses' thoughts as he deals with the events surrounding the giving of the Torah at Sinai and Israel's beginnings as a nation. Or, students can write the diary from the perspective of Miriam or Aaron or one of the multitude.

4. Make a matching pairs card game. Using about 20 3" x 5" cards, make up 10 sets of matching pairs (e.g., a person and an event, a symbol or ritual object and its meaning or importance). Make several sets so that when groups of 3 to 5 students are formed, the entire class can play at the same time. This can be a student-made review game for Shavuot or for the entire holiday cycle. If the class works in teams, each team can make a set of holiday

cards which are then used with the other groups.

5. Go to the sanctuary and look at a Torah, specifically at the Ten Commandments. Can students read Hebrew words they know (e.g., *Shabbat, Anochi, Lo, Kabayd*, etc.)? If your synagogue has a representation of the Ten Commandments, compare the version in the Torah with the words in the sanctuary. (NSM)

6. Give groups of students passages from the Torah which describe Shavuot. What different names can they find for this holiday? How does each name add to our understanding of the observance? What else do they learn about the holiday? (You might make a chart to help them make comparisons. Consider the following headings: Name Given to the Day, How Observed, Passage of Time Mentioned, Special "Offerings.") See: Deuteronomy 26:1-11, Numbers 28:6, Numbers 28:26-31, Exodus 23:16, Leviticus 23:15-16, Deuteronomy 16:16-17. (NSM)

7. Invite a high school student to discuss his or her experiences and feelings about Confirmation. (NSM)

8. Divide students into groups of two or three. Have each group read Leviticus 19:9-10 and Deuteronomy 24:19-21 (passages about leaving the gleanings in your fields after a harvest) and Ruth 1 and 2 (the first chapter sets the context and the second describes Ruth gleaning in the field). Without giving students background or summaries of the passages, have them read both sets of readings and figure out what the first two have to do with the second two. Have students brainstorm ways non-farmers can help out the poor in similar ways. (NSM)

9. Invite in one or more Jews-by-choice to discuss their decision to convert to Judaism.

Introduce your guest in the context of reading the Book of Ruth (about a convert) on Shavuot. (NSM)

10. Have students decode the statement that follows. (To do so, they must go back one letter in the alphabet.) You may either give the students the key to the code or ask them to "break the code" on their own. Students who finish first can make up other sentences using the same code.

QMFBTFEPOPUBTL
PLEASEDONOTASK

NFUPMFBWFZPV.
METOLEAVEYOU.

GPSXIFSFZPVHP
FORWHEREYOUGO,

JXJMMHPZPVS
IWILLGO.YOUR

QFPQMFTIBMMCFNZ
PEOPLESHALLBEMY

QFPQMFBOEZPVS
PEOPLANDYOUR

HPENZHPE
GODMYGOD.

11. Have each student make up a "Five Sense Poem" about Shavuot. Writing as if he or she was there, the student describes what "color" the scene was at Mount Sinai, tells of the emotion the Israelites felt when Moses came down, describes the sounds and smells at the base of the mountain, describes what the scene looks like, and how it makes the student feel. Add these poems to the students' poetry books. If desired, as a review of each holiday, have students illustrate the poetry they wrote during the year.

12. Which One Doesn't Belong? In each group of words or phrases, find the one that does not belong:

a.   Moses, Ruth, Naomi, Boaz (Moses)
b.   Wheat, barley, peaches, grapes (peaches)
c.   Mount Sinai, Jacob, Decalogue, Moses (Jacob)
d.   Naomi, Jesse, King David, Samson (Samson)
e.   Feast of Booths, Feast of Weeks, Feast of the Giving of the Law, Feast of Bikkurim (Feast of Booths)

13.   Have half the class write a letter to an Israelite who was at Mount Sinai when the Law was given to Israel, inquiring what it was like to be present at such an historic occasion. Have the other half of the class answer the letters. Ask for volunteers to read aloud both sets of letters or you read aloud some of the letters written by the students.

14.   Give each student ten or so minutes to write a prayer related to the holiday of Shavuot and reflecting the theme of Torah and Torah in our lives. Some or all of the prayers can then be used for a school worship service. The Rabbi may wish to invite some of the students to read their prayers as part of the congregational holiday worship service. The prayers can be added to students' original prayer books.

15.   Give each student a map of Israel and the surrounding areas. Indicate key locations, especially those related to the holiday of Shavuot. Give the students two tasks: (1) to locate the places on the map that are connected to the holiday of Shavuot, and (2) to identify those sites by listing the places and identifying their significance in one sentence. Use this map to trace the route of the wandering of the Israelites through the Wilderness of Sinai.

16.   Prepare a list of Shavuot key words. Give each student one key word (orally). The student says the first thing that comes to mind. Or, do this as a written activity and then ask students to read their lists.

17.   Divide the class into teams of 3 to 5 students each. The task of each group is to write one or more headlines to describe the events that they have been studying. The teams can prepare one main headline and several sub-headings or several main headlines. Decide which team has the best headlines. This can also be done as a brainstorming activity with the whole class. In the latter case, write the suggested headlines on the blackboard and have the class decide which headlines they like the best. Encourage a bit of humor.

18.   Because Shavuot occurs at the conclusion of the school year, this is a good time to review the highlights of all of the holidays that occur throughout the year. Form small groups. Give each group 10 or so minutes to make up questions about Shavuot and the other Jewish holidays/festivals. Reassemble the class for a Holiday Quiz Bowl. Administer the questions, giving teams 1 point for correct answers to easy questions and 2 points for correct answers to difficult questions. Give the team with the most points some special year-end responsibility.

19.   Ask students to collect old clothes, scraps of materials, etc. Each student creates a costume that reflects one of the characters in the Shavuot story. After putting on the homemade costumes, the students can act out the momentous events at Sinai. One student can be Moses, with the rest of the class being the Israelites.

20.   Help children to make a *tallit* out of strips of muslin approximately 6" x 2'. Make the *tzitzit* out of macramé.
Resource: *The First Jewish Catalog* by Richard Siegel, Michael Strassfeld, and Sharon Strassfeld, pp. 52-53.

21.   Teach students how to do simple Hebrew calligraphy. To demonstrate the difficult task of a *sofer*, throw away any sheets with errors on them.
Resource: *The First Jewish Catalog* by Richard

Siegel, Michael Strassfeld, and Sharon Strassfeld, pp. 184-209.

22. Give each student a sheet with "The Ten Commandments" written on the top and an outline of two tablets below. Inside the "tablets," number 1 to 5 on the left side and 6 to 10 on the right side. Either individually or as a class, have students write in the Ten Commandments in simple English. Discuss what each commandment means. Use simple, direct explanations for such difficult terms as adultery. As a follow-up activity, a second sheet that is identical to the first can be given out. Divide the class into groups of 3 to 5 students each. Their task is to think of ten additional commandments for contemporary society.

23. Students write questions about Shavuot on cards which are collected and read aloud. With the help of the teacher, the class decides where to took for an answer — the newspaper, the library, a prayer book, the Rabbi, the Cantor, etc. Establish teams and give each team a set amount of time to research at least one question from each category. Teams present their research to the class.

24. Have students write to pen pals in Israel and other countries to find out how they celebrate Shavuot.

25. Read and discuss some of the stories in *God's Top Ten: The Meaning of the Ten Commandments* by Roberta Louis Goodman.

26. On some holidays and festivals, our participation symbolically links us to events in the distant past and creates a symbolic continuum that reaches to the present. Examine this phenomenon: Ask the students to imagine that they were living when the Torah was given to Israel at Mount Sinai. Role play the event with the class.

27. Divide the class into pairs. One person in each pair is a reporter, while the second person becomes Moses who has just come down from spending 40 days on Mount Sinai. The reporter interviews Moses. Then the students reverse roles, and the second student serves as the reporter. Next, have the reporter interview Aaron about the golden calf.

28. Divide the Book of Ruth into small segments. Then break the class into groups of 2 or 3 students each. Give the groups 10 to 15 minutes to work out a dramatization of their scene in the story. Then have each group act out its segment.

29. Simulate a "You Are There" broadcast from the time Moses ascends the mountain the first time until he comes down the second time.

30. Complete the pages on Shavuot in *Jewish Holiday Copy Pak*™ *4-6* by Marji Gold-Vukson (pages 21 and 22).

31. Perform the play "Fair Exchange" in *Kings and Things: 20 Jewish Plays for Kids 8 to 18* by Meridith Shaw Patera (page 123) for parents and/or other classes.

Secondary

1. Divide students into groups. Give each group a copy of the Ten Commandments from Exodus 20:2-14 and Deuteronomy 5:6-18. Ask them to study the two versions to compare the differences in the wording. Have them research some opinions as to the differences (check the commentators, both traditional and modern). (NSM)

2. In small groups, ask students to examine and summarize for the class one of the biblical passages related to Shavuot.

3. Divide the class into teams. Each team has 10 minutes to think of reasons why the Torah is meaningful, special, and important to Jews.

The class then votes on which is the best reason, the most original reason, etc.

4. Examine each of the names for Shavuot. Why is each name used? What makes each significant?

5. Tell the story and/or read selections from the Book of Ruth. Many important ideas can be brought out in the ensuing classroom discussion, which might cover some of the following topics:

   a. The role of the convert. If King David could have a non-Jew in his family tree (i.e., Ruth), and still be a great king, then converts do indeed occupy an important place in Judaism.

   b. The idea of commitment and devotion to family, friends, and religion as shown by Ruth.

   c. How the agricultural background of the Book of Ruth links the story with Shavuot.

   d. An examination of the role of women in Judaism. How does the Book of Ruth reflect the role of women? How is the role of women different today?

6. Have the class "become" the Board of Trustees of the synagogue, which is faced with a dilemma. The holiday of Shavuot is approaching in a few weeks. This year it falls on a Tuesday night and Wednesday with the second day on Wednesday night and Thursday. Confirmation is usually held on the evening or the morning of Shavuot. It is feared that holding Confirmation on a weekday will greatly diminish congregational participation in this important festival. The Board is further concerned that people are not fully appreciating the importance of Shavuot in Jewish life. Board members are therefore forced to make a decision about the celebration of Shavuot from among the following choices. Which will it be?

   a. Celebrate Shavuot on Tuesday night and Wednesday, with Confirmation on Wednesday morning.

   b. Celebrate Shavuot on Tuesday night and Wednesday, with Confirmation on Tuesday evening.

   c. Celebrate Shavuot on Tuesday evening and Wednesday, with Confirmation on Friday.

   d. Celebrate Shavuot on the following Shabbat, with Confirmation taking place on Friday evening.

   When the students have reached a decision, have them list the reasons for the Board's choice.

7. Discuss why Shavuot was chosen by the early Reform Jews as the holiday to celebrate Confirmation. Why do students think Confirmation was to take place two to three years after Bar/Bat Mitzvah? In what ways does the Confirmation ceremony still have meaning today?

8. Have students poll the other congregations in your community to see if they observe Confirmation and how the observance differs from that of your congregation.

9. In his book *For Those Who Cannot Believe* (pp. 204, 205), Rabbi Harold Schulweis refers to Rabbinic commentary which says that the words of the Ten Commandments were cut through the stone so that both the leaders and the people could read them at the same time. Discuss: What are the ethical implications of this idea? To whom do these commandments apply? Why did the Rabbis also say that, at the moment the Ten Commandments were given to Israel, they were being simultaneously translated into every human language? What idea is present in both of these *midrashim*?

10. Divide the class into small groups. Give each student a copy of the Ten Commandments. Ask each group to list as many Jewish values as possible that they see in the words of the Ten Commandments or that they see implied

in the Ten Commandments. Bring the groups back together and create a composite list.

11. Passover speaks of the departure from slavery in Egypt to a life of freedom. Shavuot celebrates the giving of the Torah to Israel. Ask students if they see these two festivals as two sides of the same coin. (The connection is freedom and responsibility.)

12. Taking the Jewish and the secular calendars into consideration, ask students why they think Shavuot is observed less and studied less than most other Jewish holidays.

13. Rabbi Harold Kushner, in his book *To Life!* (p. 131), describes Shavuot as the "holiday of youth, truth, and Ruth." Have students discuss what Kushner means by this.

14. Some holidays and festivals are celebrated for two days outside of Israel: Rosh HaShanah, two days at the beginning of Sukkot, two days at the end of Sukkot, two days at the beginning of Passover, two days at the end of Passover, and two days of Shavuot. In ancient times, there was some uncertainly about when a festival actually began, but for nearly 2000 years Jews have been able to calculate with precision when a festival starts. Ask: Why then do Conservative and Orthodox Jews outside of Israel continue to celebrate two days instead of one?

15. Examine the role that study plays in the celebration of Shavuot. Discuss the concept of the *Tikkun Layl Shavuot,* which takes place on the first night of Shavuot. It traditionally involves studying a small portion from each book in the Hebrew Bible or a selection from every chapter in the Talmud. Students could plan a Shavuot "Study-thon" modeled after *Tikkun Layl Shavuot.*

16. There has been a long-standing debate about the whereabouts of Mount Sinai. Jewish and non-Jewish scholars have suggested more than a dozen different locations. For 1600 years, Christian authorities have said that Jebel Musa in the south-central Sinai Desert is the actual mountain. St. Catherine's Monastery was built there. When we consider all of the information about the various places the Israelites visited during the Sinai experience, identifying Jebel Musa with Mount Sinai is somewhat questionable. Discuss: Does it really matter which mountain is actually the biblical Sinai? How important is location compared with the events that occurred? (RAZ)

17. In Deuteronomy 29 and 30, the *parashah* read on Yom Kippur, the Torah includes everyone, even the stranger, in the process of receiving the Torah. Ask: What does this suggest about Judaism's relationship with the non-Jewish world?

18. Divide the class into pairs. One person becomes Naomi and the other Ruth. One speaks while the other listens. The partners take turns explaining to each other their thoughts and feelings. Then, they role play the interaction as it occurs in the book of Ruth. Reverse roles and repeat the process.

19. Working in pairs, one person takes the role of God and the second person of Israel/the Jewish People. God explains the divine side of the covenant while Israel listens. Then Israel explains its side of the agreement while God listens. After 5 to 10 minutes, reverse roles and repeat the process. As a class, spell out clearly on the blackboard the basic conditions of the covenant between God and Israel.

20. Have a discussion on the *mitzvah* of *Ahavat HaGer* (loving the convert). Read and discuss the Book of Ruth 1:1-16. For other activities on the subject, consult *Teaching Jewish Life Cycle* by Barbara Binder Kadden and Bruce Kadden, Chapter 3, "Conversion."

21. Have students complete the Instant Lesson *Ten x Ten: Ten Things about the Ten Commandments*.

22. Perform the play "The Story of Ruth (A Puppet Play)" in *Kings and Things: 20 Jewish Plays for Kids 8 to 18* by Meridith Shaw Patera (page 128) for parents and/or other classes. (This play can also be adapted as a conventional play instead of a puppet play.)

23. Perform "And There Was Light" (page 121) or "Emet V'Emunah — True and Certain It Is That There Is One God" (page 132), both of which are Confirmation cantatas from *Class Acts: Plays & Skits for Jewish Settings* by Stan J. Beiner.

All School

1. Have a Shavuot family holiday dinner at the synagogue. Such an event enables children to teach their parents in a way that does not embarrass the parents, yet exposes them to the beauty of Shavuot observance. Following such a dinner, the children and their parents can participate in a brief Shavuot worship service.

2. Have a congregational cheesecake baking contest. Read and study the Book of Ruth and enjoy the dessert. (RAZ)

3. Invite a scribe to visit and demonstrate to students and their families how a *sofer* works. (Or, consider having the scribe prepare a complete *Sefer Torah* for the congregation. Such a Torah project emphasizes the importance of Torah in our lives and helps congregants to be in touch with their feelings of religiosity and religious commitment.)

   Before the *sofer's* visit, spend a little while discussing with students various aspects of writing a *Sefer Torah*. This can include a visit to the sanctuary to see one of the congregation's Torah scrolls. Then, when the scribe arrives, students will be better able to appreciate the difficulty of the scribe's task, whether it be the writing of a *Sefer Torah*, a *Megillah*, or the parchment for *mezuzah* or for *tefillin*. Prior to the *sofer's* visit, provide everyone with the following information on the *mitzvah* of writing a Torah.

The Mitzvah of Writing a Torah

It is regarded as a positive biblical commandment for every Jew to possess a *Sefer Torah*. Deuteronomy 31:19 states: "Therefore, write down this poem and teach it to the people of Israel; put it in their mouths, in order that this poem may be my witness with the people of Israel." While the "poem" here refers to the last speech of Moses, it has come to refer to the Torah as a whole.

In *Pirke Avot* 5:7, it is stated that "ten things were created (by God) on the eve of the first Sabbath: . . . the writing, and the pen, and the tables." This is taken to refer to the instruments used for writing a *Sefer Torah* and emphasizes the sacredness of the task.

Maimonides, in a volume of the *Mishneh Torah* entitled *Sefer Torah*, declares that every Jew should write a Torah, and if this is not possible, that person should engage a scribe to help fulfill this *mitzvah*.

The First Jewish Catalog states: "On the basis of the statement of the Talmud [*Menahot* 30a] to the effect that he who corrects even one letter in a Sefer Torah is regarded as though he had himself written it, a custom has developed which both gives every Jew a portion in a *Sefer Torah* and symbolically regards him as having fulfilled the command of writing one. The *sofer* writes only the outlines of the words in the first and last passages of the *Sefer Torah* and they are completed at a ceremony known as *Siyyum HaTorah* ('the Completion of the Torah'). Those present are honored by each being invited to fill in one of the hollow letters, or formally authorize the *sofer* to do so" (p. 205).

Scribes

Ezra came to Jerusalem from Babylon between 458 and 444 B.C.E. He was a priest, and is also known as the first scribe. His importance in our tradition is so great that he is referred to as the second Moses. In all likelihood, Ezra put the Torah in its final form. Those who followed on the heels of Ezra and became *soferim*, not only copied books and documents, but also became conversant with their content. In a sense, they were the forerunners of the Rabbis.

There have come to be two types of scribes: those who write *Sifre Torah*, *tefillin*, and *mezuzot*, and those who write "legal" documents, such as divorce decrees, marriage documents, wills, etc. A scribe could engage himself in both areas, but often specialized in one or the other.

Writing a Sefer Torah

A *sofer* uses parchment, quill, ink, stylus, a ruler, and a *Tikkun* (a book with the entire Torah text). The Torah is written on parchment prepared from specified sections of the hide of a kosher animal, usually lamb, goat, calf, or deer. Deer skin is the finest type of parchment because it is translucent (and the letters can be seen from both sides). Sephardic and Oriental Jews often use the leather of cows.

Quills are usually of turkey feathers, as these are sturdy and long lasting. The ink is also specially prepared. It must be black, durable, but not indelible. Metal may not be used in writing a Torah.

Since the beginning of the nineteenth century, a standard pattern of 248 columns of 42 lines each is used for writing a Torah. A column is generally 4" to 5" wide. It takes a scribe about a day to write a column. As a result, it takes nearly a year to write one *Sefer Torah*. Each word is read aloud from a *Tikkun*, copied onto the parchment, and read from the scroll aloud and checked against the *Tikkun*. This slow process is meant to avoid mistakes.

Mistakes may be corrected, since the ink can be flaked off with a knife and a pumice stone. However, a mistake in the writing of a Name of God may not be corrected or erased, and a *klaf* (parchment sheet) with such a mistake — if it contains God's Name elsewhere — must be buried along with other sacred prayer works in a *genizah* or in a portion of a Jewish cemetery reserved for such artifacts.

Key Terms

The following are key terms that relate to the Torah Scrolls:

Wooden roller(s) - *Aytz Chayim (Atzay Chayim)* (Tree(s) of Life)
The silver breastplate - *Hoshen*
Torah Crown (covers both rollers) - *Keter Torah*
Individual Crowns - *Rimmonim* (pomegranates)
Ark of the Covenant - *Aron HaKodesh*
Ark Curtain - *Parochet*

Family

1. Help families organize an age appropriate *Tikkun Layl Shavuot*. What could parents teach their children with such an opportunity? What Jewish games could they play? What foods would they eat? (NSM)

2. Organize a family education program for two to four-year-olds (there are two already designed Shavuot programs in *Head Start on Holidays: Jewish Programs for Preschoolers and Their Parents* by Roberta Louis Goodman and Andye Honigman Zell).

3. Send home the Torah portions that are read on Shavuot. Suggest that each family member be given a few verses to study and summarize for the rest of the family. When all are ready, each reads the selection from the Torah and then restates it in his/her own words. To conclude, the family discusses the meaning of the passage from the Torah.

4. Suggest that families create a newspaper around Shavuot. Include the activities of siblings and pets, preparations and cooking, celebrations, events (the Confirmation of a family member or friend). Have them mail it

to friends and out of town family. Children can bring their family's newspaper to class to share with other students.

5. Tell families to investigate the special foods eaten on Shavuot, such as *kreplach,* cheese products, ladder-decorated *challot,* etc. Plan a menu, help cook the meal, and enjoy Shavuot as a family.

6. Look up passages in the Bible which mention various fruits and make a Shavuot fruit salad: grapes (Isaiah 5:2), figs (Proverbs 27:18), almonds (Ecclesiastes 12:5), apples (Song of Songs 2:3), pomegranates (Deuteronomy 8:8), dates (Joel 1:12), peanuts (Genesis 43:11), walnuts (Song of Songs 6:11), berries (II Samuel 5:23), melons (Numbers 11:5), oranges (Proverbs 25:11). Describe the context in which each ingredient is mentioned in the Bible. Can you find other fruits, vegetables, spices also?

BIBLIOGRAPHY

See pages 303-304.

CHAPTER SIXTEEN

TISHAH B'AV

VOCABULARY

Asarah B'Tevet: "The tenth day of the tenth month." On this day in 586 B.C.E., the Babylonian general Nebuchadnezzar began his siege of Jerusalem and of the First Temple. It is a minor fast day.

Av: The fifth month of the year. It corresponds to July/August, has the zodiac sign of Leo the lion, and is 30 days long. Tishah B'Av, Judaism's second most important fast day (next to Yom Kippur), takes place on the ninth day of the month of Av.

Avaylut: "Mourning." Technically the period of time between the death of a loved one and the funeral. The mourner uses this "no time" to make all of the necessary arrangements for burial without the strictures of *shivah*. In general, it is also the sense of mourning for those times and those places in which the Jewish people has suffered and died.

Aychah: The Book of Lamentations (*Megillat Aychah*) is read on the eve of Tishah B'Av.

Bakashah: "Request." *Bakashah* is one of the three reasons for fasting in Judaism. It involves a special request or plea of a public or private nature. In times of misfortune, fasts took the form of a plea or supplication. Some biblical examples are found in Judges 20:26, I Samuel 7:6, Isaiah 56:3ff., Jeremiah 14:12, and Jonah 3:5-8.

Bar Kochba, Shimon: The leader of the second major revolt against Rome from 132-135 C.E. Bar Kochba and his soldiers made a last stand against the Romans at Betar, southwest of Jerusalem in the Judean mountains. Tradition indicates that on Tishah B'Av, the fortress at Betar fell.

Chorban HaBayit: "Destruction of the House" [of God]. The First Temple fell in 586 B.C.E. at the hands of Nebuchadnezzar, the Babylonian general. The Second Temple was destroyed by the Roman General Titus in 70 C.E. Both were destroyed on Tishah B'Av.

Kinot: "Lamentations" or "Elegies." *Kinot* are hymns, dirges, and elegies written at different periods of Jewish history by Jewish poets. These speak of Jewish suffering and pain throughout the ages. Several *kinot* are read after *Megillat Aychah* during the evening service on Tishah B'Av, but many more are read on the morning of Tishah B'Av. The Book of Lamentations is sometimes referred to as *Sefer Kinot*.

Shabbat Chazon: "Shabbat of Vision." This is the Shabbat immediately preceding Tishah B'Av. It derives its name from the *Haftarah* of the day, Isaiah 1:1-27 which begins with the words: "*Chazon Yisha'yahu*," meaning "The vision of Isaiah . . ."

Shabbat Nachamu: "Shabbat of Consolation," or "Shabbat of Comfort." This Shabbat, which immediately follows Tishah B'Av, derives its name from the opening words of Isaiah 40:1-26, the *Haftarah* for that day — "*Nachamu, Nachamu Ami*," meaning "Comfort ye, comfort ye, My people."

Shivah Asar B'Tammuz: "The l7th day of the month of Tammuz." The fasts which are widely known and more commonly observed are those fasts which commemorate events connected with the fall of Jerusalem and the destruction of the Temples. Zechariah 8:19 refers to the "fast of the fourth month," which is Tammuz. It was on the 17th of Tammuz that the Romans succeeded in breaching the walls of Jerusalem in 70 C.E. The Mishnah *(Ta'anit 4:6)* mentions four other misfortunes that occurred on this date, including the breaking of the tablets of the Ten Commandments by Moses, and the setting up of an idol in the Temple and the burning of Torah scrolls by a Syrian Greek general, Apostomus.

Shivah Asar B'Tammuz marks the beginning of the three week period before Tishah B'Av, a time of solemnity. Weddings are not traditionally permitted during this three week period.

Ta'anit B'chorim: "The Fast of the Firstborn." It occurs in the eve of Passover and is an expression of gratitude to God for saving alive the firstborn of the Hebrews while the firstborn of the Egyptians died in the tenth plague.

Ta'anit Esther: "The Fast of Esther" which takes place on the day before Purim. It was instituted in remembrance of Queen Esther's fast before she went before King Ahasuerus to ask him to spare her people.

Ta'anit Tzadikkim: "Fast of Righteous Ones." The Talmud and later Rabbinic literature contains mention of fasts in memory of outstanding personalities. The following fasts of the righteous have been observed at different times and by various

groups during the past 2000 years: 10th of Nisan (the death of Miriam); the 26th of Nisan (the death of Joshua); the 28th of Iyar (the death of Samuel); 1st of Av (the death of Aaron); the 5th of Tishre (the death of Rabbi Akiba), and the 7th of Adar (the death of Moses).

Ta'anit Tzibur: "Public Fast." Most fasts were either universally acknowledged, such as Tishah B'Av, or were fasts instituted by a community in memory of an important act of deliverance.

Ta'anit Yachid: " Private Fast." Sometimes a person chooses to fast in supplication for a private need or request.

Teshuvah: Literally, "Returning," but meaning "Repentance" or "Atonement." Yom Kippur is the only fast which is mentioned in the Torah for the purpose of *teshuvah*. *Teshuvah* is the act of returning to the right path, the path of right living as commanded in Torah and prescribed in subsequent teachings.

Tishah B'Av: "Ninth day [of the month] of Av." This is the traditional day of mourning and fasting for the destruction of the Temples in Jerusalem. *Kinot* and the Book of Lamentations are read in the synagogue. Tishah B'Av has become a symbol of all the persecutions and misfortunes of the Jewish people throughout history.

Tzom: "A Fast."

Tzom Gedaliah: "Fast of Gedaliah." It takes place on the third of Tishre, the day after the second day of Rosh HaShanah. It commemorates the murder of Gedaliah, the governor of the Jews in Jerusalem, who had been appointed to that position by Nebuchadnezzar, the King. His assassination brought great suffering for the Jewish people and hastened the destruction of the First Temple.

Yerushalayim: "Jerusalem." The word means "City of Peace."

BACKGROUND

Tishah B'Av has become the collective day of mourning in the Jewish calendar. Many tragic events are reputed to have occurred on this date. In some cases there is a question as to the precise dating of an event. For instance, with regard to the destruction of the First and Second Temples some 656 years apart, but on the same date — the 9th of Av — some sources indicate that the First Temple was destroyed on either the 7th or the 10th of Av, and the Second Temple was destroyed on the 10th of Av. Rabbinic authorities, however, decided to mark the ninth of Av as the official date for remembering the destruction of both.

Tishah B'Av serves to bind all of the following tragic events together in one day of mourning and remembering. On the ninth of Av:

- It was decreed that the Israelites, after leaving Egypt, would wander in the desert for 40 years, until a new generation would be ready to enter the Promised Land.

- Betar, the fortress headquarters of Simon bar Kochba, fell to the Romans in 135 C.E.

- Hadrian, the Roman ruler of Jerusalem, in 136 C.E., established a heathen temple and rebuilt Jerusalem as a pagan city.

- The First Temple (that Solomon built) was destroyed by Nebuchadnezzar, King of Babylonia, in 586 B.C.E.

- The Second Temple (that returning exiles built and then Herod rebuilt) was destroyed by Titus and the Romans in 70 C.E.

- The Edict of Expulsion of the Jews from England was signed by King Edward I in 1290.

- Ferdinand and Isabella decreed this to be the official date of the expulsion of the Jews from Spain in 1492. Led by Isaac Abarbanel, 300,000 Jews began to leave Spain on that date. Columbus set out on his first voyage of discovery on the day after Tishah B'Av (after delaying his sailing by one day).

Observance

The three weeks prior to and ending with Tishah B'Av are known as *Bayn HaMaytzarim*, which means "in the Straits." The *Haftarah* portions for these three weeks are Jeremiah 1:2-28, 2:4-28, 3:4, and Isaiah 1:1-27. They call for the people to perform acts of repentance and to be firm in their faith. God will not abandon them even though all seems lost.

While these are three weeks of mourning, the nine days prior to Tishah B'Av are more intense in observance of the rules of mourning than the first 12 days. No weddings or other joyous festivities are held during the entire 21 day period. During the last nine days of the period, no meat is eaten, there are to be no haircuts, no clothes are washed unless they are to be worn again during these nine days, and no ironed clothes are worn. The practice among Reconstructionist, Reform, and Conservative Jews ranges from full observance of the 21 days to observance of the nine day period to observance of only Tishah B'Av itself.

On the eve of Tishah B'Av, at the final meal before fasting, it is customary to eat a boiled egg as a symbol of mourning and to sprinkle ashes on the egg. Grace after this meal is said individually and in silence.

The traditional mourning code governs the day itself — abstinence from eating, drinking, bathing or participating in any kind of festive occasion from sunset to sunset; washing of the body is forbidden except to clean the face; sexual intimacy is not permitted; shoes made of leather are not to be worn; in the home or synagogue, shoes are removed and everyone sits on low benches as if to emulate mourners sitting *shivah*.

Only melancholy passages from the Torah, the Book of Job, prophecies of misfortune in Jeremiah, and the laws of mourning and other similar passages which serve to sadden the heart are studied. Visiting the cemetery is encouraged as if to heighten the sadness of the day.

In the synagogue, the *parochet* is removed from before the Ark, the pulpit cover is taken away, the lights are turned low, the reader and other congregants sit on low stools, and they do not greet each other. *Tallit* and *tefillin* are not worn during the morning service, but instead are worn for Minchah. It is as if the Jewish world is turned upside down.

Highlights of the Liturgy

Modifications are also made in the liturgy of the synagogue for Tishah B'Av. The regular weekday services are used; however, in the evening service, the Book of Lamentations is read, followed by several *kinot*. An extra prayer is inserted in the *Amidah*. Both the morning and the afternoon services contain a Torah and a *Haftarah* reading.

A variety of customs unique to specific communities have been linked to Tishah B'Av, but none has become universally adopted.

Other Fast Days

There are three reasons for observing fasts:

For *Teshuvah:* To repent for an action or for a life style. (It had to be accompanied by a sincere resolve to change.)

For *Avaylut:* To mourn sad occurrences in the history of the Jewish people (for more on the issue of fasting, see the chapter on Yom Kippur).

For *Bakashah:* To make a special request or plea of a public or a private nature (as in times of oppression, misfortune, and suffering; to counter evil decrees and edicts; or to stave off the effects of famine, disease, and drought). Such fasts were either either declared on behalf of a specific community, were held in remembrance of a calamity affecting the entire Jewish people (such as Tishah B'Av), or they were private fasts by an individual to serve a personal purpose.

The single most important fast day in the Jewish calendar is Yom Kippur. It is the only *Yom Tzom* that can be observed on Shabbat. If any other fast date falls on Shabbat, the fast is postponed to the following day. Other fasts which are commonly observed include Tishah B'Av, Shevah Asar B'Tammuz (17th of Tammuz), Tzom Gedaliah (3rd of Tishre), and Ta'anit Esther (13th of Adar).

ACTIVITIES

Note: Tishah B'Av is a somber fast day. It falls when school is generally not in session. All of the activities which follow are also appropriate for use at camp. Because of the nature of the observance, there are few activities for younger children.

Preschool/Kindergarten

1. Students sit in a circle. The leader whispers a message such as "Let us hope for happy events and not sad ones" to one child, who in turn whispers it to the next. The message is transmitted from person to person until it returns to the leader. The final message and original message are compared.

Primary

1. Seat the children in a circle. Explain that things happen to us that make us sad. While it is not good to think about sad things all of the time, it can be helpful to remember them from time to time. Remembering sad things can sometimes lead us to look for happy things that also have happened to us. Ask each child to complete the following sentence: "One sad thing I remember is _____." After everyone has had a chance to respond, let the children react to each other's recollections.

2. What are some things people do when they have lost something important to them? (Try and find it, get impatient or angry, cry, pout, pray for help, don't care about what they wear or look like, eat a lot or don't eat at all). Elicit from students what Jews do as a response to very important and/or traumatic events (e.g., Yom Kippur or mourning a death). Relate these actions to the Tishah B'Av observance. (NSM)

3. Provide large pieces of felt, fabric, and yarn and have students make banners/murals to

illustrate "If I forget you Jerusalem, may my right hand wither." (NSM)

4. Go around the room asking students to respond to the statement "When I am hungry, I feel _____." Then discuss fasting and the children's responses to the statement. Some of the children may have fasted on Yom Kippur until breakfast or slightly later. Have them tell how they felt when they fasted. Other questions to discuss: Why do we fast? What can we learn from fasting? How old should a child be before they fast? What can very young children do that accomplishes the same goals as fasting (e.g., give up a favorite toy or dessert, etc.).

Intermediate

1. With the students, brainstorm the key themes of Tishah B'Av. Write the list on the blackboard. Give students 5 to 10 minutes to write a prayer related to the fast day of Tishah B'Av. The prayer should reflect the themes of self-examination and remembering sad events in the history of the Jewish people. Some or all of the prayers can then be used for a congregational, school, or camp worship service.

2. Ask groups of students to research how holidays were celebrated in the time of the Temple in Jerusalem. Give each student group a carton (the kind which holds 10 reams of copy paper) to make a diorama showing the celebration. Include a short written description of the observance. When groups share the artwork with the class, ask questions which help students focus on the celebratory differences in the time of the Temple and today. (NSM) Resource: *The Jewish Festivals* by Hayyim Schauss.

3. Give students a list of Jewish events that have occurred on Tishah B'Av (see page 233). Working individually, the students make a chart of these tragic events. Have a follow-up discussion about the merits of having a fast day in the Jewish calendar that serves to remind us of many of the tragic events in Jewish history.

4. Obtain enough copies of *The Tenth of Av* by Kenneth Roseman so that individuals can work their way through this do-it-yourself-adventure. Or, allow small groups of students to make decisions through the book, then ask groups to share their adventures with the rest of the class. (NSM)

5. Ask around to see if someone who visited the Second Temple model at the Holy Land Hotel in Jerusalem has slides or pictures. Make enough copies for small groups of students to each have a set. Ask students to study the pictures and make hypotheses of what life might have been like in the time when the Temple was in existence. Compare the living conditions and life-style with students' own surrounding and lives. (NSM)

6. Have each student write a letter to the prophet Jeremiah. (He is said to have written the Book of Lamentations, which is read on Tishah B'Av.) While expressing sorrow that Jeremiah had to witness the destruction of Jerusalem and the Temple, the letters can also express gratitude to him for not giving up hope for the future and for expressing this hope to the exiles in Babylon. When the letters have been written, ask for volunteers to read them aloud to the class.

7. Invite students to write poems about the events commemorated by Tishah B'Av or about the observance itself. Let them use whatever poetic form they wish. Compare the mood, form, and content of their poems to *kinot*. Have them add the poems to their poetry books

8. Visit a local Jewish museum (or the Jewish book section of a public library, or the library in your synagogue, Jewish Day School, the

Jewish Community Center, or the Central Agency for Jewish Education). While there, take particular note of those exhibits (books) related to the Holocaust and other tragic events in Jewish history. Discuss how Jews have survived despite all of the persecution and oppression. Have students create a Tishah B'Av exhibit or display for the school, camp, and/or community.

9. Search through art and history books to find pictures of Jerusalem through the ages. Have small groups of students study the pictures and discuss the renditions (remember that artists often overlaid their own historical architectural styles on their image of Jerusalem). (NSM)

10. Prepare a special edition of a class, school, or camp newspaper devoted to Tishah B'Av. Students/campers can write about how the holiday is observed, underlying themes, interviews with famous personalities, and the like.

11. Have students research songs appropriate for Tishah B'Av and then sing some of them. Examples are: "Al *Naharot Bavel*," "Ani *Ma'amin*," "*HaTikvah*."

12. Provide an opportunity for students to study traditional Tishah B'Av observances (for example: fasting, not wearing leather, sitting on the floor or on low stools/benches, not wearing a *tallit* or *tefillin* in the morning, not reading from the Bible or studying the Talmud, reading the Book of Lamentations, covering mirrors, not shaving, greeting people in subdued ways). Then, ask each person to write a personal *brit* (covenant), stating how the individual has chosen to observe the day to make it personally meaningful. (NSM)

13. Make a large scale replica of the *Kotel* (the Western Wall) and hold a Tishah B'Av memorial service at "the Wall."

14. As a group, make a large scale Tishah B'Av time line covering the period from Abraham to the present. Illustrate various events with pictures and drawings, as well as with religious symbolism. A perfect material for a time line is window shade remnants left over from cut-to-order shades. Obtain them from window specialty stores. Write on them with felt markers. Erase errors with a damp sponge. The strips can be rolled for storage.

15. Make a list of reasons why it is permissible not to fast on fast days (e.g., too young, health problems, old age, etc.).

16. Ask for volunteers to take turns being Jeremiah speaking to the Israelites, telling them not to give up hope for the future. Look at selections from Lamentations and the Book of Jeremiah in preparation for this role playing.

Secondary
1. Divide students into groups of 3 to 4 to research and then debate the following: On Tishah B'Av, we can take the perspective of looking at Jewish history through a veil of tears, seeing the past as a series of tragedies and persecutions. (NSM)

2. Some argue that since the foundation of the State of Israel in 1948, we have no reason to commemorate Tishah B'Av . . . the Jewish state has been restored. Others say that it is important to remember the events which occured in history on Tishah B'Av, and the sufferings of our ancestors. Divide students into groups to research and debate this issue. When the debate is concluded, ask students to write their personal reactions to this issue. (NSM)

3. Plan a Tishah B'Av worship service using selections from various prayer books, readings for Tishah B'Av, and the like.

4. Divide class into small groups. Each group writes a song based on any section of Lamentations. They can set it to a known blues melody or other sad tune. Have each group sing its song for the others.

5. Tishah B'Av occurs during the summer, and thus is often observed by youngsters at camp. There are those who believe that it is appropriate to create emotionally charged educational programs (i.e., burning a model of the Temple which campers have been working on for days) and/or to create worship services designed to make campers cry (i.e., with candles lighting the darkness and with readings from Jews, including young children, who have been violently killed).

   There are also those who believe that while Tishah B'Av is certainly a day of mourning, children's emotions should not be played with. They would say that while the tone of the day should be solemn and filled with historical remembrances, camping staff should be sensitive to the developmental and emotional needs of their campers; (hysterical) theatrics are not part of their Tishah B'Av observances.

   Divide into groups to discuss the issues brought forth by these two viewpoints. Provide opportunities for members to research the viewpoints — perhaps by interviewing others, checking the Internet, reading about Tishah B'Av observances. After enough information has been gathered, ask each person to write his or her own opinion on this issue, providing one or two pieces of supporting evidence. Then, redivide members so that those with the same opinion are together.
   Ask each new group to write a full position statement on this issue to submit to a camp director. (NSM)

6. Tishah B'Av is a day of mourning for the destruction of the Jerusalem Temple. Yet, by default, it also marks a remarkable change in Judaism. It was then that the Rabbis, led by Yochanan ben Zakkai, made decisions which allowed Judaism to flourish in spite of the loss of its central place of worship. Tell the story of Yochanan ben Zakkai, and then have students research the some of the decisions the Rabbis made at Yavneh following the destruction of Jerusalem. Which ones are still part of your congregation's observances today? (NSM)

7. Discuss: What is the relationship of Tishah B'Av to the statement: "Masada shall never fall again"?

8. Discuss episodes of anti-Semitism that the students may have encountered. Consider the question: Will Jews ever be free from irrational anger, hatred, and prejudice? If Jews give the anti-Semites no ammunition, will others invent the ammunition they need?

9. Discuss: Do Jews, as sensitive, caring human beings, have a responsibility not to allow the world to forget the lessons of the Holocaust? What can each student do to assure that the world remembers? Some ideas: Observances such as Holocaust Awareness Week; a Holocaust curriculum in every high school; oral histories of survivors, such as those being done by Steven Spielberg's Survivors of the Shoah Visual History Foundation.

10. Examine the list of events that are said to have occurred on Tishah B'Av (page 233). Ask students if they think that all of them actually did occur on the ninth of Av. If not, do they think that a collective fast day and day of memorial for tragic events in Jewish history is important?

11. Examine the section entitled "Why Fast?" in the chapter on Yom Kippur (page 42). Discuss fasting. What reasons can students think of to fast? At what age did they start fasting on Yom Kippur? Discuss how they feel when they are

fasting and what effect it has on them. Ask students if they fast on Tishah B'Av? Will they consider doing so, now that they understand the reasons for this fast day? Do they think that fasting is an effective practice?

12. Have students decide if they agree or disagree with the statement: "There should be a fast day when Jews collectively mourn for all of the tragic events that have occurred in Jewish history. Tishah B'Av should serve as that day." Tally the responses and discuss.

13. On Tishah B'Av, we are asked to look at Jewish history through a "veil of tears." The Jewish past is related in terms of one tragedy and persecution after another. Some Jews feel that this is typical of Judaism and there is no happiness. Discuss this attitude and the reasons for it.

14. Investigate the various practices involved with Tishah B'Av. Find out why some Jews consider the three weeks prior to Tishah B'Av a period of mourning, while others observe only nine days, and still others only the day itself.

15. Discuss: What makes Tishah B'Av unique? How does this fast day in the middle of the summer contribute to a Jew's sense of history? How does it link the modern Jew to nearly 4000 years of Jewish life?

16. During the year, Jews come together for a Yizkor service in order to remember their own deceased loved ones. On Tishah B'Av, Jews come together as a community to remember Jews of any era who were victims of calamitous acts and to commemorate specific sad events in Jewish history. How are these two observances the same? How different? Are both types of services useful?

17. Lead students in a guided fantasy. Ask everyone to be comfortable and begin: "Close your eyes. I want you to pretend that you are in the place where my words will take you. Keep your eyes closed and try to imagine that you are . . . ." Paint a word picture of an episode or a religious experience related to one of the events that took place on Tishah B'Av. After the exercise, students open their eyes and discuss how they felt to have been, in effect, a part of such an experience.

18. Divide the group into pairs. One person in each pair becomes the Grand Inquisitor and the other a Jewish leader. The Grand Inquisitor demands that Jews either convert to Christianity, submit to the rules of the Inquisition, or leave Spain. The Jewish leader pleads the cause of the Jews, telling how valuable the Jews have been to Spain. After a few minutes, reverse roles and repeat the role playing. Remaining in pairs, process the experience, each person telling the other how it felt in each role. Then come together as a large group for additional feedback.

All-school/All-camp

1. Plan a day of Remembering the Past. Have older students plan a brief prayer service that incorporates the themes of remembering the past, even when those memories are painful. Have them incorporate in their service the idea of a collective day of memorial. Part of their task would be to explain the meaning of Tishah B'av to younger children who would also attend. As these students work to prepare the service, they will be sensitized to the difficult and often tragic chapters in the history of the Jewish People, and how Jews have overcome obstacles to become stronger in the process. Students can search out readings in the *Siddur*, the Bible, and also write their own prayers and meditations.

2. Organize a simulated trip to various memorials in Israel and the U.S. Stations might include the U.S. Memorial Holocaust Museum in

Washington, D.C., Yad VaShem, Kibbutz Lochamei HaGetaot, the Holocaust Memorial on Mount Zion, the military cemetery at Mount Herzl, etc. At each site, a "guide" can explain what is there and the rationale for the memorial.

Family

1. Encourage families to attend a Tishah B'Av worship service. Afterward, talk about the ideas and feelings elicited by the service.

BIBLIOGRAPHY

See pages 304-305.

CHAPTER SEVENTEEN

ROSH CHODESH

VOCABULARY

Adar: The twelfth month of the Jewish year, corresponds to February/March, and has the zodiac sign of Pisces. Purim takes place on the 14th of Adar.

Adar Shayni: Also called "v'Adar." On leap years, a second month of Adar is added. This occurs seven times every 19 years. When a leap year occurs, Purim takes place on the 14th of II Adar — Adar Shayni.

Av: The fifth month of the year, it corresponds to July/August, has 30 days, and its zodiac sign is Leo. Tishah B'Av takes place on the 9th of Av.

Birkat HaChodesh: "The Blessing Over the New Month" is recited on Shabbat Mevarchim, the Shabbat prior to the new month.

Chatzi Chag: Rosh Chodesh is treated as a half holiday, which means that the *Hallel* is recited along with other minor liturgical changes. No fasting is permitted.

Cheshvan: Also called Marcheshvan. The eighth month of the year, corresponding to October/ November, it has 29 or 30 days, and its zodiac sign is Scorpio. No Jewish holidays occur in this month. The name Marcheshvan comes from a misreading of the Babylonia equivalent of "*Yarayach Shemini*" — eighth month. The first letter of the phrase became a *mem*, hence Marcheshvan. This word is not in Tanach. The month is referred to as Bul in I Kings 6:38.

Chodesh: "Month." All Hebrew months have either 29 or 30 days.

Elul: The sixth month of the calendar, it corresponds to August/September, has 29 days, and its zodiac sign is Virgo. The Selichot service takes place on a Saturday night immediately preceding Rosh HaShanah.

Hallel: "Praise." Consists of Psalms 113-118 and sometimes Psalm 136. A shorter version of the *Hallel* is read on Rosh Chodesh, while the full *Hallel* is read on the festivals.

Iyar: The second month of the year, it corresponds to April/May, has 29 days, and its zodiac sign is Taurus. Yom HaZikaron takes place on the 4th of Iyar. Yom HaAtzma'ut takes place on the 5th, and Lag B'Omer occurs on the 18th.

Kislev: The ninth month of the year, it corresponds to November/December, has 29 or 30 days, and its zodiac sign is Sagittarius. Chanukah begins on the 25th of Kislev.

Luach: "Calendar." Since the earliest calendar was inscribed on a tablet, *luach* also means "tablet," "schedule," or "blackboard." For a brief discussion of the Jewish calendar, see page 243.

Machar Chodesh: Literally, "Tomorrow Month," this actually indicates the arrival of the "new moon." The term is taken from I Samuel 20:18: "Jonathan said to (David): 'Tomorrow is the new moon.'" Because it contains this phrase, I Samuel 20:18-42 is read on those Sabbaths which occur the day before a new moon.

Nisan: First month of the Jewish year, it corresponds to March/April, has 30 days, and its zodiac sign is Aries. Pesach begins on the 15th of Nisan.

Rosh Chodesh: Literally, "Head of the Month," but actually used to denote a "new month." Rosh Chodesh is considered to be a half holiday and takes place when the crescent of the new moon is first sighted after a brief period when the moon is not visible.

Shabbat Mevarchim: "Shabbat of blessing," the Shabbat prior to Rosh Chodesh. On this Shabbat, the forthcoming Rosh Chodesh is announced in the synagogue.

Shevat: The eleventh month of the calendar, it corresponds to January/February, has 30 days, and its zodiac sign is Aquarius. Tu B'Shevat takes place on the 15th.

Shofar: A ram's horn which is sounded to proclaim the beginning of the new month.

Sivan: The third month of the year, it corresponds to May/June, has 30 days, and its zodiac sign is Gemini. Shavuot begins on the 6th.

Tammuz: The fourth month of the year, it corresponds with June/July, has 29 days, and its zodiac sign is Cancer. The 17th is a fast day commemorating the beginning of the seige of Jerusalem by the Babylonians.

Tevet: The tenth month of the year; corresponds to December/January, has 29 days, and its zodiac sign is Capricorn. The first two to three days of Tevet conclude the festival of Chanukah. The 10th is a fast day comemorating the seige of Jerusalem by the Romans.

Tishre: The seventh month of the calendar, it corresponds to September/October, has 30 days, and its zodiac sign is Libra. The 1st is Rosh HaShanah, the 10th is Yom Kippur, the 15th is Sukkot, the 22nd is Shemini Atzeret, and the 23rd day is Simchat Torah.

Ya'aleh v'Yavo: "May It Ascend and Come." This prayer is recited as part of the *Amidah* on new moons and on festivals, and at the Grace after Meals on these occasions. It reads: "Our God and God of our ancestors. May our remembrance ascend and come and be accepted before You, with the remembrance of our ancestors, the Messiah, the son of David Your servant, of Jerusalem Your holy city, and of all Your people the house of Israel; bring deliverance and well-being, grace, loving-kindness and mercy, life and peace on this day of the New Moon."

Yehi Ratzon: "May It Be Your Will." This is the blessing over the new month: "May it be Your will, O God, Who is Eternal and God of our ancestors, to renew for us this coming month for good and for blessing. May the Holy One to whom all praises are due bless us and all our people, the house of Israel, with life and with peace, with gladness and with joy, with help and loving care. And let us say, Amen."

BACKGROUND

The Jewish month begins when the first crescent of the new moon (in the shape of the Hebrew letter *resh*) appears. It is a time of new beginnings, both literally and spiritually. Rosh Chodesh is mentioned in Tanach along with Shabbat and the Festivals as a day of special importance in the Jewish calendar. Numbers 10:10 states: "And on your joyous occasions, your fixed festivals and new moon days, you shall sound the trumpets over your burnt offerings and your sacrifices of well being. They shall be a reminder to you before . . . your God."

In I Samuel 20:18-34, Jonathan tells David that his presence at the King's table will be missed on the new moon . . . and on the third day . . .

Jonathan will signal with a flight of arrows to a David in hiding. From this we might surmise that the new moon was celebrated for two days on which no work (e.g., hunting, shooting) was done. From the account of Elisha and the Shunamite's son (II Kings 4:8-37, especially verse 23), it might be inferred that a "man of God" may have been called upon to aid in the celebration of Shabbat and the new moon. In Numbers 28:11-15 the sacrifices for the new moon are listed. From the prophets we learn that the new moon was celebrated as a time on which work and trade ceased (see Amos 8:5 and Isaiah 1:13-14).

About the Calendar

The Jewish calendar is both a lunar calendar (linked to the phases of the moon) and a solar calendar (linked to the time it takes the earth to make one complete rotation around the sun). The moon rotates around the earth every 29½ days. The months in the Jewish year are, therefore, assigned a length of either 29 or 30 days each. The solar year is 365¼ days in length. But the lunar year is only 354 days. This 11 day annual disparity must be addressed in order to keep Jewish festivals which have a seasonal component (Sukkot is a fall harvest festival, Pesach a spring holiday, and Shavuot celebrates the first fruits) in sync with nature. This is accomplished by adding a leap month of 30 days (II Adar/v'Adar/Adar Shayni) seven times in every 19 year cycle. In biblical times, this intercalated month was added by the priests who went into the fields at the end of Adar to see if the barley was earing up. If it was still immature, they announced a leap year.

A month concludes with a brief period (approximately 12 hours) called the *molad,* during which time the moon is precisely between the sun and the earth, hence not visible. In ancient Israel, Rosh Chodesh was determined by direct observation of the new moon emerging. Persons who observed it came before the Sanhedrin to testify as to its shape and location in the sky. If their testimony was accepted, the month was declared *Mekudash* — sanctified. If no witnesses came forth on the 29th day of a month, or if the witnesses were unable to sustain their evidence, a day was added to the current month giving it 30 days. In such cases, that day and the next were both declared to be Rosh Chodesh. This eliminated the possibility of not celebrating Rosh Chodesh on the proper day.

As soon as the new month was *Mekudash,* signal fires were lit on the hilltops around Jerusalem. When spotted miles away, signal fires were lit on distant hilltops. In this way, everyone throughout Israel and even those living outside of *Eretz Yisrael* were notified of the beginning of the new month.

In about 365 C.E., Hillel the Elder showed how each Rosh Chodesh and every leap year could be calculated for decades, even centuries in advance. This obviated the need for observation and witnessing. Everyone now had access to dates and holidays. For our usage today, leap years occur in the 3rd, 6th, 8th, 11th, 14th, 17th, and 19th year of each 19 year cycle. The 19 year cycle is determined by dividing the Jewish calendar year by 19. Thus, 5758 is the beginning of a cycle, and 5760 (remainder of 3 when dividing by 19) is the first leap year of that cycle.

The table on the following page shows the Hebrew month, the zodiac sign, and the holidays-dates that take place during that month.

Liturgy

Rosh Chodesh is announced (*Birkat HaChodesh*) on Shabbat Mevarchim, the Shabbat prior to the new moon, just after the reading of the Torah. *Birkat HaChodesh* is recited with the congregation standing and the leader holding the Torah. It consists of the *Yehi Ratzon,* which asks that the new month be for health, peace, long life, honor, love of Torah, followed by the brief *Mi She'asah* and the *Y'chadshayhu* petitions.

Because Rosh Chodesh is treated as a minor festival or half festival (special offerings were made at the Temple in Jerusalem), a special prayer stressing God's role as Creator (*Atah Yatzarta*) is substituted for *Tikanta Shabbat* in the Musaf *Amidah,* no fasting is allowed, and *Ya'aleh v'Yavo* is added to the liturgy. In addition, an abbreviated *Hallel* prayer is recited.

Days	Months (Corresponds to)	Zodiac	Holidays - Dates
30	Nisan (March/April)	Aries	Pesach - 15-21/22
29	Iyar (April/May)	Taurus	Yom HaZikaron -4
			Yom HaAtzma'ut - 5
			Lag B'Omer - 18
			Yom Yerushalayim - 28
30	Sivan (May/June)	Gemini	Shavuot - 6/7
29	Tammuz (June/July)	Cancer	Shivah Asar B'Tammuz - 17
30	Av (July/August)	Leo	Tishah B'Av - 9
29	Elul (August/September)	Virgo	None
30	Tishre (September/October)	Libra	Rosh HaShanah - 1
			Yom Kippur - 10
			Sukkot - 15/21
			Hoshana Rabbah - 21
			Shemini Atzereth - 22
			Simchat Torah - 23
29/30	Heshvan (October/November)	Scorpio	None
30/29	Kislev (November/December)	Sagittarus	Chanukah - 25/Tevet 2/3
29	Tevet (December/January)	Capricorn	Chanukah - 2/3
			Asarah B'Tevet - 10
30	Shevat (January/February)	Aquarius	Tu B'Shevat - 15
29	Adar (February/March)	Pisces	Purim - 14
(30	v'Adar (February/March)		Purim - 14)

Either from a statement in Talmud (*Sanhedrin* 42a), "Whoever pronounces the benediction over the new moon in its time . . . invites the presence of the *Shechinah*" (the femine indwelling divine spirit), or because the moon is symbolically associated with the monthly bodily cycle, Rosh Chodesh came to be regarded by women as especially meaningful. On this holiday, women were excused from all work. This was said to be a reward for women's refusal to contribute jewelry toward the making of the Golden Calf *(Pirke de Rabbi Eliezer,* Chapter 45). Today, observance of Rosh Chodesh is experiencing a revival among women, many of whom gather together in groups each month to celebrate. Usually included in the service is a *Kiddush Levanah* (blessing over the moon), *Kiddush* over wine, candle lighting, blessings for transitions in life and life experiences, the sharing of feelings and wisdom through poetry and song, storytelling about being female and Jewish, prayers for health, and more.

ACTIVITIES

Preschool/Kindergarten

1. Develop a Rosh Chodesh ritual each month in your classroom. Children are just beginning to understand the idea of a general calendar, so they may not connect immediately with another way of measuring time. But they can understand that something special is happening on a given day within the Jewish framework. You might have a special icon you place on your calendar for Rosh Chodesh and sing a simple Rosh Chodesh song (e.g., "Happy Rosh Chodesh To Us" sung to the tune of "Happy Birthday To You").

2. Play *Duck, Duck, Goose,* but substitute *Rosh, Rosh, Chodesh*! (NSM)

3. Bake sugar cookies in the shape of new moons. (AFM)

Primary

1. On butcher paper, have students make a collage of the Jewish year with the names of the holidays appearing in their respective places and with appropriate art work to accompany each holiday. This can be presented at an assembly, at a worship service, or displayed on a wall in the classroom or hall. (NSM)

2. Work on a class calendar which you can distribute to families. Have students work in 13 groups to create a picture which goes with each Hebrew month, or they can use Jewish clip art for their pictures. Print a calendar off a computer (one which notes the Jewish holidays) or use the Calendar Repro Pak published by Kar-Ben Copies, Inc. Have students match each month with the corresponding picture. Run off one for each child, bind at the top, and send home. (NSM)

3. After students are familiar with the names of the Hebrew months (see previous page for list) and have worked a while matching Jewish holidays to their corresponding months, pin the name of a month on the back of each students. Have youngsters mill around the classroom, asking friends questions which will help them guess the month on their back (e.g., Does my month have warm weather? Do we act silly during my month?) As students guess their own months, they may have a classmate take the sign off their back. (NSM)

4. For additional ideas for Rosh Chodesh, see The Melton Curriculum, *Teaching Holidays/ Mitzvot/Prayer — Alef Level*, Vol. 1, page 11. (NSM)

Intermediate

1. Have students memorize the Hebrew months in order. (NSM)

2. Divide students into groups of 2 or 3. Give each group a Jewish calendar (obtain from funeral home or borrow enough from families for the class). Also give each group a piece of paper with 13 squares labeled with the names of the Hebrew months. Have students use the calendars as a reference and figure out the names of the holidays and festivals which match each month. Group members should collaborate to write the names of the Jewish holidays in the corresponding months. (NSM)

3. Have students circle the words related to Rosh Chodesh in the following word search:

```
A Z C O R C H O D E S H N A B
X A D A R H N B C I R S T E D
T U R C E A V A I N E R O L D
I N C F R L G S H E V A T U E
S Z T A M L U Z V N G U L L B
H E E J L E V U W T H I E Z K
R V V U M L P I I O N S V I I
E R E A I S T S I V A N A Y S
B R T A M M U Z Y Q U O N A L
C A L E N D A R E R R Y A R E
S Q U B C X I O L U A C H X V
R R S T S H A B B A T O Q R T
A O N I Z R Q P I M N I S A N
V S C H E S H V A N A S T I A
N H Q U P S H A L O M A C H V
```

(Answers: Rosh, Adar, Elul, Hallel, Cheshvan, Tevet, Shevat, Sivan, Nisan, Luach, Tishre, Iyar, Av, Tammuz, Levanah, Kislev, Shabbat, Chodesh, Calendar, Shalom)

4. Keep a Hebrew calendar in the room (if possible, one which has the Hebrew month at the top of page and not the English month, and which counts day one from Rosh Chodesh. Each time the class meets, note the date in the Hebrew calendar. The week before Rosh Chodesh, announce the new month. Use the prayer in your congregation's *Siddur* or have students write their own Rosh Chodesh ritual.

5. Ask two students to volunteer to portray a month in the Jewish calendar. They interact using pantomime only. The class must figure out who they are.

6. Invite students to write their hopes for and thoughts about each new month on a graffiti board made of 9" x 12" pieces of construction paper or butcher paper.

7. Investigate how the way of calculating the new moon has changed over the centuries. Also look into whether the way that Rosh Chodesh is celebrated has changed.

8. Have students make a bulletin board that provides a chance to match the phases of the moon to specific holidays. (NSM) Resource: "Moon Watch" in *Original Bulletin Boards on Jewish Themes* by Nachama Skolnik Moskowitz.

9. Using the information on page 244, have students design an artistic chart with the Jewish months and their zodiac signs. (AFM)

Secondary

1. Read the Rosh Chodesh prayers in your congregation's *Siddur*. Brainstorm the key themes of the observance of Rosh Chodesh and write the list on the blackboard. Give each student ten or so minutes to write a prayer related to Rosh Chodesh that reflects one of its themes. You may want to suggest that girls write prayers that deal with women's interest in and relationship to Rosh Chodesh — the cycles of the month, birth and rebirth, etc. Some or all of the prayers can then be used for a school Rosh Chodesh worship service. The Rabbi may wish to invite some of the students to read their prayers as part of the congregational holiday worship service.
Resources: *A Ceremonies Sampler: New Rites, Celebrations, and Observances of Jewish Women*, edited by Elizabeth Resnick Levine; *Celebrating the New Moon: A Rosh Chodesh Anthology*, edited by Susan Berrin.

2. Ask: Why do you think Jews celebrate the beginning of each new month? Is it important to pay special attention to new beginnings, and to celebrate them? Ask students what kind of new beginnings they have in their lives. How could these events be marked with a ritual?

3. Together as a class, read the *Yehi Ratzon* prayer. Ask: What are the key ideas in the prayer? What does it say to you?

4. Examine the Jewish months in relation to the zodiac. What relationship, if any, is there between the months of the Jewish year and astrology?

5. Read and discuss with students the paired words in the prayer which announces Rosh Chodesh (see your congregation's *Siddur*). Ask students why they think the words were joined together. Have students work in pairs to create linked pictures which show the connection between the words. You might give each pair two sheets of one color of construction paper and two sheets of another color. One students chooses one color for his/her background and the other student chooses the second color for the background; they should then have contrasting colors for their foregrounds. Have one student tear his/her foreground sheet into a design which would illustrate one of the words of the pair. The other student creates a design for the word paired with the first one, also by tearing his/her foreground sheet. Glue down the designs and tape (on the back) the two connected background sheets together. (NSM)

6. Compare and contrast the Jewish lunar calendar and the Moslem lunar calendar. The Moslems do not have a leap year, only 12 lunar months of 29 to 30 days each year. Find out how the Moslem calendar affects the timing of the key Moslem festivals.

7. Have students look into Rosh Chodesh as a specifically women's holiday. Discuss the findings. (AFM)

Resources: See Secondary Activity #1 above.

8. Divide students into groups of 2 or 3 and give each group a copy of a hundred year calendar (ask your Rabbi or obtain from the first volume of the *Encyclopaedia Judaica*). Ask students to work with 19 years of their choosing. (They may want to try and focus on several months, especially Tishre and Adar). See if they can figure out the pattern the Rabbis developed to keep the Jewish calendar in sync with the solar calendar. (NSM)

9. Listen to some songs related to Rosh Chodesh and compare them. Have students write their own songs and/or poems. (AFM)
    Resources: "Rosh Chodesh Moon" on *A Moon Note* by Miraj; "Rosh Chodesh" on *The Length of Our Days* by Marsha Rose Attie; "*Birkat Levanah*" on *Debbie Friedman at Carnegie Hall*.

10. Invite someone from a women's prayer group or a Jewish women's resource center to tell students about their Rosh Chodesh observance. (AFM)

11. Research how the addition of a leap month seven times every 19 years affects the timing of Jewish holidays. Why is there a swing period of about 30 days for each Jewish holiday? Why is it, for example, that Chanukah can occur right after Thanksgiving one year and begin around Christmas and run into January a few years later?

12. Do the dance *midrash* "New Moons" in *Torah in Motion: Creating Dance Midrash* by JoAnne Tucker and Susan Freeman (page 186.). This exercise includes three motiving movements related to Rosh Chodesh and a dance *midrash*

on Numbers 28:11, the bringing of burnt offerings to God on the occasion of a new moon. Suggest that students carry out the challenge presented in the book — choreographing a moon dance for Rosh Chodesh. Afterward, come together as a group and process the experience.

All-school

1. Take a field trip one night to an observatory to view the new moon. During the next session, each class discusses what they saw and how they felt. Did they feel like saying a prayer? What is it about the moon that causes such feelings of awe and reverence? (AFM)

Family

1. Suggest that families study a Torah portion read on the forthcoming Rosh Chodesh or study the *Machar Chodesh Haftarah* portion, which is read on each Rosh Chodesh. Each member of the family is given a few verses to study and summarize for the rest of the family. When all are ready, the family members read the selection from the Torah and then restate it in their own words. To conclude, the family discusses the meaning of the passage from the Torah.

2. Encourage families to plan a festive meal for the celebration of Rosh Chodesh. Since Rosh Chodesh is, in effect, the celebration of a new beginning, they might make one Jewish dish each month that the family has not previously tasted. In this way, the family eating experience will become a new beginning also.

BIBLIOGRAPHY

See page 305.

EPILOGUE: ISRU CHAG

No one wants a good thing to end! So it is with the Pilgrimage Festivals — Sukkot, Pesach, and Shavuot. Somehow, if the festival could only be extended just a bit more, then . . . perhaps the Messiah will arrive just a little sooner.

Isru Chag means "Bind a Festival." It is the name given to the day following each of the Sh'losh Regalim. The phrase is taken from Psalm 118:27 which reads: "God is Sovereign and God has shown us light; bind the festival sacrifice with cords, even to the horns of the altar." From this reference to the sacrifices at the Temple in Jerusalem, the term has come to mean "hold on to the festival even as it departs."

The Talmud (*Sukkah* 45b) states: "Whoever makes an addition (*isur*) to the festival (*chag*) is considered to have built an altar and sacrificed on it." *Sukkah* 25b also notes that one who observes *Isru Chag* as a festive day with eating and drinking is as one who has offered sacrifices upon the altar of the Temple in Jerusalem. Rashi was the first to note that some people refer to Isru Chag as the day after a Festival. The Jerusalem Talmud refers to Isru *Chag* as "the son of the festival."

Liturgically, Isru Chag is observed as a semi-festive day, a kind of minor holiday. On this day, the *Tanchuma* supplications are omitted from the Shacharit and Minchah worship services and no penitential prayers are said.

All good things must draw to a conclusion. It is hoped that this volume will serve you well for many years to come as a valuable reference in the teaching of the Jewish holidays and festivals. May it be a source of new ideas and a catalyst for creativity and innovation.

APPENDIX: BLESSINGS

Shabbat

בָּרוּךְ אַתָּה יְיָ אֱלֹהֵינוּ מֶלֶךְ הָעוֹלָם אֲשֶׁר קִדְּשָׁנוּ בְּמִצְוֹתָיו וְצִוָּנוּ לְהַדְלִיק נֵר שֶׁל שַׁבָּת.

Baruch Atah Adonai Elohaynu Melech HaOlam Asher Kid'shanu b'Mitzvotav v'Tzivanu L'hadleek Nayr Shel Shabbat.

Blessed is the Eternal our God, Sovereign of the universe, who sanctifies us through Your commandments and commands us to kindle the Sabbath lights.

בָּרוּךְ אַתָּה יְיָ אֱלֹהֵינוּ מֶלֶךְ הָעוֹלָם בּוֹרֵא פְּרִי הַגָּפֶן.

Baruch Atah Adonai Elohaynu Melech HaOlam Boray P'ri HaGafen.

Blessed is the Eternal our God, Sovereign of the Universe, Creator of the fruit of the vine.

בָּרוּךְ אַתָּה יְיָ אֱלֹהֵינוּ מֶלֶךְ הָעוֹלָם הַמּוֹצִיא לֶחֶם מִן הָאָרֶץ.

Baruch Atah Adonai Elohaynu Melech HaOlam HaMotzi Lechem Min HaAretz.

Blessed is the Eternal our God, Sovereign of the Universe, who brings forth bread from the earth.

יְשִׂימְךָ אֱלֹהִים כְּאֶפְרַיִם וְכִמְנַשֶּׁה.

Y'simcha Elohim k'Ephraim v'chiMenasheh.

May God make you as Ephraim and as Menasseh.

יְשִׂימֵךְ אֱלֹהִים כְּשָׂרָה רִבְקָה רָחֵל וְלֵאָה.

Y'simaych Elohim k'Sarah, Rifka, Rachel, v'Leah.

May God make you as Sarah, Rebekah, Rachel, and Leah.

Havdalah

For the blessing over wine, see Shabbat, above.

בָּרוּךְ אַתָּה יְיָ אֱלֹהֵינוּ מֶלֶךְ הָעוֹלָם בּוֹרֵא מִינֵי בְשָׂמִים.

Baruch Atah Adonai Elohaynu Melech HaOlam Boray Minay Besamin.

Blessed is the Eternal our God, Sovereign of the universe, who creates diverse kinds of spices.

בָּרוּךְ אַתָּה יְיָ אֱלֹהֵינוּ מֶלֶךְ הָעוֹלָם בּוֹרֵא מְאוֹרֵי הָאֵשׁ.

Baruch Atah Adonai Elohaynu Melech HaOlam Boray M'oray HaAysh.

Blessed is the Eternal our God, Sovereign of the universe, who creates the lights of fire.

בָּרוּךְ אַתָּה יְיָ אֱלֹהֵינוּ מֶלֶךְ הָעוֹלָם הַמַּבְדִּיל בֵּין קֹדֶשׁ לְחוֹל בֵּין אוֹר לְחֹשֶׁךְ בֵּין יוֹם הַשְּׁבִיעִי לְשֵׁשֶׁת יְמֵי הַמַּעֲשֶׂה. בָּרוּךְ אַתָּה יְיָ הַמַּבְדִּיל בֵּין קֹדֶשׁ לְחוֹל.

Baruch Atah Adonai Elohaynu Melech HaOlam HaMavdil Bayn Kodesh l'Chol Bayn Or l'Choshech Bayn Yom HaShvi'i l'Shayshet Y'may HaMa'aseh. Baruch Atah Adonai HaMavdil Bayn Kodesh l'Chol.

Blessed is the Eternal our God, Sovereign of the universe, who separates the sacred from profane, light from darkness, the seventh day of rest from the six days of labor. Blessed is the Eternal who separates the sacred from the profane.

Rosh HaShanah

בָּרוּךְ אַתָּה יְיָ אֱלֹהֵינוּ מֶלֶךְ הָעוֹלָם בּוֹרֵא פְּרִי הָעֵץ.

Baruch Atah Adonai Elohaynu Melech HaOlam Boray P'ri HaAytz.

Blessed is the Eternal our God, Sovereign of the universe, who creates the fruits of the tree.

יְהִי רָצוֹן מִלְּפָנֶיךָ יְיָ אֱלֹהֵינוּ וֵאלֹהֵי אֲבוֹתֵינוּ שֶׁתְּחַדֵּשׁ עָלֵינוּ שָׁנָה טוֹבָה וּמְתוּקָה.

Yehi Ratzon Milfanecha Adonai Elohaynu Vaylohay Avotaynu Sheh'teh'chadaysh Alaynu Shanah Tovah u'Metukah.

May it be Your will, O Eternal our God and God of our ancestors, that You renew us for a good and sweet year.

Sukkot

בָּרוּךְ אַתָּה יְיָ אֱלֹהֵינוּ מֶלֶךְ הָעוֹלָם אֲשֶׁר קִדְּשָׁנוּ בְּמִצְוֹתָיו וְצִוָּנוּ לֵישֵׁב בַּסֻּכָּה.

Baruch Atah Adonai Elohaynu Melech HaOlam Asher Kid'shanu b'Mitzvotav v'Tzivanu Layshayv BaSukkah.

Blessed is the Eternal our God, Sovereign of the universe, who sanctifies us through Your commandments and commands us to dwell in the *sukkah*.

בָּרוּךְ אַתָּה יְיָ אֱלֹהֵינוּ מֶלֶךְ הָעוֹלָם אֲשֶׁר קִדְּשָׁנוּ בְּמִצְוֹתָיו וְצִוָּנוּ עַל נְטִילַת לוּלָב.

Baruch Atah Adonai Elohaynu Melech HaOlam Asher Kid'shanu b'Mitzvotav v'Tzivanu Al Netilat Lulav.

Blessed is the Eternal our God, Sovereign of the universe, who sanctifies us through Your commandments and commands us concerning lifting up the *lulav*.

Chanukah

בָּרוּךְ אַתָּה יְיָ אֱלֹהֵינוּ מֶלֶךְ הָעוֹלָם אֲשֶׁר קִדְּשָׁנוּ בְּמִצְוֹתָיו וְצִוָּנוּ לְהַדְלִיק נֵר שֶׁל חֲנֻכָּה.

Baruch Atah Adonai Elohaynu Melech HaOlam Asher Kid'shanu b'Mitzvotav v'Tzivanu l'Hadleek Nayr Shel Chanukah.

Blessed is the Eternal our God, Sovereign of the universe, who sanctifies us through Your commandments and commands us to kindle the Chanukah lights.

בָּרוּךְ אַתָּה יְיָ אֱלֹהֵינוּ מֶלֶךְ הָעוֹלָם שֶׁעָשָׂה נִסִּים לַאֲבוֹתֵינוּ בַּיָּמִים הָהֵם בַּזְּמַן הַזֶּה.

Baruch Atah Adonai Elohaynu Melech HaOlam Sheh'asah Nisim La'Avotaynu BaYamim HaHaym BaZ'man HaZeh.

Blessed is the Eternal our God, Sovereign of the universe, who performed miracles for our ancestors in days of old, at this season.

Purim

בָּרוּךְ אַתָּה יְיָ אֱלֹהֵינוּ מֶלֶךְ הָעוֹלָם אֲשֶׁר קִדְּשָׁנוּ בְּמִצְוֹתָיו וְצִוָּנוּ עַל מִקְרָא מְגִלָּה.

Baruch Atah Adonai Elohaynu Melech HaOlam Asher Kid'shanu b'Mitzvotav v'Tzivanu Al Mikra Megillah.

Blessed is the Eternal our God, Sovereign of the universe, who sanctifies us through Your commandments and commands us to read the *Megillah*.

בָּרוּךְ אַתָּה יְיָ אֱלֹהֵינוּ מֶלֶךְ הָעוֹלָם שֶׁעָשָׂה נִסִּים לַאֲבוֹתֵינוּ בַּיָּמִים הָהֵם בַּזְּמַן הַזֶּה.

Baruch Atah Adonai Elohaynu Melech HaOlam Sheh'asah Nisim La'Avotaynu BaYamim HaHaym BaZ'man HaZeh.

Blessed is the Eternal our God, Sovereign of the universe, who performed miracles for our ancestors in days of old, at this season.

Pesach

For the blessing over wine, see Shabbat.

בָּרוּךְ אַתָּה יְיָ אֱלֹהֵינוּ מֶלֶךְ הָעוֹלָם בּוֹרֵא פְּרִי הָאֲדָמָה.

Baruch Atah Adonai Elohaynu Melech HaOlam, Boray P'ri HaAdamah.

Blessed is the Eternal our God, Sovereign of the universe, Creator of the fruit of the earth. (*Karpas*)

בָּרוּךְ אַתָּה יְיָ אֱלֹהֵינוּ מֶלֶךְ הָעוֹלָם אֲשֶׁר קִדְּשָׁנוּ בְּמִצְוֹתָיו וְצִוָּנוּ עַל אֲכִילַת מָרוֹר.

Baruch Atah Adonai Elohaynu Melech HaOlam Asher Kid'shanu b'Mitzvotav v'Tzivanu Al Achilat Maror.

Blessed is the Eternal our God, Sovereign of the universe, who sanctifies us through Your commandments and commands us concerning the eating of bitter herbs.

בָּרוּךְ אַתָּה יְיָ אֱלֹהֵינוּ מֶלֶךְ הָעוֹלָם אֲשֶׁר קִדְּשָׁנוּ בְּמִצְוֹתָיו וְצִוָּנוּ עַל אֲכִילַת מַצָּה.

Baruch Atah Adonai Elohaynu Melech HaOlam Asher Kid'shanu b'Mitzvotav v'Tzivanu Al Achilat Matzah.

Blessed is the Eternal our God, Sovereign of the universe, who sanctifies us through Your commandments and commands us concerning the eating of *matzah*.

For the blessing over bread, see Shabbat.

בָּרוּךְ אַתָּה יְיָ אֱלֹהֵינוּ מֶלֶךְ הָעוֹלָם אֲשֶׁר קִדְּשָׁנוּ בְּמִצְוֹתָיו וְצִוָּנוּ עַל נְטִילַת יָדַיִם.

Baruch Atah Adonai Elohaynu Melech HaOlam Asher Kid'shanu b'Mitzvotav v'Tzivanu Al Netilat Yadayim.

Blessed is the Eternal our God, Sovereign of the universe, who sanctifies us through Your commandments and commands us concerning the washing of hands.

Candlelighting for a Festival

בָּרוּךְ אַתָּה יְיָ אֱלֹהֵינוּ מֶלֶךְ הָעוֹלָם אֲשֶׁר קִדְּשָׁנוּ בְּמִצְוֹתָיו וְצִוָּנוּ לְהַדְלִיק נֵר שֶׁל (שַׁבָּת וְשֶׁל) יוֹם טוֹב.

Baruch Atah Adonai Elohaynu Melech HaOlam Asher Kid'shanu b'Mitzvotav v'Tzivanu l'Hadleek Nayr Shel (Shabbat v'Shel) Yom Tov.

Blessed is the Eternal our God, Sovereign of the universe, who sanctifies us through Your commandments and commands us to kindle the (Shabbat and) Festival lights.

בָּרוּךְ אַתָּה יְיָ אֱלֹהֵינוּ מֶלֶךְ הָעוֹלָם שֶׁהֶחֱיָנוּ וְקִיְּמָנוּ וְהִגִּיעָנוּ לַזְּמַן הַזֶּה.

Baruch Atah Adonai Elohaynu Melech HaOlam Shehecheyanu v'Keeyamanu v'Higeeyanu LaZ'man HaZeh.

Blessed is the Eternal our God, Sovereign of the universe, who has kept us alive, watched over us, and enabled us to reach this season.

BIBLIOGRAPHY

Carolyn Starman Hessel

Note: A majority of the materials listed in this Revised Edition date from 1990 forward. Exceptions are made for a few major works that have stood the test of time. A new feature is the annotation accompanying each suggested title, which offers the opportunity for a more informed selection. Most books included are published by the major Jewish and general publishing houses. This was a purposeful decision to provide resources which are readily accessible and are available through your local Jewish bookstore or a large general bookstore.

This book by itself is complete with background and a wealth of programmatic suggestions, thereby reducing the need for an extensive library of additional guides. These resources, therefore, are intended as a supplement and enrichment to Dr. Goodman's work. There is no attempt to list every book available. Rather, the effort is made to provide a well-rounded list to meet the many needs within the diverse Jewish community.

The Bibliography begins with a listing of general titles on the holiday cycle. These are listed in the categories "For Students" and "For Teachers and Parents." Entries follow for each holiday categorized in the same two divisions. Additionally, you will find listings of audiotapes, videos, and CD-ROMs. Following the Bibliography are addresses of publishers of Jewish materials and distributors of videos, audiotapes, and software.

While an age group is specified for all student materials, please be aware that these are just guidelines, and that many listings can be adapted for children in other grades.

You will note an extensive listing of adult selections and teaching materials for Yom HaShoah, Holocaust Day. The form of observance of this mournful episode is still emerging; thus, there is a proliferation of materials. So, too, there are many materials for Yom Ha'Atzmaut, Israel Independence Day. This holiday, celebrated just days after Yom HaShoah, is gaining recognition within the American Jewish community, and there is as yet no uniformity of celebration.

A word about the media resources. This section is most reflective of changes in materials that have taken place since the first edition of this book. Videos and CD-ROMs were just a glimmer on the horizon at that time. Now they are the major media tools and very much a part of every child's life. However, in the case of CDs, this is still a relatively new field and Jewish education is struggling to stay abreast. Whatever is listed here is but a "tip of the iceberg." So this material is merely intended to whet the appetite. New products, emerging daily, are announced in your local Anglo-Jewish newspaper and Jewish periodicals and journals. Or, keep in touch with your local Board of Jewish Education, the Director of Education and/or Early Childhood specialist at your synagogue, or the local Jewish Community Center for news of the latest resources.

My thanks to Susan March of Los Angeles and Dr. Marcia Posner of Long Island, New York for their assistance.

GENERAL HOLIDAY BOOKS/MATERIALS

For Students

Adler, David A. *The Kids' Catalog of Jewish Holidays.* Philadelphia, PA: Jewish Publication Society, 1996, ISBN 0-8276-0581-1.

Easy-to-use introduction to each Jewish holiday with stories, poems, recipes, crafts, puzzles, cartoons and more. Also included are stories from around the world from the best of children's holiday literature. There is a substantive bibliography and a resource section. Grades 3 up.

Apelbaum, Shiffy. *Moshe Mendel the Mitza Maven and His Amazing Mitzva Quest.* Spring Valley, NY: Feldheim Publishers, 1993, ISBN 0-87306-662-6.

Following the *Where's Waldo* "search and find" format, readers are challenged to locate depictions of Moshe Mendel fulfilling various *mitzvot* (commandments) within densely illustrated scenes from religious Jewish neighborhoods. Each page contains a myriad of activities connected with Jewish holidays and/or Jewish values. Grades K-5.

Beiner, Stan J. *Class Acts: Plays & Skits for Jewish Settings.* Denver: A.R.E. Publishing, Inc., 1992, ISBN 0-86705-028-4.

A book of plays related to holidays and other subjects. Grades K-12.

Berman, Bonnie, and Laura Glatstein. *Holiday Game Pak.* Denver: A.R.E. Publishing, Inc., 1977.

Five games that teach and reinforce facts, symbols, and practices of the Jewish holidays. Grades K-3.

Blue. Rose. *Good Yontif: A Picture Book of the Jewish Year.* Brookfield, CT: Millbrook Press, 1997, ISBN 0-7613-0142-9.

Follow one family through the cycle of holidays in the Jewish year. There is no narration, so small children can create their own stories from the descriptive full-color illustrations. Grades PK-1.

Brinn, Ruth Esrig. *Jewish Holiday Crafts for Little Hands.* Rockville, MD: Kar-Ben Copies, Inc., 1993, ISBN 0-929371-47-X.

One hundred craft projects designed to help young children relate to, and feel part of, each Jewish holiday or festival. Directions are clear and illustrations make them easy to follow. An excellent book for the entire family. Grades PK-6, Families.

———. *Jewish Holiday Games for Little Hands.* Rockville, MD: Kar-Ben Copies, Inc., 1995, ISBN 0-929371-86-0.

Forty-eight games for children to play with one other or for families to play together. Brinn also describes 10 types of card games and six word games. All games have clear instructions. A glossary is included. Grades PK-6, Families.

Building Jewish Life Activity Books. (Blue Label and Red Label). Los Angeles, CA: Torah Aura Productions.

A series of activity books for children and their parents. The focus is on the symbols related to each holiday and what they say to us. Uses hands-on activities to involve the child in the process. Books available for Shabbat, the High Holidays, Sukkot, and Simchat Torah, Chanukah, Purim, and Passover. Highly recommended for both classroom and home setting. *Blue Label* books, Grades K-1; *Red Label* books, Grades 2-4.

Burstein, Chaya. *The UAHC Kids Catalog of Jewish Living.* New York: UAHC Press, 1992, ISBN 0-8074-0464-0.

Describes the Reform movement's interpretation of Jewish life and Jewish holidays. Includes brief paragraphs, good illustrations, and many activities. Grades 4-7.

———. *The Jewish Kids Catalog.* Philadelphia, PA: Jewish Publication Society, 1993, ISBN 0-8276-02154.

A compendium of Jewish information and lore. Includes chapters on holidays with plans for celebrations and crafts activities. A good reference for every child. Grades 3-7.

———. *Make Your Own Jewish Calendar Coloring Book.* Mineola, NY: Dover Publishing, 1995, ISBN 0-486-28630-4.

A coloring book to create one's own Jewish calendar while learning the names of the Jewish months and the dates for the Jewish holidays. Includes 12 full-page, ready-to-color illustrations, each depicting an appropriate holiday. Grades K-4.

Drucker, Malka. *The Family Treasury of Jewish Holidays*. New York: Little, Brown and Co., 1994, ISBN 0-316-19343-7.

A holiday book with stories, poems, songs, and activities for all ages. Information is given on each of the holidays, including *Shabbat*. All Hebrew is transliterated and translated. A glossary and suggestions for further reading are included. The illustrations were influenced by Hebrew illuminated manuscript paintings. This is a delightful book to be read alone or out loud with others. Grades 1 up.

———. *A Jewish Holiday ABC*. San Diego, CA: Gulliver Books, Harcourt Brace Jovanovich, 1992, ISBN 0-15-200482-2.

Bright paper cuts compliment this alphabet book. In addition to reading, parents can also ask their children to identify what they see in the illustrations. At the end of the text, a brief explanation of each holiday is presented. A glossary and pronunciation guide are included. A *Children's Book of the Month Club* Alternate Selection. Grades PK-2.

Farber, Michael, and Anne Klein Farber. *Bagelhead to the Rescue*. Maple Shade, NJ: KF Classics, 1995, ISBN 0-9646094-0-1.

Using the Bagelhead character throughout, the authors provide four stories that teach good values and reinforce the children's exposure to Jewish holidays and symbols. The focus is on Shabbat, Sukkot, and Yom Kippur. Grades 2-5.

Feldman, Sarah. *Let's Discover the Holidays (Set 1: Let's Discover the Fall Holidays, Set 2: Let's Discover the Spring Holidays)*. West Orange, NJ: Behrman House, 1997, ISBN 0-87441-624-8 and 623-X.

Set 1 and Set 2 of this publication each include eight full-color folders. Each introduces children to the holidays through photographs, illustrations, activities, and a simple text. Grades K-1.

Fisher, Adam. *My Jewish Year: Celebrating Our Holidays*. West Orange, NJ: Behrman House, 1993, ISBN 0-87441-540-3.

A first introduction to the major holidays. Contains activities, stories, and information on rituals, symbols, history, traditions, and legends. A Teacher's Guide by Jessica Weber is also available. Grades 2-3.

Gootel, Rifka. *My First Learn and Do Jewish Holiday Book*. West Orange, NJ: Behrman House, 1988, ISBN: 0-86705-475-X.

Hands-on activities reinforce customs, special foods, and blessings. Grades K-2.

Greenberg, Melanie. *Celebrations: Our Jewish Holidays*. Philadelphia, PA: Jewish Publication Society, 1991, ISBN 0-8276-0505-6.

A few lines capture the flavor of each holiday and tell how we practice it. Grades PK-3.

Groner, Judyth, and Madeline Wikler. *Thank You, God: A Jewish Child's Book of Prayers*. Rockville, MD: Kar-Ben Copies, Inc., 1993, ISBN 0-929371-65-8.

A first prayer book in simple Hebrew, which is transliterated and translated. Includes blessings for a new day, for food, Shabbat and holiday rituals, life and health, comfort and forgiveness. Prayer is a wonderful way to introduce a child to Jewish traditions. Grades PK-1.

Home Start (Level 1). West Orange, NJ: Behrman House, 1985.

Material delivered to the home before the start of the school year. Level 1 includes Fall Holidays, Chanukah, Purim, and Passover, and features picture books, activity books, cassette tapes, and a parent handbook. Includes Teacher's Handbook. Grades PK-K.

Home Start (Level 2). West Orange, NJ: Behrman House, 1985.

Material delivered to the home before the start of the school year. Level 2 includes Fall Holidays, Chanukah, Purim, Passover, Shavuot, and Shabbat, and features picture books, play and learn magazines, cassette tapes, and a parent handbook. Teacher's Handbook also included. Grades 1 and 2.

Illions, Yehudis. *Things I Like to See on Shabbos; on Hanukah.* Spring Valley, NY: Feldheim's Young Reader's Division, 1993.

Two board books for toddlers about the Jewish holidays show Jewish symbols and traditions. Attractively illustrated and designed. Ages 2-3.

Isaacs, Ron, and Kerry Olitzky. *Sacred Celebrations: A Jewish Holiday Handbook.* Hoboken, NJ: KTAV Publishing House, 1994, ISBN 0-88125-496-7.

Each chapter includes insights from Jewish tradition related to the holiday; basic description of the holiday; major rituals, customs, and celebrations in synagogue and home; family activities, games, and recipes; blessings; and a glossary of holiday terms. Grades 7-9.

Kozodoy, Ruth. *The Book of Jewish Holidays.* 2d ed. West Orange, NJ: Behrman House, 1997, ISBN 0-87441-629-9.

Everything the student needs to know about the celebrations, feasts, and fasts of the Jewish year can be found in this text and activity book. Contains Hebrew lessons, primary source texts, information on how we share our celebrations with others, a holiday planner, and ideas for family celebration. A Teacher's Guide is available. Grades 4-5.

Lepon, Shoshana. *Holiday Rhymes and Riddles.* Brooklyn, NY: Mesorah Publications, Ltd., 1994, ISBN 0-89906-820-6.

This text assumes the reader has a high level of knowledge about the holidays. All Hebrew is transliterated, following the Ashkenazic pronunciation. The answers to the rhymes and riddles appear at the bottom of each page. A text that children can use together or for parents and their children. Grades 3 up.

Let's Celebrate. West Orange, NJ: Behrman House, 1995, ISBN 0-87441-573-X.

A package of seven full-color 16-page magazines on the major holidays. Each retells the story of the holiday, describes specific rituals and values, and includes activities for home or school to expand and enrich the material. Each includes a special parent page. A Teacher's Guide is also available. Grades K-2.

Musleah, Rahel, and Michael Klayman. *Sharing Blessings: Children's Stories for Exploring the Spirit of the Jewish Holidays.* Woodstock, VT: Jewish Lights Publishing, 1997, ISBN 1-879045-71-0.

For 13 different holidays, there is a story about David and Ilana and their parents that focuses on the spiritual value embodied in each holiday. Each story begins with a brief explanation of the holiday and concludes with a special prayer that child and adult can share. Appropriate for children in Grades 1-5.

Patera, Meridith Shaw. *Kings and Things: 20 Jewish Plays for Kids 8 to 18.* Denver: A.R.E. Publishing, Inc., 1996, ISBN 0-86705-038-1.

Twenty plays on some of the Jewish holidays, as well as Bible, Israel, Holocaust, folktales, and Jewish values. Grades 3-12.

Pearl, Sydelle. *Elijah's Tears: Stories for the Jewish Holidays.* New York: Henry Holt, 1996, ISBN 0-8050-4627-5.

After introducing Elijah's role in Jewish folklore, five stories follow which conform to the ideas of helping the needy or warning of impending doom. There are two with a Passover theme, one each with Sukkot, Chanukah, and Passover themes. Grades 2-5.

Ross, Kathy. *The Jewish Holiday Craft Book.* Brookfield, CT: Millbrook Press, 1997, ISBN 0-7613-0175-5.

96 pages filled with easy-to-follow and fun-to-make crafts suggestions for the major holidays. The selection of projects is interesting. Grades PK-3.

Rouss, Sylvia. *Fun with Jewish Holiday Rhymes.* New York: UAHC Press, 1992, ISBN 0-8074-0463-2.

This book introduces young children to Shabbat and holidays through the recitation of playful rhymes and movement activities. Appropriate for Shabbat and holiday services for young children. Grade PK.

Silverman, Maida. *The Glass Menorah and Other Stories for Jewish Holidays*. New York: Four Winds Press, 1992, ISBN 0-02-782682-1.

A collection of eight stories describes how the Berg family celebrates the holidays. Includes a glossary and an explanation of why the Jewish day begins the night before. Grades 2 up.

———. *My First Book of Jewish Holidays*. New York: Dial Books for Young Readers, 1994, ISBN 0-8037-1427-0.

Ten holidays, including Shabbat, are described in this collection. A glossary and pronunciation guide provides additional information for adults. The text accompanied by a series of collagraphs, is appropriate as a read aloud for parents and their children. Grades PK-3.

Van Hansel, Esther. *A Children's Treasury of Holiday Tales*. Brooklyn, NY: Mesorah Publications, Ltd., 1992, ISBN 0-89906-416-7.

This collection consists of ten stories about holidays and Shabbat. The text assumes the reader has a high level of knowledge about traditional ritual and celebration. Ashkenazic pronunciation of Hebrew. Part of the *Art Scroll Youth Series*. Includes a glossary. Grades 3 up.

Weilerstein, Sadie Rose. *The Best of K'tonton*. Philadelphia, PA: Jewish Publication Society, 1995, ISBN 0-8276-0187-5.

Sixteen stories, one for each holiday, are brought together in this paperback edition for both the home and group setting. Every young child of today should be introduced to the "Jewish Tom Thumb." Grades 1-5.

Wylen, Stephen M. *The Book of the Jewish Year*. New York: UAHC Press, 1996, ISBN 0-8074-0537-X.

An introduction to the Jewish holiday cycle with the rituals, foods, symbols, stories, and legends as well as Hebrew and English blessings. Excellent color photos of contemporary families celebrating the holidays. Suggested for the formal education setting. Grades 4-6.

Yolen, Jane. *Milk and Honey: A Year of Jewish Holidays*. New York: Putnam's Sons, 1996. ISBN 0-399-22652-4.

A well-illustrated accompaniment for families celebrating the cycle of Jewish holidays. Divided according to the occasion, each section includes an account of the respective history and customs followed by appropriate poems, folktales, and traditional songs. Grades 1-7.

Zalban, Jane Breskin. *Beni's Family Cookbook*. New York: Henry Holt, 1996, ISBN 0-8050-3735-7.

The cookbook is arranged around the Jewish holiday calendar. The author contributes a brief introduction to each celebration and humorous recipe headnotes. The recipes are for family sharing, not for children alone. All Ages.

Zeldin, Florence. *A Mouse in Our Jewish House*. Los Angeles, CA: Torah Aura, 1990, ISBN 0-933873-43-3.

The mouse (*akbar* in Hebrew) is busy eating his way through the Jewish holiday year. Archie Akhbar isn't just eating; he is introducing 12 Jewish holiday celebrations while also teaching how to count from one to twelve. Grades PK-2.

Zwebner, Janet. *Uh! Oh!: Hidden Objects You'll (Almost) Never Find: Jewish Holidays*. St. Helier, NJ: Yellow Brick Road Press Ltd., 1993, ISBN 0-943706-15-7.

Based on the *Where is Waldo* format, *Uh! Oh!* is an entertaining text covering ten holidays of the year. Appropriate for anyone who likes to search and find. Grades K up.

Zwerin, Raymond A., and Audrey Friedman Marcus. *Shabbat Can Be*. New York: UAHC Press, 1979, ISBN 0-8074-0023-8.

The emotional tone of Shabbat and the warm feelings and images familiar to a small child are evoked in the simple text and full-color illustrations. Grades PK-3.

For Teachers and Parents

Alper, Janice P., ed. *Learning Together: A Sourcebook on Jewish Family Education.* Denver: A.R.E. Publishing, Inc., 1987, ISBN 0-86705-019-5.

Contains some 50 how-to chapters featuring models of family education programs ready to implement in synagogues, J.C.C.'s, camps, Family Service Agencies, and other settings. The contributors are educators from every movement and type of agency in the Jewish community.

Fellner, Judith. *In the Jewish Tradition: A Year of Food and Festivals.* New York: Smithmark, 1994, 0-8317-5268-8.

From historic origins and traditional rituals of the major Jewish holidays comes stories, poems, music, and recipes. Included is extensive resource guide.

Fox, Karen L., and Phyllis Zimbler Miller. *Seasons for Celebration: A Contemporary Guide to the Joys, Practices, and Traditions of the Jewish Holidays.* New York: Perigee Books, 1992, ISBN 0-399051764-2.

This book features separate chapters for each major holiday. Within each chapter are sections about home and synagogue traditions, appropriate activities, recipes, and insights. Personal anecdotes are interspersed throughout the text. All Hebrew is transliterated and translated. The appendix explains the Jewish calendar and lists Jewish holiday dates through 2005. The addresses of selected Jewish organizations and an index are also included.

Goodman, Philip. *JPS Holiday Anthologies.* Philadelphia, PA: Jewish Publication Society, 1970-1974. *Rosh Hashanah* ISBN 0-8276-0302-9; *Yom Kippur* ISBN 0-8276-0409-2; *Sukkot/Simchat Torah* ISBN 0-8276-0302-9; *Hanukkah* ISBN 0-8276-0401-7; *Purim* ISBN 0-8276-0319-3; *Passover* ISBN 0-8276-0410-6; *Shavuot* ISBN 0-8276-0391-6.

This outstanding series is one that has stood the test of time, and the books remain a reliable guide to authentic and rewarding holiday celebration. Each volume includes biblical selections, ancient and modern prose and poetry, history of the holiday and its traditional observance in America, traditional foods, songs, and art. The children's sections carry stories and holiday activities. Now available in complete seven volume set in paperback or may be purchased individually.

Goodman, Roberta Lewis, and Andye Honigman Zell. *Head Start on Holidays: Jewish Programs for Preschoolers and Their Parents.* Denver: A.R.E. Publishing, 1991, ISBN 0-87605-026-8.

Two master teachers bring together many years of programming in this ready-to-implement book of suggestions for leaders of early childhood programs and their families. It contains everything you ever need to know and more, and will serve as an excellent resource for every group.

Grundleger, Barbara. *Hands On! Teacher-made Games for Jewish Early Childhood Settings.* Denver: A.R.E. Publishing, Inc., 1991, ISBN 0-86705-027-6.

Contains instructions for many games appropriate for preschool and kindergarten children that combine skills with Jewish themes.

Klagsbrun, Francine. *Jewish Days: A Book of Jewish Life and Culture Around the Year.* Mark Podwal, illus. New York: Farrar, Straus & Giroux, 1996, ISBN 0-374-17923-9.

With legends, stories, and interpretative essays, Klagsbrun takes the reader through every month of the Hebrew calendar, discussing and analyzing its special days. Podwal's stunning paintings reflect the mystical view of the world.

Kops, Simon. *Fast Clean & Cheap: Or Everything the Jewish Teacher (Or Parent) Needs to Know about Art.* Los Angeles, CA: Torah Aura Productions, 1989, ISBN 0-933873-25-5.

This creative work includes magic tricks, more than 70 projects, and a dozen ways to reconsider the simple tasks related to doing art projects.

Mandelkern, Nicholas D., and Vicki L. Weber. *The Jewish Holiday Home Companion: A Parent's Guide to Family Celebration.* West Orange, NJ: Behrman House, 1994, ISBN 0-87441-566-7.

The first part of this book consists of short chapters on each holiday, each of which provides some of the respective history and celebrations. Suggestions for involving children are also included. The second section contains blessings, prayers, and songs appropriate for each holiday. All Hebrew is translated and transliterated. A calendar listing the secular dates of the holidays through the year 2001 is included, as well as selected holiday recipes. The text is accompanied by black and white photographs.

Miller, Helena. *The Magic Box: A Source Book of Craft Ideas for Jewish Festivals and Projects*. Los Angeles, CA: Torah Aura Productions, 1995, ISBN 0-933873-92-1.

A source book for those with little or no experience in the visual arts. Includes projects for the holidays, Bible, and Jewish history and many other Jewish themes.

Moskowitz, Nachama Skolnik. *Original Bulletin Boards on Jewish Themes*. Denver: A.R.E. Publishing, Inc., 1986, ISBN 0-86705-019-5.

Contains instructions for making creative bulletin boards that enhance learning on a variety of subjects.

Nathan, Joan. *The Children's Jewish Holiday Kitchen*. New York: Schocken Books, ISBN 0-8052-4130-2.

Expanded from the 1987 edition, this cookbook aims for fun in the making of Jewish holiday recipes the whole family can enjoy. The book is divided into nine holidays and Shabbat with menus and recipes for each, and includes a chapter explaining what is and is not kosher.

————. *Jewish Cooking in America*. New York: Alfred A. Knopf, 1994, ISBN 0-394-58405-8.

A collection of over 300 recipes representing both Sephardic and Ashkenazic traditions makes this a valuable resource. The introduction includes a section on holidays and there is a chapter on Passover foods. More than 100 photographs and illustrations accompany the text. Includes suggested holiday menus, a list of kosher dry wines, a glossary of Jewish food terms, bibliography, and index.

Nowak, Nancy Cohen. *Jewish Preschool/Kindergarten Copy Pak*™. Denver: A.R.E. Publishing, Inc., 1988.

Contains 56 original activity pages to photocopy for preschool and kindergarten children on Jewish holidays, symbols, values, and Hebrew.

Olitzky, Kerry M., and Ronald H. Isaacs. *The How To Handbook for Jewish Living*. Hoboken, NJ: KTAV Publishing House, 1993, ISBN 0-88125-290-5.

Using a step-by-step format, this text is a guide to Jewish customs, rituals, and practices. All Hebrew is translated and transliterated. Includes a list of additional resources. Along with Shabbat and holidays, the text includes chapters on a variety of Jewish topics.

————. *The Second How-To Handbook for Jewish Living*. Hoboken, NJ: KTAV Publishing, 1996, ISBN 0-88125-550-5.

This second edition includes holiday how-to's with recipes for preparing for Shabbat and Rosh HaShanah.

Ross, Lesli Koppelman. *Celebrate! The Complete Jewish Holidays Handbook*. Northvale, NJ: Jason Aronson Inc. 1994, ISBN 1-56821-154-6.

Celebrate! aims to introduce or enhance holiday traditions in the home. The text is comprehensive and nondenominational in approach and contains the historical development, religious importance, and personal significance of each holiday that is useful to both beginners and those who are well versed. Chapters are divided into two main sections: why we celebrate, and how we celebrate. A recommended reading list for adults and children is included in each chapter.

Schauss, Hayyim. *The Jewish Festivals: A Guide to Their History and Observance*. New York: UAHC, 1938, reissued by Schocken Books, 1996, ISBN 0-805-20937-9.

This book, originally published decades ago, has stood the test of generations, for its message is timeless. It provides background on all of the major Jewish holidays including origin, meaning, significance, and forms of celebration during different time periods and in different geographic locations.

Sher, Nina Streisand, and Margaret A. Feldman. *100+ Jewish Art Projects for Children*. Denver: A.R.E. Publishing, Inc., 1996, ISBN 0-86705-039-X.

A delightful compilation of art projects for children in Grades PK-6 in Jewish settings. Complete instructions and photographs of finished products included.

Silberman, Mel. *101 Strategies to Teach Any Subject*. Boston: Allyn and Bacon, 1996, ISBN 0-205-17866-9.

No teacher should be without this comprehensive collection of active learning techniques that can be adapted to any age group or setting. Every strategy is explained in clear, step-by-step instructions.

Tucker, JoAnne. *Creative Movement for a Song: Activities for Young Children*. Denver: A.R.E. Publishing, Inc., 1993, ISBN 0-86705-024-1.

This book features ideas for movement activities that accompany songs from popular audiotapes. Grades PK-3.

Tucker, JoAnne, and Susan Freeman. *Torah in Motion: Creating Dance Midrash*. Denver: A.R.E. Publishing, Inc., 1990, ISBN 0-86705-024-1.

Contains easy-to-follow instructions for movement exercises based on over 100 Torah passages, as well as a brief description of the biblical passage, discussion ideas, and a special dance challenge for each verse. An appendix organizes the Dance *Midrashim* by Torah portion, holidays, and life cycle events.

Warshawsky, Gale Solotar. *Creative Puppetry for Jewish Kids*. Denver: A.R.E. Publishing, Inc., 1985, ISBN 0-86705-017-9.

Contains complete, easy-to-follow instructions for helping children in Grades PK-7 make a variety of puppets.

Wolf, Sandy Furfine, and Nancy Cohen Nowak. *The Jewish Preschool Teachers Handbook*. Rev. ed. Denver: A.R.E. Publishing, Inc., 1991, ISBN 0-86705-004-7.

An ideal resource for teachers and parents of children in Grades PK and Kindergarten, this book features chapters on holidays, symbols, Bible, Hebrew, values, faith development, and more. Also contains a developmental overview of the child from ages 3 to 5, ideas for involving parents, and ways to enrich the classroom environment.

Audiotapes

Aleph Bet Boogie. Joe Black. Available from A.R.E. Publishing, Inc.

Catchy songs about holidays and more. All Ages.

Apples on Holidays & Other Days. Leah Rubin. Tara Publications.

Original songs and poems for holidays and year round. Includes suggestions for children's activites for school and home, melody line, chords, and transliterations. Grades PK-3.

Celebrate with Cindy (vols. 1 and 2). Cindy Paley. Sounds Write Productions.

Two extensive collections of holiday songs, including traditional and English favorites, as well as familiar Israeli melodies. All Ages.

Especially Wonderful Days. Steve Reuben. A.R.E. Publishing, Inc.

Sing-along songs that teach the Jewish holidays. Songbook with scores, guitar chords, and lyrics included. Grades PK-3.

Everybody's Got a Little Music. Joe Black. Available from A.R.E. Publishing, Inc.

A playful collection of songs for holidays and history. All Ages.

Growin' (Vols. I and 2). Kol B'Seder. Available from A.R.E. Publishing, Inc.

Songs which teach holidays, blessings, simple Hebrew phrases, and the value of family. Grades PK-6, Families.

Holiday Songs Kids Love to Sing. Deborah Bard. Sounds Write Productions.

Traditional and contemporary music selections that are easy to sing are presented. Grades PK-3.

Shanah Tovah: A Good Year. Debbie Friedman. Available from A.R.E. Publishing, Inc.

Cycle through the Jewish year with Debbie in this fun loving recording of 13 original English songs. Hebrew words and symbols appropriate to the holidays are introduced. The music and lyrics for most of the songs were created for *Home Start* (Behrman House). Grades PK-6.

Shirim Al Galgalim. Debbie Friedman. Available from A.R.E. Publishing, Inc.

Commissioned by Hadassah for their "Training Wheels" program, these songs follow the holiday cycle and are meant to strengthen identity and family life. Grades PK-K.

Video
The Jewish Holidays Video Guide. 75 min. color. Board of Jewish Education of Greater New York.

Simon and Dinah Cohen lead their two children through a cycle of the Jewish calendar as they celebrate each of the major Jewish holidays in their warm family home. Well organized, sometimes shmaltzy (and with a few subtle promotions for sponsors Empire, Kedem, and Hebrew National), this video is best used one holiday at a time. All Ages.

CD-ROM
Sammy's Guide to the Jewish Holidays. Available from Jewish Software Center.

An interactive CD-ROM for PC and MAC featuring the music of Cindy Paley that teaches the history and traditions of each of the Jewish holidays. Sammy acts as the guide through each experience. Grades PK-3.

SHABBAT

For Students
Bogot, Howard; Robert Orkand; and Joyce Orkand. *Gates of Wonder; A Prayerbook for Very Young Children.* New York: CCAR Press, 1990, ISBN 0-88123-009-X.

This is the first official prayer book for young children ever produced by the Reform Movement. Charmingly illustrated, it is educational and entertaining. Grades PK-1.

Erev Shabbat. Los Angeles, CA: Torah Aura Productions.

This lesson introduces the blessings and practices of the Friday night Shabbat table ritual. Separate guide for teachers is called *The Celebration Lessons Teacher's Guide.* Grades K-2.

Golding, Goldie. *Dovy and the Surprise Guests.* Brooklyn, NY: Mesorah Publications, Ltd., 1993, ISBN 0-89906-512-0.

Ari, the Lion, Dovy's Shabbat guest, gets the chicken pox and has to cancel. Dovy and Debbie invite others, but they already have plans. While Dovy cleans for Shabbat, Debbie goes to the market and finds many animals who are happy to be invited for Shabbat. Ashkenazic pronunciation is used. Includes Debbie Bear's *cholent* recipe. Appropriate as a read aloud. Grades 3 up.

Fettman, Surie. *My Shabbos 1,2,3's.* Brooklyn, NY: Hachai Publications, Inc., 1996. ISBN 0-922613-61-3.

A counting book with numbers one through ten helps children set the *Shabbos* table. Beginning with 1, *Kiddush* cup, it proceeds to ten napkins on the table. Following is a page that has the blessings for candle lighting plus a brief glossary. Grades PK-1.

Kobre, Faige. *A Sense of Shabbat.* Los Angeles, CA: Torah Aura, 1990, ISBN 0-933873-44-1.

Experience the Sabbath through a child's senses. Shabbat is the taste of *challah,* the splashing water used to wash small hands, the aroma of the Havdalah cloves, the sound of the Shabbat songs, and the warmth one feels as the family celebrates the Shabbat together. Grades PK-3.

Kress, Camille. *Tot Shabbat.* New York: UAHC Press, 1996, ISBN 0-8074-0607-4.

A first board book for the very young. Only 36 words are used, with bright illustrations of the Shabbat ritual objects. Ages 1-3.

Manushkin, Fran. *Starlight and Candles: The Joys of the Sabbath*. New York: Simon & Schuster, 1995, ISBN 0-689-80274-9.

Jake and Rosy are very busy helping their parents prepare for Shabbat. When Shabbat arrives, it is a peaceful time for the family and they are able to enjoy their time together. Appropriate as a read aloud for younger children. Grades 3 up.

Mastering the Shabbat Table Service. Los Angeles, CA: Torah Aura Productions.

Through a series of exercises, students learn to master oral performance and basic understanding of the Shabbat table blessings. Grades 2-4.

Motzei Shabbat. Los Angeles, CA: Torah Aura Productions.

This Instant Lesson focuses on the Havdalah service. It introduces the symbols and the meaning of the ceremony. Separate guide for teachers is called *The Celebration Lessons Teacher's Guide*. Grades K-2.

Rosenfeld, Dina. *Peanut Butter & Jelly for Shabbos*. Brooklyn, NY: Hachai Publications, Inc., 1995, ISBN 0- 922613-69-9.

It is a cold, snowy Friday when the father of Yossi and Laibel goes to the hospital to bring their mother and baby sister home. Because of the bad weather, their parents are delayed, so the boys decide to prepare Shabbat dinner. Written as a rhyme. Ashkenazic pronunciation is used. Includes a glossary. Grades 3 up.

Schwartz, Amy. *Mrs. Moskowitz and the Sabbath Candles*. Philadelphia, PA: Jewish Publication Society, 1990, ISBN 0-8276-0372-X.

A winner of the National Jewish Book Award, this is a story about a lonely widow during her move to a new home. When she unpacks the Shabbat candlesticks and lights them for the first time in her new apartment they make her feel at home in her new surroundings. Grades K-4.

Shiefman, Vicky. *Sunday Potatoes. Monday Potatoes*. New York: Simon & Schuster, 1994, ISBN 0-671-86596-X.

A family is so poor that it exists on potatoes, but Mama uses her ingenuity to serve the potatoes in different disguises and on Shabbat — a feast! Grades PK-3.

Schur, Maxine Rose. *Day of Delight: A Jewish Sabbath in Ethiopia*. New York: Dial Books for Young Readers, 1994, ISBN 8037-1413-0.

A story about Menelik, the son of a blacksmith, as he and the members of his village prepare for and celebrate Shabbat. A wonderful presentation of a life that is quickly vanishing. Grades 4-6.

Schwartz, Howard, and Barbara Rush. *The Sabbath Lion: A Jewish Folktale from Algeria*. New York: HarperCollins Publishers, 1992, ISBN 0-06-020853-8.

A ten-year-old Algerian boy named Yosef worked hard all week to help support his family. Yosef had to travel across the desert to Cairo to receive a bequest from a relative who died. He joined a caravan with the condition that he be allowed to rest on Shabbat. When the caravan leader broke this promise, Yosef decided not to travel and spent Shabbat in the desert. As Shabbat began, something wonderful happened, and Yosef was able to receive the inheritance. Grades 3 up.

Schweiger-Dmi'el, Itzhak. *Hanna's Sabbath Dress*. New York: Simon & Schuster, 1996, ISBN 0-689-80517-9.

Hanna knows Shabbat is a very special. But what will happen when she ruins her Shabbat dress while doing a *mitzvah*? Grades PK-2.

Swartz, Daniel. *Bim and Bom: A Shabbat Tale*. Rockville, MD: Kar-Ben Copies, Inc., 1996, ISBN 0929371-12-7.

A short tale based on a child's Shabbat folktale. Bim and Bom are sister and brother who toil all week and look forward to being together on Shabbat. The story is presented in 24 pages, with the words and music to the song *"Shabbat Shalom"* on the back cover. Grades PK-K.

Symbols of Shabbat. Los Angeles, CA: Torah Aura Productions.

This Instant Lesson introduces six basic Shabbat symbols. Grades K-2.

Yom Shabbat. Los Angeles, CA: Torah Aura Productions.

This Instant Lesson provides a "visit" to a Shabbat morning service. It introduces the key symbols and events of the worship experience. Separate guide for teachers is called *The Celebration Lessons Teacher's Guide*. Grades K-2.

For Teachers and Parents

The Harvard Hillel Sabbath Songbook. Boston, MA: David R. Godine, 1992, ISBN 0-87923-900-X.

The text contains the complete Shabbat ritual for the home, beginning with the lighting of the candles through the *Birkat HaMazon* (Grace after Meals). The main part of this book is devoted to *zemirot* (songs). The words are written in Hebrew and Yiddish and are translated and transliterated. Full musical notation is included.

Palatnik, Lori. *Friday Night and Beyond: The Shabbat Experience Step-by-Step.* Northvale, NJ: Jason Aronson Inc., 1994, ISBN 1-56821-035-3.

A practical guide to traditional Shabbat observance starting with candle lighting on Friday night and ending with Havdalah on Saturday night. All Hebrew is translated and transliterated. Includes recipes, suggestions for further reading, a listing of beginner's services (all Orthodox), a listing of Aish HaTorah centers (Orthodox), glossary, and index.

Rosman, Steven. *The Bird of Paradise and Other Sabbath Stories.* New York: UAHC Press, 1994, ISBN 0-8074-0529-9.

A collection of stories and tales adapted from traditional sources as well as modern literature. Each story is preceded by a verse or verses from the weekly Torah portion upon which its main idea is based. Shabbat provides a good opportunity for parents and children to enjoy Torah learning through storytelling.

Shaarei Shabbat (Gates of Sabbath): A Guide for Observing Shabbat. New York: CCAR Press, 1991, ISBN 0-88123-010-3.

Published by the organization of Reform Rabbis, this book is a guide to observing Shabbat. It includes information on the basic ceremonies of home observance, background material on the origins of the rituals, music, prose, poetry, and discussion of the meaning of "rest" for the contemporary Jew.

Wolfson, Ron. *The Art of Jewish Living. The Shabbat Seder.* Woodstock, VT: Jewish Lights Publishing, reissued 1995, ISBN 1-879045-90-7.

The first volume of the Art of Jewish Living series for families (with or without children, and of every denomination) focuses on the *erev* Shabbat (Friday night) experience, teaching the meaning, importance, and practices. The reader is led through every step of the process, including the traditional rituals and prayers, with many creative ideas along the way.

Audiocassettes

Around Our Shabbat Table. Margie Rosenthal and Ilene Safyan. Available from A.R.E. Publishing, Inc.

Shabbat melodies from around the world in Hebrew and English will delight the entire family. All Ages.

Because We Love Shabbat. Leah Abrams. Tara Publications.

Presents the many facets of Shabbat with warmth and humor. Melody line, chords, texts, and transliteration included. Grades PK-3.

It's Time to Sing. Margie Rosenthal and Ilene Safyan. Available from A.R.E. Publishing, Inc.

Contains 16 upbeat Hebrew and English songs for Shabbat and every day. All Ages.

Shabbat Shalom. Cindy Paley. Sounds Write Productions.

Twenty beautiful Shabbat songs in English and Hebrew that encourage singing along. A good mood setter for home and classroom. All Ages.

ROSH HASHANAH AND YOM KIPPUR

For Students

Abrams, Judith. *Selichot: A Family Service; Rosh Hashanah: A Family Service;* and *Yom Kippur: A Family Service.* Rockville, MD: Kar-Ben Copies, Inc., 1990, ISBN 0-929371-15-1; 0-929371-16-X; 0-929311-17-8.

Three books that follow the order of the service, but dramatize the themes of the holiday with story, song, and suggested activities. A 30 minute cassette with four original songs as well as the traditional tunes is also available. Grades PK-4, Families.

Bayar, Steven. *Did Darth Vader Repent?* Los Angeles, CA: Torah Aura Productions.

Bassed on the movie *Return of the Jedi*, this Instant Lesson teaches insights from Maimonides, *Avot de Rabbi Natan*, the Talmud, and other sources to answer the question. Grades 6-Adult.

Bogot. Howard; Robert Orkand; and Joyce Orkand. *Gates of Awe: Holy Day Prayers for Very Young Children.* New York: CCAR Press, 1991. ISBN 0-88123-014-6.

Gates of Awe allows very young children to explore prayers appropriate for the High Holy Days. Each page is filled with direct, easily accessible text. Grades PK-1.

Cohen, Barbara. *Yussel's Prayer.* New York: Lothrop, 1981, 0-688-00461-X.

A retelling of the well-known tale of the shepherd boy whose fervent prayers open the gates of heaven at the end of the Yom Kippur service. The story demonstrates that sincere *tefillah* is more valued by God than rote prayer. Grades 1-4.

Epstein, Sylvia B. *How the Rosh Hashanah Challah Became Round.* Jerusalem: Gefen Publishing House, 1993, ISBN 965-229-095-5.

Yossi's father is a baker who makes delicious braided *challah*. Yossi enjoys being his father's helper. One day, as Yossi took the *challah* to the oven, he tripped, and the Rosh Hashanah *challah* rolled down the stairs. The community questioned the *challah's* shape until the Rabbi came up with a wonderful explanation. Appropriate as a read aloud for younger children. Grades 2 up.

The Feather Story. Los Angeles, CA: Torah Aura Productions.

During this Instant Lesson, students read a Jewish folk tale and use it to talk about the power of words to hurt and heal. Grades K-2.

Goldin, Barbara Diamond. *The World's Birthday: A Rosh Hashanah Story.* New York: Harcourt Brace, 1990, ISBN 0-15-20045-3.

A tenderly told tale of the concept of creation on the world's birthday. A little boy gives the world a party on Rosh HaShanah by setting a cake with candles outside. In the morning, the candles are blown out. Grades PK-3.

Groner, Judyth, and Madeline Wikler. *The Shofar Calls To Us.* Rockville, MD: Kar-Ben Copies, Inc., 1991, ISBN 0-929371-61-5.

A board book that tells the toddler what the *shofar* is saying to them. Ages 1-4.

———. *My Very Own Rosh Hashanah;* and *My Very Own Yom Kippur.* Rockville, MD: Kar-Ben Copies, Inc., 1978, ISBN 0-929371-06-7; 0-929371-05-9.

These two books remain "staples" in every Jewish home with young children, as well as every early childhood facility. They are the introduction to all that follows. Grades PK-2.

Kimmel, Eric. *Days of Awe: Stories for Rosh Hashanah and Yom Kippur.* New York: Viking, 1993, 0-14-050271-8.

The background to each holiday precedes three tales adapted from traditional sources focusing on charity, prayer, and forgiveness. Grades 3-7.

Oppenheim, Peter A., and Diane E. Berg. *The Yom Kippur Crisis.* Los Angeles, CA: Torah Aura Productions.

In Vilna in 1848, Rabbi Israel Salanter is forced to decide whether to urge his community to observe

Yom Kippur as usual or — in order to prevent the spread of a cholera epidemic — to urge them to break the fast and eat. Grades 6-Adult.

Rosh ha-Shanah. Los Angeles, CA: Torah Aura Productions.

In this Instant Lesson, children learn about the meaning of the holiday's name and about the *shofar*, the *Machzor*, and apples and honey. Separate guide for teachers is called *The Celebrations Lessons Teacher's Guide*. Grades K-2.

Rouss, Sylvia. *Sammy Spider's First Rosh Hashanah*. Rockville, MD: Kar-Ben Copies, Inc., 1996, ISBN 0-929371-98-4.

When he sees the mail carrier deliver greeting cards, Sammy Spider learns that another Jewish holiday is coming. It's Rosh HaShanah, and the Shapiro family is getting ready to celebrate. Grades PK-2.

Springer, Sally. *High Holiday Fun for Little Hands*. Rockville, MD: Kar-Ben Copies, Inc., 1993, ISBN 0-929371-76-3.

The sixteen activities in this book are designed for preschoolers and beginning readers. Parental supervision is necessary. Includes a glossary. Grades PK-2.

Weilerstein, Sadie Rose. *K'tonton's Yom Kippur Adventure*. Philadelphia, PA: Jewish Publication Society, 1995, ISBN 0-8276-0541-2.

A kitchen mishap presents K'tonton (a Jewish Tom Thumb-like character) with a sticky problem as he is preparing for Yom Kippur. Grades PK-3.

Wise, Ira J. *A Long, Penitent Season*. Los Angeles, CA: Torah Aura Productions.

A sticker-based Instant Lesson that helps student learn the major Jewish events in Elul and Tishre, and to uncover the story of repentance locked into the calendar's progression. Grades 2-4.

———. *Missing the Mark*. Los Angeles, CA: Torah Aura Productions.

This Instant Lesson teaches the Jewish understanding of *Chet*, that everyone "misses the mark" sometimes and needs to start again. Grades 4-6.

———. *T'shuvah, She Wrote*. Los Angeles, CA: Torah Aura Productions.

This Instant Lesson uses both case studies and classical texts to make clear the difficult process of *teshuvah*. Grades 4-6.

Yom Kippur. Los Angeles, CA: Torah Aura Productions.

An Instant Lesson that teaches about the meaning of the holiday's name; the idea of *Chet*, missing the mark; *Teshuvah*, repentance; and other Yom Kippur customs. A separate guide for teachers is called *The Celebration Lessons Teacher's Guide*. Grades K-2.

Zalben, Jane Breskin. *Happy New Year, Beni*. New York: Henry Holt and Co., 1993, ISBN 0-8050-1961-8.

Beni and Sara and their extended family are going to their grandparents for the holiday. After constantly fighting with his cousin Max during Rosh HaShanah, Beni discovers that the new year is an opportunity to put his mistakes behind him and start over. Includes a recipe for *challah* and a glossary. Grades PK-2.

For Teachers and Parents

Apisdorf, Shimon. *Rosh Hashanah Yom Kippur Survival Kit*. Columbus, OH: Leviathan Press, 1992, ISBN 1-881927-00-8.

Apisdorf wrote this text for three types of people: those who are not planning to attend High Holy Day services, those planning to attend services and are dreading the experience, and those who already have some sense of the meaning of the two holidays. The author walks the reader through the Rosh HaShanah and Yom Kippur service so that he/she will have an understanding of the prayers before saying them. All Hebrew is transliterated and translated.

Finkel, Avraham Yaakov. *The Essence of the Holy Days: Insights from the Jewish Sages*. Northvale, NJ: Jason Aronson Inc. 1993, ISBN 0-87688-524-6.

This text offers a rich selection of insights on the festivals of the year, from the greatest Jewish teachers of the Talmud, *Midrash*, and other Jewish sources. Each section begins with a description of the historical background and significance of the holiday, as well as concise treatment of laws and customs. Finkel's translations of the words of the sages gives the reader access to material that has not been readily available in English. Includes glossary, bibliography, index of sages, scripture, and subjects.

Olitzky, Kerry M., and Rachel T. Sabeth. *Preparing Your Heart for the High Holy Days*. Philadelphia, PA: Jewish Publication Society, 1996, ISBN 0-8276-0578-1.

Guides one through the preparations during the month before the onset of the High Holy Days and the ten days between Rosh HaShanah and Yom Kippur. Helps the reader turn inward to take a moral and spiritual inventory.

SUKKOT AND SIMCHAT TORAH

For Students

Abrams, Judith Z. *Simchat Torah: A Family Celebration with Consecration Service*. Rockville, MD: Kar-Ben Copies, Inc., 1995, ISBN 0-929371-24-0.

The book begins with a mini-service leading into the Torah service. It ends with the traditional parents' blessing and an explanation of the rituals. For each of the seven *hakafot,* there is an explanation and musical accompaniment. Grades PK-3.

Etrog, Palm, Myrtle, and Willow. A Lifetime of Torah. Los Angeles, CA: Torah Aura Productions.

Using Rabbinic sources and values clarification, inquiry, and personal exploration, this Instant Lesson helps students make meaning of the symbols of Sukkot. Grades 2-4.

Goldin, Barbara Diamond. *Night Lights*. San Diego, CA: Gulliver Books/ Harcourt Brace & Co., 1995, ISBN 0-15-200536-6.

Daniel and his father are building the *sukkah*. Daniel wants to put a real roof on the *sukkah* because he is

afraid of the dark. Since his grandpa is sick, Daniel and his sister Naomi will be sleeping in the *sukkah* all by themselves. As the *sukkah* is built, Daniel learns the history of the holiday. He also is able to overcome his fear of the dark. Grades PK-3.

Goodman, Roberta Louis. *God's Top Ten: The Meaning of the Ten Commandments*. Los Angeles, CA: Torah Aura Productions, 1992, ISBN 0-933873-73-5.

Here you will find an original story for each of the Ten Commandments. A Teacher's Guide is also available. Grades 4-6.

Groner, Judye, and Madeline Wikler. *Sukkot and Simchat Torah Fun*. Rockville, MD: Kar-Ben Copies, Inc., 1993, ISBN 0-929371-77-1.

Young children learn about the holidays through simple craft and activity pages, including making a Simchat Torah flag, seeing what's wrong with the *sukkah*, dot-to-dot activities, and mazes. Features full-color board game. Grades PK-2.

Lepon, Shoshana. *Hillel Builds a House*. Rockville, MD: Kar-Ben Copies, Inc., 1993, ISBN 0-929371-41-0.

Hillel loves to build houses. He wants to light Chanukah candles in his cardboard house until his father tells him it is dangerous. Hillel's Purim costume is a house which gets ruined by the rain. When Sukkot comes, Hillel learns that this is the perfect time to build a house. Includes a glossary. Grades 1-4.

A Lifetime of Torah. Los Angeles, CA: Torah Aura Productions.

This Instant Lesson presents the Jewish life cycle in terms of eight important Torah events: covenant ceremony, consecration, going to a Jewish school, Bar/Bat Mitzvah, Jewish youth group, Jewish summer camp, Confirmation, and adult education. Appropriate for teaching the holidays of Simchat Torah and Shavuot, as well as for life cycle or synagogue. Grades K-2.

Polacco, Patricia. *Tikvah Means Hope*. New York: Bantam Doubleday Dell Publishing Group, 1994, ISBN 0-385-32059-0.

Mr. and Mrs. Roth are building their *sukkah* with help from their young neighbors Justine and Duane. As the holiday approaches, a terrible fire causes them to be evacuated from their homes. When the fire is out and they return to their neighborhood, they find that only the chimneys remain. While the Roths are looking for their cat Tikvah, Justine and Duane find that the *sukkah* is still standing. That evening, as they were eating in the *sukkah*, they heard a tiny sound. It was Tikvah, who had survived the fire. Includes a note about the Oakland fire. Appropriate as a read aloud for younger children. Grades 4 up.

Portnoy, Mindy Avra. *Ima on the Bima: My Mommy Is a Rabbi*. Rockville, MD: Kar-Ben Copies, Inc., 1986, ISBN 0-930494-55-5.

Rebecca calls her mommy 'Ima," but everyone else calls her "Rabbi," because that is her job. Helps young children to understand the Rabbi's role in a variety of settings, at home, and at work. Grades PK-3.

Simhat Torah. Los Angeles, CA: Torah Aura Productions.

In this Instant Lesson, students learn about the Torah and *hakafot*, as well as other Simchat Torah customs. The separate guide for teachers is called *The Celebration Lessons Teacher's Guide*. Grades K-2.

Sukkot. Los Angeles, CA: Torah Aura Productions.

In this Instant Lesson, students follow along and place stickers to learn the history, customs, and meaning of Sukkot. The separate guide for teacher's is called *The Celebration Lessons Teacher's Guide*. Grades K-2.

The Torah. Los Angeles, CA: Torah Aura Productions.

In this Instant Lesson, students learn about how the Torah is written and about the things we use to dress the Torah and show that it is holy. The separate guide for teachers is called *The Celebration Lessons Teacher's Guide*. Grades K-2.

Weilerstein, Sadie Rose. *K'tonton's Sukkot Adventure*. Philadelphia, PA: Jewish Publication Society, 1993, ISBN 0-8276-0502-1.

Once there was a couple who dearly wanted a child. An older woman at synagogue told the wife to eat the end of the *etrog* and that she would have a child. And so it was. K'tonton, no bigger than a thumb, grows and gets into mischief. Includes a glossary. Grades 2-6.

For Teachers and Parents

Strassfeld, Michael. "Shemini Atzeret/Simhat Torah: Reveling with the Torah" In *The Jewish Holidays: A Guide & Commentary*. New York: Harper & Row, Publishers, 1985, pp. 149-159.

Contains an overview of these holidays, traditions, and commentary.

———. "Sukkot: Creating Shelter." In *The Jewish Holidays: A Guide & Commentary*. New York: Harper & Row, Publishers, 1985, pp. 125-147.

An overview of the holiday, including the traditions, rituals, Ushpizin, the Four Species, Chol HaMo'ed, Hoshana Rabbah, activities, food and crafts, and commentary.

Waskow, Arthur. "Dancing with Torah — Simchat Torah." In *Seasons of Our Joy: A Celebration of Modern Jewish Renewal*. Toronto: Bantam Books, 1982, pp. 77-85.

Contains information on origins, present practice, and new approaches.

———. "Harvest Moon — Fulfillment at Sukkot" In *Seasons of Our Joy: A Celebration of Modern Jewish Renewal*. Toronto: Bantam Books, 1982, pp. 47-65.

Contains information on origins, practice, blessing over the *lulav*, biblical readings, Hoshana Rabbah, and food.

———. "Seed for winter — Sh'mini Atzeret." In *Seasons of Our Joy: A Celebration of Modern Jewish Renewal*. Toronto: Bantam Books, 1982, pp. 67-75.

Contains information on origins, present practice, foods, and new approaches.

Video

For Out of Zion. Ergo Media Inc.

A vivid introduction to Torah and its centrality in Jewish life. Special attention is given to the making, ornamentation, and reading of the scroll. Grades 4 up.

CHANUKAH

For Students

Adler, David. *One Yellow Daffodil: A Hanukkah Story*. San Diego, CA: Gulliver Books/Harcourt Brace & Co. 1995, ISBN 0-15-200537-4.

During Chanukah, two children help Morris, a Holocaust survivor, once again to embrace his religious tradition. He tells the children about his experiences during the war years when he was a young man. Also appropriate for Yom HaShoah. Grades 3 up.

Backman, Aidel. *One Night, One Hanukkah Night*. Philadelphia, PA: Jewish Publication Society, 1990, ISBN 0-8276-0368-1.

The same *chanukiah* that shone in a grandparent's home now shines in a modern Jewish home. The book shows both the past and the present. There is a new form of celebration as another candle is added to the *chanukiah* each night of the holiday. Grades PK-2.

Benjamin, Alan. *Chanukah*. New York: Simon & Schuster, 1993, ISBN 0-671-87069-6.

A beginning board book with single sentences and cheery, full-color illustrations describing what one family does on Chanukah. They listen to grandpa tell a story, light the first candle, and more. Ages 1-4.

Channen, Don. *Uh! Oh!: Hidden Object You'll (Almost) Never Find: Hanukkah*. St. Helier, NJ: Yellow Brick Road Press Ltd., 1993, ISBN 0-943706-15-7.

Based on the format of the *Where's Waldo* books, *Uh! Oh!* is an entertaining text. Appropriate for anyone who likes to search and find. Grades K up.

Cohn, Janice. *The Christmas Menorahs: How a Town Fought Hate*. Morton Grove, IL: Albert Whitman & Co., 1995, ISBN 0-8075-11522-8.

On the third night of Chanukah in Billings, Montana, a rock crashes through the window of Isaac Schnitzer's bedroom. The people of Billings show their support to the Schnitzers by hanging *chanukiot* in their windows and on their doors. This action reminds us of the support the Danish people gave the Jews during World War II. Based on events in Billings, Montana in 1993. Grades 3 up.

Conway, Diana Cohn. *Northern Lights: A Hanukkah Story*. Rockville, MD: Kar-Ben Copies, Inc., 1994, ISBN 0-929371-79-8.

When Sara joins her father on medical rounds to remote Eskimo villages, neither foresees missing the first night of Chanukah. A storm grounds their small plane and causes a power outage. Sara spends the evening with a Yupik Eskimo family by the light of an old oil lamp, and she shares the Chanukah story and learns Yupik traditions. Grades 2 up.

Corwin, Judith Hoffman. *Hanukkah Crafts: A Holiday Craft Book*. New York: Watts, 1996, ISBN 0-531-11269-1.

Begins with a history of the holiday and an introduction to crafts, and includes many holiday related projects focusing primarily on the symbols. Grades 3-5.

The December Dilemma: Living in Two Civilizations or Trouble in Short Hills. Los Angeles, CA: Torah Aura Productions.

This Instant lesson deals with the conflict between community interfaith dialogue and the separation of church and state. It is based on a community's deliberations in regard to the public display of a crèche. Grades 6-Adult.

Drucker, Malka. *Grandma's Latkes*. San Diego, CA: Harcourt Brace Jovanovich, 1992, ISBN 0-15-200468-8.

Molly is finally old enough to help her grandmother make *latkes*. As they cook together, Grandma tells Molly the Chanukah story and the significance of *latkes* frying in oil. Includes a *latke* recipe. Grades PK-3.

Frank, Daniel. *Chanukah*. New York: Macmillan/First Aladdin Books, 1993, ISBN 0-689-71733-4.

A square shaped board book with a square shaped hole on every page. The hole stands for something different on each leaf, i.e., on the cover, the square is part of the *dreidel*, and on another page, it is part of a cabinet where the gifts are hidden. Ages 1-3.

Gantz, David. *David's Hanukkah Golem*. Philadelphia, PA: Jewish Publication Society, 1991, ISBN 0-8276- 0380-0.

A frightened boy, hiding from two boys he mistakenly thinks are out to steal the scooter he received as a Chanukah present, is inspired by his grandfather's golem story to fashion a mini-golem for protection. Grades K-4.

Gellman, Ellie. *Jeremy's Dreidel*. Rockville, MD: Kar-Ben Copies, Inc., 1992, ISBN 0-929371-33-X.

Jeremy signs up for a *dreidel* making class at the JCC. He decides to make a Braille *dreidel* for his father, who is blind. Through the making of his *dreidel*, Jeremy's friends learn that being blind is not how you look, but how you see. Includes directions to make three different *dreidels*, instructions to play *dreidel*, and information about Braille. Grades K-4.

Goldin, Barbara Diamond. *While the Candles Burn: Eight Stories for Hanukkah*. New York: Viking, 1996, ISBN 0-670-85875-7.

Eight stories, traditional and original, from different countries and across the generations, which reflect the concepts at the heart of the holiday of

Chanukah; dedication, faith, and religious freedom. Grades 3-7.

Golub, Jane. *Mastering the Hanukkah Brakhot*. Los Angeles, CA: Torah Aura Productions.

An Instant Lesson that helps students recite the Chanukah *brachot* fluently. Grades 3-5.

Gordon, Yosi. *The Tannenbaum's Tree*. Los Angeles: Torah Aura Productions.

An Instant Lesson about a family struggling with the boundary between "appreciating" Christmas and coveting it. Grades 4-8.

Grishaver, Joel Lurie. *The True Story of Chanukah*. Los Angeles, CA: Torah Aura Productions.

An Instant Lesson that presents Chanukah as the evolution of a social struggle between two different groups of Jews. Grades 6-Adult.

Hanukah Kit. Available from A.R.E. Publishing, Inc.

An exciting kit that contains information filled booklets; Chanukah stories; easy recipes; a cassette tape; a board game; an overview and history of Chanukah; ritual, prayers, and readings. All Grades, Families.

Hanukkah Board Game. Los Angeles, CA: Torah Aura Productions.

In this game, the facts of the Chanukah story and the details of observance are woven into personal value statements and basic social perceptions. Grades 4-Adult.

Hanukkah, Oh Hanukkah! Rockville, MD: Kar-Ben Copies, Inc., 1995, ISBN 0-929371-88-7.

An illustrated board book with the words to the song *"Hanukkah, Oh Hanukkah."* The score and words are on the back of the book. Ages 1-3.

Hanukkah — The Story. Los Angeles, CA: Torah Aura Productions.

Through this Instant Lesson, students learn the basics of the Chanukah story. Grades K-2.

Hanukkah — What We Do. Los Angeles, CA: Torah Aura Productions.

This Instant Lesson introduces the major blessings and customs of Chanukah as students stick down eight stickers, one for each of the eight nights. Grades K-2.

Hoyt-Goldsmith, Diane. *Celebrating Hanukkah.* New York: Holiday House, 1996, ISBN 0-8234-1252-0.

A photo-essay in full color about the celebration of the festival of Chanukah in America. In addition to the history, legend, and significance of the holiday, there are instructions for playing *dreidel*, and a *latke* recipe. A very contemporary selection. Grades 2-7.

Jaffe, Nina. *In the Month of Kislev: A Story for Hanukkah.* New York: Viking, 1992, ISBN 0-670-82863-7.

Mendel, his wife, and children lived in a small Polish town. One Chanukah, they were so poor that they were unable to buy even a single potato. Fivel, on the other hand was very wealthy, and also very stingy. He even took Mendel's children to court for smelling his *latkes*. Eventually, Fivel learned an important lesson from Rabbi Jonah about the meaning of giving. Grades PK-3.

Kessler, Raizy. *A Tale of Two Wagons and Other Chanukah Stories.* Lakewood, NJ: C.I.S. Publishers, 1994, ISBN 1-56062-286-5.

The common theme of celebrating Chanukah and lighting the candles serves as inspiration for the characters in the 11 stories of this collection. The setting is Eastern Europe during the first half of the twentieth century. A glossary of Yiddish and Hebrew terms is included. Ashkenazic pronunciation is used. Grades 8 up.

Kimmel, Eric. *The Chanukkah Guest.* New York: Holiday House, 1991, ISBN 0-8234-0788-8.

On the first night of Chanukah, Old Bear wanders into Bubba Brayna's house and receives a delicious helping of potato *latkes* when she mistakes him for the Rabbi.

———. *Asher and the Capmakers: A Hanukkah Story.* New York, Holiday House, 1992, ISBN 0-8234-1031-5.

This fantasy takes place one Chanukah eve in the Carpathian mountains. Asher is on his way to get an egg for the *latke* batter. He gets lost in a snowstorm and finds himself in the home of several capmakers. Asher discovers that these women are more than capmakers as they take him on a journey to Jerusalem. Grades 5 up.

———. *The Spotted Pony: A Collection of Hanukkah Stories.* New York: Holiday House, 1992, ISBN 0-8234-0936-8.

Eight folktales, including stories of King Solomon and his magic ring, a mysterious spotted pony, the trickster Hershel of Ostropol, and a cast of Rabbis, demons, ghosts, and fools. Grades 2-5.

———. *The Magic Dreidels: A Hanukkah Story.* New York: Holiday House, 1996, ISBN 0-8234-1256-3.

Jacob drops his new brass *dreidel* down the well by accident and meets a goblin. Greedy Fruma Sarah foils the boy several times, but with the goblin's help, Jacob gets revenge along with *latkes*, applesauce, and sour cream. At the end is a note about the holiday traditions for adults. The back cover carries instructions for playing *dreidel*. Grades PK-3.

Kimmelman, Leslie. *Hanukkah Lights, Hanukkah Nights.* New York: HarperCollins Publishers, 1992, ISBN 0-06-020368-4.

A counting book describing how an extended family prepares and celebrates Chanukah. Includes an explanation of the history of Chanukah and how the holiday is celebrated today. Grades PK-K.

Kuskin, Karla. *A Great Miracle Happened There: A Chanukah Story.* New York: HarperCollins Publishers, 1993, ISBN 0-06-023618-3.

On the first night of Chanukah, the young narrator of this book invites his friend Henry to join the family celebration. Henry has never seen the Chanukah rituals and asks many questions which prompt a retelling of the Chanukah story. Grades PK-3.

Levine, Arthur. *All the Lights in the Night*. New York: Tambourine/Morrow, 1991, ISBN 0-688-10107-0.

Two boys find a way to celebrate Chanukah as they make their perilous way to Palestine after the Czar's pogrom. The story captures the essence of the holiday in a new setting. Grades 1-5.

Manushkin, Fran. *Latkes and Applesauce: A Hanukkah Story*. New York: Scholastic Books, 1990, ISBN 0-590-42261-8.

The Menashe family was ready to celebrate Chanukah. Suddenly, a blizzard covered all the apples and potatoes, and there was no way to make *latkes* and applesauce. Despite that, they shared what little food they had with some starving stray animals, who later return the favor. Grades PK-3.

Mastering the Hanukkah Brakhot. Los Angeles, CA: Torah Aura Productions.

An Instant Lesson that helps students to learn and master the Chanukah *brachot*. Grades 4-6.

Minelli, Tali Marcus. *Chanukah Fun*. New York: Tupelo/William Morrow, 1996, ISBN 0-688-13560-9.

Lighting the candles, playing the *dreidel* game, and exchanging gifts are all a part of the holiday fun. This book offers stimulating activities for young children to accompany the more traditional activities. Adult supervision required. Grades 1-3.

Moss, Marissa. *The Ugly Menorah*. New York: Farrar, Straus & Giroux, 1996, ISBN 0-374-38027-9.

Weaving together past and present, Moss brings wonderful memories of Grandpa to a little girl's Chanukah celebration. Includes overview of Chanukah for adults. Grades PK-2.

Penn, Malka. *The Miracle of the Potato Latkes*. New York: Holiday House, 1994, ISBN 0-8234-1118-4.

Tanta Golda makes the best *latkes* in all of Russia. This year, due to drought, there is only one tiny potato, but she always said that in times of trouble, God will provide. In the end, Tanta Golda is able to make *latkes* for her family and friends. Grades 3 up.

———. *The Hanukkah Ghosts*. New York: Holiday House, 1995, ISBN 0-8234-1145-1.

A Chanukah story combined with the themes of Holocaust and prejudice, set in an English countryside manor house. High interest, low reading level. Grades 3-5.

Polacco, Patricia. *The Trees of the Dancing Goats*. New York: Simon & Schuster, 1996, ISBN 0-689-80862-3.

During a scarlet fever epidemic one winter in Michigan, a Jewish family helps make Christmas special for their sick neighbors by making their own Chanukah miracle. Grades K-5.

Rojany, Lisa. *Story of Hanukkah: A Lift-the-Flap Rebus Book*. New York: Hyperion, 1993, ISBN 1-56282-420-1.

The story of Chanukah has rebus flaps covering words and four pages of attractive pop-ups in realistic watercolors. Particularly fascinating is the pop-up in which a boy's hand holding the *shammas* moves down to light the *chanukiah* when the page is turned. Grades PK-3.

Rosen, Michael. *Elijah's Angel*. San Diego, CA: Harcourt Brace Jovanovich, 1992, ISBN 0-15-225394-7.

Michael, a Jewish nine year old, and Elijah, a Christian black man in his eighties, are friends. Michael likes to visit Elijah at his barbershop and watch him cut hair and carve items out of wood. Elijah shows his affection for Michael by giving him a carved angel for Christmas. This bothers Michael because he is Jewish. His parents explain that the angel is a gift of friendship. Michael reciprocates by giving Elijah a *chanukiah* he made at Hebrew school. Grades 4 up.

Rosenberg, Amye. *Melly's Menorah: A Hanukkah Story*. New York: Simon & Schuster, 1991, ISBN 0-671-74495-X.

When this Jewish beaver family's Chanukah *menorah* is lost in their move to a new house, little Melly's cookie dough *menorah* saves the day. Includes 50 full-color pull off stickers. Grades PK-1.

Ross, Kathy. *Crafts for Chanukah*. Brookfield, CT: Millbrook Press, 1997, ISBN 0-7613-0078-3.

Draws on Chanukah themes and also ideas for the year round, such as the *Magen David* and *kipah*. Some projects are actually games. Most activities call for adult supervision. Grades 2-5.

Ruedor, Illustrator. *The Doodle Family Hanukkah*. Huntington Beach, CA: Atara Publishing, 1996, ISBN 0-885511-114.

The Israeli author/illustrator presents Chanukah to the MTV generation with a comic-strip family posing as a typical American-Jewish family. The story of Chanukah is presented in 19 fun-filled, clever chapters. Yiddish and Hebrew words appear as integral to the story. Grades 2 up.

Rothenberg, Joan. *Inside-Out Grandma*. New York: Hyperion Books, 1995, ISBN 0-7868-0107-7.

Rosie wants to know why Grandma is wearing her clothes inside out. As Grandma explains, it is so that she remembers to buy oil in which to fry the *latkes*. Rosie thinks this is strange, but as Grandma continues, it all makes sense to Rosie. Includes a *latke* recipe. Appropriate as a read aloud for younger children. Grades 2 up.

Rouss, Sylvia A. *Sammy Spider's First Hanukkah*. Rockville, MD: Kar-Ben Copies, Inc., 1993, ISBN 0-929371-45-3.

Sammy Spider wants to spin a *dreidel*. His mother tells him that spiders spin webs. In this colorful counting book, Sammy learns about Chanukah, and in the end, gets to spin like a *dreidel*. Appropriate as a read aloud for younger children. Grades PK-1.

Scharfstein, Sol. *Are You Ready for Hanukah?: A Hanukah Surprise Book*. Hoboken, NJ: KTAV Publishing House, 1992, ISBN 0-87068-475-4.

A brightly illustrated picture book for parents to read with their young children. There is a surprise text on each page. Grades PK-1.

Schnur, Steven. *The Tie Man's Miracle: A Chanukah Tale*. New York: Morrow Junior Books, 1995, ISBN 0-688-13463.

On the last night of Chanukah, Mr. Hoffman, the tie man, stops at Seth's home. Mr. Hoffman joins the family in lighting the *chanukiah*. After the lighting, Seth learns that Mr. Hoffman's family perished in the Holocaust. Mr. Hoffman also tells the family that when all nine candles go out at the same time, a person's wishes are carried straight to the ear of God. Grades 4 up.

Schotter, Roni. *Hanukkah*. New York: Little Brown, 1990, ISBN 0-316-77466-9.

Describes the meaning and traditions of Chanukah as five young children and their family celebrate the holiday with all its special traditions, from the lighting of the *chanukiah* to making and spinning the *dreidel*, to the singing of songs and the eating of *latkes*. Grades PK-3.

Springer, Sally. *Let's Make Latkes*. Rockville, MD: Kar-Ben Copies, Inc., 1991, ISBN 0-929371-58-5.

With a text of five verbs and brightly colored figures, this board book is most suitable for toddlers and even babies. Ages 1-3.

Topek, Susan Remick. *A Turn for Noah*. Rockville, MD: Kar-Ben Copies, Inc., 1992, ISBN 0-929371-37-2.

Noah is having a hard week at nursery school. He has trouble learning to spin the *dreidel*, he spilled his paint cup, and his donut dripped on his new shirt. At the end of the week, Noah has success and spins the *dreidel*. Grades PK-K.

Trouble in Jewish Cheyenne. Los Angeles, CA: Torah Aura Productions.

This Instant Lesson allows students and teachers to confront responses to anti-Semitism and to apply Jewish values to those responses. Grades 6-Adult.

Weiss, Nicki. *The First Night of Hanukkah*. New York: Grosset & Dunlap, 1992, ISBN 0-448-40389-7.

As preparations are made for the first night of Chanukah, Uncle Dan tells Molly the story of Chanukah. Appropriate as a read aloud for younger children. Grades 3 up.

Zalben, Jane Breskin. *Papa's Latkes*. New York: Henry Holt, 1994, ISBN 0-8050-3099-9.

Mama Bear doesn't feel like making *latkes* this year, so Papa and the little bears have a *latke* making contest. Includes the music for *"O Chanukah"* and a *latke* recipe. Grades 1-5.

Ziefert, Harriet. *What is Hanukkah?* New York: HarperCollins Publishers, 1994, ISBN 0-694-00483-9.

As Josh helps his parents prepare for Chanukah, he learns the rituals and history of the holiday. A Lift-the-Flap Story. Appropriate as a read aloud for younger children. Grades PK-2.

Zwerin, Raymond A., and Audrey Friedman Marcus. *Like a Maccabee*. New York: UAHC Press, 1991, ISBN 8074-0445-4.

This beautifully illustrated book explores the themes of leadership, bravery, determination, problem solving, and pride through the story of the Maccabees and Chanukah. Young readers will learn to be *like a Maccabee*. Grades PK-3.

For Teachers and Parents

Berman, Nancy. *The Art of Hanukkah*. Southport CT: Hugh Lauter Levin (Distributed by Simon & Schuster), 1996, ISBN 0-88363-046-X.

Chanukiot, paintings, *dreidels* — all symbols of the joyous holiday — are gathered from around the world and across the years — and brought together in this visually beautiful book featuring 48 masterpieces. They tell the story of the desecration of the Holy Temple, its subsequent reclaiming and rededication, and how the holiday has been carried by the Jewish people to every area of the Diaspora throughout the ages.

Ganzfried, Solomon. *Code of Jewish Law: Kitzur Schulhan Aruch*. Hyman E. Goldin, trans. New York: Hebrew Publishing Co., 1963, ISBN 0-88482-423-3.

The comprehensive compilation of Jewish laws and customs related to every facet of traditional Jewish observance.

Modesitt, Jeanne. *Songs of Chanukah*. Boston, MA: Little Brown & Co., 1992, ISBN 0-316-57739-1.

The Chanukah blessings and 13 songs, both traditional and contemporary, make up this collection. The music, for piano and guitar, includes Hebrew and English lyrics. Each song is accompanied by an explanation of an aspect of Chanukah.

Olitzky, Kerry M. *Eight Nights, Eight Lights: Family Values for Each Night of Hanukkah*. Los Angeles: Alef Design Group, 1994, ISBN 0-831283-08-9.

Eight chapters are divided into three sections: Learning; Doing; and Sacred Sources for Inspiration and Insight. A practical and spiritual guide to Chanukah for the family. Includes blessings in Hebrew and English, recipes, glossary, and sources for further reflection.

Schram, Peninnah, and Steven Rosman. *Eight Tales for Eight Nights*. Northvale, NJ: Jason Aronson Inc., 1990, ISBN 0-87668-234-4.

The authors have gathered stories from the many corners of the Jewish world that reflect the customs and traditions of our people through the ages. They are meant to be read by adults to children as they celebrate the holiday together. There are love stories and humorous stories, some from Eastern Europe, from the Holocaust, from the Marrano community, and more.

Schwartz, Cherie Karo. *My Lucky Dreidel: Hanukkah Stories, Songs, Poems, Crafts, Recipes, and Fun for Kids.* New York: Smithmark, 1994, ISBN 0-8317-6285-3.

The eight chapters of this book highlight holiday themes: light, family, freedom, challenge, rededication, miracle, hope, and peace. Each chapter is filled with information and activities: a story, poem, songs, a recipe, a craft, and folklore from Jewish communities worldwide. A book for the whole family. Includes a glossary, bibliography, and index.

Wax, Wendy. *Hanukkah, Oh, Hanukkah! A Treasury of Stories, Songs and Games to Share.* New York: Bantam Books, 1993, ISBN 0-533-09551-X.

As the title indicates, this text is chock full of crafts, stories, songs, poems, games, dances, and recipes. All Hebrew is transliterated. Music accompanies all songs. For parents to enjoy with their children.

Wolfson, Ron. *The Art of Jewish Living: Hanukkah.* Woodstock, VT: Jewish Lights Publishing, 1990, reprinted 1996, ISBN 1-879045-97-4.

A guide to celebration covering the origins of Chanukah, the customs, blessings, songs, and recipes. A section titled "December Dilemma" discusses how a Jewish family copes with Christmas.

Audiocassettes

Chanukah: A Singing Celebration. Cindy Paley. Sounds Write Productions.

Twenty contemporary and traditional Chanukah songs in English and Hebrew. All Ages.

Happy Chanukah! A Collection of Holiday Songs. Fran Avni. Available from A.R.E. Publishing, Inc.

Joyous interpretations of traditional holiday songs. All Ages.

Just in Time for Chanukah. Margie Rosenthal and Ilene Safyan. Available from A.R.E. Publishing, Inc.

This tape of festive songs to enrich the Chanukah celebration was recommended by the American Library Association. All Ages.

Miracles and Wonders. Debbie Friedman. Available from A.R.E. Publishing, Inc.

Two complete musicals, one for Chanukah and one for Purim, including instructions for stage setting, performance notes, scripts, melody line, and chords. All Ages.

Videos

Benjamin and the Miracle of Hanukkah. 24 min. color. Ergo Media Inc.

The story of the arduous journey of a young boy sent by Judah Maccabee to obtain oil for the Temple light. Narrated by Herschel Bernardi. Grades PK-4.

A Hanukah Celebration. 25 min. color. Ergo Media Inc.

Mike Burstyn and his puppet friends introduce the meaning and symbols of the holiday through story and song. Includes the candle lighting ritual and playing *dreidel.* Grades PK-6.

Lights: A Hanukah Fable. 24 min. color. Ergo Media Inc.

A retelling of the Chanukah story through animation and music. Narration by Judd Hirsch. Also available in Russian language version. Grades PK-6.

In the Month of Kislev. 12 min. color. Weston Woods Studios, Inc.

Produced by Nina Jaffe and narrated by Theodore Bikel, this video is about a wealthy, arrogant merchant who learns the true meaning of Chanukah when he takes the family of a poor peddler to court for savoring the smell of his wife's *latkes* from outside their window. Grades PK-4.

CD-ROMs

Hanukah Activity Center. Windows. Davka Corporation.

Celebrating and learning about the holiday will be aided by this CD-ROM intended for families. Eight activities including *Dreidel Drama,* in which one can spin the *dreidel* in the traditional way or try one's luck at new games. Grades 1 up.

The Hyperhanukkah. Mac only. Jewish Software Center.

A program that brings the traditions of the holiday to life with graphics, digital sound, and animation. Also includes art and cooking activities. Grades 2 up.

TU B'SHEVAT

Note: For the most complete description of Tu B'Shevat materials, write to the Department of Education of the Jewish National Fund for a catalog of free items, some of which are listed below.

For Students

Appelman, Harlene, and Jane Shapiro. *A Seder for Tu B'Shevat*. Rockville, MD: Kar-Ben Copies, Inc., 1984, ISBN 0-930494-39-3.

This Tu B'Shevat *Seder* traces the history of the New Year for Trees and highlights the importance of conservation and ecology today. Features stories, readings, blessings, fruit tasting, and seed planting. All Ages.

Cone, Molly. *Listen to the Trees*. New York: UAHC Press, 1995, ISBN 0-8074-0536-1.

Through quotations from Torah and Rabbinic sources, this text provides a view of the Jewish connection to the natural world and shows that taking care of the earth is an important part of Judaism. Grades 6 up.

Gershator, Phyllis. *Honi's Circle of Trees*. Philadelphia, PA: Jewish Publication Society, 1994, ISBN 0-8276-0511-0.

Honi the Circle Maker is a wanderer and a doer of good deeds. He plants carob seeds for the future generations who will enjoy the fruit of those trees. One day, after planting carobs, Honi takes a nap, to wake up 70 years later. Honi comes to realize that God has given him the gift of seeing the carob trees bear fruit. Grades 3 up.

Kirschen, Ya'akov. *Trees: The Green Testament*. New York: Vital Media Enterprises, 1993, ISBN 0-9641252-1-8.

Kirschen, famous for the Shuldig and his dog Doobie cartoons, uses the same format to tell the history of the Land of Israel and the Jewish people through the eyes of the trees. The text explores the Jewish people's connection with the Land of Israel and the importance of trees to the land. Grades 5 up.

Sasso, Sandy Eisenberg. *A Prayer for the Earth: The Story of Naamah, Noah's Wife*. Woodstock, VT: Jewish Lights Publishing, 1997, ISBN 1-879045-60-5.

Naamah, Noah's wife, was asked to save a sample of each plant on earth before the flood. The real work begins when she returns the plants to earth. The story inspires children, and adult, too, to care for earth's garden. A fitting Tu B'Shevat message. Grades PK-3.

Tu BiShvat. Los Angeles, CA: Torah Aura Productions.

This Instant Lesson presents a wonderful story and a series of beautiful paper tears to introduce the holiday. The separate guide for teachers is called *The Celebration Lessons Teacher's Guide*. Grades K-2.

Zalben, Jane Breskin. *Pearl Plants a Tree*. New York: Simon & Schuster Books for Young Readers, 1995, ISBN 0-689-80034-7.

When Pearl joins her grandfather to see his first home in America, she is shown the apple tree that he planted. Pearl is inspired by this to plant her own tree. When spring arrives, Pearl and her grandfather plant her tree in the yard, imagining the day when Pearl will show it to her grandchildren. A delightful story. The author includes pages on tree planting holidays, Tu B'Shevat, *midrashim*, and how to grow a tree. Ages 3-6.

For Teachers and Parents

Bernstein, Ellen, and Dan Fink. *Let the Earth Teach You Torah*. Wyncote, PA: Shomrei Adamah, 1992.

An excellent resource that explores biological and ecological concepts within the context of Jewish tradition and values. Grades 9 up.

Fisher, Adam. S*eder Tu Bishevat: The Festival of Trees*. New York: CCAR Press, 1989, 0-88123-008-1.

Contains two *Sedarim*, one for adults and children of various ages and one designed specifically for younger children. Both mark the observance of Tu B'Shevat and celebrate Judaism's appreciation of the larger cycles of nature as the work of God. Ideal for congregational and family use.

Stein, David E., ed. *A Garden of Choice Fruits: 200 Classic Jewish Quotes on Human Beings and the Environment*. Wyncote, PA: Shomrei Adamah, 1991, ISBN 0-9632-848-0-0.

A valuable resource for teachers. Quotes are fully referenced and organized into ten categories, such as wise land use, trees, and farming.

Audiocassettes

Daisies and Ducklings. Fran Avni. Available from A.R.E. Publishing, Inc.

Cheerful songs and strories about the environment. Grades PK-3.

Guarding the Garden: A Journey from Eden to the Edge. Sounds Write Productions.

This musical play is about Judaism and the environment. It features lively, thought provoking songs and stars Lilith, Eve, Adam, and God and *Shechinah*. Grades 7 up.

Shalom BaAretz — Nature Songs. Chaim Parchi. Tara Publications.

Composer-musician Chaim Parchi celebrates the nature and Land of Israel with a group of songs perfect for Tu B'shevat celebrations or nature/ecology awareness programs. All Ages.

Video

Grandpa's Tree. 24 min. color. Ergo Media Inc.

An American Jewish student comes to Israel to locate his grandfather's tree, planted a half century earlier. In the course of his search, we learn about Israel today. Grades 4 up.

PURIM

For Students

Gettinger, Shifrah. *A Very Special Gift*. Brooklyn, NY: Hachai Publications, Inc., 1993, ISBN 0-922613-52-4.

Gali wanted to buy a present for her mother. She decided on a special *hamentashen* plate and decorated the plate with pictures of the Purim story. Her mother loved the gift. When the plate broke, Gali took the pieces and made a *gragger* for her mother. Grades 1-5.

Goldin, Barbara Diamond. *Cakes and Miracles: A Purim Tale*. New York: Viking, 1991, ISBN 0-670-83047-X.

The story about a blind boy who can "see" with his mind. With this talent, he is able to help his mother with the Purim goodies. Grades PK-2.

The Gonzo Megillah Game. Los Angeles, CA: Torah Aura Productions.

This Instant Lesson helps students master the full complexity of the Purim story and learn some lessons from it. Grades 6-Adult.

Nerlove, Miriam. *Purim*. Morton Grove, IL: Albert Whitman & Co., 1992, ISBN 0-8075-6682-9.

A read aloud story in rhyme. A young boy finds his Purim costume and describes what happens at the synagogue on Purim eve. Includes the history of Purim and how it is celebrated. Grades K-2.

Our Purim Problem. Los Angeles, CA: Torah Aura Productions.

This Instant Lesson contrasts the value of celebrating *"Ad de-Lo Yada"* with concerns about substance abuse. Grades 4-6.

Purim Fun for Little Hands. Rockville, MD: Kar-Ben Copies, Inc., 1994, ISBN 0-929371-48-8.

The activities are designed for preschoolers and beginning readers and consist of coloring, cut and paste, games, and dot-to-dots. For children to do on their own or with help from their parents. Grades PK-3.

Purim Megillah. Los Angeles, CA: Torah Aura Productions.

Through this Instant Lesson, students make their own *Megillot.* The separate guide for teachers is called *The Celebration Lessons Teacher's Guide.* Grades K-2.

Purim — The Story. Los Angeles, CA: Torah Aura Productions.

In this Instant Lesson, an intergenerational cast of actors act out the Purim story. The separate guide for teachers is called *The Celebration Lessons Teacher's Guide.* Grades K-2.

Purim — What We Do. Los Angeles, CA: Torah Aura Productions.

An Instant Lesson that teaches the customs of Purim. The separate guide for teachers is called *The Celebration Lessons Teacher's Guide.* Grades K-2.

Topek, Susan Remick. *A Costume for Noah.* Rockville, MD: Kar-Ben Copies, Inc., 1995, ISBN 0-929371-91-7.

Noah's classmates have planned their Purim costumes, but Noah's costume isn't ready because his household is too preoccupied with the arrival of a new baby. But, in the end, Noah's costume appears just in time. Grades K-3.

Two Mitzvot of Giving. Los Angeles, CA: Torah Aura Productions.

This Instant Lesson shows how *Shelach Manot* and *Matanot l'Evyonim* came to be important Jewish practices. Grades 4-6.

Wolkstein, Diane. *Esther's Story.* New York: Morrow Junior Books, 1996, ISBN 0-688-12127-6.

Written in diary form, Esther describes how she became queen and foiled Haman's terrible plan to kill the Jews of Persia. The author uses the biblical Book of Esther, and oral legends to retell the Purim story from Esther's point of view. Grades 3-7.

Zwerin, Raymond A., and Audrey Friedman Marcus. *A Purim Album.* New York: UAHC Press, 1981, ISBN 0-8074-0154-4.

This charming book tells the traditional story of Purim and a new tale about the personal experience of a young girl who plays the part of Esther in her school play. Grades PK-3.

For Teachers and Parents

Strassfeld, Michael. "Purim: Self-Mockery and Masquerade." In *The Jewish Holidays: A Guide & Commentary.* New York: Harper & Row, Publishers, 1985, pp. 187-199.

An overview of the holiday, including the story, traditions, special Purims, food and crafts, and commentary.

Waskow, Arthur. "Spring Fever — Purim." In *Seasons of Our Joy: A Celebration of Modern Jewish Renewal.* Toronto: Bantam Books, 1982, pp. 115-131.

Contains information on origins, practice, songs and food, and meaning of the holiday, as well as new approaches.

Audiocassette

Latkes and Hamentashen. Fran Avni. Available from A.R.E. Publishing, Inc.

Brings to life in song and story the people who symbolize Chanukah (Side 1) and Purim (Side 2). Grades PK-3.

Miracles and Wonders. Debbie Friedman. Available from A.R.E. Publishing, Inc.

Two complete musicals, one for Chanukah and one for Purim, including instructions for stage setting, performance notes, scripts, melody line, and chords. All Ages.

PESACH

For Students

Atlas, Susan. *Passover Passage*. Los Angeles, CA: Torah Aura Productions, 1991, ISBN 0-933873-46-8.

Rebecca Abel is having a most memorable Passover sailing the Caribbean with her grandparents aboard their sailing ship, the Diaspora. She learns not only how a *Seder* is celebrated on the open seas, but also about freedom, family, and Judaism. Grades 2-5.

Backman, Aidel. *Pesach 1-2-3: A Passover Mitzvah Book*. Brooklyn, NY: Mesorah Publications, Ltd., 1992, ISBN 0-89906-988-6.

The numbers 1 to10 help explain many aspects of the Passover story and ritual. Ashkenazic pronunciation is used. Definitions of Passover terms are provided for the adult reader. Grades PK-2.

Bat-Ami, Miriam. *Dear Elijah*. Philadelphia, PA: Jewish Publication Society, 1994, ISBN 0-8276-0592-7.

Rebecca's father is hospitalized and she is distressed that he can't be with the family for Passover. She bears her soul to Elijah the prophet in a series of

letters which address issues of importance to girls entering their teens. Grades 4-8.

Bogot, Howard I., and Mary K. Bogot. *Seder with the Animals*. New York: CCAR Press, 1995, ISBN 0-88123-067-7.

This volume, with its playful rhymes and fantastic images, provides a perfect way to introduce the youngest *Seder* guests to the magical themes and wonders of the celebration. Grades PK-2.

Bogot, Howard I., and Robert J. Orkand. *A Children's Haggadah*. New York: CCAR Press, 1995, ISBN 0-88123-059-6.

An egalitarian *Haggadah* which can be used at home or in a school setting. Appropriate for families with young children. This *Haggadah* is accessible to those with a limited knowledge of Passover. Holiday songs, with musical notations, are translated and transliterated. Grades 2-5.

Cohen, Barbara. *Make a Wish Molly*. New York: Doubleday, 1994. ISBN 0-385-31079-X.

By the author of the award-winning *Molly's Pilgrim*, this wonderful story is about a Jewish child, new to America, who celebrates her birthday during Passover. She wants her party to be very special, as a sign of accommodation to the ways of this new culture. But how can she have a birthday cake during Passover? Grades 3-6.

dePaola, Tomie. *My First Passover*. New York: Putnam, 1991, ISBN 0-399-21784-3.

A board book with basic concepts and vocabulary for young children. The illustrations of the Passover symbols introduce the holiday. Ages 1-3.

Drucker, Malka, and Michael Halpern. *Jacob's Rescue*. New York: Bantam Books, 1993, ISBN 0-553-08976-5.

Young Marissa wants to know why Alex and Mela Roslan have joined her family for the Passover *Seder*. She is told the story of how the Roslans hid her father and uncle in their Warsaw home during the Holocaust and saved their lives at great risk to their own. Marissa is also told that the Israeli government will bestow the Righteous among the Nations award to the Roslans. Also appropriate for Yom HaShoah. Grades 5 up.

Fifteen Steps to Freedom. Los Angeles, CA: Torah Aura Productions.

An Instant Lesson that uses the 15 steps in the *Seder* as a way of explaining the *Seder* as a spiritual journey. Grades 6-Adult.

Fluek, Toby Knobel, and Lillian Fluek Finkler. *Passover As I Remember It*. New York: Alfred A. Knopf, 1994, ISBN 0-679-83876-7.

The author describes how her family prepared for and celebrated Passover in the years before World War II while living in Czernica, a small Polish village. Grades K-5.

Gikow, Louise. *Kippi and the Missing Matzah: A Sesame Street Passover*. New York: Comet International/ Children's Television Workshop, 1994.

Kippi, the porcupine, on a visit from Israel's *Sesame Street*, invites his friends to a Passover *Seder*, but first they must find the *matzah* stolen by Oscar the Grouch. An accompanying audiocassette, *Shalom Sesame Sing-along Songs for Passover*, contains a narration of this story, an activity book, a board game, and a card game. Grades PK-1.

Goldin, Barbara Diamond. *The Magician's Visit: A Passover Tale*. New York: Viking, 1993, ISBN 0-670-84840-9.

On the night of the first *Seder*, a guest appears at the door of a poor couple, bringing with him all that is needed for the Passover holiday. An adaptation of the I. L. Peretz story, written in 1904, which tells how Elijah, in the guise of a magician, comes to the aid of a poor and pious couple at the time of the *Seder*. Appropriate as a read aloud for younger children. Grades 2 up.

Heymsfeld, Carla. *The Matzah Ball Fairy*. New York: UAHC Press, 1996, ISBN 0-8074-0600-7.

Frieda Pinsky wants her *matzah* balls to be light and fluffy. Instead, they are heavy as stones. All is not

lost as the *matzah* ball fairy comes to Frieda's rescue and gives her a magic potion which will make the *matzah* balls light and fluffy. At the *Seder* meal, after eating the *matzah* balls, the members of the Pinsky family rise up in the air like balloons and float through the house. The *matzah* ball fairy returns and finds the perfect antidote. Grades 4 up.

Kimmelman, Leslie. *Hooray! It's Passover!* New York: HarperCollins Publishers, 1996, ISBN 0-06-024673-1.

A read aloud book for parents and their children describing the activities that take place during the *Seder*. Includes a summary of the Passover story. Grades PK-1.

Krulik, Nancy. *Penny and the Four Questions*. New York: Scholastic Books, 1993, ISBN 0-590-46339-X.

Penny is so excited about reciting the four questions at her first *Seder* until she learns that Natasha, a recent immigrant from Russia, will be saying them. Penny changes her mind as she learns more about the difficult life Natasha had in Russia. In the process, Penny makes a new friend. Grades 3 up.

Mamet, David. *Passover*. New York: St. Martin's Press, 1995, ISBN 0-312-13141-0.

A grandmother and granddaughter are cooking for the *Seder*. As they prepare the meal, the grandmother reminds the girl of the significance of each dish, and begins to retell the Passover story. She also tells her granddaughter how her family survived the Polish pogroms. Grades 8 up.

Manushkin, Fran. *The Matzah That Papa Brought Home*. New York: Scholastic Inc., 1995, ISBN 0-590-47146-5.

Inspired by the Passover song *"Chad Gadya,"* this rhythmic tale describes how one family prepares for and celebrates the *Seder*. Includes a glossary of *Seder* vocabulary. Grades 3 up.

Markovic, Debra, and Lisa Rauchwerger. *Seder Symbols and Their Stories*. Los Angeles, CA: Torah Aura Productions.

An Instant Lesson that introduces the basic symbols of the *Seder*: wine, *matzah*, *charoset*, shank bone, bitter herbs, roasted egg, greens, salt water, and Elijah's cup. Grades K-2.

Mastering the Four Questions. Los Angeles, CA: Torah Aura Productions.

An Instant Lesson excerpted from *The Words Know the Way* helps students polish their performance and understanding of the Four Questions. Grades 3-7.

Passover — The Story. Los Angeles, CA: Torah Aura Productions.

In this Instant Lesson, the story of Passover emerges through the symbols of the *Seder*. The separate guide for teachers is called *The Celebration Lessons Teacher's Guide*. Grades K-2.

Passover — What We Do. Los Angeles, CA: Torah Aura Productions.

Through this Instant Lesson, students learn the names of the items found on the *Seder* table. The separate guide for teachers is called *The Celebration Lessons Teacher's Guide*. Grades K-2.

Polacco, Patricia. *Mrs. Katz and Tush*. New York: Bantam Books, 1992, ISBN 0-553-08122-5.

A Passover story about an elderly Jewish woman, an African-American child, and a cat. Grades PK-3.

Portnoy, Mindy Avra. *Matzah Ball: A Passover Story*. Rockville, MD: Kar-Ben Copies, Inc., 1994, ISBN 0-929371-68-2.

Larry invites Aaron to an Orioles baseball game. A problem arises as the event is during Passover and Aaron will have to bring his lunch. This upsets Aaron because he doesn't like to feel different from his non-Jewish friends. At the game, Aaron gives his lunch to his buddies. When they go to the concession stand, an older man sits next to Aaron and tells him that when he was a kid, he took a Passover lunch to Ebbets Field. While the two were sitting together, a ball is hit and Aaron catches it. Perhaps it was Elijah? How else would the older man know Aaron's name. Grades 4 up.

Schotter, Roni. *Passover Magic*. Boston, MA: Little Brown & Co., 1995, ISBN 0-316-77468-5.

Molly and Ben prepare for Passover and the *Seder*. When Uncle Harry arrives at the house, there's no telling what will happen, especially when its time to search for the *Afikoman*. Includes an explanation of the Passover story. Grades 2 up.

Schram, Peninnah. *Elijah's Mysterious Ways*. Los Angeles, CA: Torah Aura Productions.

This Instant Lesson gives students an opportunity to discuss the difficult questions that seem to have no answer, such as why bad things happen, and why people often seem to receive rewards and punishments they don't deserve. Grades 4-6.

Silberman, Shoshana. *A Family Haggadah*. Rockville, MD: Kar-Ben Copies, Inc., 1987, 0-930494-66-0.

A *Haggadah* that, through discussion questions and activities, encourages the active participation of everyone at the *Seder*. Ideal for families with young children. Grades PK-4, Families.

———. *A Family Haggadah 2*. Rockville, MD: Kar-Ben Copies, Inc., 1997, ISBN 0-929371-968.

An all-new *Haggadah* for families whose children are preteens and older. Distinguished from the original volume by different commentaries and activities and an expanded story of Passover. Grades 5-Adult.

Sonnenfeld, Leah. *My Pesach Play and Learn Book*. Translated and adapted by J. Bennet from *Iton-li*, a monthly Hebrew magazine. Jerusalem: Feldheim Publishers, 1993.

An activity book with stories, riddles, rhymes, cut and paste, and puzzles. Uses Ashkenazic pronunciation. Grades 2 up.

Swartz, Leslie. *A First Passover*. New York: Simon & Schuster, 1992, ISBN 0-8136-2305-7.

Jasha remembers how he and his family secretly celebrated Passover in the Soviet Union. One day, the family receives permission to leave and go to America. Jasha compares his leaving to the Exodus from Egypt. He also compares celebrating Passover in America with the way his family celebrated in the Soviet Union. Includes a glossary. *A First Passover* is part of the *Multicultural Celebrations* series

developed under the auspices of The Children's
Museum, Boston. Grades 2 up.

Topek, Susan Remick. *A Taste for Noah*. Rockville, MD:
Kar-Ben Copies, Inc., 1993, ISBN 0-929371-39-9.

Noah is having a hard week at nursery school. His
class is getting ready for Passover by preparing all
that they will need for the *Seder*. Noah is worried
because he doesn't like *charoset*. Noah's friends help
him discover that *charoset* tastes good! Grades PK-1.

Ziefert, Harriet. *What Is Passover?* New York: Harper-
Collins Publishers, 1994, ISBN 0-694-00482-0.

As Jake helps his parents prepare for Passover, he
learns the rituals and history of the holiday. A Lift-
the-Flap Story. Grades PK-2.

For Teachers and Parents

Apisdorf, Shimon. *Passover Survival Kit*. Columbus, OH:
Leviathan Press, 1994, ISBN 1-881927-01-6.

Apisdorf walks the reader through the *Haggadah*
and *Seder* experience. All Hebrew is translated and
transliterated. The author's goal is to transform the
Seder into an experience of personal growth and
spiritual insight.

———. *The Survival Kit Family Haggadah*. Columbus,
OH: Leviathan Press, 1997, ISBN 1-881927-11-3.

This selection incorporates three elements that set it
apart: the Matzahbrei family that guides one
through the *Seder* experience, the "talking *Haggadah*" translation with 1990s English usage and
explanations, and a running commentary to the text
in question and answer format.

Bronstein, Herbert, ed. *A Passover Haggadah*. 2d rev. ed.
New York: CCAR Press, 1992, ISBN 0-916694-
05-4.

This gender sensitive, revised edition of the now classic
Baskin Haggadah features 23 original, full-color
watercolors by Leonard Baskin. It contains a
complete service for the *Seder*, an extensive song
section, and supplemental readings and meditations.
Also available in a Russian-Hebrew edition.

Cohen, Jeffrey. *1001 Questions and Answers on Passover*.
Northvale, NJ: Jason Aronson Inc., 1996, ISBN
1-56821-523-1.

A comprehensive look at Passover including background and ritual. Presented in an easy-to-use
question and answer format for the contemporary
reader. It serves as a reference guide as the author
addresses the laws and customs of the holiday, along
with their historical and sociological evolution.

Friedland, Susan R. *The Passover Table: New and
Traditional Recipes for Your Seders and the Entire
Passover Week*. New York: HarperPerennial, 1994,
ISBN 0-06-095062-9.

This cookbook is full of Passover information.
History, rituals, and over 40 recipes are included.
Sephardic and Ashkenazic traditions are represented.

Goldin, Barbara Diamond. *The Passover Journey: A Seder
Companion*. New York: Viking, 1994, ISBN 0-670-
82421-6.

Biblical and *midrashic* texts are used to tell the story
of the Exodus. The second part of the text describes
how Passover is celebrated today with a description
of the fourteen parts of the *Seder*. Customs from
other lands are included. Most Hebrew is transliterated. A glossary with a pronunciation guide is
provided.

Heine, Heinrich. *The Rabbi of Bachrach*. New York:
Schocken Books, 1947, o.p.

While conducting the *Seder*, the Rabbi sees the body
of a child beneath the table. The novella deals with
the escape by the Rabbi and his followers. While
out of print, the book can be found in many
libraries.

Rabinowicz, Rachel Anne. *Passover Haggadah: The Feast
of Freedom*. New York: The Rabbinical Assembly,
1982, ISBN 0-87068-782-4.

Bright illustrations and comprehensive commentary
mark this *Haggadah*, published by the national
organization of Conservative Rabbis.

A Passover Haggadah. With comments by Elie Wiesel. Illus. By Mark Podwal. New York: Simon & Schuster, 1993, ISBN 0-671-73541-1.

Wiesel presents a poetic translation of the Hebrew text, enhancing its meaning with personal reflections including a reminiscence of a *Seder* conducted in whispers in his Nazi occupied hometown, a poem about Passover in a concentration camp, and thoughts on Israel and the Middle East. The historical significance of each *Seder* ritual is discussed.

Steingroot, Ira. *Keeping Passover: Everything You Need to Know to Bring the Ancient Tradition to Life and to Create Your Own Passover Celebration*. New York: HarperSanFrancisco, 1995, ISBN 0-06-067553-5.

An outstanding text for those who want to understand the rationale behind the observances and who want to create or add to their Passover experience. Written for those familiar with the *Seder* and those who are beginners. Hebrew, Aramaic, Yiddish, and Ladino are transliterated. Includes a calendar of Passover dates through 2012, recipes, glossary, and extensive bibliography of *Haggadot*, background books, sheet music, and recordings.

Wolfson, Ron. *The Art of Jewish Living: The Passover Seder*. Woodstock, VT: Jewish Lights Publishing, reissued 1996. ISBN 1-879045-95-8.

Dr. Wolfson presents a unique approach to making the *Seder* experience a meaningful one for both the liberal and traditional minded Jew through guidance and direction for both leaders and participants. Also available with workbook, audiocassette, and teacher guide.

Yerushalmi, Yosef Hayim. *Haggadah and History*. Philadelphia, PA: Jewish Publication Society, 1997, 0-8276-0624-9.

A panoramic view of the evolution of the *Haggadah*, from the beginnings of Hebrew printing in the fifteenth century to modern times. Features commentary by the author and 200 facsimile plates (unfortunately, all in black and white).

Zion, Noam, and David Dishon. *A Different Night: A Traditional Pesach Haggadah*. Jerusalem: Hartman Institute, 1996. (Available from A.R.E. Publishing, Inc.)

A major contribution to a family *Seder* experience. How can the *Seder*, observed year after year, remain stimulating for the participants and still remain faithful to the tradition? This selection, complete with Leader's Guide, will provide many suggestions.

Audiocassettes

Celebrate with Us: Passover. Available from A.R.E. Publishing, Inc.

Stories and songs related to the Passover holiday. PK-3.

Mostly Matzah. Fran Avni. Available from A.R.E. Publishing, Inc.

A collection of songs in a variety of musical styles which tell the story of the Exodus from ancient Egypt. PK-3.

A Singing Seder. Cindy Paley. Sounds Write Productions.

Upbeat arrangements for more than 20 traditional and modern melodies appropriate to Passover. All Ages.

Videos

The Animated Haggadah. 30 min. color. Ergo Media Inc.

A delightful redition of the whole Passover story from the burning bush to Pharaoh's court, the Ten Plagues, and the liberation of the children of Israel. All Grades.

My Exodus: An Oral History of Leaving Egypt. 30 min. color. Torah Aura Productions.

In this video, six delightful kids give personal accounts of their "experiences" leaving Egypt. Grades 4-6.

Passover Adventure. 28 min. color. Ergo Media Inc.

An Israeli guide leads an exploration through the history and traditions of Passover and celebrates the

Seder on a *kibbutz* with American *olim* (immigrants). Grades 4 and up.

Passover at Bubbe's. 30 min. color. Ergo Media Inc.

An adorable cast of puppets (Muffin, Zachary, and Chester) help Bubbe prepare for her *Seder* and are surprised by a talking *Haggadah*. Grades PK-Adult.

A Passover Seder. 30. min. color. BJE of Greater New York.

A combination of live action, original illustrations, and animation guide the viewer through the *Seder* with a multi-generational family. Presented by Elie Wiesel, this video includes some of his special memories and poetic interpretations. Grades PK-Adult.

Passover: Traditions of Freedom. 58 min. color. National Center for Jewish Film.

Shot on location in Israel and the U.S., this documentary intertwines ancient customs and individual family stories with the history of the holidays and discussion of its special foods. Grades 7-Adult.

A Rugrats Passover. 25 min. color. Available from Tara Publications.

Nickleodeon's series has Angelica as Pharaoh, Tommy as Moses, and the babies as the Hebrews in the Rugrat's version of Passover. Ages PK-3.

CD-ROM

The Interactive Haggadah. Windows. JEMM Productions. Available from Davka Corporation.

Combines traditions and technology to bring the *Seder* to life, in three languages — English, Russian, or Hebrew. Features colorful animation, songs, games, and much more. Grades 1 up.

YOM HASHOAH

Note: This observance requires the utmost sensitivity on the part of teachers, leaders, and parents. While the enormity of the Nazi crime must not be minimized, the subject needs to be presented in an age appropriate manner. Extra care has been taken here to define the appropriate age level, but materials should be evaluated carefully before presenting them.

For Students

Ackerman, Karen. *The Night Crossing*. New York: Alfred A. Knopf, 1994, ISBN 0-679-83169-X.

A fine introduction to the Holocaust, this story takes place in 1938 and focuses on the escape from Austria. The mother's candlesticks provide the vehicle to freedom. Grades 3-5.

Adler, David. *Child of the Warsaw Ghetto*. New York: Holiday House, 1995, ISBN 0-8234-1160-5.

The story of the Warsaw Ghetto told through the eyes of a boy who moved in and out of the ghetto to find food, then lived in Korczak's orphanage until deportation to Dachau. He was liberated by American soldiers. The photos portray the drama and hopelessness of the child's plight. Grades 7-11.

———. Hilde and Eli: *Children of the Holocaust*. New York: Holiday House, 1994, ISBN 3-8234-1091-9.

Describes the fate of two Jewish children from their happy childhood (one in Germany and one in Czechoslovakia) to the escalating Nazi persecution of the Jews. Grades 3-6.

———. *One Yellow Daffodil: A Hanukkah Story*. San Diego, CA: Gulliver Books/Harcourt Brace & Co., 1995, ISBN 0-15-200537-4.

During Chanukah, two children help Morris, a Holocaust survivor, once again to embrace his religious tradition. He tells the children about his experiences during the war years when he was a young man. Also appropriate for Chanukah. Grades 3 up.

Bachman, Susan. *Tell Them We Remember: The Story of the Holocaust*. Boston, MA: Little, Brown, 1994, ISBN 0-316-69264-6.

If you can select only one book on the subject, this should be your choice! Using the photos of the U.S. Holocaust Museum in Washington, D.C., the reader is able to follow several young Holocaust victims through their identity cards and to see how they fared. This personalizes the event in a meaningful way for the young reader. Grades 6 up.

Boaz, Jacob. *We Are Witnesses: The Diaries of Five Teenagers Who Died in the Holocaust.* New York: Henry Holt, 1995, ISBN 0-8050-3702-0.

Five teenagers who died in the Holocaust reveal in their diaries their innermost feelings about coping. Boaz, a Holocaust survivor, incorporates his own commentary using excerpts from each diary to personalize history and to compare individual experiences. He remarks that Anne Frank's experiences were atypical. The diaries exhibit a sense of false optimism. Grades 5 up.

Brodmann, Aliana. *The Gift.* New York: Simon & Schuster, 1993, ISBN 0-671-75110-7.

A recollection of the narrator's childhood in Germany. She was given a gift of a five mark coin for Chanukah and, instead of selecting a gift for herself, she gave the money to a street musician who, in turn, taught her to play. Grades K-3.

Bunting, Eve. *Terrible Things: An Allegory of the Holocaust.* Philadelphia, PA: Jewish Publication Society, 1994, ISBN 0-8276-0507-2.

Little Rabbit wonders why the "Terrible Things" take away all creatures with feathers. There is no direct reference or mention of the Holocaust. Grades 1-3.

Ginsburg, Marvell. *The Tattooed Torah.* New York: UAHC Press, Reissued 1994, ISBN 0-8074-0252-4.

This popular title prepares very young children for Yom HaShoah, and lays the groundwork for more intensive understanding at a later time. It is the story of the Torahs that were stolen by the Nazis in their drive to make the world *judenrein.* These were hidden with the intention of showing them in a museum. Instead, after the war, they were located and given to Jewish congregations. A beautiful story. Grades K-3.

Grishaver, Joel Lurie. *Schindler's List.* Los Angeles, CA: Torah Aura Productions.

This Instant Lesson contrasts the movie account of Oskar Schindler's life with that found in Thomas Keneally's novel of the same name. Grades 6-Adult.

Handler, Andrew, and Susan V. Michael, eds. *Young People Speak: Surviving the Holocaust in Hungary.* New York: Franklin Watts, 1993, ISBN 0-531-11044-3.

The contributors share three characteristics: they were all children during World War II; they were all born and reared in Hungary (the last country to be occupied by Hitler, where 75 percent of the Jews perished). There are no discussions here of concentration camp experiences. The individual accounts are of living in the ghetto, avoiding being caught and deported, and adjustment to a life in hiding or under an assumed name. The book opens with a succinct, eight page introduction. Excellent stories for teens. Grades 9 up.

Herman, Erwin, and Agnes Herman. *The Yanov Torah.* Rockville, MD: Kar-Ben Copies, Inc., 1985, 0-930494-46-6, o.p.

Jews in a work camp in Yanov, during the Nazi occupation of Lvov, Poland, smuggle in a Torah piece by piece despite enormous personal danger. Availabe in many libraries. Grades 4-6.

Ippisch, Hanneke. *Sky: A True Story of Resistance During World War Two.* New York: Simon & Schuster, 1996, ISBN 0-689-80508-X.

The book describes how a young woman was incarcerated by the Germans after joining the Dutch Resistance. The autobiography includes documents, verses, clippings, historical notes, and photographs of places and artifacts. Grades 6-9.

Jules, Jacqueline. *The Grey Striped Shirt: How Grandma and Grandpa Survived The Holocaust.* Los Angeles, CA: Alef Design, 1995, ISBN 1-881283-06-2.

While Fannie is looking for Grandma's purple hat, she accidently discovers hidden in the back of the closet a grey striped shirt with a yellow star. Frannie asks her grandparents questions, and slowly they begin to unfold the story of their Holocaust experiences. Grades 5-8.

Lakin, Patricia. *Don't Forget*. New York: William Morrow & Co., 1994, ISBN 0-688-02076-8.

Each shopkeeper gives eight-year-old Sarah a tip on how to bake a cake, but it is the advice of Mrs. Singer — whose number tattooed on her arm always made the little girl a bit uneasy — that Sarah will never forget. An effective introduction to Yom HaShoah. Grades 1-4.

Matas, Carol. *Daniel's Story*. New York: Scholastic Books, 1993, ISBN 0-590-4692-7.

The author succeeds in bringing to life Daniel's family and the children in the photographs found at the U.S. Holocaust Museum in Washington, D.C. Follow Daniel from his home in Germany to the Lodz Ghetto, to Auschwitz, and then to survival. Grades 5 up.

Perl, Lila, and Marian Blumenthal Lazan. *Four Perfect Pebbles: A Holocaust Story*. New York: Greenwillow, 1996, ISBN 0-688-14294-X.

A memoir which recalls the devastating years that shaped Marian's childhood. Caught in Nazi Germany, the family fled to Holland and during the next six years lived in camps including Bergen-Belsen. It is a story of horror and of courage. Grades 5-9.

Pomeranc, Marion Hess. *The Hand-Me-Down Horse*. Morton Grove, IL: Albert Whitman Co, 1996, ISBN 0-8075-3141-3.

After surviving the Holocaust, David and his family are awaiting their turn to go to America. The wait seems endless until David receives a rocking horse from his friend whose turn has come. David must promise to give it to another waiting child when he leaves for America. Grades 1-5.

Rosenberg, Maxine. *Hiding to Survive: Stories of Jewish Children Rescued from the Holocaust*. New York: Clarion Books, 1994, ISBN 0-395-65014-3.

First person accounts by European children who were forced to hide during the Holocaust in their effort to survive. Grades 5-9.

Sandman, Rachel. *As Big As An Egg; A Story about Giving*. Brooklyn, NY, Hachai Publications, Inc., 1995, ISBN 0-922613-77-X.

The story takes place in Russia when food is scarce. It reads like a folktale, and is about sharing. Because it tells of life during the hard times of the Holocaust without ever mentioning the Holocaust or the Nazis, It provides a good introduction for the very young. Grades PK-1.

Schlemer, Sarah M. *Far from the Place We Called Home*. New York/Jerusalem: Feldheim, 1994, ISBN 0-87306-667-7.

An emotional story about the famous *Kindertransport*, groups of children whose parents sent them to England just before the War. The goal was survival. The children hardly knew English, and it was rare that the placement was with a Jewish family, but their lives were saved. This is their story presented as a historical novel. Grades 7 up.

Schnur, Steven. *The Shadow Children*. New York: Morrow Junior Books, 1994, ISBN 0-688-13831-4.

Set in a small French village years after World War II, the story addresses the guilt still experienced because of the death of Jewish children. Grades 4-6.

Seven Weeks of Remembrance. Los Angeles, CA: Torah Aura Productions.

This Instant Lesson introduces all the holidays between Passover and Shavuot — Yom HaAtzma'ut, Yom HaZikaron, Yom Yerushalayim, and Yom HaShoah. The separate guide for teachers is called *The Celebration Lessons Teacher's Guide*. Grades K-2.

Spiegelman, Art. *Maus: Vol. I: The Father Bleeds History; Vol. II: And Here My Troubles Began*. New York: Schocken Books, reissued 1995, ISBN 0-394-55655-0.

Maus is presented in cartoon format, with the Nazis represented as cats and the Jews as mice. Both volumes tell two stories. The first story moves back and forth from Poland to Rego Park, New York, as the author's father tells how he and his wife survived the Holocaust in Europe and Spiegelman himself tells his story of his difficult relationship with his father. The second volume is set in the Catskills and tells of the father's tale of survival and the author's attempt to lead a normal life with aging survivor parents. Grades 9 up.

Toll, Nelly S. *Behind the Secret Window: A Memoir of a Hidden Childhood.* New York: Dial, 1993, ISBN 0-8037-1362-2.

Features 29 full-color reproductions of paintings made by the author when she was an eight-year-old in hiding, waiting endlessly in a bricked up room. Toll also describes the tense relationship with the couple that hid her and her mother, and their eventual escape. Grades 5-9.

Volavkova, Hana, ed. *I Never Saw Another Butterfly.* New York: Schocken Books, 1994, ISBN 0-8052-1015-6.

This book of poems and drawings from children in the concentration camp is a classic. It allows us to see, through the eyes of the child, what life was like there. The verses and drawings reveal their courage and optimism as well as their fears. Now also available as a video (see page 291). Grades 3 up.

Wiesel, Elie. *Night.* New York: Bantam Books, 1982, ISBN 0-553-27253-5, o.p.

Wiesel's own story of his life in the concentration camp. While this book is out of print, it is available in many libraries. Grades 7-Adult.

Williams, Laura E. *Behind the Bedroom Wall.* New York: Milkweed Editions, 1996, ISBN 1-57131-606-X.

A young girl's involvement in a Nazi youth group raises questions about her loyalties and asks," why Nazism held so many in its deadly thrall." Grades 5-9.

Zwerin, Raymond A.; Audrey Friedman Marcus; and Leonard Kramish. *Gestapo: A Learning Experience about the Holocaust.* Denver: A.R.E. Publishing, Inc., 1976.

Students face situations parallel to those faced by Jews in the Nazi era and must risk their values and make choices. Grades 8-Adult.

Zwerin, Raymond A.; Audrey Friedman Marcus; and Leonard Kramish. *The Holocaust: A Study in Values.* Denver: A.R.E. Publishing, Inc., 1976.

A mini-course that features interviews with "personalities" from the Nazi era. Students must decide if these individuals are guilty or not guilty. An engrossing way to involve students in the background and history of the Holocaust. The Leader Guide includes the history of anti-Semitism in Germany, reasons for Hitler's rise to power, and more. Designed for 5-10 hours of group study. Grades 7-Adult.

For Teachers and Parents
Note: This focused choice of books is intended to heighten awareness of the kind of records being left for future generations. What will the population in 2100 learn about the Holocaust? Our collective memory, such as it is, will be their textbooks. The best recommendations to readers will include the understandings provided by those closest to the event, as well as the views of historians, sociologists, psychologists, and other specialists in related fields.

Each generation must come to grips with the event. The children of survivors have been profoundly affected by the experience of their parents. This second generation has had its own Holocaust visions: pictures of murdered family members; behavioral patterns related to survivor syndrome; and the pressures of small, intense families. But this generation is also intimately aware of survivor strengths and is committed to sharing their Holocaust stories. They wonder, as parents themselves now, how to tell their own children, the third generation, about the Holocaust.

Remembrance is an essential component of Jewish tradition. While Judaism emphasizes the retelling of a story, the responsibility to hand it down has been placed on our writers. At the same time, Raul Hilberg, a foremost historian of the period, has cautioned that " . . . some people might read what I have written in the mistaken belief that here on my printed pages, they will find the true ultimate Holocaust as it really happened. Nevertheless, we must continue to uncover truths and, above all, to remember."

Alex Krieger is a child of survivors. At the Founders Dinner of the New England Holocaust Memorial Committee (November 29, 1989, Boston), referring to a new Holocaust memorial, he said: "The memorial will be for me. Because I was not there, and did not suffer, I cannot remember. Therefore I very much need to be reminded. [It will be for my daughter] who will need to be reminded even more. It will be for her children who will need to be reminded still more. We must build . . . for all the generations to come who, by distance from the actual events and people, will depend on it to activate [memory]" (In *The Texture of Memory*, James Young, p. 285).

Elie Wiesel says: "The danger lies in forgetting. Forgetting, however, will not affect only the dead. Should it triumph, the ashes of yesterday will cover our hopes for tomorrow."

Berenbaum, Michael. *The World Must Know: The History of the Holocaust as Told in the United States Holocaust Memorial Museum*. Boston, MA: Little, Brown, 1993, ISBN 0-316-09135-9.

Remembrance is at the heart of the mission of the U.S. Holocaust Memorial Museum. Written by its educational director, this volume is intended to help future generations as well as our own learn from the past. The book draws upon the museum's extensive resources, including eyewitness accounts, artifacts, and photographs to provide a comprehensive historical overview and to tell the human story from pre-Holocaust days through the aftermath. The book is aimed at a general audience and should be available in every institution.

Block, Gay, and Malka Drucker. *Rescuers: Portraits of Moral Courage in the Holocaust*. New York: Holmes & Meier, Publishers, Inc., 1992, ISBN 0-8419-1323-4.

The authors spent three years interviewing 105 rescuers from ten countries. Forty-nine of them are represented in this book. Each tells an unforgettable story of hiding and helping Jews during the Nazi era and why — at the risk of their own lives — they acted with humanity in a time of barbarism. Includes full-color photographs by Block of each rescuer, maps, historic photographs from family collections, and a Prologue by Cynthia Ozick.

Bohm-Duchen, Monica. *After Auschwitz: Responses to the Holocaust in Contemporary Art*. London: North Centre for Contemporary Art, Lund Humphries Publishers, 1995, ISBN 0-85331-666-X.

A series of illustrated essays by leading artists addressing the impact of the Holocaust on contemporary art. It looks at the art produced by victims during the Holocaust, the influence of the Holocaust on artists who were not camp inmates during and after the war, Holocaust memorials and their significance, and the work of younger generations of artists whose relationship to the event is even more oblique.

Brecher, Elinor J. *Schindler's Legacy: True Stories of the List Survivors*. New York: NAL Dutton, 1994, 0-452-27353-6.

Thirty stories of survival from among the more than 1,100 Jews saved by Oskar Schindler by employing them in his factory. These survivors tell of how they met Schindler, how they got on his list, and what it meant in their battle for life. The book continues into the postwar era and period of rehabilitation. Over 100 photos of the survivors are included.

Delbo, Charlotte. *Auschwitz and After*. Rosette C. Lamont, trans. New Haven, CT: Yale University Press, 1995, ISBN 0-300-062-08.

Vignettes, poems, and prose poems of life in the concentration camp and afterward by a female resistance leader. A non-Jew speaks of horror and heroism, of everyday deprivation and abuse, and the difficulties of survivors in returning to normal life.

Gilbert, Martin. *Atlas of the Holocaust*. New York: William Morrow & Co., 1993, ISBN 0-688-12364-3.

Detailed maps of events that took place during the Holocaust. An invaluable reference.

Gold, Ruth Glasberg. *A Survivor's Memoir: Ruth's Journey*. Gainesville, FL: University of Florida Press, 1996, ISBN 0-8130-1400-X.

Ms. Gold's memoir is both a record of a child's survival in the camps and a study of the growth and development of an orphaned survivor of the Holocaust. She describes the cruel, terrifying journey through the savagery of the wartime years and the bewildering emotional journey of trauma, loss, and bitterness, followed by a process of reintegration and self-discovery. She devotes much space to her struggle to integrate into a new society after the war, first in Palestine, then South America, and finally Miami. Each time she had to learn a new language and adapt to a new culture.

Goldhagen, Daniel J. *Hitler's Willing Executioners: Ordinary Germans and the Holocaust.* New York: Alfred A. Knopf, 1996, ISBN 0-679-44695-8.

An explosive and thought provoking investigation into the response of German society to the murder of six million Jews. Goldhagen posits that the Nazi regime successfully harnessed much of Germany's energies for the anti-Semitic crusade, and did so with little opposition. He revolutionizes our understanding of the problem and exposes as myth the belief that most Germans did not know what the Nazi regime was doing in their name. A book to be read by every adult for a deeper perception of the *Shoah*. There are those who believe Goldhagen, a Harvard University professor, has put in writing what many people have thought all these years.

Grobman, Alex, ed. *Those Who Dared: Rescuers and Rescued: A Teaching Guide for Secondary Schools.* Los Angeles, CA: Martyrs Memorial and Museum of the Holocaust, 1995.

This guide provides background and information about the Holocaust, with a focus on individuals known as the "Righteous among the Nations." Included are stories of how individuals reacted to the Holocaust and how they acted to help rescue Jews. There are stories about well-known figures, such as Raoul Wallenberg and Oskar Schindler, but also stories about less familiar heroes.

Halpern, Sam. *Darkness and Hope.* New York: Shengold Publishers, 1996, ISBN 0-88400-181-4.

This survivor's story gives the reader insight into the daily courage that was required simply to survive the thousands of Nazi-inflicted torments. In seven chapters, the book tells of Halpern's life in Eastern Galicia, and offers some important understandings of Polish-Jewish and Ukrainian-Jewish relations during the Holocaust.

Hartman, Geoffrey H., ed. *Holocaust Remembrance: The Shapes of Memory.* Cambridge, MA: Blackwell, 1993, ISBN 1-55786-367-9.

Scholars, artists, and writers consider the ways in which the events of 1939-1945 have been, might be and will be remembered. Through remembering, they believe, an understanding of the past can emerge, and humanity be redeemed from the forces of humiliation and guilt. Essays include: "The Library of Jewish Catastrophe" by David Roskies; "Remembering Survival" by Lawrence Langer; "Jewish Memory in Poland" by James E. Young; and "Trauma, Memory and Transference" by Saul Friedlander.

Hass, Aaron. *The Aftermath: Living with the Holocaust.* New York: Cambridge University Press, 1996, ISBN 0-521-57459-5.

In a look at the postwar adjustment of survivors, the author's thesis is that psychologists who write about the immobilization of survivors are speaking of theory, not fact. The author writes of 58 survivors who reassembled their lives and revived their self-respect. This provides a case study of the elasticity of endurance and the capacity to bounce back.

Helmreich, William. *Against All Odds: Holocaust Survivors and the Successful Lives They Made in America.* New York: Simon and Schuster, 1992, reissued by Transaction, 1996, ISBN 1-56000-865-2.

What lessons can be learned from the survivors about coping with tragedy and adversity? How did they pick up the threads of their lives and learn to trust and have faith? This popular, not scholarly, book discusses ten traits possessed by successful survivors and highlights the story of 170 people and their impact on America. Chapters deal with "The Struggle to Rebuild," "Living With Memories," and "Overcoming Tragedy."

Kahn, Leora, and Rachel Hager, eds. *When They Came to Take My Father: Voices of the Holocaust.* New York: Arcade Publishers, 1996, ISBN 1-55970-305-9.

"How do people carry on?" is a question asked over and over. Every answer is as unique as the individual. Here are the voices of 50 survivors, along with powerful photographic testimony to their bravery, resilience, and will to survive. The story of Sandra Brand and her German officer is but one example. Punctuating the accompanying narrative are essays by Arthur Hertzberg, Ann Roiphe, and Abe Foxman.

Kornberg, Jacques, "On Teaching the Holocaust as History." In *Shofar: An Interdisciplinary Journal of Jewish Studies,* Vol. 11, No. 1, Fall, 1992.

An excellent discussion of the pros and cons of attempts to engage students sympathetically and morally through the study of the Holocaust, and the opposite strategy of maintaining a scholarly detachment.

Linenthal, Edward T. *Preserving Memory: The Struggle to Create America's Holocaust Museum.* New York: Penguin, 1995, ISBN 0-670-86067-0.

This volume considers the struggles which trans-pired to define and delimit the ideas, objects, persons, and representations that would capture the meaning of the Holocaust in the museum. Through the museum, the memory is no longer the sole possession of American Jews — it is now a national trust. It has an impact on political decision making, as well as on the relationship of Christians and Jews to their respective traditions. Included is a discus-sion of "Who Owns the Memory?" Enhanced by black and white photos.

Lipstadt, Deborah E. *Denying the Holocaust: The Growing Assault on Truth and Memory.* New York: NAL/Dutton, 1994.

A scholar brilliantly defends the actuality of the Holocaust in the face of the deniers.

Littell, Marcia S., and Sharon W. Gutman, eds. *Liturgies on the Holocaust: An Interfaith Anthology.*. Valley Forge, PA: Trinity Press International, 1996, ISBN 1-56338-138-9.

The editors present 33 program samples of worship services appropriate for observance of Yom HaShoah in different settings. Some synagogue programs of a more traditional nature are included, as well as examples of programs for interfaith

groups, college campuses, the military, and general civic observances. Certain classical texts have seemingly *become* liturgy, as their repeated use has given them ritual and symbolic recognition. Among these are the poems of Nellic Sachs, *The Diary of Anne Frank,* the poems of the children of Theresienstadt, and the writings of Elie Wiesel. An outstanding collection.

Millen, Rochelle. *New Perspectives on the Holocaust.* New York: New York University Press, 1996. ISBN 0-8147-5540-2.

This multidisciplinary volume offers guidance to those in the teaching professions, and describes innovative research and guidance for those in secular universities and Religious Schools.

Miller, Judith. *One by One by One: Facing the Holocaust.* New York: Simon and Schuster, 1991, 0-671-74034-2.

This book is about the obligations of memory — about what we owe to those who survived and to those who did not. How can we pass on the Holocaust most effectively and honestly? If the Holocaust is indeed unique, how can it be compared to other tragedies? If, on the other hand, it cannot be compared, how is it relevant? The author asked these questions in six countries: Germany, Austria, Holland, France, USSR (before the fall of Communism), and the United States. Each interviewee was asked to describe the Holocaust as he or she remembered it. In these countries, the author found, there does not seem to be a collective memory. But Jews, on the other hand, *do* have something resembling a collective memory. Miller concludes that it is the specific that fosters memory. For example, for her, it was a single infant's leather shoe encased in glass at Yad Vashem that was most powerful.

Mokotoff, Gary, and Sallyann Amdur Sack. *Where Once We Walked: A Guide to the Jewish Communities Destroyed in the Holocaust.* Teaneck, NJ: Avotaynu, 1991, ISBN 0-9626373-1-9.

Twenty-two thousand Central and Eastern Euro-pean communities were home to Jews before the Holocaust. The authors provide information for those seeking their roots and/or doing research. This fascinating book lists name and alternate name(s) of each community, Jewish population, proximity to closest major city, and more. A must for every community library.

Mokotoff, Gary. *How to Document Victims and Locate Survivors of the Holocaust.* Teaneck, NJ: Avotaynu, 1995, ISBN 0-9626373-8-6.

A second-generation American who thought he was removed from the Holocaust learns he lost 250 family members who had remained in Europe. This book leads the reader through the research process. There is excellent reference material on "The Principal Sources of Information about Holocaust Victims and Survivors" and "Facilities with Collections of Holocaust Materials." Eight appendixes include European research locations and other significant resources. Highly recommended for every synagogue and community library.

Pfefferkorn, Eli. *Commemorative Observances for Days of Remembrance.* Washington, DC: U.S. Holocaust Memorial Council, 1985.

This collection is intended to provide a platform for the words used by the victims. In reading their testimonies, future generations join in the human effort to foil oblivion. Their memoirs appear as stories, poems, dialogues, and diaries. Examples are "Portraits of Auschwitz," which includes two dramatic presentations for groups, "An Address in Premonition" by Elie Wiesel.

Rittner, Carol, and John K. Roth, eds. *Different Voices: Women and the Holocaust.* New York: Paragon House, 1993, ISBN 1-55778-503-1.

A book that asks questions about memory and morality regarding women at the time of the Holocaust. Here is a selection of the best writings by and about adult women during that period. It is divided into three parts: "First Voices," the experiences of those who survived to bear witness, all pivoting around Auschwitz, a microcosm of extremity; "Second Voices," interpretations, primarily by historians who study the larger picture of the ways Nazi theory and practice made an impact on women; and "Third Voices," those of

reflection from Holocaust survivors and a child of survivors.

Segev, Tom. *The Seventh Million: The Israelis and the Holocaust.* trans. by Haim Watzman. New York: Hill & Wang, 1993, ISBN 0-8090-8563-1.

The Israelis' vision of the Holocaust has shaped their idea of themselves, even as their changing sense of self has altered their view of the Holocaust and its meaning over the decades of Israeli statehood. The subject contains great human drama involving, first, repression, and then recognition of the agonizing lessons of the past. The author suggests ways in which the bitter events of the past continue to shape the life of a nation, e.g., the Israeli view of *yekkes* (German-born Jews), Israel's acceptance of refugees, The Eichmann Trial, restitution payments, etc. The Holocaust formed the collective identity of Israel —for all Israel, then and now.

Shermer, Michael, and Alex Grobman. *Denying History: Who Says the Holocaust Never Happened & Why Do They Say It?* Santa Cruz, CA: Millenium Press, 1997, 0-9655047-5-1.

The authors take up the contentions of the Holocaust deniers and refute them point by point.

Stephens, Elaine C.; Jean E. Brown; and Janet E. Rubins. *Learning about the Holocaust: Literature and Other Resources for Young People.* North Haven, CT: Shoe String Press, Inc., 1995, 0-208-02408-5.

The intention is to have young people become actively involved in the literature and to help as they learn. The chapters survey books by medium. Chapter titles are "We Must Remember, It Really Happened," "Informational Books," "It Must Not Happen Again," "They Were There," "Personal Narratives," "We Create Through Drama," and "We Learn From Stories." Designed for a broad, secular audience, this volume includes a list of media resources and educational materials. Each book noted is accompanied by a summary and considerations for the classroom teacher.

Sutin, Jack, and Rochelle Sutin. *Jack and Rochelle: A Holocaust Story of Love & Resistance.* Lawrence Sutin, ed. St. Paul, MN: Graywolf Press, 1995, ISBN 1-55597-243-8.

A fine example of the genre of survivors' stories, this book tells of a couple who knew each other before the war in Poland and were reunited. They had each escaped from Nazi ghetto labor camps and met again when they were part of a resistance group. The story is presented in their words, with their two voices intertwined in the narrative. Their son's words tie the story together. He adds the preface and final chapter.

Wiesel, Elie. *All Rivers Run to the Sea*. New York: Alfred A. Knopf, 1995, ISBN 0-679-43916-1.

In this book Wiesel explores his early years in Sighet, the Holocaust experiences, and the first 25 years after liberation. He impresses upon readers that each of those who perished "was once a human being — living, creative human being — working, fighting, dancing, singing." As a survivor of Auschwitz and Buchenwald, Wiesel remains the foremost voice of the Holocaust, and is credited with affixing the name to it. He believes "that the experience of the *Shoah* is incommunicable," yet his writings come the closest to communicating it successfully. Highly recommended for ages 15 and up.

Wyman, David S. *The Abandonment of the Jews*. New York: Pantheon Books, 1986, 0-394-74077-7.

A searing indictment of the failure of the U.S. State Department, the president, the public, the press, and even the Jewish community, to make a substantial commitment to rescue the Jews of Europe during the Nazi era.

Young, James E. *The Texture of Memory*. New Haven, CT: Yale University Press, 1993, ISBN 0-300-05383-5.

Winner of the 1994 National Jewish Book Award, this selection seeks to heighten awareness of the effect of Holocaust memorials, of the uses and abuses of officially cast memory, and of the contemporary consequences of past events in their memorial representations. In 1959, the Israeli Knesset designated that Yom HaShoah be put on the Jewish calendar. Already we see a generational change in America's public memorialization of the Holocaust from its early place along the margins of historical consciousness to its more recent overshadowing of nearly all other Jewish events. Reading this book, one remembers that the memorials also reflect the tastes and the values of the country they are in. Highly recommended!

Audiocassettes

Ani Ma-amin. Debbie Friedman. Available from A.R.E. Publishing, Inc.

A musical montage spanning generations of Jewish liturgical and biblical vision. An affirmation of humankind's hope for brighter tomorrows. (Contains a version of the title song.)

A Brighter Day. Safam. Sounds Write Productions.

A musical drama dedicated to victims and survivors of the Holocaust. Grades 7 up.

Hineni. Sam Glaser. Available from A.R.E. Publishing, Inc.

Fourteen spiritual and energetic rock, jazz, and soulful tunes combine with biblical, liturgical, and holiday motifs. (Contains an original version of *Ani Ma'amin*.)

Life's a Lesson. Ben Sidran. Sounds Write Productions.

Jazz versions of 15 selections in Hebrew and English. (Contains a version of *Ani Ma'amin*.)

Videos

Angst. 56 min. color. National Center for Jewish Film.

Laughter through tears. A look inside the lives of three Jewish comedians, all of whom are children of Holocaust survivors. Amidst the comedy, one sees a painful, yet penetrating glimpse of the difficulties of the second generation. The film provides a means to transmit the pain to the uninitiated and help the "children" tell the story to yet another generation. Grades 10-Adult.

Diamonds in the Snow. 59 min. color. Cinema Guild.

Of the thousands of children who lived in the Polish city of Bendzin before the Holocaust, barely a dozen survived. This documentary tells the story of three of these children, one of whom is the filmmaker. Grades 6 up.

The Journey of a Butterfly. 62 min. color. Available from United States Holocaust Memorial Council.

Poetry and songs of children of Terezin, 1941-1945. The poetry from the book *I Never Saw Another Butterfly* has been set to music and accompanies the drawings in this video. Grades 3 up.

Live from the Past: The Holocaust. 3 videotapes, 16-17 min. each. color. Available from United States Holocaust Memorial Council.

Designed especially for classroom (group) use, each tape focuses on one aspect of the Holocaust: the Background; the Death Camp; The Eichmann Trial. On the first two videos, Elie Wiesel talks about his experiences as a 15-year-old during the *Shoah*. Includes guides for the leader. Grades 7 up.

One Survivor Remembers. 40 min. color. HBO Video, Inc.

Gerda Weissman Klein was a teenager when the Nazis invaded her home town in Poland. This is a first person account of what followed that provides an incredible story as well as an affirmation of life. Grades 7 up.

Schindler's List. 185 min. color. Available at video stores.

The story of one man's stuggle to save the lives of over 1,000 Polish Jews during the Third Reich's implementation of Hitler's "final solution." Grades 10 up.

Sorrow: The Nazi Legacy. 33 min. color. Ergo Media Inc.

Six Swedish teens, two of whom are Jewish, make a trip to Auschwitz in an attempt to understand the incomprehensible. Their meeting with a survivor is filled with pain and sorrow, yet also with hope for the future. The pilgrimage comes full circle when the group meets with the son of a ranking Nazi upon their return to Stockholm. Grades 6 up.

Tzvi Nussbaum: A Boy from Warsaw. 50 min. color. Ergo Media Inc.

This is the story of the life of the little boy with his arms raised in surrender in the famous photograph. Grades 6 up.

The Warsaw Ghetto Uprising. 23 min. color. Ergo Media Inc.

Archival film footage, authentic still photographs, and actual testimonies of survivors help the viewer to understand this brief and courageous chapter in Jewish history. Grades 10 up.

Weapons of the Spirit. 90 min. color. Ergo Media Inc.

In Le Chambon, a Nazi occupied village in France, 5,000 Jews were taken in and sheltered by the Christian population. A great story of humanity's capacity for choosing good over evil. Pierre Sauvage, who was born in Le Chambon and was one of the fortunate survivors, returned to the town to interview rescuers and to make this film. Grades 7 up.

CD-ROMs

The Complete Maus: A Survivor's Tale. Available for Mac or Windows. United States Holocaust Memorial Museum.

Explore the novel and see hundreds of preliminary sketches and archival photos along with interviews with the author and his father that were the basis for the narrative. Grades 9 up.

The Holocaust. Windows only. Jewish Software Center.

An interactive multi-media database presenting a close-up of the *Shoah*. Provides a complete historical and pictorial review including camp-by-camp documentation. Grades 7-Adult.

Lest We Forget. Windows and Mac. Jewish Software Center.

Combines photos, film footage and sound with information to permit a study of the Holocaust from persecution to aftermath. Recommended for classroom settings. Grades 7-Adult.

YOM HAATZMA'UT

For Students

Abramson, Lori L., and Joel K. Abramson. *Shirah B'Tiyul: A Musical Israel Curriculum.* Denver: A.R.E. Publishing, Inc., 1993.

A curriculum and cassette tape in which ten geographic areas of Israel are introduced through songs. Lesson modules and activities include explorations of such topics as holidays; Zionism; Diaspora communities; biblical stories, characters and places; Torah; Jewish cultural diversity; halachah, God, and mysticism. Provides a unique method of introducing and connecting students to Israel. Grades 5-Adult.

Almagor, Gila. *Under the Domim Tree.* Hillel Schenker, trans. New York: Simon & Schuster, 1995, ISBN 0-671-89020-4.

Set in 1953, in Udim, a youth village along Israel's coastal plain, this is a story of three girls living in the aftermath of the Holocaust. The Holocaust took their memory from them, but in Israel they grow toward womanhood and new lives. Grades 7-10.

ArtScroll Youth Series. *Jerusalem Diaries and Other Stories* by Miriam Stark Zakon, 1988; *Jerusalem Gems* by S. Sonnenfeld, 1987; *Tales from Old Jerusalem* by S. Sonnenfeld. Brooklyn, NY: Mesorah Publications, Ltd., 1988.

Short stories about Jerusalem, the old and the emerging new, outside the gates. The stories are filled with warmth, family values, and Torah learning. Grades 5 up.

Artson, Bradley Shavit. "Ahavat Tziyon: Zionism and Israel." In *It's a Mitzvah! Step-by-Step to Jewish Living.* West Orange, NJ: Behrman House and New York: Rabbinical Assembly, 1995, ISBN 0-87441-585-3.

In this chapter, the author asks: "Why should the State of Israel matter to us today?" Answers include concise historical overviews that are clearly directed at the reading audience and are followed by ways to become involved with the Israel scene. A good choice for groups which include Israel as part of a larger curriculum focus. Grades 8-Adult.

Bamberger, David. *A Young Person's History of Israel.* 2d. ed. West Orange, NJ: Behrman House, 1994, ISBN 0-87441-393-1.

A Hebrew school text on Israel which views the Homeland through rose colored glasses. It follows the history of *Eeretz Yisrael* from early times through the growth of Zionism, the establishment of the State of Israel, and the major events in the first 40+ years of its existence. Good photos enhance the narrative. Grades 5-9.

Banks, Lynne Reid. *One More River.* New York: Avon, 1992, ISBN 0-380-72755-2.

A rich Canadian girl reluctantly moves to Israel with her parents, and is drawn to the Arab boy she sees across the Jordan. Grades 5 up.

———. *Broken Bridges.* New York: Avon, 1995, ISBN 0-380-72384-0.

The Canadian girl from the book *One More River* by the same author is now a mother of a daughter. Set in the time of the Intifada. There is some violence — a friend of the daughter is killed. Grades 5 up.

Borovetz, Frances. *Israel Copy Pak™ K-3.* Denver: A.R.E. Publishing, Inc., 1989.

Twenty-eight original, read-to-photocopy activity pages which introduce and reinforce the teaching of Israel, including special places, life-style, culture and customs, famous people and events, and more. Teacher Guide included. Grades K-3.

———. *Israel Copy Pak™ 4-6.* Denver: A.R.E. Publishing, Inc., 1993.

Twenty-five original, ready-to-photocopy activity pages which introduce or reinforce the teaching of Israel, including geography, history, famous people, government, orgniazations, and more. Teacher Guide included. Grades 4-6.

Burstein, Chaya. *Our Land of Israel.* New York: UAHC Press, 1994, ISBN 0-8074-0533-7.

A textbook, primarily for the supplementary school classroom, which presents the story of Israel through actual Israelis of different backgrounds and ages. The first of these is an American *olah*, Naama

Kelman, the first woman to be ordained a Rabbi in Israel. The goal is for the American reader to "connect" with Israel and find commonality with its residents. Topics cover history, geography, and culture. Fine graphs and color photos make it an attractive choice in spite of the "sugar-coated" view it projects. Grades 4-7.

Carmi, Giora. *And Shira Imagined*. Philadelphia, PA: Jewish Publication Society, reissued 1995, ISBN 0-8276-0288-X.

A small child hears about Israel, but how do the young translate these descriptions into visual pictures? In this full-color book, Shira takes her stuffed animals on an imaginary first trip from America to Israel. Grades PK-2.

Cytron, Phyliss, and Barry Cytron. *Myriam Mendilow: The Mother of Jerusalem*. Minneapolis, MN: Lerner Group, 1992, ISBN 0-8225-4949-0.

The story of Myriam Mendilow's lifetime in Jerusalem includes a description of her many righteous projects, among them *Yad LaKashish* (Lifeline for the Old), which began as a book-binding workshop and grew into an extensive network of programs designed to help the elderly. Myriam's life is a testimony to the saying "One person *can* make a difference." Her efforts continue to impact upon the lives of many, many residents of her native city. Grades 5-9.

David, Justin. *One Has to Make Peace With One's Enemies — Not With One's Friends*. Los Angeles, CA: Torah Aura Productions, 1995.

In this Instant Lesson, students address the peace process through use of copies of the actual peace accord documents. These will be the source for better understanding and enlightened predictions about future prospects for peace. Grades 6-Adult.

Dolphin, Laurie. *Neve Shalom/Wahat al-Salam: Oasis of Peace*. New York: Scholastic Books, 1993, ISBN 0-590-45799-3.

This story follows two ten-year-old boys, Shlomo Franklin, an Israeli Jew, and Muhammed Jubar, an Israeli Arab Moslem, on their first day in an experimental school in Israel that brings together Arabs and Jews. Each boy travels through soldier-occupied territories to reach school. Over time, the students find shared interests and the beginnings of friendship. Also includes brief history of Arab-Israeli conflict. Beautiful photos. Grades 3 up.

Edwards, Michelle. *Chicken Man*. New York: Lothrop, 1991, ISBN 0-688-09708-1.

This happy *kibbutznik* loves all his jobs so much that that the other *kibbutzniks* grow jealous of him, causing him to be temporarily removed from his beloved chickens. Winner of the 1992 National Jewish Book Award for Picture Books. Grades K-3.

Epstein-Asor, Kyla. *Places in Israel*. Los Angeles, CA: Torah Aura Productions, 1995.

An Instant Lesson that introduces the child to eight popular Israeli sites including a *kibbutz*, the Negev Desert, the Dead Sea, and the big cities. Grades K-2.

Feldman, Sarah. "Israel: A City Tour" and "Israel: People and Places." In *Let's Explore Being Jewish*. West Orange, NJ: Behrman House, 1995, ISBN 0-87441-586-1; 0-87441-587-X.

Each of these magazines brings Israeli history, geography, and daily life together using stories, art photos, and hands-on activities. In addition, each section includes activities for parents and children to enjoy together. Grades 1-2.

Fine, Steve. *Peace in Jericho*. Los Angeles, CA: Torah Aura Productions, 1995.

In Jericho there is an ancient synagogue called "Peace upon Israel." In this Instant Lesson, students explore the site and gain a better understanding about the current peace process. Grades 6-Adult.

Geras, Adele. *Golden Windows and Other Stories of Jerusalem*. San Francisco, CA: HarperCollins, 1993, ISBN 0-06-022941-1.

Five stories about a widow and her seven children set in Jerusalem during the early part of the twentieth century. Winner of the 1993 National Jewish Book Award. Grades 3-7.

Gold-Vukson, Marji. *Imagine . . . Exploring Israel: Creative Drawing Adventures.* Rockville, MD: Kar-Ben Copies, Inc., 1993, ISBN 0-929371-64-X.

Here is an opportunity for children to learn about a site or event related to Israel and then draw what they think it looks like or as they imagine it. For example: "What do you think an El Al plane will look like when you grow up?" Or, seeing a falafel in pita which is not quite recognizable, the young person is asked, "What strange things do you see in the pita?" Grades K-5.

Goldsmith, Mark. *My Israel.* London: Centre for Jewish Education, 1994.

A series of work units that involves active student participation. The unit on Jerusalem opens with an explanation of the words to "Jerusalem of Gold" and goes on to explore the golden city, both the old and the new. There is reference to the Intifada and words of caution about visiting the Old City. The intended audience is children in Reform Movement schools in England, and there are references to London sites and the situation in Ireland to relate to the children's immediate situation. However, there are some good ideas which can easily be adapted to the schools in North America. Grades 4-6.

Goodman, Ruth Fisher. *Pen Pals: What it Means to Be Jewish in Israel and America.* Santa Barbara, CA: Fithian Press, 1996. ISBN 1-56474-159-1.

Jonathan in Pennsylvania and David in the Israeli seaside resort of Netanya exchange letters and discover similarities and differences in their respective Jewish observances and feelings. Their friendship is further explored when Jonathan's family plans a trip to Israel. This selection is highly recommended as a catalyst to classroom pen pal projects. Grades 3 up.

Gordon, Yosi. *Neighbors in a Crowded House.* Los Angeles, CA: Torah Aura Productions, 1995.

An Instant Lesson with an overview of the background to the Arab-Israeli conflict and addressing the myth and reality of the current problem. Grades 6 up.

Jerusalem Resource Kit. Boston: Bureau of Jewish Education of Greater Boston, 1994.

The eight gates of Jerusalem provide the guide to this 122-page well planned tour which covers sites, observance of Jewish ritual in the Holy City, literature, history, and a visit to a Sephardic home. The kit includes separate age appropriate activities, a song packet, a bibliography, and media suggestions. The material is educationally appropriate and current. Grades 2-7.

Lerner, Sharon. *Passport to Israel Series.* Los Angeles, CA: Torah Aura Productions, 1995,

Introduces children to the major geographic regions in Israel together with the country's three largest cities. The Instant Lesson packets include 15 passports and an equal number of stickers for classroom use. Grades 3-5.

Paris, Alan. *Jerusalem 3000: Kids Discover the City of Gold.* New York and Jerusalem: Pitspopany, 1995, ISBN 0-943706-59-9.

A well-illustrated, large-size book with painted scenes of Israel past and present side by side. This is preceded by concise written information about the various sites pictured. The travelers visit the Cardo, City of David, The Jewish Quarter, Yemin Moshe, and four other places of interest. Grades 3-7.

Passport to Israel. Los Angeles, CA: Torah Aura Productions.

This is a series of eight Instant Lessons plus a passport. Each takes students to a different region of Israel: The Judean Desert, Tel Aviv, The Negev, The Coast, Ha'Ir Ha-Atikah, The Galilee, Modern Jerusalem, and Haifa. Students learn related Hebrew vocabulary and earn a regional "stamp" for their passport. Teacher's guide included. Grades 3-5.

Rabinovich, Abraham. *Teddy Kollek: Builder of Jerusalem.* Philadelphia, PA: Jewish Publication Society, 1995, ISBN 0-8276-0559-5.

For 25 years, Teddy Kollek served as mayor of Jerusalem. He brought the city from a small town to a thriving metropolis. It can truly be said that his policies and visions shaped modern Jerusalem into a city for all peoples and an old/new capital for the State of Israel. His story will give youngsters a better understanding of what it is to be a builder and a leader. Grades 4-8.

The Record/Jerusalem: City of David. New York: Anti-Defamation League, 1995.

A quick overview of a long story. Using a newspaper tabloid format, this publication features articles covering the 3,000 years of Jerusalem's history. Grades 9-Adult.

Schwartz, Howard. *Next Year in Jerusalem: 3000 Years of Jewish Stories.* New York: Viking, 1996, ISBN 0-670-86110-3.

Winner of the 1996 National Jewish Book Award for Children's Literature, this is a collection of folktales all centering on Jerusalem. The stories, printed in boldface, take up two-thirds of the page while in the wide margins, Schwartz has provided italicized commentary on the story. Neil Waldman's illustrations enrich the visual understanding of Jerusalem. Grades 3-7.

Segal, Sheila F. *Joshua's Dream: A Journey to the Land of Israel.* New York: UAHC Press, 1992, ISBN 0-8074-0476-4.

Amazed by the deeds of his great-aunt who was one of the *chalutzim* (pioneers) in Israel, Joshua dreams of taking part in the cultivation of the Land. One day, he fulfills his dream by planting a tree in the Negev. Grades K-3.

Semel, Nava. *Becoming Gershona.* New York: Puffin Books/Penguin Publishers, 1992, ISBN 0-14-036071-9.

A young girl comes of age in Tel Aviv in 1958, in the shadow of Holocaust survivors, when the State of Israel is in existence only 10 years. Gershona's grandfather comes to live with her and helps her establish her own self-awareness among a sea of changes. Winner of the National Jewish Book Award. Grades 5-9.

———. *Flying Lessons.* New York: Simon and Schuster, 1995, ISBN 0-689-80161-0.

A young, motherless girl in a small Israeli agricultural village in 1955 dreams of flying away from her problems. In one painful year, she learns about flying and about courage. Grades 5 up.

Seven Weeks of Remembrance. Los Angeles, CA: Torah Aura Productions.

This Instant Lesson introduces all the holidays between Passover and Shavuot — Yom HaAtzma'ut, Yom HaZikaron, Yom Yerushalayim, and Yom HaShoah. The separate guide for teachers is called *The Celebration Lessons Teacher's Guide.* Grades K-2.

Sofer, Barbara. *Kids Love Israel, Israel Loves Kids.* Rockville, MD: Kar-Ben Copies, Inc., 1996, ISBN 0-929371-89-5.

A one-of-a-kind guide to Israel for family travel. Suggests over 200 child friendly places in Israel, as well as hints for planning the trip together and information about the recommended sites. No one with children along can go to Israel without this book, which features over 300 tourist sites that are of interest to families. All Ages.

———. *Shalom Haver, Goodbye Friend.* Rockville, MD: Kar-Ben Copies, Inc., 1996, ISBN 0-929371-97-6.

Saying good-bye to a friend is not easy, so says author Barbara Sofer. In beautiful simultaneous Hebrew/English text, she describes the life of Yitzhak Rabin in tribute. Vivid photos accompany this outstanding selection. Grades 3 up.

Sokolow, Moshe. *Yakirei Yerushalayim: A Modular Approach to the History of Jewish Jerusalem.* New York: Joint Authority for Jewish Zionist Education, Torah Education Department, 1995.

This new curriculum piece consider's Jerusalem's social, economic, political, and cultural history through the significant contributions of 12 distinctive personalities whose lives were centered in Jerusalem. Beginning with Rabbi Yehuda HaLevi during the Middle Ages, it includes, among others, Dona Gracia Nasi in the Post-Expulsion time, Sir Moses Montefiore in the Early Modern Period, Yosef Rivlin connected with Nachalat Shiva, and Shmuel Agnon in the Modern Period. Seven others are also included. An excellent approach for young people to become acquainted with the city through its famous inhabitants. Grades 4-12.

Speregen, Devra Newberger. *Yoni Netanyahu: Commando at Entebbe.* Philadelphia, PA: Jewish Publication Society, 1995, ISBN 0-8276-0523-4.

A modern day hero for young people, Yoni Netanyahu symbolizes bravery and patriotism in his service to Israel. The story takes the reader through Yoni's short life, highlighting his path toward leadership even at a young age. Netanyahu's name is synonymous with the Entebbe Rescue, now called "Operation Jonathan" in his memory. Grades 4-7.

Springer, Sally. *Israel Fun for Little Hands.* Rockville, MD: Kar-Ben Copies, Inc., 1994, ISBN 0929371-74-7.

Games, riddles, puzzles, and mazes introduce young children to favorite sites in Israel. With full-color postcards for tourists. Grades PK-2.

Starr, Joyce. *God Now Has a Fax Number.* San Francisco, CA: HarperSanFranciso, 1995, ISBN 0-06-007585-3.

Technology is making it easier to "talk to God." This small book provides actual messages received by Bezek, the Israeli telephone company, for placement in the *Kotel.* They include passionate pleas for love, urgent appeals for divine intervention, hopes for peace, and humorous requests. Grades 6 up.

Topek, Susan Remick. *Israel Is . . . .* Rockville, MD: Kar-Ben Copies, Inc., 1992, ISBN 0930494-92-X.

A board book of 12 pages with pictures of cities, sandy deserts, tall mountains, salty seas, and many people. Ages 1-3.

Waldman, Neil. *The Golden City: Jerusalem's 3,000 Years.* New York: Atheneum, 1995, ISBN 0-670-86110-3.

If the stones of Jerusalem could speak, what a story they would tell! Waldman, known primarily as an artist, presents a concise and very sensitive overview of the city's long and interesting history. Beautiful illustrations accompany the sensitive text for children of all religions. Grades 2-5.

Yolen, Jane. *O Jerusalem.* New York: Scholastic Books, 1996, ISBN 0-590-48426-5.

Yolen captures the ecumenical feeling of Jerusalem, holy to three religions. Through poems and exquisite paintings, the story of Jerusalem is told. Grades 4-7.

For Teachers and Parents

A Walk through Jerusalem. Boston: Bureau of Jewish Education of Greater Boston.

This is a multi-media, hands-on exhibit for the entire community. It is available for rental throughout the country.

Collins, Larry, and Dominique Lapierre. *O Jerusalem!* New York: Simon & Schuster, 1972, 1988, ISBN 0-671-66241-4.

A massive book about the people and events in Jerusalem which take the reader from the decision to partition Palestine in November, 1947, to the end of Israel's War of Independence. It tells the drama of 1948 when Arab and Jew fought each other for the city and for its symbolic importance to their respective peoples.

Decter, Moshe. "Passion for Jerusalem." *Midstream*, Vol. XXXXI, No. 4, May, 1995. (Published by Theodor Herzl Foundation)

This excellent article, provides a succinct overview of Israel's claim to Jerusalem, all of Jerusalem, as its rightful capital. The approach is chronological and secular, but adament in its view. For leaders in a hurry, there is enough information in six pages to provide a basic background on the subject. It is also suggested for parents and lay readers who merely wish to stay abreast of current issues.

Frankel, Glenn. *Beyond the Promised Land: Jews and Arabs on the Hard Road To a New Israel.* New York: Simon and Schuster, 1994, 0-684-82347-0.

Beyond the first 40 years, what will be the next period of Israeli history bring? How will Israelis handle their new circumstance bearing peace and prosperity? The author, an award-winning *Washington Post* journalist, guides his readers through the events and names that are leading to this new era. Winner of the 1995 National Jewish Book Award.

Furstenberg, Rochelle. *Images of Jerusalem: City of David in Modern Hebrew Literature.* Carol Diament, ed. New York: Hadassah, 1995, ISBN 0-889525-2.

A presentation of Jerusalem in literature (from early *midrashim* to the modern literary works of Agnon, Oz, Yehoshua, Amichai, and others), with discussion questions and guides for the leader of adult study groups. See the city through the literary perceptions of *sabras*, *olim*, and *vatikim*.

Gilbert, Martin. *Atlas of the Arab-Israeli Conflict.* New York: Oxford University Press, 1993, ISBN 0-19-521062-X.

Detailed maps of all the conflicts between the Arabs and the Israelis.

———. *The Atlas of Jewish History.* New York: William Morrow & Co., 1993, ISBN 0-688-12264-7.

A comprehensive series of maps detailing the events in Jewish history.

Hammer, Reuven., comp. *The Jerusalem Anthology: A Literary Guide.* Philadelphia, PA: Jewish Publication Society, 1995, ISBN 0-8276-0554-4.

A collection of literature, poetry, songs, and history of Jerusalem from biblical to modern times. A wonderful classroom and home resource.

Hareven, Shulamith. *City of Many Days: A Novel.* San Francisco, CA: Mercury House, reissued 1993, ISBN 1- 56279-050-1.

A work of fiction which traces the interwoven lives of many Jerusalemites during the period of the British Mandate. The award winning author brings the reader into the daily lives, homes, and difficulties of the residents at the time. Highly recommended!

Herzog, Chaim, *Living History.* New York: Pantheon, 1996, ISBN 0-679-43478-X.

This is the memoirs of a former president of Israel and one who has lived the history of the modern state since his *aliyah* in 1935. As a warrior and a statesman, Herzog's astute observations add even greater depth to his interesting life story.

Holzer, Margie; Alvin Schiff; and Carolyn Starman Hessel. *Jerusalem: A Resource Guide for Jerusalem 3000 and Beyond.* New York: Coalition for the Advancement of Jewish Education, 1996.

This fine resource contains *aggadot* and *midrashim* related to Jerusalem, as well as a bibliography that includes a listing of books for adults and children, materials for teachers/leaders, tour guides, videos, and more.

Horovitz, David, ed., and *The Jerusalem Post* Staff. *Shalom, Friend: The Life and Legacy of Yitzhak Rabin.* New York: Newmarket Press, 1996, ISBN 1-55704-287-X.

The biography of a great leader and soldier as well as a history of modern Israel. Incisive, informative, and balanced, *Shalom, Friend* does justice — if that is possible — to the memory of a hero,

Jelinek, Nancy Block. *Jerusalem: An Annotated Bibliography.* Melrose Park, PA: Auerbach Central Agency for Jewish Education, 1994.

Intended specifically for the Jewish educator and appropriate for informal and formal educational settings, this is an annotated list of educational resources including general educational materials, materials in Hebrew, and multi-media releases. The author has unearthed items that are educationally sound and often overlooked, thus giving the teacher the opportunity to use something different. Send for this catalog for further information.

Magid, Anna, and Heddy Swartz, eds. *Jerusalem Catalog.* Jerusalem: Joint Authority for Jewish Zionist Education, Departments for Education, 1994.

This all-purpose guide to materials for teaching Jerusalem includes items which are available in English and Hebrew, as well as French, Spanish, and Russian. The English section contains close to 100 entries of curricula, literature, media, posters, and games. Each listing includes an annotation, age recommendation, and distributor.

Jerusalem through the Ages. Tel Aviv: Israel's Open University, 1986. (Available through Gefen Publishers, New York and Jerusalem)

A ten-unit course for adult education programs. The course spans 3,000 years of the Holy City's long and often stormy history. Each unit is self-contained, and includes questions and activities. No previous background is necessary. Some of the titles are: "From a Jebusite City to the Capital of the People of Israel," "Jerusalem the Capital of the Crusader Kingdom," and eight more.

Jerusalem thru the Ages Timeline. New York: Joint Authority for Jewish Zionist Education, Torah Education Dept., 1994.

An easy-to-read and attractive piece which covers 23 periods in Jerusalem's 3,000 year history. Each sheet, representing a specific period, contains a concise historical synopsis, biblical or post-biblical quotation, and photo.

Reisman, Ofra, and Miriam Snapir, eds. *Jerusalem: Curriculum for Young Children.* Jerusalem: Department of Jewish Education and Culture in the Diaspora, 1992.

Included in this curriculum is an activity booklet, six illustrated story booklets, and a teacher guide. The guide aims to help the teacher relate the stories to the theme, Jerusalem. The suggestions are creative and applicable to the age group and to settings in North America. The booklets are annotated in the *Jerusalem Catalog* (see Magid and Swartz, above).

Rothenberg, Naftali; Leora Tanenbaum; and Sara Silberman. *Reflections on Jerusalem: City of David in Classical Text.* New York: Hadassah, 1995, ISBN 1-889525-03-0.

Jerusalem's history has been recorded through the written word from its founding during biblical times. Any understanding of this historic location is enriched by going back and traveling through the years with the authentic sources. This rich guide for both formal and informal adult study groups divides the city's history into six periods and for each provides classical text, historical background, thought questions, and answers.

The Sources of Jerusalem. Jerusalem: Joint Authority for Jewish Zionist Education, 1995.

A five-part series of booklets that tells the story of Jerusalem through primary sources integrated into a narration of the city's development. The series is recommended for a pre-trip preview, a trip companion, for adult education mini-courses, and to prepare for the International Jerusalem Quiz. The important highlights are provided in a concise, easy-to-digest manner.

Stahl, Abraham. *Jerusalem through the Windows of Time.* Jerusalem: Joint Authority for Jewish Zionist Education, 1995.

This textbook is suitable for high school students, college, and adult study groups in the Diaspora. The book, in 12 chapters (referred to as windows), affords insight into periods of Jerusalem's history in chronological order. Each era has a historical account, selections from Jewish literature, and color pictures and maps. This is a concise, well presented piece.

Teveth, Shabatei. *Ben Gurion and the Holocaust.* New York: Harcourt Brace, 1996, ISBN 0-15-100237-1.

Israel's founding father has been blamed for not taking greater action during the Holocaust. What did Ben Gurion actually do? Could he have done more?

Wheatcroft, Geoffrey. *The Controversy of Zion: Jewish Nationalism, the Jewish State and the Unresolved Jewish Dilemma.* New York: Addison Wesley Longman, 1996, ISBN 0-201-56234-0.

A richly detailed and fair account of the impact of one hundred years of Zionist thought and action on Jewish self-understanding, tracing the themes that have echoed from the days of Ahad Ha'Am and Herzl to the assassination of Rabin.

Audiocassettes

El Eretz Yisrael: A Child's Tour of Israel. Ralph Dalin and Michael Stein. Available from A.R.E. Publishing, Inc.

This cassette brings to life in song and story a young girl's dream of being in Israel. Transported on the wings of a dove from her home in Moscow, she meets a friend who guides her through Israel. By way of original and classic Israeli songs, children learn of Israel's geography, history, language, and way of life. Grades PK-3.

Z'man LaShir: Time To Sing Hebrew. Fran Avni. Available from A.R.E. Publishing, Inc.

Fourteen original songs feature catchy tunes and bouncy rhythms that teach simple Hebrew words and phrases. Grades 1-5.

Videos

Note: Some films about Israel have stood the test of time and are classics. Fortunately, many of these are now readily available on video for both group and home use. In addition, new videos about Israel appear with each important occasion. In 1996, there was the 3000th anniversary of Jerusalem, in 1997, there was the 100th anniversary of the Zionist Congress, and in 1998, the 50th anniversary of the modern State of Israel.

The Century of Teddy Kollek. 60 min. color. Ergo Media Inc.

Teddy Kollek, mayor of Jerusalem from 1965-1993, is the man most responsible for the shape of Jerusalem as it stands today. Here is the story of how one man made a difference from his days as a pre-State activist to his retirement. Grades 7 up.

Children of Jerusalem through Videos. 30 min. each. color. National Film Board of Canada.

A series of five 30 minute videos which gives insights into the lives of five children growing up in a culturally divided city. Each is followed through a typical day: showing homes, schools, families, houses of worship, and activities. Grades 2 up.

Exodus. 128 min. b/w. Available from Ergo Media Inc., or your local video store.

Adapted from the Leon Uris novel of the same name, this film directed by Otto Preminger documents the concentration camp refugees and the growth of the Jewish homeland following World War II. Grades 7 up.

Hill 24 Doesn't Answer. 101 min. b/w. Available from Ergo Media Inc. or your local video store.

Four young Zionists are assigned to defend strategic Hill 24 outside of Jerusalem, which is critical to getting to the city during the 1948 War of Independence. Through their personal stories, one gains a critical perspective on the creation of the modern State of Israel and the lives that were risked to make it a reality. Grades 9 up.

Jerusalem: Soul of a People. 30 min. color. Ergo Media Inc.

To understand Jerusalem's overwhelming importance today requires an understanding of its 3,000 year history. This video presents the history using animation, photos, and documentary footage as it takes the viewer through the centuries. Grades 9 up.

Jinja's Israeli Safari. 40 min. color. Ergo Media Inc.

Join Jinja, Israel's favorite lion cub, on her trip through Tel Aviv's Safari Park. Facts are set against easy-to-learn children's songs in Hebrew. Grades 1-6.

Late Summer Blues. 101 min. color. Kino International Films.

Tel Aviv, 1970 . . . a group of seven eighteen-year-olds are between final exams and their induction into *Tzahal*, the Israel Defense Force, as the War of Attrition draws on. How do Israeli teenagers make this sudden transition from student to soldier. Recommended for teen-age groups.

Lost Treasure: Rebirth of a Nation and Romance of New Palestine. 45min. b/w. English and Hebrew versions available. National Center for Jewish Film.

A 1995 documentary incorporating rare historic film footage of the early twentieth century *Yishuv* (pre-state Jewish settlement in Palestine) including scenes of boats arriving with immigrants, the building of Tel Aviv, early *kibbutzim*, and more. Grades 7 up.

One Hundred Gates in Jerusalem. 6 min. b/w. Isaac Cohen.

This 1995 documentary was filmed in Jerusalem's ultra-Orthodox neighborhood of Mea Shearim, which captures its unique way of life. The film starts at the Western Wall and proceeds into the streets showing how the people retain the Eastern European way of life from a past century. Grades 5 up.

Shalom Sesame Series. 30 min. each. color. Available from The Learning Plant.

Eleven episodes of the award winning television show that relate to Israel. Titles include, among others, "The Land of Israel," "Tel Aviv," "Kibbutz," "The People of Israel," "Jerusalem."

Summer of Aviya. 96 min. color. Ergo Media Inc.

One summer in the life of a ten-year-old girl, the daughter of a Holocaust survivor, during the first years of Israel's statehood. Aviya's mother, with a number tattooed on her arm, had been a partisan fighter during the *Shoah*. She walked the thin line between sanity and madness. Aviya has lived in orphanages most of her life. This was the summer she returned home. Grades 7-12.

Wake the Dawn: The Story of the Temple. 32 min. color. Ergo Media Inc.

The Holy Temple is more than a building. When King David wanted a home for the Ark, he selected the Temple Mount in Jerusalem, and there his son, Solomon, built the Holy Temple. Twice it was destroyed, and now it remains a vision to Jews everywhere. Here we learn of the physical dimensions of the Temple and the biblical, Talmudic, and *midrashic* sources of our knowledge. Grades 7-12.

The Wordmaker. 90 min. color. English and Hebrew with English subtitles. National Center for Jewish Film.

At the beginning of the twentieth century, a language war raged in Palestine. Eliezer Ben Yehuda led the fight to make Hebrew the everyday language of the *yishuv* and the modern state. He was zealous, stubborn, and courageous; and his driving passion breathed life into the ancient biblical tongue. A story of how one man can make a difference. Grades 9 up.

Music

Pasternak, Velvel. *Jerusalem in Song*. Cedarhurst, NY: Tara Publications, 1995, ISBN 0-933676-42-5.

Ninety-six selections all about Jerusalem. Each song is transliterated and translated and is arranged with sheet music, and chords allowing musicians of all instruments to play every composition. Also available with a 70 min. companion compact disc, redigitized and remastered from the original recordings.

CR-ROMs

Jerusalem 3000. Windows only. Ergo Media Inc.

Introduces the Jerusalem of today. One can "travel" around the city by taking one of four fully narrated tours: modern Jerusalem, Jewish, Christian, or Moslem Jerusalem. Click on a neightborhood and find out all about it. Visit the "Hall of Fame" and learn about 35 people intimately connected with the city. Includes a glossary of 200 names and terms. Grades 6 up.

Multi-Media Israel. Windows. Davka Corporation.

An in-depth course on the history, land, and people of the modern State of Israel. Material is presented through games, photographs, narration, and music. Grades 8 up.

LAG B'OMER

For Teachers and Parents

"Lag Ba-Omer." In *Encyclopaedia Judaica*. Jerusalem: Keter Publishing House Jerusalem Ltd., 1972, Vol. 10, pp. 1356-7.

SHAVUOT

For Students

The Children of America. *The 11th Commandment: Wisdom from Our Children*. Woodstock, VT, Jewish Lights Publishing, 1995, ISBN 0-879045-46-X.

Children of many religious denominations answer the question, "If there were an 11th commandment, what would it be?" The answers reveal children's thoughts and concerns about life, living with others, living with the earth, living with family, living with yourself, and living with God. An exquisite book with color illustrations. Grades 1 up.

Cone, Molly. *Who Knows Ten?: Children's Tales of the Ten Commandments*. New York: UAHC Press, 1965, ISBN 0-8074-0080-7.

This classic explains the biblical origin of each commandment, illustrating the application of each in a simple, age appropriate story. Grades K-3.

Fox, Marci. *The Ten Commandments*. Los Angeles, CA: Torah Aura Productions.

This Instant Lesson introduces the Ten Commandments and lets students match the individual commandments to actions people take to try to live by them. Grades K-2.

Ganz, Yaffa. *Shavuos with Bina, Benny and Chaggai Hayonah*. New York: Mesorah Publications, Ltd., 1992, ISBN 0-89906-982-7.

Bina, Benny, and Chaggai Hayonah (the dove) explain the history and rituals of the holiday. Ashkenazic pronunciation of Hebrew. Includes a glossary. Part of the ArtScroll Children's Holiday Series. Grades 4 up.

Goodman, Roberta Louis. *God's Top Ten: The Meaning of the Ten Commandments*. Los Angeles, CA: Torah Aura Productions, 1992, ISBN 0-933873-73-5.

Involves students in telling, expanding, interpreting, and finding meaning in ten stories — one for each of the Ten Commandments. Grades 4-Adult.

Karkowsky, Nancy. *The Ten Commandments*. West Orange, NJ: Behrman House, 1988, ISBN 0-87441-477-6.

The meaning of each commandment is explained in simple terms that are keyed to the child's level of understanding. Grades 3-4.

A Lifetime of Torah. Los Angeles, CA: Torah Aura Productions.

Presents the Jewish life cycle in terms of eight important Torah events: Covenant ceremony, consecration, going to a Jewish school, Bar/Bat Mitzvah, Jewish youth group, Jewish summer camp, Confirmation, and adult education. Grades 1-2.

Shavuot. Los Angeles, CA: Torah Aura Productions.

This Instant Lesson introduces the Shavuot basics. The guide for teachers is called *The Celebration Lessons Teacher's Guide*. Grades K-2.

Siegel, Richard; Michael Strassfeld; and Sharon Strassfeld. *The First Jewish Catalog: A Do-It-Yourself Kit*. Philadelphia, PA: Jewish Publication Society, 1973, ISBN 0-8276-0042-9.

A must reference on celebrations, ceremonies, arts and music, travel, and education. Grades 7-Adult.

10 x 10: Ten Things about the Ten Commandments. Los Angeles, CA: Torah Aura Productions.

Ten interesting lessons about the Ten Commandments. Grades 6-Adult.

For Teachers and Parents

Kadden, Barbara Binder, and Bruce Kadden. *Teaching Jewish Life Cycle*. Denver: A.R.E. Publishing, Inc., 1997, ISBN 0-86705-040-3.

Contains an excellent chapter on conversion and welcoming the convert.

Kushner, Harold. *To Life! A Celebration of Jewish Being and Thinking*. Boston: Little, Brown and Company, 1993, ISBN 0-316-50735-0.

In this practical and spiritual guide to the Jewish tradition, Kushner explains why prayer matters, how holiday and life cycle observances teach us to be human, *kashrut*, how we look at Christianity, and more.

Strassfeld, Michael. "Shavuot: Revealing the Torah." In *The Jewish Holidays: A Guide and Commentary*. New York: Harper and Row, Publishers, 1985, ISBN 0-06-015406-3, pp. 69-83.

Intended to help readers observe the holidays with more understanding, this book is a fascinating weave of the traditional and the contemporary. It contains insights into the history, traditions, and liturgy, and the brilliant and interesting commentaries of five scholars.

Waskow, Arthur. "Shavuot — Peak Experience." In *Seasons of Our Joy*. Toronto: Bantam Books, 1982, ISBN 0-0-553-01369-6, pp. 185-205.

A lively and accessible approach to Shavuot and the other holidays. The author teaches the origins, history, and seasonal significance of each. He relates how they have been celebrated in the past and offers some innovative and contemporary approaches to these celebrations and observances.

Audiocassette

And the Youth Shall See Visions. Debbie Friedman. Available from A.R.E. Publishing, Inc.

Combines both liturgy and biblical selections in a Shavuot service, and encourages listeners to create our dreams and visions.

TISHAH B'AV

For Students

Ganz, Yaffa. *Tishah B'Av: The Four Fasts with Bina, Benny and Chaggai Hayonah*. New York: Mesorah Publications, Ltd., 1992, ISBN 0-89906-983-5.

Bina, Benny, and Chaggai Hayonah (the dove) explain the history and rituals of four of the fast days of the year. Ashkenazic pronunciation of Hebrew. Includes a glossary. Part of the ArtScroll Children's Holiday Series. Grades 4 up.

Roseman, Kenneth. *The Tenth of Av*. New York: UAHC Press, 1988, ISBN 0-8074-0359-8.

The reader travels back to the year 70 of the Common Era to the city of Jerusalem which is burning at the hands of the Roman soldiers. They must decide to fight or flee — the first of many decisions throughout the book, all concerned with events in Jewish history. Grades 4-7.

For Teachers and Parents

"Av, The Ninth of." In *Encyclopaedia Judaica*. Jerusalem: Keter Publishing House Jerusalem Ltd., 1972, Vol. 3, pp. 936-940.

Strassfeld, Michael. "The Three Weeks: The Dark Time." In *The Jewish Holidays: A Guide & Commentary*. New York: Harper & Row, Publishers, 1985, pp. 85-93.

A brief overview of the three weeks leading up to Tishah B'Av and the history and traditions relating to this observance.

Waskow, Arthur I. "Burnt Offering — Tisha B'Av." In *Seasons of Our Joy: A Celebration of Modern Jewish Renewal*. Toronto: Bantam Books, 1982, ISBN 0-8070-3611-0.

An overview of the origins of Tishah B'Av, as well as preparations for it, observance, and new approaches.

ROSH CHODESH

For Teachers and Parents

Adelman, Penina V. *Miriam's Well: Rituals for Jewish Women around the Year*. 10th anniversary ed. New York: Biblio Press, 1996, ISBN 0-930395-11-5.

This popular guide contains rituals for Jewish women for Rosh Chodesh, as well as for adoption, child weaning, alternative weddings, pregnancy loss, ecological holidays, and more.

Berrin, Susan, ed. *Celebrating the New Moon: A Rosh Chodesh Anthology*. Northvale, NJ: Jason Aronson, 1996, ISBN 1-56821-459-6.

Contributors discuss the significance of Rosh Chodesh and the role it plays in the Jewish calendar.

Levine, Elizabeth Resnick, ed. *A Ceremonies Sampler: New Rites, Celebrations, and Observances of Jewish Women*. San Diego: Women's Institute for Continuing Jewish Education, 1991, ISBN 0-9608054-9-4.

A unique collection of contemporary ceremonies created to recognize significant events in a Jewish woman's life.

Solomon, Judith Y. *The Rosh Hodesh Table: Foods at the New Moon*. New York: Biblio Press, 1995, ISBN 0-9303935-23-9.

A unique book of Jewish food lore containing the history and foods for Rosh Chodesh observance.

Teaching Holidays/Mitzvot/Prayer — Alef Level, Vol. 1. New York: The Melton Research Center for Jewish Education, 1979.

An integrated, graded teaching program for 8-year-olds. Contains some information on Rosh Chodesh.

Audiocassettes

A Moon Note. Miraj. Sounds Write Productions.

A feminist recording that is a blending of beautiful harmony with 13 songs based on Psalms, Jewish holidays, and women of the Bible. (Contains a song on Rosh Chodesh.) Grades 7 up.

Chodesh Chodesh B'Shir: A Song a Month. Penina Adelman and Suri Krieger. Sounds Write Productions.

Original Hebrew songs that parallel the Hebrew months of the year. These songs complement the book Miriam's Well, and are ideal for Rosh Chodesh celebrations. Grades 7 up.

Debbie Friedman at Carnegie Hall. Debbie Friedman. Available from A.R.E. Publishing, Inc.

All 22 selections from Debbie's Carnegie Hall debut are included in this two-volume set. Includes well loved favorites, as well as new songs recorded here for the first time. Among the latter is *"Birkat Halevana."* All Ages.

The Length of Our Days. Marsha Rose Attie. Sounds Write Productions.

A meditative look at Hebrew and English liturgical and biblical texts with the theme of Jewish Renewal. (Contains a song on Rosh Chodesh.) Grades 7 up.

ADDRESSES OF JEWISH PUBLISHERS/ ORGANIZATIONS

Alef Design Group
4423 Fruitland Ave.
Los Angeles, CA 90058

Anti-Defamation League
823 United Nations Plaza
New York, NY 10017

A.R.E. Publishing, Inc.
3945 South Oneida Street
Denver, CO 80237

Auerbach Central Agency
for Jewish Education
7607 Old York Road
Melrose Park, PA 19027

Avotaynu
155 North Washington Avenue
Bergenfield, NJ 07621

Behrman House
235 Watchung Avenue
West Orange, NJ 07052

Bureau of Jewish Education
of Greater Boston
333 Nahanton Street
Newton, MA 02159

Centre for Jewish Education
80 East End Road
London N32SY
England

CCAR Press
192 Lexington Ave.
New York, NY 10016

Coalition for the Advancement
of Jewish Education
261 West 35th Street, Floor 12A
New York, NY 10001

Dept. of Jewish Education and Culture
in the Diaspora
P.O. Box 92
91920 Jerusalem
Israel

The Dreidelmaker
Mark Glickman
P.O. Box 1904
Frederick, MD 21702

Philipp Feldheim Inc.
200 Airport Executive Park
Spring Valley, NY 10977

Gefen Publishing House
12 New Street
Hewlitt, NY 11557

Hachai Publications, Inc.
156 Chester Avenue
Brooklyn, NY 11218

Hadassah
National Jewish Education Department
50 West 58th Street
New York, NY 10019

Israel's Open University
330 West 58th Street
New York, NY 10019

Jason Aronson Inc.
230 Livingston Street
Northvale, NJ 07647

Jewish Lights Publishing
P.O. Box 237
Sunset Farm Offices, Rte. 4
Woodstock, VT 05091

Jewish National Fund
Department of Education
78 Randall Avenue
Rockville Center, NY 11571

The Jewish Publication Society
1930 Chestunut Street
Philadelphia, PA 19103

Joint Authority for Jewish Zionist Education
4th Floor, Publication Dept.
110 East 59th Street
New York, NY 10022

Kar-Ben Copies, Inc.
6800 Tildenwood Lane
Rockville, MD 20852

Kiryat HaChinuch
Ha'askan Street #3
Jerusalem 93780
Israel

KTAV Publishing House Inc.
900 Jefferson Street
Hoboken, NJ 07030

Martyrs Memorial and
Museum of the Holocaust
6505 Wilshire Boulevard
Los Angeles, CA 90048

Mesorah Publications, Ltd.
4401 Second Avenue
Brooklyn, NY 11232

Schocken Books
c/o Pantheon Books
201 East 50th Street
New York, NY 10022

Shengold Publishers
18 West 45th Street
New York, NY 10036

Shomrei Adamah
50 W. 17th St., 7th floor
New York, NY 10011

Theodor Herzl Foundation
110 East 59th Street
New York, NY 10022

Torah Aura Productions
4423 Fruitland Ave.
Los Angeles, CA 90058

UAHC Press
838 Fifth Avenue
New York, NY 10021

United States Holocaust Memorial Council
Dept. TC
P.O. Box 92420
Washington, DC 20090

Woman's Institute for
Continuing Jewish Education
4126 Executive Drive
La Jolla, CA 92037

ADDRESSES OF DISTRIBUTORS OF
VIDEOS/AUDIOTAPES/SOFTWARE

A.R.E. Publishing, Inc.
3945 South Oneida Street
Denver, CO 80237

Board of Jewish Education of
Greater New York
426 West 58th Street
New York, NY 10019

Cinema Guild
1697 Broadway, Suite 802
New York, NY 10019

Davka Corporation
7074 North Western Ave.
Chicago, IL 60645

Ergo Media Inc.
P.O. Box 2037
Teaneck, NJ 07666

HBO Video, Inc.
1100 Avenue of the Americas
New York, NY 10036

Isaac Cohen
97 Perkins Street
Jamaica Plain, MA 02130

Jewish Software Center
15466 Los Gatos Blvd.
Los Gatos, CA 95032

KINO International Films
333 West 39th Street
New York, NY 10018

National Center for Jewish Film
Brandeis University, Lown 102
Waltham, MA 02254

National Film Board of Canada
1251 Avenue of the Americas
New York, NY 10020

Sounds Write Productions, Inc.
6685 Norman Lane
San Diego, CA 92120

Tara Publications
P.O. Box 707
Owings Mills, MD 21117

United States Holocaust Memorial Council
Dept TC
P.O. Box 92420
Washington, DC 20090

Weston Woods Studios, Inc.
399 Newtown Turnpike
Weston, CT 06851